TOEIC® Listening and Reading Test Prep Plus

4 Practice Tests + Proven Strategies + Online + Audio

Special thanks to the team who made this book possible: Kim Bowers, Buddy Brown, Louise Cook, Scarlet Edmonds, Jenni Fogg, Joanna Graham, Brian Holmes, Bharat Krishna, Alan Martins, Jinan Muneer, Teresa Rupp, Nimesh Shah, Noel Smaragdakis.

Published by Kaplan Publishing, a division of Kaplan, Inc.
750 Third Avenue
New York, NY 10017

10 9 8 7 6 5 4 3 2 1

ISBN: 978-1-5062-6455-4

TABLE OF CONTENTS

How to Use This Book

WELCOME TO KAPLAN TOEIC LISTENING AND READING TEST PREP PLUS, SECOND EDITION

Congratulations on your decision to improve your English proficiency, and thank you for choosing Kaplan for your TOEIC preparation. You've made the right choice in acquiring this book—you're now armed with a comprehensive TOEIC program that is the result of decades of researching the TOEIC and similar tests and teaching many thousands of students the skills they need to succeed. You have everything you need to score higher—let's start by walking through what you need to know to take advantage of this book and the Online Study Plan.

Your Book

There are two main components to your *Kaplan TOEIC Prep Plus* study package: your book and your Online Study Plan. This book contains the following:

- Detailed instruction covering the essential concepts and skills for the seven parts of the TOEIC Listening and Reading test.
- Time-tested and effective Kaplan Methods and strategies for every question type.
- Four full-length practice tests and a chapter full of practice questions for each of the seven parts of the TOEIC.

Your Online Study Plan

Your Online Study Plan lets you access additional instruction and practice materials to reinforce key concepts and sharpen your TOEIC skills. Resources include the following:

- Online answer grids for the practice tests in this book.
- Listening tracks that accompany the chapters and practice tests in this book.

GETTING STARTED

1. Register your Online Study Plan.
2. Take a TOEIC practice test to identify your strengths and weaknesses.
3. Create a study plan.
4. Learn and practice using this book and your Online Study Plan.

Step 1: Register Your Online Study Plan

To listen to the audio for this book, access your audio tracks and other online resources through the Online Study Plan.

Register your Online Study Plan using these simple steps:

1. Go to **kaptest.com/moreonline**.
2. Follow the instructions. You will need to have your book with you to register.

When registering, make sure you select the correct book title and ISBN (you can find this book's ISBN number at the front of the book).

Once you have registered, login at **kaptest.com/login**.

You should listen to your audio wherever you see this icon 🎧 in your book.

If you have any issues finding your audio online, please email us at **booksupport@kaplan.com**.

Step 2: Take the TOEIC Practice Test

It's a good idea to take a practice test early on. Doing so will give you the initial feedback and diagnostic information that you need to achieve your maximum score.

You can use Practice Test 1 (in Part Five of this book) as your diagnostic test. This practice test will give you a chance to familiarize yourself with the various question types. It also allows you to accurately gauge the content you know and identify areas for practice and review. Print out a copy of the answer sheet from your Online Study Plan to use as you take this practice test. After completing the test, copy your answers from your answer sheet into the online answer grid available in your Online Study Plan.

Review the detailed answer explanations to better understand your performance. Look for patterns in the questions you answered correctly and incorrectly. Were you stronger in some areas than others? This analysis will help you target your practice time to specific concepts.

Step 3: Create a Study Plan

Use what you've learned from your diagnostic test to identify areas for closer study and practice. Take time to familiarize yourself with the key components of your book and Online Study Plan. Think about how many hours you can consistently devote to TOEIC study. We have found that most students have success with about three months of committed preparation before Test Day.

Schedule time for study, practice, and review. One of the most frequent mistakes in approaching study is to take practice tests and not review them thoroughly—review time is your best chance to gain points. It works best for many people to block out short, frequent periods of study time throughout the week. Check in with yourself frequently to make sure you're not falling behind your plan or forgetting about any of your resources.

Step 4: Learn and Practice

Your book and Online Study Plan come with many opportunities to develop and practice the skills you'll need on Test Day. Read each chapter of this book and complete the practice questions. Depending on how much time you have to study, you can do this work methodically, covering every chapter, or you can focus your study on those question types and content areas that are most challenging for you. You will inevitably need more work in some areas than in others, but know that the more thoroughly you prepare, the better your score will be.

Initially, your practice should focus on mastering the needed skills and not on timing. Add timing to your practice as you improve fundamental proficiency. As soon as you are comfortable with the question types and Kaplan Methods, take and review the additional full-length practice tests in your Online Study Plan.

Thanks for choosing Kaplan. We wish you the best of luck on your journey to English fluency.

PART ONE

The Basics

CHAPTER 1

Taking the TOEIC Exam

LEARNING OBJECTIVES

In this section, you'll learn to:

- Identify where and how to take the TOEIC exam
- Explain how the TOEIC is scored
- Identify the 7 different Parts of the TOEIC exam

UNDERSTANDING THE TOEIC EXAM

Before looking at the questions on the TOEIC exam, let's look at some background information about it.

What Is the TOEIC Exam?

The TOEIC exam was set up around 40 years ago to test the English abilities of non-native speakers in business and professional situations. The TOEIC is currently taken in more than 160 countries and used by more than 14,000 companies around the world.

The TOEIC Reading and Listening exam covers two main areas: your ability to understand real-life conversations and speeches in English (spoken English), and your ability to read and understand materials in English, such as manuals, reports, advertisements, periodicals, correspondence, and technical articles (written English). The language tested on the TOEIC exam is not specialized language. It is the everyday language that people use in the workplace to communicate about their jobs and business, and when they communicate with friends or acquaintances about common subject areas such as health, weekend activities, and travel.

Who Produces the TOEIC Exam?

The TOEIC exam was developed by the Educational Testing Service (ETS), a private, not-for-profit organization located in Princeton, New Jersey, in the United States. ETS is a leading center for educational and psychometric research in the United States and is well known as an organization that prepares and administers a variety of tests for school, college, and graduate program admission as well as occupational and professional certification and licensing.

Who Uses the TOEIC Exam?

Corporations and government offices worldwide use the TOEIC exam for many reasons:

- Assessing how well their current employees understand English
- Hiring new employees
- Tracking the progress of employees in English-language training programs

When Did the TOEIC Exam Change?

In April 2018, ETS released updates to the TOEIC Reading and Listening Test. The content in this book reflects these test changes.

Test changes include:

- Some Reading passages feature more modern formats, such as text messages.
- Some conversations in Part III have three speakers instead of two.
- Some Listening questions include a visual component, such as a graph or chart. You must answer questions by combining the visual information with what the speakers say.

Check the official TOEIC website at **ets.org/toeic** for the most up to date information on test changes.

How Do the TOEIC Exam and the TOEFL Exam Compare?

The TOEIC exam and the TOEFL (Test of English as a Foreign Language) exam were both developed to test English listening and reading, but they differ in their purpose, content, and design.

Purpose

The TOEFL exam is designed to determine how well a candidate can use English in colleges and universities in the United States. Its purpose is to identify candidates who can perform successfully in an academic setting. The TOEIC exam, on the other hand, tests everyday English used in business settings.

Content

Content for TOEFL exam material is taken from lectures, texts, and other documents found in the academic environment. TOEIC exam materials reflect the needs of people accomplishing work tasks, providing services, communicating with others, traveling, and manufacturing and distributing products.

Design

Because the primary purpose of the TOEFL exam is to identify those students who can perform successfully in an English-based academic environment, it focuses on test takers of intermediate to fluent English language ability.

The TOEIC exam, on the other hand, measures a wider range, from the lowest proficiency level to high professional-level competence. In addition, the Internet-based TOEFL iBT has speaking and writing sections, as well as listening and reading sections, whereas the TOEIC Reading and Listening exam tests only listening and reading.

ETS offers separate Internet-based speaking and writing tests for TOEIC exam takers. These will not be covered in this book. For more information about the TOEIC Speaking and Writing Test, visit **toeic.org**.

HOW AND WHERE THE TOEIC EXAM IS ADMINISTERED

The TOEIC exam is available internationally through two separate programs. Your local representative will help you decide the best way for you to take the exam.

Choice 1: Taking the Exam in an Open Public Session

These sessions are held on selected dates at different locations across the globe. Companies might want to send their employees to an open session exam rather than administering the exam on their own premises. People who wish to take the exam but who are not affiliated with an organization that conducts on-site exam administration must take the exam at an open public session. Because public sessions are not yet available in every country, you should check with the ETS representative in your country regarding the availability of these open sessions.

Choice 2: On-Site Exam Administration

The TOEIC exam serves the needs of corporations and government organizations that have a number of people who require a test at the same time. On-site exams are administered under secure conditions, supervised by both the client organization's staff and by ETS. Exams that are taken on-site or at an open session are all scored only by ETS or its representatives.

To find out more information about taking the TOEIC exam via either method, be sure to contact your TOEIC representative. Information on contacting your TOEIC representative can be found at **toeic.org**.

AN OVERVIEW OF THE TOEIC EXAM

The TOEIC exam is a standardized test, meaning that it consists of certain types of multiple-choice questions, is given to a large number of people at the same time, is graded by computer, and is timed. Complex statistical procedures ensure that test scores from different forms of the test can be compared directly.

Total Questions	200 questions
Total Time	2.5 hours (includes time for filling out forms)
Total Score Range	10–990

Format and Content

The TOEIC exam is approximately two hours long and consists of 200 multiple-choice questions. If you include the time it takes to fill in the answer sheet and background questions, the exam is about two and a half hours long. See the following chart for a breakdown of the exam sections.

LISTENING TEST

Part	Questions	Format
1 – Photograph Questions	6	Choose the answer that best describes the photograph.
2 – Question Response	25	For each question, you hear a question or statement with 3 possible responses. Choose the answer that best responds to the question or statement.
3 – Conversations	39	13 conversations with 3 questions for each conversation. You will hear conversations between two or three speakers. Choose the answer that is true according to what the speakers say.
4 – Talks	30	10 talks with 3 questions for each talk. You will hear one speaker talk. Choose the answer that is true according to what the speaker says.

READING TEST

Part	Questions	Format
5 – Incomplete Sentences	30	Choose the answer that best completes the sentence.
6 – Text Completion	16	4 texts with 4 questions per text. Read the text, then choose the word, phrase or sentence that best completes the text.
7 – Reading Comprehension	29	Single Passage sets. You must answer 2–4 questions about a single text.
	25	Multiple Passage sets. 2 sets with 2 passages and 3 sets with 3 passages. You must answer 5 questions about each multiple passage set.

Scoring

TOEIC scores are worked out by adding up the total number of correct responses in the Listening Comprehension Section and the Reading Comprehension Section. These two totals are converted to a scaled score ranging from 5 to 495 for each section, with a combined total from 10 to 990. These scaled scores allow scores from different TOEIC exams to be compared accurately.

Something to remember when you are looking at your TOEIC score is that there is no failing or passing score for this exam. The TOEIC exam was developed to assess the English proficiency of people who will need to use English in a professional capacity. It does not measure achievement, which is why there is no passing or failing score. Nevertheless, many companies who use the TOEIC exam to set their own standards may require employees to obtain a certain minimum score due to the corresponding level of English needed for that job. This does not mean that people pass or fail the TOEIC exam; it just means they meet or do not meet the specific standards set by a specific organization.

An important thing to note is that because the exam calculates only the number of correct responses, and because you do not lose points for incorrect responses, you should answer *every* question rather than leave any blank. This book will teach you how to narrow down the possible options for each answer so that you come closest to picking the correct one, but even if you do not know the answer, guess! After all, you may, with luck, score a point; if you leave an answer blank, however, you receive no credit.

ANSWER EVERY QUESTION

On the TOEIC exam, you do not lose points for incorrect responses, so you should try to answer every question. If you do not know the answer, guess!

TOEIC exam writers recommend that a TOEIC score be considered valid for up to two years. However, if you took the TOEIC exam fewer than two years previously, and if you have greatly boosted your language skills during that period, you may find that your previous TOEIC exam score has become outdated.

Your TOEIC exam score is confidential. Information about your performance is available only to you and to the administering institution. Institutions may provide individual candidate information to staff only on a need-to-know basis and are not allowed to post scores on bulletin boards or other public places without the permission of the test takers.

Timing

As previously described, the TOEIC exam is timed. This means that your score greatly depends on being able to complete the questions within the time allowed.

We will indicate the amount of time you should budget for each part of the exam at the beginning of each chapter. At first, this might seem like an extremely short amount of time to answer all of the questions. However, at Kaplan, we have designed our test-taking strategies to help you eliminate incorrect answers as efficiently as possible. By practicing the strategies, you should be able to get through nearly all of the exam questions. Remember also, that even if you are not able to complete a whole section before the time limit, you should still fill in the answer grid for any unanswered questions. You may choose a correct answer by luck and get additional points; if you leave those answers choices blank, you will receive no points.

When you do the practice questions for each section, pay attention to the amount of time you spend on each question. You do not have to be strict about time at this point, but you do want to note where you are moving too slowly. Then, when you are ready to take the Practice Test, be sure to time yourself very carefully. This way, you will have as close to a real exam experience as possible, and you will see exactly where you need improvement.

FILLING OUT FORMS

Like other standardized tests, the TOEIC exam requires you to fill out a number of forms. For all of these forms, you will need a No. 2 or HB pencil and an eraser.

Before you start the exam you will have to complete a background questionnaire. Practice filling it out before you take the TOEIC exam so that are fully comfortable with it on Test Day.

The next form you will use is the answer grid. On the answer grid, you will first fill in ovals to indicate your name, the center where you are taking the exam, and other identifying information. You will use the rest of the grid to indicate your answer choices.

When taking the exam, it is common to lose track of which question you are on. Check that you are on the right question after every five questions. That way, if you have accidentally skipped an oval, you have to correct only a few of them.

It is important that you *fill in the ovals completely*; a check mark or an *X* will confuse the computer that scores the exam. Also, be sure that you do not go too far outside the oval and that if you erase, you do so completely. The Practice Tests in the back of the book include answer grids. Practice filling these out so that you are prepared on Test Day.

USE THE RIGHT PENCIL

You must use a No. 2 or HB pencil. The computer that scores the exam cannot read any other type of pencil or pen.

CHAPTER 2

Preparing for Test Day

LEARNING OBJECTIVES

In this section, you'll learn to:

- Plan your study schedule
- Explain the 4 key strategies for the TOEIC exam
- Apply the Kaplan Stress Busting Tips to maximize performance on Test Day

STUDY PLANNER

You will find calendars on pages 11 and 12. Use them to fill in a specific study schedule. Be realistic about the amount of time you have to study and practice your English-language skills. Do not worry about your current level of English; just make sure that you give yourself the amount of time you need to get the most out of this book. Remember to update the schedule as necessary.

Do not forget to schedule vocabulary practice and the practice tests along with the rest of the chapters of the book. Take the practice tests after you have reviewed all of the other chapters of the book. Be sure to leave enough time before the exam so you will be able to review your weak areas from each practice test. Take each practice test as if it were the real thing: Find a quiet place where you will not be interrupted and take it in one session. Time yourself accurately. In this way, you will be more prepared for your actual Test Day.

On page 10 are some broad guidelines for setting up your schedule. Remember that everyone is different and your pace may be far slower or faster than what is listed here. These are just to give you a general sense of the amount of time you will need. In addition to the hours noted here, you will want to schedule in time for a second or third review of certain chapters, depending on your strengths and weaknesses. Finally, do not schedule too much studying immediately before Test Day. As described later in this chapter, studying up to the last minute will only make you more anxious and will probably not raise your score.

Sharpening Your Listening Comprehension and Reading Comprehension Skills	
Part I: Listening Comprehension: Photographs	2 to 4 hours
Part II: Listening Comprehension: Question-Response	2 to 4 hours
Part III: Listening Comprehension: Short Conversations	2 to 4 hours
Part IV: Listening Comprehension: Short Talks	2 to 4 hours
Part V: Reading Comprehension: Incomplete Sentences	2 to 4 hours
Part VI: Reading Comprehension: Text Completion	2 to 4 hours
Part VII: Reading Comprehension: Reading Comprehension	2 to 4 hours

Vocabulary Review	
List 1	2.5 to 4 hours
List 2	2.5 to 4 hours
List 3	2.5 to 4 hours
List 4	2.5 to 4 hours
List 5	2.5 to 4 hours

Practice Test	
Practice Test 1	2 hours
Practice Test 1 Review	1 to 3 hours
Practice Test 2	2 hours
Practice Test 2 Review	1 to 3 hours
Practice Test 3	2 hours
Practice Test 3 Review	1 to 3 hours
Practice Test 4	2 hours
Practice Test 4 Review	1 to 3 hours

KAPLAN TOEIC Study Planner

Month: ____________________

Sunday	Monday	Tuesday	Wednesday	Thursday	Friday	Saturday

To Do This Month:

KAPLAN TOEIC Study Planner

Month: ______________________

Sunday	Monday	Tuesday	Wednesday	Thursday	Friday	Saturday

To Do This Month:

NINE KEY STRATEGIES FOR THE TOEIC EXAM

Strategy 1: Know the Directions

Each part of the TOEIC exam has its own directions. Knowing what they are before you take the exam will help you manage your time—you will not have to waste valuable test time listening to or reading the directions if you already know what they are. In the Listening Comprehension Section, you will hear the directions for each part before the actual questions begin. The directions will also be printed in your exam book. While the directions are playing, you can use this time to look ahead at the questions that you will be asked to answer. Knowing what the questions are in advance will help you focus on what to listen for.

In the Reading Comprehension Section, the directions are printed at the beginning of each part. Again, by knowing what the directions are in advance, you will be able to begin answering the questions immediately rather than after reading and understanding the directions.

Strategy 2: Read Each Question Carefully

Before looking at the answer choices, read the question closely to find out what you are being asked. Often, incorrect answer choices are designed to trap you if you misread the question. If you do not understand a question, reread it slowly. On the exam, the language of the questions and answers is simpler and easier to understand than the language of the material being tested. If you understood the passage (conversation, short talk, reading passage) but do not understand the question, reread the question and focus on the keywords in the question to understand what you need to do.

Strategy 3: Predict the Answer

After you are clear on what you are required to do, try to predict the answer in your own words—before looking at the answer choices. The questions on the exam are very straightforward—there are no trick questions or any questions that require you to make calculations or make a conclusion that is not already in the provided in the text or audio. Information is provided in the listening and reading materials, and the questions try to determine whether you understood that information. If you understand the question, you should be able to answer it in your own words. Your predicted answer should be among the answer choices.

Strategy 4: Evaluate the Answer Choices

After you have predicted the answer in your own words, check to see if your answer is among the choices. If the choices do not match your predicted answer exactly, select the choice that best matches. Reread the question to make sure it is a good match, and mark your answer choice on the answer sheet.

Strategy 5: Eliminate Wrong Answer Choices

If the answer you have predicted is not among the answer choices, eliminate any answer choices that you know are wrong and choose the best answer from the remaining choices. If you can eliminate even one wrong choice, you will increase your chances of guessing the correct answer. When there are four answer choices, you have a one-in-four chance of guessing the correct one. By eliminating one choice, you have improved your chances to one in three. If you can eliminate two wrong choices, you have a one in two chance of choosing the correct answer.

Strategy 6: Answer Easy Questions First

The Listening Comprehension Section of the exam is controlled by the recording. You will not be able to skip ahead, nor can you go back to review your answers. You must answer the questions in the Listening Comprehension Section in the order they are presented. In the Reading Comprehension Section, however, you may answer the questions in any order you like.

Generally, the Reading Comprehension Section is organized from easy to hard. Part V is the easiest, Part VI is more difficult, and Part VII is the most difficult. Within each part, the questions are generally ordered from easy to hard. The easiest items appear in the beginning, and the most difficult items appear at the end. For this reason, it is best to work through the Reading Comprehension Section in the order it is presented in the exam book. As you work through this section, do not spend too much time on any one question. Each question is worth the same number of points. If you spend a lot of time on one question, you risk losing time that you could spend answering easier questions that appear later on. If you are having trouble answering a question, either guess at the answer choice or circle the question number on your answer sheet so that you can return to it later if there is time. When you have finished all the easy questions, go back and try answering the difficult questions you left blank. If you don't know which answer is correct, remember to eliminate any answers that you know are not correct, and guess the answer from the remaining choices.

In Part VII of the Reading Comprehension Section, the reading text sets have between two and five questions each. Generally, passages with fewer questions are shorter and easier than passages with more questions. You will not need to spend as much time answering these questions. For some of the reading passages, there will be a question that asks about how a particular word is used in the passage. These are generally easy questions that can be answered quickly. If you are running out of time, look for these questions, find the word in the passage, and try to answer the question. Often, if you know the word being tested, you can eliminate one or two answer choices without even reading the passage.

Strategy 7: Answer Every Question

Do not leave any questions unanswered. There is no scoring penalty for an incorrect answer on the TOEIC exam. Your score is the total of all questions answered correctly. If you do not know the answer to a question, guess. Choose one letter—(A, B, C, or D)—to use as a "guessing letter." Using the same letter for every guessed question ensures that, on average, 25 percent of your guesses will be correct. The TOEIC exam is designed so that in each part, the number of times each letter is correct is about equal. This means there are approximately the same numbers of As, Bs, Cs, and Ds in each part. For example, if you choose answer choice D to guess at ten questions in Part VII, you should expect at least two or three of your guesses to be correct. However, if you guess randomly—picking a different letter for every question—you might not get any correct! Remember to try eliminating answer choices first, so if your guessing letter is D, but you know that answer choice D cannot be correct, you should pick a different answer choice.

Strategy 8: Manage Your Time

The TOEIC exam is a timed test; you are given 45 minutes to complete the Listening Comprehension Section and 75 minutes to complete the Reading Comprehension Section. As mentioned earlier, in the Listening Comprehension Section, the timing is controlled by the recording. After each question, there will be a pause of between five and eight seconds, during which you must choose and mark your answer (five seconds for Part I and eight seconds for Parts II–IV). After the pause, the next question, conversation, or passage will begin. You must work quickly so that you do not fall behind the recording. For the Reading Comprehension Section, you are given 75 minutes to finish, and you work at your own pace. Be sure to watch the clock so you know how much time you have left. Work as quickly as you can, but avoid making careless mistakes by working too fast.

Strategy 9: Check Your Answer Sheet for Mistakes or Unanswered Questions

If you finish the test before time is called, check your answer sheet to make sure you have filled in each oval completely and that there are no extra marks on it. Be sure you have filled in only one answer choice for each question. Be sure that you have answered every question and that there are no unanswered questions. If time is running out and you will not be able to finish the test, pick one letter (A, B, or C for questions with three answer choices or A, B, C, or D for questions with four answer choices) and fill in the remaining questions on your answer sheet. It is much better to guess at the remaining questions than to leave them unanswered. Your guesses might be correct, which would earn you score points.

Strategy Summary

1. Know the directions.
2. Read each question carefully before you look at the answer choices.
3. Predict the answer before looking at the choices.
4. Evaluate the answer choices and mark the answer if you know it.
5. Eliminate wrong answer choices and choose the best answer from the answer choices that remain.
6. Answer easy questions before the hard ones. Usually, Part V is easier than Part VI, which is easier than Part VII.
7. Answer every question, and choose one letter (A, B, or C for questions with three answer choices and A, B, C, or D for answers with four answer choices) to use when guessing the answers.
8. Manage your time.
9. Check your answer sheet for mistakes or unanswered questions before you turn it in.

TIPS FOR THE FINAL WEEK

The tendency among test takers is to study too hard during the last few days before the exam and then to leave the important practical matters until the last minute.

The Week Before Test Day

Do not try to study too hard on the days immediately before the exam. Instead, you should:

- Recheck your admission ticket for accuracy; call the TOEIC exam administrator if there are any problems.
- Visit the testing center if you can. Sometimes seeing the actual room where your exam will be administered may help to calm any anxiety. In addition, by visiting the center you can see how long it takes to arrive there, ensuring that you do not get lost on the day of the exam.
- Practice getting up early and working on exam material as if it were Test Day. Be sure to listen to the audio tracks so that you get in the habit of listening to English early in the day.
- Evaluate thoroughly where you stand. Use the last week before Test Day to focus on your weaker points and reread those chapters of this book. Do not neglect your strong areas, however; after all, this is where you will score most of your points.
- Make sure all of your practices are timed, even if you are not doing a full length test.

TEST KIT

The night before the exam, collect the following items to bring with you to the exam:

- admission ticket
- photo ID card
- a watch (you must shut off any alarms, cell phones, or beepers while taking the exam)
- Headache medicine, just in case

The Day Before Test Day

Try to avoid doing intensive studying the day before the exam. You have probably learned a good amount about the TOEIC at this stage, and it is difficult to learn a lot of new information the day before a test, so you should focus on revising what you already know. Review key strategies, get together everything you will need for Test Day, and then do something relaxing.

Test Day

Plan to arrive early to your exam center; the administrators will not admit latecomers. Make sure you have your test kit with you, especially your admission ticket and photo ID. Most centers have a clock, but you may still want to bring a watch, just in case. Bear in mind that smart watches and mobile phones are not permitted in the exam.

After the exam booklets are handed out and you have filled out all the necessary forms, the TOEIC exam will begin. The administrator will either write or call out the starting time for each section and will also usually announce the time at specified intervals.

The exam begins with the Listening Comprehension Section, followed by the Reading Comprehension Section. Between the two sections, the administrator will tell you that the time has expired and it is time to go on to the next section. You should then immediately go from the Listening Comprehension

Section to the Reading Comprehension Section. Use this time to take a deep breath and refocus your concentration. Remember, if you finish the Reading Comprehension Section early, you will not be able to go back to the Listening Comprehension Section. Use this time to review your work on the Reading Comprehension Section.

During the exam, try not to think about how you are scoring. Instead, focus on the task of selecting the right answer. Remember, you do not have to create the correct answer—it is right there in front of you. Think about how well you have prepared and be confident and positive about your abilities.

After the TOEIC Exam

After all your hard work in preparing for the TOEIC exam, be sure to celebrate once it is over. Get together with your family and friends, relax, and have fun. You have a lot to celebrate: You prepared for the exam ahead of time. You did your best. You are going to get a good score.

STRESS BUSTERS

If you are like most people preparing for the TOEIC exam, you may be feeling anxious about it. You may be worried about your listening comprehension skills, for example, or all those new words you just learned, or what will happen if you do not get a certain score. All those stressful thoughts and fears can make you nervous, sleepless, and ultimately less able to perform well on the exam.

At Kaplan, we believe that learning to control stress and anxiety is a key part to boosting your TOEIC exam score. That is why we have included the following stress-busting techniques. By practicing them—no matter how silly they may seem—you will lessen your exam anxiety, and let all the hard studying you have done pay off.

Before the Test

Just as an athlete needs to train to perform well in a sports event, you can train to do your best on the TOEIC exam. Here are some tips for getting into peak condition, both mentally and physically.

Make English a Part of Every Day

Surround yourself with the English language in the weeks and months leading up to your exam. Get in the habit of reading or listening to something in English every day, separate from your study time. Even if it is just ten or fifteen minutes a day, listening to something in English and trying to figure out who is talking, why they are talking, and what they are talking about will help you improve your listening comprehension. You can do the same thing with reading. By reading anything you see written in English, such as advertisements, signs, or directions, and by asking yourself what their meaning is, you will be working on your reading comprehension. Even more importantly, you will become more and more familiar, and therefore more comfortable, with English. The level of comfort you have with English, whether it is listening or reading, will help reduce stress and nervousness when you take the actual TOEIC exam.

Talk

Talk to other friends or colleagues who are taking the TOEIC exam. Chances are, they are feeling the same sort of stress that you are. Sharing your fears and worries with people who can understand them is a proven way to alleviate stress.

Think

Positive thinking is also a good way to ward off anxiety. Tell yourself things such as "I choose to take this exam," rather than "I have to"; "I will do well," rather than "I hope things go well"; "I can," rather than "I cannot." Any time a negative thought occurs, conquer it with a positive one. This builds your self-esteem and confidence.

This technique is especially useful at night when you are just about to fall asleep. Because your mind is very open to suggestion then, think about all your positive accomplishments and skills (*I performed well at work today*; *I like where I'm living*; *I relate well to my friends*; etc.). You will wake up feeling a lot more positive in the morning.

Eat

Try to eat healthy foods before the exam: fruits and vegetables, low-fat foods, proteins, and whole grains. Do not fill up on sugary or high-fat snacks. Sugar makes stress worse and fatty foods are not healthy. Steer clear of heavily salted foods, too; they can deplete potassium, which you need for nerve function.

Exercise

Whether it is walking, jogging, biking, swimming, skating, or aerobics, physical exercise is a proven way to stimulate your mind and body and to improve your ability to concentrate. After all, exercise pumps more oxygen into the blood, which helps you think better. Even if you do not regularly exercise, take a five- to ten-minute activity break for every hour that you study. This will help keep your body and mind in balance.

One warning about exercise: It is not a good idea to exercise vigorously immediately before bedtime.

Take a Break

Do not study up to the moment you go to sleep. You need some time for your mind to relax; otherwise, you will lie awake worrying about your studies.

Breathe

Breathing deeply and regularly is an excellent way to stay relaxed. Try closing your eyes and breathing in slowly and deeply through your nose. Hold the breath for a bit and then release it through your mouth. The key is to take in air slowly and to use your diaphragm. Breathing with your diaphragm encourages relaxation and helps minimize tension.

Imagine

When you are feeling very anxious, it is helpful to take a break, find a quiet place, and sit comfortably. If you wear glasses, take them off. Then close your eyes and breathe deeply for a few minutes, as previously described. Fill your diaphragm and lungs as fully as you can and then exhale the air completely. While you're doing this, imagine yourself in a relaxing situation. It might be a special place you have visited—a garden or beach, for example—or one you have read about. Imagine the smells, the sounds, and the way things feel in that place. Stay in that place for as long as you feel comfortable. Then, take a moment to check how you are feeling. Focus on staying relaxed and then imagine you are taking the TOEIC exam with this same calm feeling.

Practice this exercise often, especially when you are starting to feel anxious. The more you practice it, the more effective the exercise will be for you.

During the Test

The TOEIC exam requires a high level of concentration and quick responses. Your state of mind as you take the exam will affect your score. Here are some tips for performing your best as you take the TOEIC exam.

Keep Moving

Do not get stuck on a difficult question or passage. You do not have to get everything right to achieve a good score, so do not spend an excessive amount of time on a question that is too difficult for you. Select the best possible choice and then move on! While you cannot go back to review the listening items after the recording has played, in the Reading Comprehension Section you can always go back to the more difficult questions later.

Concentrate

Other test takers may seem to be working more busily than you are, but do not pay attention to them! Other people's activity levels are not necessarily signs of progress or higher scores. Continue to work carefully and thoroughly, especially on the Reading Comprehension Section of the exam.

Breathe

Weak test takers tend to share one major characteristic: They forget to breathe properly as the exam proceeds. They start holding their breath without realizing it, or they breathe without a normal rhythm. Improper breathing hurts confidence and accuracy, and it interferes with clear thinking. Breathe deeply and steadily, and remember your relaxation exercises.

Think Positively!

If you get discouraged during the exam, remember:

- You do not have to get every single question right to achieve a high score.
- By having studied the strategies in this book, you are better prepared than the majority of other test takers are.
- You are probably doing better than you realize. Think to yourself: "I can do well on this exam!"

PART TWO

The Listening Comprehension Section

CHAPTER 3

Exam Part I—Photograph Questions

LEARNING OBJECTIVES

In this section, you'll learn to:

- Identify the key features of the photographs
- Use the Kaplan Strategies to evaluate the statements
- Identify the common distractors used in Part I

Time Budget for Part I: Approximately 5 minutes

For this part of the TOEIC exam, you will look at six photographs. For each photograph, you will hear four different statements. You must decide which of the four statements best describes each photograph. There will be a five-second pause between the end of the last statement for a photograph and the first statement of the next photograph.

TEST-TAKING STRATEGIES

Strategy 1: Know the Directions

It is important to understand what you are being asked to do *before* you take the test. The directions will look something like this:

> **Listening Comprehension Section**
>
> In the Listening Comprehension Section, you will have the chance to demonstrate how well you understand spoken English. The Listening Comprehension Section will take approximately 45 minutes. There are four parts, and directions are given for each part. You must mark your answers on the separate answer sheet. Do not write them in the test book.

Directions: For each question, you will hear four statements about the photograph in your test book. When you hear the statements, choose the one statement that best describes what you see in the photograph. Then, find the number of the question on your answer sheet and mark your answer. The statements will not be written in your test book and will be spoken just once.

For the example photograph shown, you will hear:

Narrator:	*A.*
Woman:	*They're making coffee.*
Narrator:	*B.*
Woman:	*They're planting the seeds.*
Narrator:	*C.*
Woman:	*They're discussing a project.*
Narrator:	*D.*
Woman:	*They're standing on the table.*

Choice (C), *They're discussing a project,* best describes what you see in the photograph.

Strategy 2: Look at the First Few Photographs

The directions are the same for each photograph: you must choose the statement which best describes what you see. Because you already know the directions, look at the first few photographs in your test book while the directions are playing. This will let you know what to expect and what you will need to listen for.

As you look at the photographs, think about what they are showing and how that might be described in English.

Strategy 3: Focus on the Photograph

As you look at each photograph, decide what the main action or idea is. The correct statement about the photograph will almost always deal with the most important element in the photograph.

The correct answer will not usually be a minor detail; it will be the answer to this question: "What is this a photograph of?"

In the example photograph, the man who is standing is also holding a tea cup. TOEIC exam writers would not make the correct answer "*The man is holding a tea cup.*" While this statement is true, it is not the main action or element shown in the photograph. Ask yourself, "What is this a photograph of?" It is a photograph of four people having a conversation about something.

When there are people in the photographs, it can be easy to decide what the main action is. The people are usually doing something. The correct statement will probably be about whatever it is they are doing. However, some photographs on the TOEIC exam do not have any people in them; they might show a group of objects or a landscape, for example. With these photographs, it can be more difficult to say what is being shown.

To help focus on the main action or element in a photograph without people in it, ask yourself:

- Where was the photograph taken? If the location is very obvious, such as the beach or a parking lot, then the answer may be about where the photograph was taken.
- What objects are being shown? The answer may be testing whether you know what they are called.
- How are the objects located or positioned? If the photograph shows several objects, the answer may involve the location or position of the objects—for example, whether one object is in front of, on top of, or behind another.

Look at each photograph quickly and decide in your own words what it shows. Each photograph shows one main action or idea; the answer for each photograph is the statement that best describes what is happening, which almost always refers to the most obvious action or object in the photograph.

Look again at the example photograph in the directions. What is it a photograph of? Your answer is probably something very close to this: "Four people are around a table talking." The correct statement is choice (C), *They're discussing a project.*

Most of the time, your first thought will be the correct answer.

Strategy 4: Evaluate the Statements

Once you have decided in your own words what the photograph is showing and have decided on the main action, you must listen to and evaluate the statements you hear. Because each statement will be spoken only once, you must listen carefully.

Listen for a statement that is a close match to what you decided the photograph was of. Be sure to listen to all four statements before you mark your answer sheet. If one of the statements is a close match to the answer you have been expecting, find the number for the question on your answer sheet and mark the oval for the letter that matches your answer.

Strategy 5: Eliminate False Statements

If it seems like none of the statements match your expected answer very well, then you must start eliminating any choices that are false. The best way to do that is to repeat each statement to yourself and ask whether or not it is true.

Look at directions example again.

Statement (A) *They're making coffee.*

This is clearly false. One man is holding a cup that might contain coffee, but no one is making coffee. You can eliminate this choice.

Statement (B) *They're planting the seeds.*

This is also false. There are no seeds and they are not planting anything. You can eliminate this choice.

Statement (C) *They're discussing a project.*

This is true; they are talking together. Therefore, you should keep this choice.

Statement (D) *They're standing on the table.*

This is false. The people are at a table, but three are seated around the table, while another is standing nearby. No one is standing on the table. You can eliminate this choice.

In this example, only choice (C), *They're discussing a project*, is true. Choices (A), (B), and (D) can be eliminated because they are false.

In the example, the main action was very clear, and it was easy to identify the statements that were false. If only one or two choices seem false to you, or if you cannot eliminate all the wrong answers, then you must select the best match from what is left.

You have already decided what the answer should be in your own words. Consider whether any of the answer choices contain words that are similar to what you expected the correct answer to use. In the directions example, you might expect the word *talking* or *working*. The only choice that contains a similar word is 'discussing' in (C), which is the correct answer. If you are unable to eliminate answer choices, select the choice that uses words or phrases that are similar to your expected answer.

Strategy 6: Answer the Current Question Before the Next One Begins

You should answer every question as quickly as you can. You have only about five seconds to choose your answer for each photograph. You should be finished with the current question before the next set of statements begins. If you are still answering a question when the next one begins, you might not hear the first statement.

As soon as you have finished a question, look ahead to the next photograph and ask yourself what it is a photograph of. Answer in your own words, and listen for the statement that most closely matches yours.

Strategy 7: Know the Distractors

There are several kinds of distractors used in Part I. Here are the most common:

- wrong word usage
- similar-sounding words
- reasonable statements/assumptions
- irrelevant statements
- hybrids

More than one type of distractor may be used in a photograph. Not all distractors fit into these categories; some may belong to more than one category. Note also that each of these distractor types is similar because, in the end, they are false and do not describe what is happening in the photograph. However, it is useful to look at *why* they are false and to understand what it is you must listen for. The following pages will look at each distractor in turn.

Wrong Word Usage

This type of distractor essentially asks you to identify the correct vocabulary word, or the correct form of a word. Each of the choices might, for example, use the same form of a verb but change the nouns they refer to. Alternatively, they might use the correct noun throughout, but change the verbs. Prepositions can also be tested this way. This distractor type is often easy to eliminate.

Example 1

Narrator:	*Look at the photograph marked number 1 in your test book.*
Narrator:	*A.*
Woman:	*They're examining the documents.*
Narrator:	*B.*
Woman:	*They're copying the documents.*
Narrator:	*C.*
Woman:	*They're writing on the documents.*
Narrator:	*D.*
Woman:	*They're emailing the documents.*

The correct statement is choice (A), *They're examining the documents.* Choices (B), (C), and (D) all use the wrong verb to describe what is happening. This is essentially a vocabulary item.

Similar-Sounding Words

This type of distractor uses words that sound similar to the correct answer.

Example 2

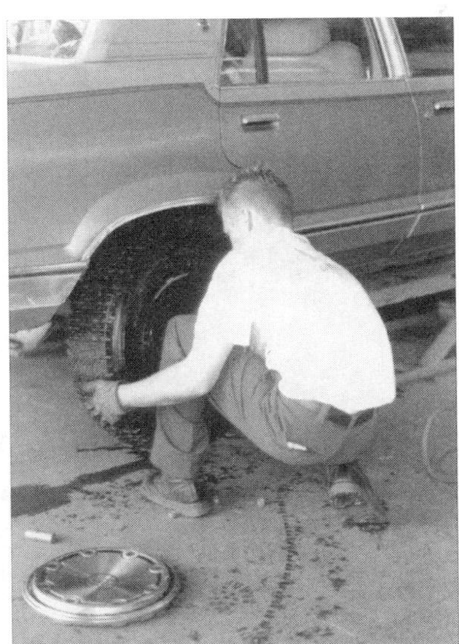

Narrator:	*Look at the photograph marked number 2 in your test book.*
Narrator:	*A.*
Woman:	*The man is changing his tie.*
Narrator:	*B.*
Woman:	*The man is putting out a fire.*
Narrator:	*C.*
Woman:	*The man is changing a tire.*
Narrator:	*D.*
Woman:	*The man is going to retire.*

The correct statement is choice (C), *The man is changing a tire.* Choices (A), (B), and (D) all use words that sound similar to *tire* (e.g. *tie, fire, retire*). Sometimes the similar-sounding words will be nouns—as in choices (A) and (B). At other times, the similar-sounding words may be verbs—as in choice (D)—or other parts of speech.

Reasonable Statements/Assumptions

This type of distractor may refer to objects or actions in the photograph and, therefore, may seem reasonable, but the statement does not correctly describe what you see. It may also make assumptions about what may (or may not) be happening in the photograph. When a statement makes an assumption, it is usually wrong.

Example 3

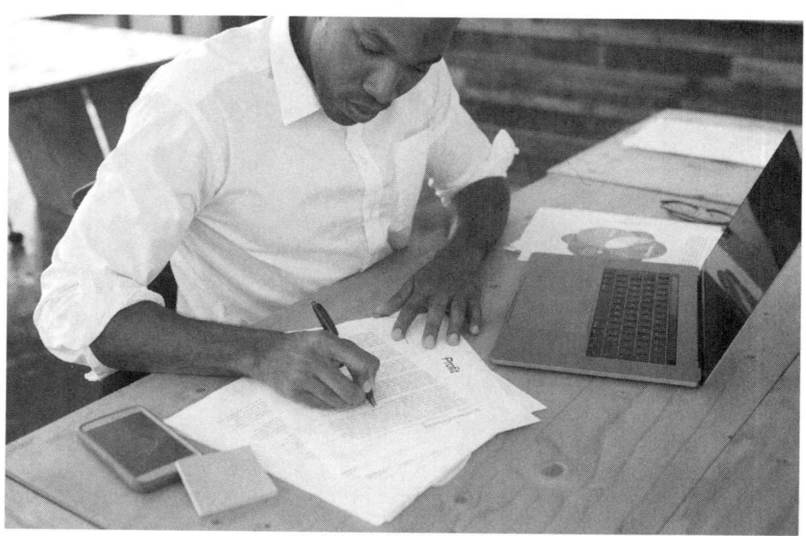

Narrator:	*Look at the photograph marked number 3 in your test book.*
Narrator:	*A.*
Woman:	*The man is working at his desk.*
Narrator:	*B.*
Woman:	*The man just sat down in the chair.*
Narrator:	*C.*
Woman:	*The man is installing software on his computer.*
Narrator:	*D.*
Woman:	*The man is deleting an email.*

The correct statement is choice (A), *The man is working at his desk.* Choice (B) uses the words *sat down* and *chair* because the man is, in fact, sitting in a chair; however, we do not know whether or not he *just sat down*—meaning he sat down very recently. He may have been sitting there for several hours. This is an example of a reasonable statement that also makes an assumption. Choice (C) uses the word *computer* because we can see a computer in the photograph; however, we do not know if the man is *installing software.* Again, this is an example of a reasonable statement that also makes an assumption. Choice (D) uses the phrase *deleting an email,* because that is an activity that can be associated with using a computer; however, we do not know whether or not he is deleting an email, writing an email, opening a document, or performing some other activity.

Irrelevant Statements

This type of distractor uses statements that do not describe anything in the photograph. It often uses words or phrases that may seem like they should go with the objects or main action in the photograph.

Example 4

Narrator:	*Look at the photograph marked number 4 in your test book.*
Narrator:	*A.*
Man:	*The waiter is setting the table.*
Narrator:	*B.*
Man:	*The spoons are next to the forks.*
Narrator:	*C.*
Man:	*The food is in the refrigerator.*
Narrator:	*D.*
Man:	*The dishes are stacked on shelves.*

The correct statement is choice (D), *The dishes are stacked on shelves.* Choice (A) refers to a *waiter* and *setting the table*, which can both be associated with *dishes*; however, this statement does not describe anything that can be seen in the photograph. Choice (B) refers to *spoons* and *forks*, which again are both associated with *dishes*; however, this statement does not describe anything that can be seen in the photograph. Choice (C) refers to *food* and a *refrigerator*, which can both be associated with *dishes*; however, this statement does not describe anything that can be seen in the photograph.

Hybrids

This type of distractor combines similar-sounding words, references to objects that may be seen in the photograph, or words and phrases that seem like they should go with the objects or main action in the photograph. These distractors are working to distract you on several levels at once. They are very common, and they are usually the most difficult to eliminate.

Example 5

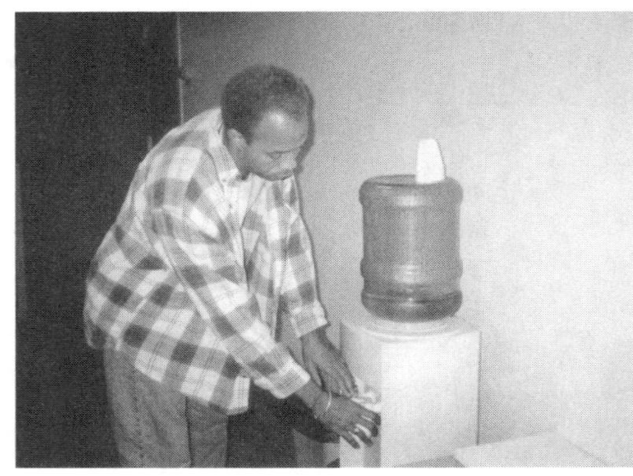

Narrator:	*Look at the photograph marked number 5 in your test book.*
Narrator:	*A.*
Woman:	*He's watering the plants.*
Narrator:	*B.*
Woman:	*He's putting on glasses.*
Narrator:	*C.*
Woman:	*He's getting some water.*
Narrator:	*D.*
Woman:	*He's spilling water from a cup.*

The correct statement is choice (C), *He's getting some water.* Choice (A) uses the word *watering*, which is similar to the expected word, *water*. It is also an irrelevant statement because there are no *plants* in the photograph, and the statement does not describe what is happening. This hybrid distractor is a combination of similar-sounding words and an irrelevant statement. Choice (B) uses the word *glasses*. We might expect the correct answer to use the word *cup* or *glass*. The word *glasses* sounds similar to the word *glass,* but *glasses* refers in this case to *eyeglasses*. There are no *glasses* in the photograph, so the statement does not describe what is happening. This hybrid distractor is a combination of similar-sounding words and an irrelevant statement. Choice (D) uses the word *spilling*, which sounds similar to the expected word *filling*. It also uses the expected words *water* and *cup*; however, the statement does not describe what is happening. This hybrid distractor is a combination of similar-sounding words and a reasonable statement.

Strategy Summary

1. Know the directions.
2. Look ahead at the photographs while the directions are playing.
3. Focus on the main action and ask, "What is this a photograph of?"
4. Evaluate the answer choices.
5. Eliminate as many answer choices as you can.
6. Answer each question before the next one starts.
7. Understand the common distractor types.

PHOTOGRAPH PRACTICE SET

Now you are ready to listen to the audio and practice some Photograph questions on your own. You may turn the audio on or off at any point, but try playing the statements for at least two photographs at a time. You will find the script for each set of questions in Part 6 of this book, but we suggest listening without the script so you will be better prepared for the real exam.

You will hear four short statements for each photograph. When you hear the four statements, look at the photograph and choose the statement that best describes what is in the photograph.

You can mark your answers in the ovals next to the photographs and then check them against the answer key that follows the practice questions. (Remember that on Test Day you will mark your answers on the answer grid.) Once you have checked your answers, be sure to read the review that follows the answer key.

PART I: PHOTOGRAPHS

Directions: For each question, you will hear four statements about the photograph in your test book. When you hear the statements, choose the one statement that best describes what you see in the photograph. Then, find the number of the question on your answer sheet and mark your answer. The statements will not be written in your test book and will be spoken just once.

Now listen to the four statements. Ⓐ Ⓑ Ⓒ Ⓓ

Choice (C), "They're gathered around the table," best describes what you see in the picture. Therefore, you should fill in choice (C) in your answer sheet.

Track 1

Play Track 1 to hear the statements for the Photograph practice questions.

1. 

Ⓐ Ⓑ Ⓒ Ⓓ

2. 

Ⓐ Ⓑ Ⓒ Ⓓ

3. 

4. 

(A) (B) (C) (D)

5. 

Ⓐ Ⓑ Ⓒ Ⓓ

6. 

Ⓐ Ⓑ Ⓒ Ⓓ

7. 

8. 

Ⓐ Ⓑ Ⓒ Ⓓ

9.

10.

(A) (B) (C) (D)

11. 

12. 

13.

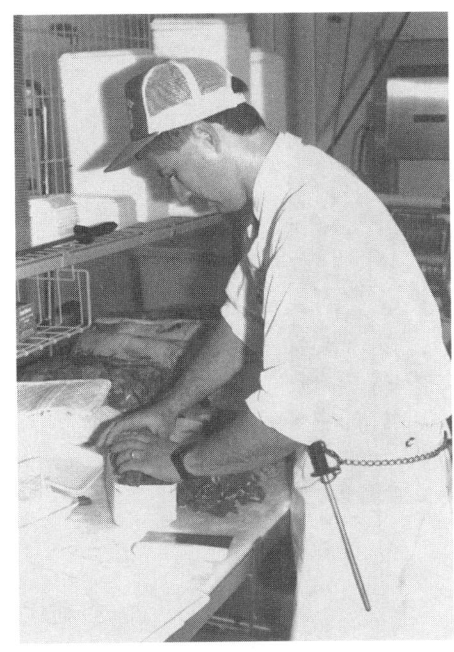

14.

Ⓐ Ⓑ Ⓒ Ⓓ

15. 

16. 

17.

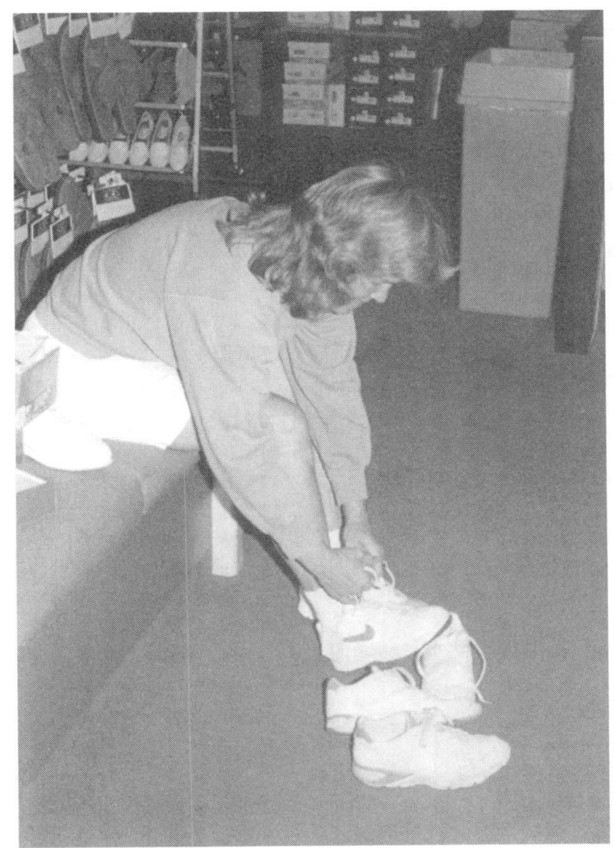

Ⓐ Ⓑ Ⓒ Ⓓ

18.

Ⓐ Ⓑ Ⓒ Ⓓ

19. 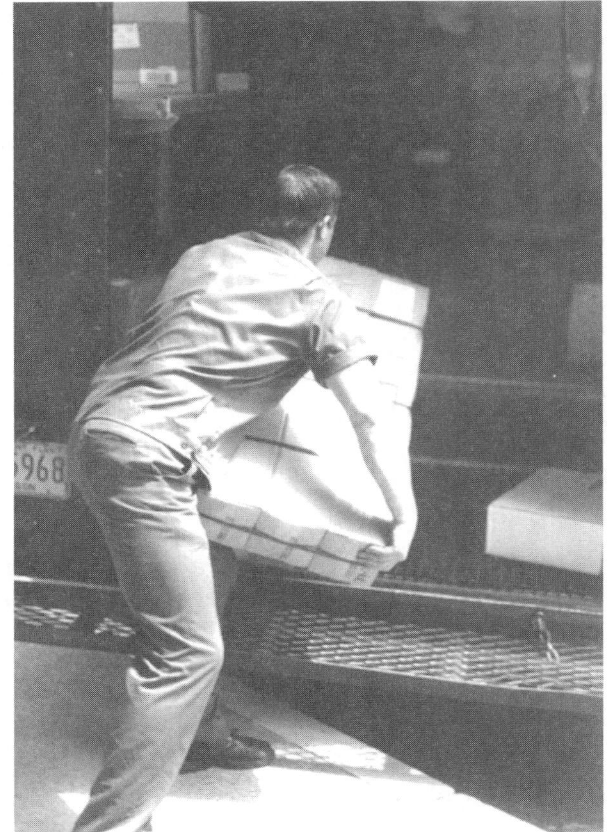

Ⓐ Ⓑ Ⓒ Ⓓ

20. 

Ⓐ Ⓑ Ⓒ Ⓓ

21. 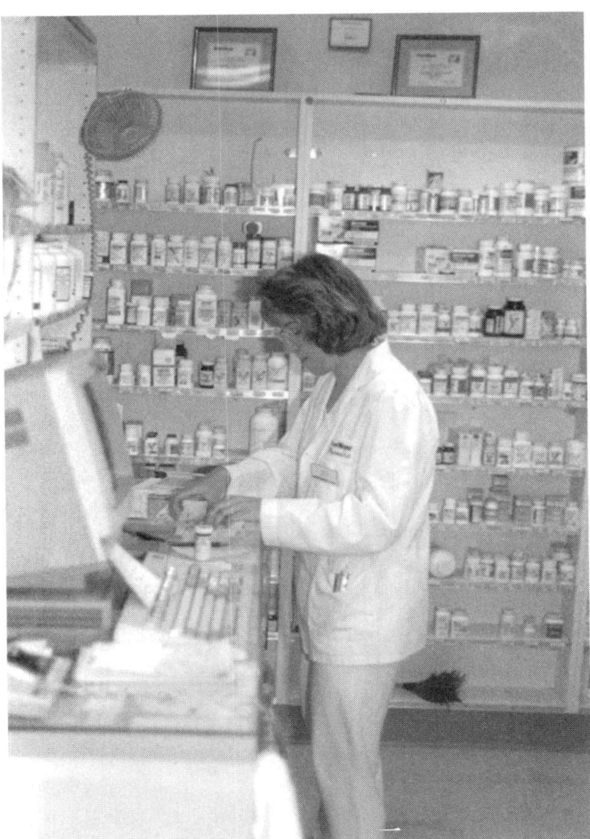

Ⓐ Ⓑ Ⓒ Ⓓ

22. 

Ⓐ Ⓑ Ⓒ Ⓓ

23. 

24. 

(A) (B) (C) (D)

ANSWER KEY

1. A
2. C
3. A
4. C
5. B
6. B
7. A
8. D
9. C
10. D
11. C
12. D
13. B
14. A
15. D
16. D
17. B
18. B
19. D
20. A
21. D
22. C
23. C
24. B

ANSWERS AND EXPLANATIONS

All of the answer choices are included for each question with an explanation of exactly why the wrong answer choices are incorrect. For some questions, we have left the wrong answer explanations blank so that you can fill them in. The more you can analyze and explain the errors in the wrong answer choices, the more skillful and efficient you will become at eliminating incorrect choices and selecting the correct ones.

Sample responses for these "Identify the Error" answer explanations are included at the end of the Answers and Explanations section.

1. A. He is sorting envelopes into the boxes. CORRECT
   B. All of the boxes are filled to capacity. (Most of the boxes are filled, but not to capacity.)
   C. He is writing letters to his colleagues. (He is sorting letters, not writing them.)
   D. The squares are stacked on top of each other. (The boxes are not squares.)

2. A. The cable is old and rusty. (The cable is not rusty in the photograph.)
   B. The wire is in front of the school. (The photograph is of a spool, not a school.)
   C. The cable is coiled on spools. CORRECT
   D. The spools are being delivered by truck. (We do not know from looking at the photograph whether they are being delivered, or how they might be delivered.)

3. A. Several parking spots are available. CORRECT
   B. A parking attendant is counting the cars. (There is no attendant in the photograph.)
   C. The people are getting into their cars. (There are no people in the photograph.)
   D. The parking lot is completely filled. (You can see empty spaces in the parking lot.)

4. A. The woman is watching television. (There is no television.)
   B. The woman is sending a business contract from her cell phone. (This cannot be determined from the photograph.)
   C. The phone is being used. CORRECT
   D. The woman is walking down the staircase. (The woman is standing still.)

5. A. He is taking inventory at the store. (There is no paperwork to suggest inventory.)
   B. He is putting pants on the hanger. CORRECT
   C. He is hanging the pictures on the wall. (He is hanging something, but not pictures.)
   D. He is hemming the pants at the shop. (He is hanging pants, not hemming them.)

6. A. They are checking all the boxes. (They are checking their flights.)
   B. They are looking at the departure board. CORRECT
   C. They have just departed from an airplane. (They are waiting for their flight.)
   D. They are all looking bored. (They are looking at the board, but they are not bored.)

7. A. The housekeeper is making the bed. CORRECT
   B. The woman is going to bed. ____________
   ____
   C. The sheets need changing. ____________
   ____
   D. The maid is folding towels. ____________
   ____

8. A. The equipment is full of dirt. ____________
   ____
   B. The vehicle is being driven on the highway. ____________
   C. He's working under the trees. ____________
   ____
   D. The man is operating construction equipment. CORRECT

9. A. The man is leaving the store with the boards. (The exit is not in the photograph.)
   B. The boards are being sawed in the back room. (Nothing is being sawed.)
   C. The store sells lumber. CORRECT
   D. The store is filled with many customers. (Only one customer is in the photograph.)

10. A. The women are being shown to their table. (The women have already been seated at their table.)
    B. The waitress has spilled soup on her sleeve. (We do not know what happened in the past.)
    C. The women are getting ready to leave. (The women are being served dessert, not getting ready to leave.)
    D. The waitress is serving dessert to her customers. CORRECT

11. A. He is looking at his watch. (This is the noun form of *watch*.)
    B. He watches his step while he walks. (He is not walking.)
    C. He is watching something below. CORRECT
    D. He is washing the glass under the railing. (Washing is the wrong action.)

12. A. The nurse is entering patient information into the computer. (She is entering information into a form.)
    B. She attends to the sick patient all by herself. (She is not helping a patient.)
    C. She is standing patiently while she waits for the doctor. (She is writing, not standing patiently.)
    D. The nurse is writing notes on the paper. CORRECT

13. A. He is cooking meat at the restaurant. (He is packing meat, not cooking.)
    B. The butcher packs meat on small trays. CORRECT
    C. He meets his deadline for unpacking the trays. (This is using the verb *meet*, not the noun *meat*.)
    D. The chef is chopping the meat into small pieces. (He is packing meat that is already chopped.)

14. A. She is stacking boxes on top of each other. CORRECT
    B. She is putting groceries on the shelf. (She is stacking boxes, not putting groceries on the shelf.)
    C. She is getting a refund at the store. (It is not clear that she is in a store or is getting a refund.)
    D. She is purchasing office supplies. (There are no office supplies in the photograph.)

15. A. The man is buying a new tennis racquet.

    ____

    B. The woman is writing a check for the merchandise.

    ____

    C. The woman is helping a couple move furniture.

    ____

    D. The woman is assisting the customers with a purchase. CORRECT

16. A. He is driving his car to the construction site. ______________________________
    B. The truck is leaving the construction area. ______________________________
    C. He is burning garbage at the construction site.

    ____

    D. The construction debris is being loaded into the trash container. CORRECT

17. A. The shoes are stacked on the floor. (The shoes are stacked on racks and shelves.)
    B. She is trying the shoes on for size. CORRECT
    C. The shoes are all on sale. (We do not know whether they are on sale.)
    D. She is walking into the shoe store. (She is already in the shoe store.)

18. A. The material is displayed on racks. (There are no racks.)
    B. The material is stacked on pallets. CORRECT
    C. The stack of materials is wet. (We cannot see if it is wet in the photograph.)
    D. The man is stacking the material. (There is no man in the photograph.)

19. A. The package fell out of the truck. (We do not know what happened in the past.)
    B. There is no room in the truck for the package. (There is a lot of room in the truck.)
    C. The package has already been opened. (We cannot know whether it has been opened.)
    D. He's loading the package into the truck. CORRECT

20. A. He wears headphones while he is on the air. CORRECT
    B. The air inside the studio is chilly. (We cannot know whether it is chilly. He is wearing short sleeves, so it is actually probably comfortable.)
    C. He is using a remote to change the channel. (He is adjusting a knob, on a control panel, not changing a channel.)
    D. He is speaking into a telephone. (He is speaking into a microphone, not a telephone.)

21. A. The pharmacist is taking an order for a prescription. (She is not taking an order.)
    B. The farmer is buying fertilizer for her crops. (There is no farmer, fertilizer, or crops.)
    C. The woman is reaching for a bottle from the shelf. (She is not reaching for the shelf.)
    D. The pharmacist is filling a customer's prescription. CORRECT

22. A. The camera crew is carrying the equipment. (They are not carrying anything.)
    B. The camera man is talking on the phone. (There are several people, and none is on the phone.)
    C. The camera crew is taking a break. CORRECT
    D. The camera man is loading film into the camera. (No one is loading film.)

23. A. They are balancing the company's books.

    ____

    B. The woman waits while the man looks.

    ____

    C. The man and woman are reviewing a document. CORRECT
    D. The woman watches the man prepare the invoice.

    ____

24. A. The boys are ignoring the speaker.

    ____

    B. The boys listen and watch while the man speaks. CORRECT
    C. He's teaching the boys how to paint the fence.

    ____

    D. The man is coaching a football team.

    ____

Responses for the Identify the Error Questions

7. A. The housekeeper is making the bed. CORRECT
   B. The woman is going to bed. (*She is making the bed, not getting ready to sleep.*)
   C. The sheets need changing. (*The sheets are clean and fresh.*)
   D. The maid is folding towels. (*She is folding the bedspread.*)

8. A. The equipment is full of dirt. (*There is no dirt in the equipment.*)
   B. The vehicle is being driven on the highway. (*The vehicle is not on the highway.*)
   C. He's working under the trees. (*He is under a building structure.*)
   D. The man is operating construction equipment. CORRECT

15. A. The man is buying a new tennis racquet. (*There is no tennis racquet in the photograph.*)
    B. The woman is writing a check for the merchandise. (*The woman writing is a clerk, not a buyer.*)
    C. The woman is helping a couple move furniture. (*There is no furniture being moved.*)
    D. The woman is assisting the customers with a purchase. CORRECT

16. A. He is driving his car to the construction site. (*The vehicle is not a car and it is already at the site.*)
    B. The truck is leaving the construction area. (*It is not a truck and it is not leaving.*)
    C. He is burning garbage at the construction site. (*There is no burning garbage seen.*)
    D. The construction debris is being loaded into the trash container. CORRECT

23. A. They are balancing the company's books. (*They are not doing accounting.*)
    B. The woman waits while the man looks. (*They are interacting.*)
    C. The man and woman are reviewing a document. CORRECT
    D. The woman watches the man prepare the invoice. (*They are working together.*)

24. A. The boys are ignoring the speaker. (*They are listening to him.*)
    B. The boys listen and watch while the man speaks. CORRECT
    C. He's teaching the boys how to paint the fence. (*There is a fence, but it is a minor detail in the photograph.*)
    D. The man is coaching a football team. (*A learning activity is not necessarily a sporting activity.*)

CHAPTER 4

Exam Part II—Question-Response

LEARNING OBJECTIVES

In this section, you'll learn to:

- Identify the 4 question categories for Part II
- Identify the purpose of the question or statement
- Identify the 4 main distractors used in the responses

Time Budget for Part II: Approximately 10 minutes

For this part of the TOEIC exam, you will listen to 25 questions and will hear three spoken responses to each question. You must decide the best response for each question. There will be an eight-second pause between each question.

TEST-TAKING STRATEGIES

Strategy 1: Know the Directions

It is important to understand what you are being asked to do *before* you take the test. The directions will look something like this:

Directions: You will hear a question or statement and three responses spoken in English. They will be spoken only once and will not be printed in your test book. Choose the best response to the question or statement and mark the letter on your answer sheet.

Listen to a sample question:

Man:	*Where is the meeting room?*
Narrator:	*A.*
Woman:	*To meet the new supervisor.*
Narrator:	*B.*

Woman: *It's the second room on the left.*
Narrator: *C.*
Woman: *No, at three o'clock.*

Choice (B), *It's the second room on the left,* best answers the question.

Strategy 2: Know the Question Types

The question types for Part II can be divided into four broad categories:

1. New information
2. Choice
3. *Yes/No*
4. Tag

Knowing the different kinds of question types will help you to anticipate answers and to eliminate distractors.

New Information Questions

New information questions are the most common type of question on the exam. They use question words (*who, what, where, why, when,* and *how*). They ask about details and require answers that provide new, specific information. The correct answers are usually *not* simply "yes" or "no."

Question Word	Examples
What + verb	
Common verbs for *What* questions are:	
do	*What does Technoline Inc. charge for its services?*
be	*What aren't we supposed to delete?*
have	*What have you told Sarah regarding the mix-up?*
will	*What will George say about the cost overruns?*
can	*What can't they ship by today?*
could	*What could we do to improve office morale?*
should	*What should have been done differently?*
would	*What wouldn't you want to change in the contract?*
might	*What might be causing the delay in shipping?*

Question Word	Examples
The verbs that follow the word *what* can occur in all tenses, and they can be positive or negative. ***What + verb questions*** Cover a large number of topics. There is no "formula" for predicting the correct answers. The answers will depend on the specific verbs used in the questions.	
What + noun/noun phrase	
The word *what* can be followed by singular or plural nouns or noun phrases. *What + noun/noun phrase* questions cover a large number of topics. There is no "formula" for predicting the correct answers; the answers will depend on the specific nouns or noun phrases used in the questions.	*What reason did they give for not paying on time?* *What time is the meeting?* *What day would be best for you?* *What plans do you have for expanding your market share?* *What kind of company is Troglodyne?* *What types of products does your company sell?* *What sort of person would be good at this job?*
What collocations	
Certain collocations or fixed expressions are formed with the word *what.*	*What about . . .* *What if . . .*
The words *what about* can be used to make a suggestion. The answer will usually be either an agreement or a disagreement with the suggestion, plus a reason for agreeing or disagreeing (e.g. *That's a good idea, but...*). The words *what about* can also be used to ask the status of something.	*What about offering a discount on volume purchases?* (Suggestion) *What about their plan to downsize the workforce?* (Asking about status)
The words *what if* ask about a possibility—a situation that has not happened but that is possible.	*What if we hired temporary workers over the holidays?* *What if nobody likes the new advertisement?*
Where + verb	
Common verbs for *Where* questions are:	
do	*Where did you put the Johnson project folder?*
be	*Where's the best place in town to go for sushi?*
have	*Where have you decided to open your next store?*
will	*Where will the new secretary's desk go?*
can	*Where can I find more information on this?*
could	*Where could we go to get a better price?*

Question Word	Examples
should	*Where should I send the invoice?*
would	*Where would you like me to put these boxes?*
The verbs that follow the word *where* can occur in all tenses, and they can be positive or negative.	
The answer to a *Where* question will be a location, often with a preposition (e.g. *On Smith Street*; *On my desk*; *Over there*; *At the post office*; *To the warehouse*; *etc.*).	
Who + verb	
Common verbs for *Who* questions are:	
do	*Who didn't respond to our questionnaire?*
be	*Who's in charge of marketing at Brayburn Inc.?*
have	*Who has the authority to make budget changes?*
will	*Who will we send to the seminar?*
can	*Who can we contact to get more information?*
could	*Who could have known about our plans?*
should	*Who should we call to get the copier fixed?*
would	*Who would be the best candidate for training?*
might	*Who might be interested in partnering with us on the project?*
The verbs that follow the word *who* can occur in all tenses, and they can be positive or negative.	
The answer to a *Who* question can be a person's or a company's name (e.g. *John Wilson*; *Mrs. Smith*; *Glaxon Industries*), a group (e.g. *Our customers*; *The board of directors*), or a person's title or rank (e.g. *the accountant, President Kim*).	
Why + verb	
Common verbs for *Why* questions are:	
do	*Why don't all your stores carry the full product line?*
be	*Why were the paychecks sent out late this week?*
have	*Why hasn't more been done to increase production?*
will	*Why won't Rebecca be at the meeting?*
can	*Why can they make the same product for less money?*
could	*Why couldn't we have gotten a better discount?*

Question Word	Examples
should	*Why should we wait another month?*
would	*Why wouldn't they send the parts right away?*
The verbs that follow the *why* can occur in all tenses, and they can be positive or negative.	*Why might Tom not like the plan?*
The answer to a *Why* question will be a reason or explanation. Often, answers will began with *Because . . .* or *To . . .*	
When + verb	
Common verbs for *When* questions are:	
do	*When did they sign the agreement?*
be	*When was Alan supposed to be here?*
have	*When has the meeting been scheduled for?*
will	*When will the next train arrive?*
can	*When can I expect my order to be delivered?*
could	*When couldn't you go?*
should	*When should we leave for the airport?*
would	*When would be a good time to call back?*
might	*When might the layoffs occur?*
The verbs that follow the word *when* can occur in all tenses, and they can be positive or negative; however, negative questions are uncommon.	
The answer to a *When* question will usually indicate a time (e.g. *On Friday*; *Tomorrow*; *At five o'clock*; *In six months*).	
How + verb	
Common verbs for *How* questions are:	
do	*How did SymTech get its start?*
be	*How were you planning to advertise the products?*
have	*How have the new tax laws affected us?*
will	*How will we measure the plan's success?*
can	*How can customers contact us?*
could	*How could we better invest our profits?*
should	*How should the president have responded?*
would	*How would you improve our website?*
might	*How might we get more data about our customers?*

Question Word	Examples
The verbs that follow the word *how* can occur in all tenses, and they can be positive or negative.	
The answer to a *How + verb* question will indicate the way in which something is done, or it will indicate an action that can or should be taken. Often, the answer will begin with the word *by* (e.g. *By sending a fax*; *By filling out a form*; *By bus*).	
How + adjective	
Common adjectives for *How* questions are:	
many	*How many employees does your company have?*
much	*How much are these?*
large	*How large is the freight elevator?*
big	*How big is your largest store?*
small	*How small are the rooms?*
fast	*How fast can you get the order out?*
slow	*How slow were they to pay?*
different	*How different are the two plans?*
similar	*How similar were the offers?*
long	*How long will it take to ship?*
near	*How near the airport is the hotel?*
far	*How far is the warehouse from here?*
close	*How close are they to being finished?*
The answer to a *How + adjective* question will indicate a degree or an amount (e.g. *Very large*; *Not far*; *Ten minutes*; *Six hours*).	
How + adverb	
Common adverbs for *How* questions are:	
often	*How often is website content updated?*
quickly	*How quickly can the project be finished?*
swiftly	*How swiftly can we get it done?*
slowly	*How slowly does the machine need to run?*
cheaply	*How cheaply can we make them?*
The answer to a *How + adverb* question will indicate a degree or an amount (e.g. *Fairly often*; *In two days*; *For five dollars each*).	

Question Word	Examples
How collocations	
How come . . .	*How come nobody's ever on time to meetings?* *How come I'm always the one who has to stay late?* *How come the copier's always out of toner?*
How is it that . . .	*How is it that Sandra did all the work, but Jared got all the credit?* *How is it that our competitors are doing so well?* *How is it that profits are down when sales are up?*
How about . . .	*How about offering employees more overtime opportunities?* *How about taking a break?* *How about getting Priya's input on this?*
The words *how come* . . . and *how is it that* . . . can both be used to complain. Answers to these questions will usually be reasons or explanations, often using the words *because* . . . or *to* . . . The words *how come* . . . and *how is it that* . . . are both similar to *Why* questions. The phrase *how about* is a suggestion. The answer will usually be either an agreement or disagreement with the suggestion, plus a reason for agreeing or disagreeing (e.g. *That's a good idea, but* . . .).	

Choice Questions

Choice questions ask about choices and preferences. They require answers that provide specific information. Choice questions often use the initial question word *which*.

Which suit do you like better?

The expected answer should indicate a specific choice or preference:

The blue one.

Often, Choice questions present the choices using the word *or*:

Would you like coffee or tea?

The expected answer should indicate a specific choice or preference:

Coffee, please, with a little cream.

Common phrases used in Choice questions include:

Which one/ones . . .
Which of these/those . . .
Which kind of/kinds of . . .
Which do you prefer . . .
Which do you like better . . .
Which would you choose . . .
Would you like A or B . . .

Common verbs used in Choice questions include the following. These all indicate that a choice or preference is being asked about.

like
prefer
want
choose

If you hear a Choice question, listen for a response that indicates a preference or choice. The answer to a Choice question is usually not simply "yes" or "no."

Yes/No Questions

Yes/No questions require an answer that is "yes," "no," or an expression of uncertainty, such as "I don't know" or "I'm not sure."

Are you going to the conference in San Francisco?

This question requires a yes/no response—either "yes," "no," or an expression of uncertainty:

Yes, I am.
No, I'm not.
I'm not sure.

Of course, other information can be added to the response:

Yes, in fact, I'll be making a presentation.
No, they're sending John instead.
I'm not sure; they might send John.

Note that the yes/no can be implied—not stated directly:

I'll be making a presentation.
They're sending John instead.
They might send John.

Some common ways to say or imply "yes" include:

Okay
Sure
No problem
I'd be glad to

Some common ways to say or imply "no" include:

Not really
Unfortunately
I'm afraid not

Some common ways to say or imply uncertainty include:

I'm not sure
I don't know
I think so
I don't think so
Maybe

There are many kinds of *Yes/No* questions. Following are the most common kinds that appear on the exam.

Verb	Examples
Do + subject pronoun + infinitive	
The verb *do* can occur in the present or past tense, and it can be positive or negative.	*Do I need to work this Saturday?* *Do you go to the gym every day?* *Doesn't she work in the accounting department?* *Does it require special training to use?* *Didn't they guarantee payment within 90 days?* *Didn't we ship their order on Monday?*
Do + possessive adjective + noun	
The verb *do* can occur in the present or past tense, and it can be positive or negative.	*Does my staff need to attend the meeting?* *Do your records match ours?* *Does his boss know what he's been doing?* *Don't its parts need to be serviced soon?* *Didn't our order get sent out on time?* *Did their payment clear?*
The nouns can be singular or plural.	

Verb	Examples
Do + -ing The verb *do* can occur in the present or past tense, and it can be positive or negative.	*Does paying in cash mean we'll get a discount?* *Did hiring more workers help your production problem?* *Doesn't shipping by air cost more?* *Didn't installing the wireless network take a lot of time?*
Be + subject pronouns + adjectives The verb *be* can occur in the present or past tense, and it can be positive or negative.	*Am I late for the meeting?* *Are you happy with your new job?* *Is Mr. Murphy sick today?* *Is it faster than the old one?* *Are they expensive?* *Aren't we lucky to have Phoebe on our staff?*
Be + subject pronouns + -ing The verb *be* can occur in the present or past tense, and it can be positive or negative.	*Am I doing this correctly?* *Are you waiting to speak to Mr. Crawford?* *Isn't Julie Reiss running the department these days?* *Is it operating more efficiently since it was upgraded?* *Are they coming to the party?* *Weren't we expecting a delivery from QualComp today?*
Have + subject pronoun + past participle The verb *have* can occur in the present or past tense, and it can be positive or negative.	*Have I worked here long enough to qualify for benefits?* *Haven't you finished the Scottsdale report yet?* *Has she called you about the cost estimate?* *Hasn't it cost too much money already?* *Hadn't they asked us to bill their client directly?* *Haven't we changed vendors?*
Can/Could + subject pronoun + infinitive The verbs *can/could* can be positive or negative.	*Can I send the documents to your home instead of your office?* *Could you come to work a little early tomorrow?* *Couldn't she find a cheaper apartment?* *Can it go any faster than that?* *Couldn't they hire you on a temporary basis?* *Can't we return it if it's damaged?*

Verb	Examples
Could + subject pronoun + have + past participle The verb *could* can be positive or negative.	*Couldn't I have gone with him?* *Could you have finished quicker if you had better tools?* *Couldn't he have gotten a better price somewhere else?* *Could it have been due to a clerical error?* *Couldn't they have waited a little longer?* *Could we have raised our prices too high?*
Will + subject pronoun + infinitive The verb *will* can be positive or negative.	*Won't I need to bring my own tools?* *Will you take your laptop with you?* *Will she know where to go when she gets there?* *Will it work when the temperature is below freezing?* *Will they have enough time to finish everything?* *Won't we pay in cash?*
Will + possessive adjective + noun The verb *will* can be positive or negative.	*Will my paycheck be ready by this afternoon?* *Will your company be adding any more staff?* *Will his plan get approval from the board?* *Won't its sales just continue to decline?* *Will our software work on their system?* *Won't their website be updated daily?*
Will + -ing The verb *will* can be positive or negative.	*Will repairing the computer be cheaper than buying a new one?* *Won't making reservations online be faster?* *Will taking this medicine on an empty stomach make me feel nauseated?* *Won't traveling by yourself be lonely?*
Would + subject pronoun + infinitive The verb *would* can be positive or negative.	*Would I need to get approval first?* *Would you buy more if we lowered our price?* *Would he charge extra for overnight delivery?* *Would it look better if we painted it blue?* *Wouldn't they prefer to stay at the Wexler Hotel?* *Wouldn't we make more money by investing in high-risk bonds?*

Verb	Examples
Would + possessive adjective + noun	
The verb *would* can be positive or negative.	*Would my salary go up if I take the new position?* *Would your office be a more convenient place to meet?* *Would her boss really say something like that?* *Would its parts break less frequently if they were serviced more often?* *Would their services be of use to us?* *Would our staff be willing to work overtime on short notice?*
Would + -ing	
The verb *would* can be positive or negative.	*Would working from home be a possibility?* *Wouldn't buying in bulk quantities be less expensive?* *Would billing you monthly be more convenient?* *Wouldn't flying be quicker than driving?*
Should + subject pronoun + infinitive	
The verb *should* can be positive or negative.	*Should I arrange a meeting with John?* *Shouldn't you make your presentation first?* *Should Lisa call to make the reservations?* *Shouldn't it be held in the conference room, instead?* *Should they upgrade their entire manufacturing system?* *Should we go to a later show?*
Should + possessive adjective + noun	
The verb *should* can be positive or negative.	*Should my accountant call you back to discuss the details?* *Shouldn't your order have been delivered by now?* *Should his file be updated?* *Shouldn't its parts be oiled every day?* *Should their offer be accepted?* *Shouldn't our department handle matters like that?*
Should + -ing	
The verb *should* can be positive or negative.	*Should smoking be banned in public places?* *Shouldn't training be required for all new employees?* *Should billing be quarterly?* *Shouldn't buying online be cheaper?*

Tag Questions

Tag questions come at the end of sentences. They are used to check information, ask for agreement, or find out whether something is true. They are more common in spoken English than they are in written English.

Chris works in the accounting department, doesn't he?

In this case, the question is checking whether or not Chris works in the accounting department. The speaker thinks this might be true but is not sure. Notice that the expected answer is "yes," "no," or an expression of uncertainty:

No, he works in the marketing department.

Tag questions repeat the auxiliary verb used in the sentence:

Maxine can come on Friday, can't she?
The capital of France is Paris, isn't it?
You don't take the subway to work, do you?
You haven't seen my glasses anywhere, have you?

Notice that the tag is negative when the sentence verb is positive, and it is positive when the sentence verb is negative:

Joan Mayer is the CEO of Exitron, isn't she?
[+] [–]

Joan Mayer isn't the CEO of Exitron, is she?
[–] [+]

If the sentence does not have an auxiliary verb, the question tag always uses a form of *do*:

You remembered to send the invoices, didn't you?
Sarah made the reservations, didn't she?
Mr. Lee likes to play golf, doesn't he?
Mark goes on vacation next week, doesn't he?

Strategy 3: Know the Distractors

There are four basic types of distractors for Part II questions:

1. **Similar-sounding words**—This type of distractor uses words and phrases that sound similar to the expected correct response.
2. **Repetition of question words**—This type of distractor repeats words and phrases used in the question or statement.
3. **Irrelevant responses**—This type of distractor responds to a common misunderstanding of the question or statement. Also included in this category are yes/no answers to *Wh-* information questions and *Wh-* information answers to *Yes/No* questions.
4. **Hybrid distractors**—This type of distractor uses combinations of the first three distractor types.

Look at the Part II directions example again. You will hear:

Man: *Where is the meeting room?*

Narrator: *A.*
Woman: *To meet the new supervisor.*
Narrator: *B.*
Woman: *It's the second room on the left.*
Narrator: *C.*
Woman: *No, at three o'clock.*

Choice (A) uses the word *meet*, which is a repetition of the word *meeting* in the question. This is an example of a repetition distractor. Choice (C) does not answer the question; however, if you misunderstood the question as "When is the meeting?" this would be an appropriate response. This is an example of an irrelevant response distractor.

Here is another example.

Woman: *How many cups of coffee do you usually drink each day?*

Narrator: *A.*
Man: *No more than two.*
Narrator: *B.*
Man: *I have two copies.*
Narrator: *C.*
Man: *I think that's too many.*

The correct response is (A), *No more than two.* Choice (B) uses the word *copies*, which sounds similar to *coffee* or *coffees.* This is an example of a similar-sounding distractor. Choice (C) repeats the question word *many*, and it uses the word *too*, which sounds like the expected word *two*. This is an example of a hybrid distractor using repetition of a question word and a similar-sounding word.

A set of responses may use more than one type of distractor at a time. Not all distractors fit neatly into the categories we have outlined; some may seem to belong to more than one category. Note also that each of these distractor types is similar because, in the end, they are inappropriate responses to the question or statement. However, it is useful to look at *why* they are inappropriate and to understand what it is you must listen for.

Similar-Sounding Words

This type of distractor uses words and phrases that sound similar to the expected correct response. For example, you will hear:

Man:	*How many pairs of tickets do we need?*
Narrator:	*A.*
Woman:	*I eat chicken two or three times a week.*
Narrator:	*B.*
Woman:	*Four should be enough.*
Narrator:	*C.*
Woman:	*Get some pears, some apples, and some cherries, too.*

The correct response is (B), *Four should be enough.* Choice (A) uses the word *eat*, which sounds a little like *need*, and *chicken*, which sounds a little like *ticket*. This is an example of a similar-sounding distractor. Choice (C) uses the word *pears*, which sounds like the word *pairs*. This is another example of a similar-sounding distractor.

Repetition of Question Words

This type of distractor repeats words and phrases used in the question or statement.

Man:	*Are there any more copies of the annual report left?*
Narrator:	*A.*
Woman:	*Yes, there should be a few left on the shelf in the library.*
Narrator:	*B.*
Woman:	*No, I'm afraid he left early this afternoon.*
Narrator:	*C.*
Woman:	*Yes, turn left at the next traffic light.*

The correct response is (A), *Yes, there should be a few left on the shelf in the library.* Choice (B) repeats the question word *left*, but here it has a different meaning. This is an example of a repetition distractor. Choice (C) repeats the question word *left*, but again, it has a different meaning. This is another example of a repetition distractor.

Irrelevant Responses

This type of distractor responds to a common misunderstanding of the question or statement.

You will hear:

Woman:	*Where will you stay when you go to London?*
Narrator:	*A.*
Man:	*I'm leaving on the tenth.*
Narrator:	*B.*
Man:	*At my cousin's house.*
Narrator:	*C.*
Man:	*Yes, I'm going there for a conference.*

The correct response is choice (B) *At my cousin's house.* Choice (A) answers the question, *When will you go to London*? Choice (C) answers the *Yes/No* question, *Will you go to London?* Both choices (A) and (C) are irrelevant response distractors.

Hybrid Distractor

This type of distractor uses combinations of the first three distractor types.

You will hear:

Man:	*When's the deadline for submitting contract bids?*
Narrator:	*A.*
Woman:	*They need to be in by five P.M. on Friday.*
Narrator:	*B.*
Woman:	*No, not until all the contract bids are in.*
Narrator:	*C.*
Woman:	*You can submit your contact information by email.*

The correct response is (A), *They need to be in by five P.M. on Friday.* Choice (B) repeats the question words *contract bids,* and it uses the word *until,* which might be expected in a response to a *When* question. The response is also a yes/no answer to an *Wh*-information question. This distractor is a hybrid distractor combining repetition and an irrelevant response. Choice (C) repeats the question word *submit*, and it uses the word *contact,* which sounds similar to *contract.* It also uses the phrase *by email,* because an expected response to a *When* question often takes the form of *by* + time word. This is an example of a hybrid distractor using repetition and similar-sounding words.

Strategy 4: Focus on the Purpose

Listen carefully to the question or statement that the first speaker makes. Ask yourself what the intent of the first speaker is. Examine what kind of response the speaker expects. Determine whether the response should be "yes" or "no," provide new information, or indicate an opinion or offer advice.

Listen especially to the first word for clues as to whether the question is *Yes/No* or *Wh-* information. Knowing the intent of the first speaker is a key step in the process of choosing the correct response.

Strategy 5: Evaluate the Statements

Listen closely to the first word to determine what kind of question it is and to decide what the speaker's intent is. Once you know the intent of the question or statement, you must listen to and evaluate the responses you hear. Because each response will be spoken only once, you must listen carefully.

Listen for a response that closely matches the intent of the question. After you hear a statement that is a close match to the answer you have been expecting, find the number for the question on your answer sheet and mark the oval for the letter that matches your answer. Be sure to listen to all three responses before you mark you answer sheet.

Strategy 6: Eliminate Statements that Do Not Fit

If none of the responses match your expected answer very well, then you must eliminate any choices that do not fit the situation. Listen carefully to the first word to determine what kind of question it is. Eliminate any answers that are inappropriate. For example, eliminate a yes/no answer to a *Wh-* information question.

Listen carefully to the tense used in the question and in the responses. Eliminate any answer choices that use the wrong tense; for example, a past tense response to a question about a future action.

If you must guess, eliminate the answer choices that repeat words from the question. Very often, these are distractors—not always, but often.

Strategy 7: Answer the Current Question Before the Next One Begins

Make sure you answer every question as quickly as you can. You have only about eight seconds to choose your answer for each question or statement. You should be finished with the current question before the next one begins. If you are still answering a question when the next one begins, you might not hear the beginning of the question.

As soon as you have finished with a question, get ready to listen for the next one.

Strategy Summary

1. Know the directions.
2. Know the different kinds of question types.
3. Understand the basic types of distractors.
4. Focus on the purpose of the question or statement.
5. Evaluate the statements you hear and mark the answer if you know it.
6. Eliminate statements that do not fit the situation and select the best match from what is left.
7. Be sure to answer the current question before the next question begins.

QUESTION-RESPONSE PRACTICE SET

Play Track 2 to hear the questions

Time Budget: 10 minutes for 24 questions

1. Mark your answer on your sheet. Ⓐ Ⓑ Ⓒ
2. Mark your answer on your sheet. Ⓐ Ⓑ Ⓒ
3. Mark your answer on your sheet. Ⓐ Ⓑ Ⓒ
4. Mark your answer on your sheet. Ⓐ Ⓑ Ⓒ
5. Mark your answer on your sheet. Ⓐ Ⓑ Ⓒ
6. Mark your answer on your sheet. Ⓐ Ⓑ Ⓒ
7. Mark your answer on your sheet. Ⓐ Ⓑ Ⓒ
8. Mark your answer on your sheet. Ⓐ Ⓑ Ⓒ
9. Mark your answer on your sheet. Ⓐ Ⓑ Ⓒ
10. Mark your answer on your sheet. Ⓐ Ⓑ Ⓒ
11. Mark your answer on your sheet. Ⓐ Ⓑ Ⓒ
12. Mark your answer on your sheet. Ⓐ Ⓑ Ⓒ
13. Mark your answer on your sheet. Ⓐ Ⓑ Ⓒ
14. Mark your answer on your sheet. Ⓐ Ⓑ Ⓒ
15. Mark your answer on your sheet. Ⓐ Ⓑ Ⓒ
16. Mark your answer on your sheet. Ⓐ Ⓑ Ⓒ
17. Mark your answer on your sheet. Ⓐ Ⓑ Ⓒ
18. Mark your answer on your sheet. Ⓐ Ⓑ Ⓒ
19. Mark your answer on your sheet. Ⓐ Ⓑ Ⓒ
20. Mark your answer on your sheet. Ⓐ Ⓑ Ⓒ
21. Mark your answer on your sheet. Ⓐ Ⓑ Ⓒ
22. Mark your answer on your sheet. Ⓐ Ⓑ Ⓒ
23. Mark your answer on your sheet. Ⓐ Ⓑ Ⓒ
24. Mark your answer on your sheet. Ⓐ Ⓑ Ⓒ

Answers and explanations begin on the next page ▶ ▶ ▶

ANSWER KEY

1. A
2. C
3. C
4. B
5. C
6. C
7. C
8. C
9. B
10. A
11. A
12. C
13. C
14. A
15. C
16. B
17. A
18. C
19. C
20. B
21. B
22. C
23. A
24. A

ANSWERS AND EXPLANATIONS

For each question, we have identified the question type (*Wh-*, Choice, *Yes/No*, or Tag). All of the answer choices are included for each question, and in parentheses, there is an explanation of exactly why the wrong answer choices are incorrect. For some questions, we have left the wrong answer explanations blank so that you can fill them in. The more you can analyze and explain the errors in the wrong answer choices, the more skillful and efficient you will become at eliminating incorrect choices and selecting the correct ones.

Sample responses for these Identify the Error answer explanations are included at the end of the Answers and Explanations section.

1. Is there anything good on TV tonight? (*Yes/No*)

   A. The news comes on in about an hour. CORRECT

   B. Yes, the plant is on top of the television. (Double repetition of the words *on* and *TV/television*)

   C. Please find a different station. (Does not relate to the question)

2. Why did they cancel the reception for Mr. Chang? (*Why*)

   A. Her secretary did. (Answers a *Who* question)

   B. He received the invitation. (Does not answer the question)

   C. He got sick. CORRECT

3. Where can I buy a magazine? (*Where*)

   A. A cab just went by. (Plays on the words *by* and *buy*)

   B. The store takes credit cards, I think. (Irrelevant)

   C. The newsstand on the corner. CORRECT

4. What type of business are you in? (*What*)

   A. Because I sold the house. (Irrelevant)

   B. I'm a banker. CORRECT

   C. I'll type it tomorrow. (Uses the verb form of the word *type*)

5. Would you like to work overtime tonight? (*Yes/No*)

   A. No thanks, I have one. (Answers a question offering something)

   B. I'd rather begin at 8. (Plays on the word *work*: *begin work/work overtime*)

   C. Sure, I need the hours. CORRECT

6. Where is your final destination today? (*Where*)
   A. I'll be flying there. (Does not include a location; answers a *How* question)
   B. I'm leaving this afternoon. (Does not include a location; answers a *When* question)
   C. I'm going to Rome. CORRECT

7. It'll be a long trip, won't it? ________________
   ____
   A. She tripped on the stairs, yes. ____________
   ____
   B. No, I leave next week. ________________
   ____
   C. Yes, about four weeks. CORRECT

8. Why don't we take a short break? ____________
   ____
   A. My car got new brakes last summer. _____
   ____
   B. Yes, Lisa broke the plate by accident. _____
   ____
   C. Good idea, I'm getting tired. CORRECT

9. When will the earnings report be issued? (*When*)
   A. It will be published in the newspaper. (Does not include a time reference; answers a *Where* question)
   B. At the end of the first quarter. CORRECT
   C. Because the stock went up last week. (Wrong subject; wrong tense)

10. You subscribe to *Business Monthly Magazine*, don't you? (Tag)
   A. No, but my office does. CORRECT
   B. Yes, I heard the news on the radio. (Irrelevant)
   C. The mail is late today. (Wrong subject)

11. How are the contract negotiations coming along? (*How*)
   A. Our attorneys are reviewing the proposed changes. CORRECT
   B. We're almost finished with the progress report. (Irrelevant)
   C. They returned the rental car last night. (Answers a *When* question; irrelevant)

12. Who should we send to Buenos Aires? (*Who*)
   A. I'd recommend next week. (Answers a *When* question)
   B. Let's send out for lunch. (Answer repeats the word *send*)
   C. Jaime should go. CORRECT

13. Does Ali rent that house, or does he own it? (Choice)
   A. He used to rent a house in Alexandria. (Plays on the words *Alexandria* and *Ali*; wrong tense)
   B. His cousin just bought a home downtown. (Irrelevant)
   C. He has a one-year lease. CORRECT

14. Has Ms. Matala finished with the samples? (*Yes/No*)
   A. Yes, she was right on schedule. CORRECT
   B. No, she was born in Finland. (Plays on the words *finished* and *Finland*)
   C. She felt his action was justified. (Irrelevant)

15. What's the training workshop about? ________
   ____
   A. Sometime tomorrow afternoon. __________
   ____
   B. Somewhere in the new building. _________
   ____
   C. Something to do with team building. CORRECT

16. Why don't you apply for that new job posting? ______________________________
    A. I worked on the second shift. ______________________________
    B. I don't think I'm qualified. CORRECT
    C. I'm walking to the post office. ______________________________

17. Is that pollution or just morning haze? (*Choice*)
    A. The latter; it should be gone by noon. CORRECT
    B. The industrial zone is located in the valley. (Answers a *Where* question)
    C. The afternoon rain keeps the air clean. (Wrong subject)

18. Why don't we take a cruise for vacation? (*Why*)
    A. Because the food is so good. (Does not make sense because the question is formed negatively)
    B. So that we can get a free ticket. (Does not answer a negative question)
    C. That might be a nice change. CORRECT

19. Will Mr. Yoon write the report, or does he want me to do it? (*Choice*)
    A. He was right last time. (Plays on the words *right* and *write*)
    B. I think he reports directly to Mr. Yoon. (Verb form of the word *report*, not the noun form)
    C. He'll do it himself. CORRECT

20. How many workers will we need for the Johnston building? (*How*)
    A. Construction has been ongoing for two years. (Refers to time, not to an amount)
    B. I estimate around a hundred. CORRECT
    C. We'll need to work overtime to finish. (Repeats the words *need* and *work*)

21. Why don't you think about taking early retirement? (*Why*)
    A. I thought you retired. (Repeats part of *retirement*)
    B. Actually, I've been considering it. CORRECT
    C. I've worked for over thirty years. (Irrelevant)

22. Who's your favorite author? (*Who*)
    A. I prefer short stories over novels. (Answers a *What* question)
    B. Her favorite books are usually fiction. (Repeats the word *favorite*; wrong subject)
    C. It's hard for me to pick just one. CORRECT

23. Don't you think interest rates will continue to go up? ______________________________
    A. In the short term, I suppose so. CORRECT
    B. No, I am very interested. ______________________________
    C. I had to drive up the hill. ______________________________

24. What should we do with these files for the Wallrock lease? ______________________________
    A. Leave them until Tuesday. CORRECT
    B. Your secretary has them. ______________________________
    C. No, I sent them to Mr. Wallrock. ______________________________

Responses for Identify the Error Questions

7. It'll be a long trip, won't it? (*Yes/No*)
   - A. She tripped on the stairs, yes. (*Play on the word trip; confusing verb/noun forms*)
   - B. No, I leave next week. (*Confusion between the time the trip starts and how long it lasts*)
   - C. Yes, about four weeks. CORRECT

8. Why don't we take a short break? (*Yes/No*)
   - A. My car got new brakes last summer. (*Play on the words break and brakes*)
   - B. Yes, Lisa broke the plate by accident. (*Play on the words break and broke*)
   - C. Good idea, I'm getting tired. CORRECT

15. What's the training workshop about? (*What*)
   - A. Sometime tomorrow afternoon. (*Answers When question*)
   - B. Somewhere in the new building. (*Answers Where question*)
   - C. Something to do with team building. CORRECT

16. Why don't you apply for that new job posting? (*Why*)
   - A. I worked on the second shift. (*Irrelevant; wrong verb and tense*)
   - B. I don't think I'm qualified. CORRECT
   - C. I'm walking to the post office. (*Play on the words posting and post office*)

23. Don't you think interest rates will continue to go up? (*Yes/No*)
   - A. In the short term, I suppose so. CORRECT
   - B. No, I am very interested. (*Play on the words interest and interested*)
   - C. I had to drive up the hill. (*Play on the words go up and drive up*)

24. What should we do with these files for the Wallrock lease? (*What*)
   - A. Leave them until Tuesday. CORRECT
   - B. Your secretary has them. (*Answers a Who question*)
   - C. No, I sent them to Mr. Wallrock. (*Repeats the word Wallrock; answers a Where question*)

CHAPTER 5

Exam Part III—Short Conversations

LEARNING OBJECTIVES

In this section, you'll learn to:

- Identify the three different question types
- Understand the most common question type orders
- Use the Kaplan Strategy to identify the 4 main distractors for Part III

Time Budget for Part III: Approximately 17 minutes

For this part of the exam, you will listen to 13 short conversations. There will be two or three speakers in each conversation. In your exam booklet, you will see three questions, each with four responses; you will also hear the *question*, but *not* the answer choices. For each question, you must pick the response that best answers the question. There will be an eight-second pause between questions and an eight-second pause between the end of the last question and the start of the next conversation. For some questions, you will also be given a simple graphic, which you will need to use along with the conversation to answer one of the questions. Examples of graphics include maps, tables, diagrams, and calendars.

TEST-TAKING STRATEGIES

Strategy 1: Know the Directions

It is important to understand what you are being asked to do and to be sure you know the directions *before* you take the test. The directions will look something like this:

> **Directions**: You will now hear a number of conversations between two or more people. You will be asked to answer three questions about what the speakers say. Select the best response to each question and mark the letter on your answer sheet. The conversations will be spoken only once and will not be printed in your test book.

Be aware that for this part of the TOEIC exam, the test maker will not provide sample questions, as it does in Parts I and II.

However, here is an example illustrating the format of a typical Short Conversation, so you can begin to familiarize yourself with it.

Narrator: *Questions 41 through 43 refer to the following conversation.*

Woman: *Something smells delicious in here... what is it?*

Man: *It's vegetable lasagna. I made it for dinner last night. I made too much, and there's a lot left over, so I brought some for today's lunch.*

Woman: *Well, it really does smell wonderful. How did you learn to make this?*

Man: *It's my mother's family recipe—she got it from her grandmother. I'd be happy to bring the recipe to work tomorrow, if you'd like.*

Narrator: *Number 41. What are the speakers mainly discussing?*

You will be able to read the first question and the four answer choices in your test book:

41. What are the speakers mainly discussing?
    A. the man's family
    B. a problem the woman has
    C. the food the man has made
    D. the restaurants in the area

There will be an eight-second pause after the first question. Then you will hear:

Narrator: *Number 42. What does the man offer to do for the woman?*

You will be able to read the second question and the four answer choices in your test book:

42. What does the man offer to do for the woman?
    A. take her to lunch
    B. bring her his recipe
    C. introduce her to his family
    D. drive her to work the next day

There will be an eight-second pause after the second question. Then you will hear:

Narrator: *Number 43. What is probably true about the speakers?*

You will be able to read the third question and the four answer choices in your test book:

43. What is probably true about the speakers?
    - A. They are neighbors.
    - B. They are coworkers.
    - C. They are in a restaurant.
    - D. They are talking on the telephone.

Each question is spoken once, followed by an eight-second pause. This means for each question you have only eight seconds to read the question and answer choices and mark your answer sheet.

Usually, there are two speakers, and each speaker has two turns at speaking, though they may speak for more than two lines each. Occasionally, you will hear a conversation between three speakers. These conversations will either include one female speaker and two males, or one male speaker and two females. When you hear conversations between three speakers, the two speakers of the same gender will have distinct voices, with accents from different English speaking countries, which will help you to distinguish between the speakers of the same gender. Here is an example of a conversation between three speakers. Read through the conversation and questions now, but don't answer the questions yet, as we will do this later on in the chapter.

Narrator:	*Questions 44 through 46 refer to the following conversation with three speakers*
Woman A:	*Hey, you two. Have you seen the new rota?*
Man:	*Yeah. Goodbye social life.*
Woman B:	*Why, what's happening?*
Woman A:	*We're all down to work all of the afternoon shifts this week. Monday to Thursday.*
Man:	*So annoying! I was supposed to go to the cinema Thursday afternoon with my brother.*
Woman B:	*I don't mind, to be honest. I like to have the mornings free. I get loads done.*

You will be able to read the three questions for the conversation in your test book:

44. Why does the man say "goodbye social life"?
    - A. He hasn't made plans this week.
    - B. He's working when he would normally see people.
    - C. He wanted to go out for dinner with the women.
    - D. He has made a mistake.

45. Look at the graphic. Which group do the speakers belong to?

    A. Group 1
    B. Group 2
    C. Group 3
    D. Group 4

	MON	TUE	WED	THURS	FRI	SAT	SUN
A.M.	Group 4	Group 4	Group 4	Group 4	Group 2	Group 3	Group 3
P.M.	Group 1	Group 1	Group 1	Group 1	Group 3	Group 2	Group 2

46. Why doesn't one of the speakers mind working in the afternoon?

    A. She has a lot to do at work.
    B. She likes it when work is busier.
    C. She likes to sleep in.
    D. She accomplishes more in her time off.

Strategy 2: Read the First Few Questions

Because you already know what the directions are, look at the first few questions in your test book while the directions are playing. This will let you know what to expect and what you will need to listen for.

Strategy 3: Know the Question Types and Order

In Part III, the questions usually ask for information in the order in which it was presented in the conversation. This means that the first question will usually ask about something mentioned near the beginning, the second question will ask about something that was mentioned in the middle, and the third question will ask about something mentioned near the end.

There are five basic categories of questions for Part III:

1. **Gist**—Gist questions will ask what the main topic is, where the conversation takes place, or who the speakers are. They ask about the overall situation, rather than about specific details. Common Gist questions include:

   What are the speakers mainly discussing?
   Where does this conversation probably take place?
   Where do the speakers probably work?
   Who are the speakers?

2. **Detail**—Detail questions ask about details mentioned in the conversation, such as what someone did or has been asked to do, how a problem is being handled, or the order in which things are to be done. They can ask about general information or very specific details. Common Detail questions include:

   What did the man do?
   What did the woman ask the man to do?
   How did the speakers solve their problem?
   Which will the man do first?
   When is the report due?

3. **Implication/Inference**—Implication/Inference questions ask about things that are not stated directly by either of the speakers. They can ask about the speaker's intentions, emotions, expectations, or probable future actions. Common Implication/Inference questions include:

   What does the woman intend to do next week?
   Why is the man disappointed?
   What does the woman expect the man to do?
   What will the man probably do next?

Some Implication/Inference and Gist questions may seem to be similar. For example, a Gist question that asks about where the conversation takes place requires an inference, in that the conversation will provide enough information to make the location or setting of the conversation obvious, but this information will not be stated directly. However, while some Gist questions require you to understand an implication or make an inference, Gist questions focus on the larger picture or the overall situation. Implication/Inference questions deal with details about the speakers or the situation.

4. **Implied Meaning**—Implied Meaning questions ask you to explain the purpose of a part of speech. You will be given a quotation from the conversation, usually a phrase, and asked to choose the option that best describes what the speaker means. Here are some examples of Implied meaning questions:

   Why does the man say, "Do you know what I mean?"
   Why does the woman say, "What's up?"
   Why does the man say, "I don't get it"
   Why does the woman say, "Crazy, right?"

5. **Graphic Questions**—Graphic questions provide visual data along with the question. To answer the question correctly, you need to use the information in the conversation and the information in the visual stimulus. The visual stimulus could be a number of different things. Some examples include a price list, a calendar, a map, a floor plan, a schedule, and a budget. The graphics will be short and simple, and it will not be clear from either the graphic on its own, or the conversation on its own, what the correct answer is. You must combine both the spoken and printed information to find the correct answer. Here are some examples of Graphic questions:

Look at the price list. Which item will the woman choose?
Look at the map. Which number shows the position of the speakers?
Look at the calendar. When will they schedule their meeting?
Look at the itinerary. What time will the woman begin her speech?

Strategy 4: Know the Distractors

To understand the kinds of Part III distractors, and how they work, you first need to understand how TOEIC exam writers write TOEIC items.

All Part III distractors must answer the question *plausibly*, that is, they must be possible answers to the question. When you look at a Part III question and the answer choices by themselves—without hearing the conversation—each choice must answer the question in a logical and realistic way. For example:

What did the man do on Monday?

A. He left work early.
B. He finished a report.
C. He ate lunch at his desk.
D. He replied to John's email.

Without hearing the conversation, none of the answer choices can be eliminated. Each choice is a plausible answer to the question, and there are no "impossible" answer choices. All Part III items are written in this way.

Another feature of Part III items is that none of the questions are linked in any way. That is, the information contained in a set of question and answer choices will not help you to answer any other questions.

There are four basic types of distractors for Part III questions:

1. **Not mentioned**—This type of distractor uses words, phrases, and ideas that are not mentioned in the conversation. There is no connection to the language used in the conversation. The distractor answers the question plausibly but does not relate to the conversation.
2. **Repeated words**—This type of distractor uses words, phrases, and ideas that are mentioned in the conversation but changes them so that they are not true. The distractor answers the question plausibly but is incorrect.
3. **New words**—This type of distractor introduces new words, phrases, or ideas that may be associated with or implied by language and ideas expressed in the conversation but that are untrue. The distractor answers the question plausibly but is incorrect.
4. **Rephrase/paraphrase**—This type of distractor takes the original language used in the conversation and rephrases or paraphrases it in a way that makes it untrue. The distractor answers the questions plausibly, but incorrectly.

Note that a set of answer choices may use more than one type of distractor at a time. Not all distractors fit neatly into the categories outlined here; some may seem to belong to more than one category. Note also that each of these distractor types is similar because, in the end, they are incorrect answers to the question. However, it is useful to look at *why* they are incorrect and to understand what you must listen for.

Look at the Part III examples again. (Material in *italics* indicates what you will hear; material in **bold** indicates what is printed in your test book.)

Narrator:	*Questions 41 through 43 refer to the following conversation.*
Woman:	*Something smells delicious in here . . . what is it?*
Man:	*It's vegetable lasagna. I made it for dinner last night. I made too much, and there's a lot left over, so I brought some for today's lunch.*
Woman:	*Well, it really does smell wonderful. How did you learn to make this?*
Man:	*It's my mother's family recipe—she got it from her grandmother. I'd be happy to bring the recipe to work tomorrow, if you'd like.*
Narrator:	*Number 41. What are the speakers mainly discussing?*

41. What are the speakers mainly discussing?

A. the man's family
B. a problem the woman has
C. the food the man has made
D. the restaurants in the area

This is a Gist question. The correct answer is choice (C). Choice (A) uses words, phrases, and ideas mentioned in the conversation (*mother*, *family*, *grandmother*), but the main topic of discussion is not the man's family. This is an example of a repeated words distractor. Choice (B) is not mentioned or implied. This is an example of a not mentioned distractor. Choice (D) is not mentioned, but it uses the word *restaurant*, which is associated with food and cooking. This is an example of a new words distractor.

Narrator:	*Number 42. What does the man offer to do for the woman?*

42. What does the man offer to do for the woman?

A. take her to lunch
B. bring her his recipe
C. introduce her to his family
D. drive her to work the next day

This is a Detail question. The correct answer is (B). Choice (A) repeats the conversation word *lunch,* but the man has not offered to take the woman to lunch. This is an example of a repeated words distractor. Choice (C) repeats the conversation word *family*, which is also associated with the conversation words *mother* and *grandmother.* This is an example of a repeated words distractor but could also be seen as a rephrase/paraphrase distractor. Choice (D) plays on a rephrasing or paraphrasing of the words *I'd be happy to bring the recipe to work* tomorrow... The man offers to bring his recipe to work the next day, not drive the woman to work. This is an example of a rephrase/paraphrase distractor.

Narrator: *Number 43. What is probably true about the speakers?*

43. What is probably true about the speakers?

A. They are neighbors.

B. They are coworkers.

C. They are in a restaurant.

D. They are talking on the telephone.

This is an Inference/Implication question. The correct answer is choice (B). Choice (A) is not mentioned or implied and is an example of a not mentioned distractor. Choice (C) is not mentioned, but it uses the word *restaurant*, which is associated with the topics of food and cooking. This is an example of a new words distractor. Choice (D) is not mentioned or implied. Because the woman can smell the food, they must be in the same room at the same time. This is an example of a not mentioned distractor.

Narrator: *Questions 44 through 46 refer to the following conversation with three speakers*

Woman A: *Hey, you two. Have you seen the new rota?*

Man: *Yeah. Goodbye social life.*

Woman B: *Why, what's happening?*

Woman A: *We're all down to work most of the afternoon shifts this week. Monday to Thursday.*

Man: *So annoying! I was supposed to go to the cinema on Thursday with my brother.*

Woman B: *I don't mind, to be honest. I like to have the mornings free. I get loads done.*

44. Why does the man say, "Goodbye social life"?

- **A. He hasn't made plans this week.**
- **B. He's working when he would normally see people.**
- **C. He wanted to go out for dinner with the women.**
- **D. He has made a mistake.**

This is an Implied Meaning question. The correct answer is choice (B). Choice (A) says he hasn't made plans, but he says he wanted to see his brother. He does not mention wanting to have dinner with the women, so (C) is incorrect. There is no mention of a *mistake* so (D) cannot be correct.

45. Look at the graphic. Which group do the speakers belong to?

- **A. Group 1**
- **B. Group 2**
- **C. Group 3**
- **D. Group 4**

	MON	TUE	WED	THURS	FRI	SAT	SUN
A.M.	Group 4	Group 4	Group 4	Group 4	Group 2	Group 3	Group 3
P.M.	Group 1	Group 1	Group 1	Group 1	Group 3	Group 2	Group 2

This is a Graphic question. The graphic shows a calendar with a work schedule. A.M. means the morning and P.M. means the afternoon. The days of the week have been abbreviated, or shortened: Monday = MON. In the conversation, Woman A says *We're all down to work most of the afternoon shifts this week. Monday to Thursday* so they must belong to Group 1. The answer is therefore (A).

46. Why doesn't one of the speakers mind working in the afternoon?

- **A. She has a lot to do at work.**
- **B. She likes it when work is busier.**
- **C. She likes to sleep in.**
- **D. She accomplishes more in her time off.**

This is a Detail question. The man says he doesn't like working in the evenings, and Woman A doesn't say whether she likes or dislikes it, but Woman B says *I don't mind, to be honest. I like to have the mornings free. I get loads done*. The speaker gets more done when she's not at work in the morning during her time off, so (D) must be the answer. (A) is not the answer because she gets things done outside of work, but doesn't mention what she does at work. (B) is not correct, as they do not mention whether mornings or evenings are busier. (C) is not correct, as she says she does more, not that she sleeps more.

Notice that for each question, all the distractors are plausible answers and that none of the questions or answer choices are of any help in answering other questions.

Strategy 5: Listen for the Information

By reading the questions in your test book, you will know what information to listen for in the conversation. For example, if the first question is a Detail question asking about what one of the speakers has done, you should listen carefully for words and phrases that indicate what that speaker has done. If one of your questions contains a graphic, scan the question and the graphic to make sure that you understand the information provided and the question being asked, so that you can prepare to listen for the relevant information in the conversation.

The conversations will often contain a lot of information that is *not* tested. However, because you have the questions in front of you in your test book, you will know what information to be listening for.

Note that the questions for Part III are all *Wh-* questions. There are no *Yes/No* questions. Review the *Wh-* question material in chapter 4 to help you focus on the kinds of information the questions ask for and on the format of the expected answers. You should know, for example, that a *When* question deals with time and that you will need to listen for time words (e.g. *today, yesterday, this afternoon, at 10 o'clock*).

You will have to listen carefully to the conversation to get information you need. You will not be able to read the questions and apply logic to answer the questions. Remember, the question and answer choices used in one question will *not* help you to answer another question. The TOEIC exam writers are very careful to avoid letting the information in one question and answer choice set help to answer another question and answer choice set.

Pay attention to who each speaker is. Often, the relationship between the speakers is made very clear, and there may be a question to test whether you understood this information. Sometimes the distractors will use information that is true for one of the speakers but not the other. For example, a man and woman might be discussing the man's vacation plans. For the question "What are the speakers mainly discussing?" one of the distractors may refer to the woman's vacation plans.

When there are three speakers, the questions that ask about one of the speakers will often ask about the one person of the opposite sex. For example, if there are two men and one woman, there might be a question that is specific to the woman. When listening to conversations with three speakers, you might find it helpful to make a quick note of the speakers on the side of your paper, for example W (for woman) MA (the first male speaker) MB (the second male speaker).

Strategy 6: Answer Each Question in Your Own Words

Read each question and predict the answer in your own words *before* reading the answer choices. If you understand the conversation, you should be able to answer all the questions in your own words. For each question, your predicted answer—or one very closely matching it—should be among the answer choices. Remember, there are no trick questions on the TOEIC exam. All the information needed to answer the questions is presented in the conversation.

If you read the answer choices first without answering the question in your own words, you will be tempted to choose one of the distractors. It is much better to have your own idea about the correct answer first, *before* looking at the answer choices.

Strategy 7: Evaluate the Answer Choices

If one of the answer choices is a close match to the answer you expect, mark the oval for that letter. If none of the responses matches your expected answer very well, you must eliminate as many choices as you can. Remember, one question and answer choice set will not help you answer another, so do not look at answer choices from one question for clues to answer another question.

Often, each answer choice uses words and phrases as they were spoken in the conversation. However, if only one of the answer choices uses words and phrases from the conversation, this is likely to be the correct one.

Strategy 8: Eliminate Answer Choices

If none of the answer choices matches your expected answer very well, then you must eliminate as many wrong choices as you can. If you must guess, eliminate any choices that do not use words and phrases from the conversation—the not-mentioned distractor type. (Unless there is only *one* choice that uses words and phrases from the conversation, in which case you should choose this as the correct answer.) The not-mentioned distractors are often the easiest to eliminate.

Strategy 9: Manage Your Time

Remember that there are only eight seconds between questions. There is also an eight-second pause between the end of the last question and the introduction for the next conversation. If you spend too much time on one set of questions, you may miss the beginning of the next conversation. You will need to select your answer choice and mark it on your answer sheet as quickly as you can to keep up with the test. Because you will hear the conversations only once, you must not allow yourself to fall behind.

If you find yourself running out of time, mark your answer sheet with your wild-guess letter (see Strategy 7 from Chapter 2). Do not leave any questions unanswered.

Strategy 10: Read the Questions for the Next Conversation

For each conversation, there is a brief introduction. For example, you will hear: "*Questions 44 through 46 refer to the following conversation.*" Ideally, you should have answered all three questions for the current conversation before you hear the introduction for the next conversation. You should then immediately begin to read as many of the next set of questions as you can before the conversation begins. This will help you focus on the information you need to listen for.

Strategy Summary

1. Know the directions.
2. Read the first few questions while the directions are playing.
3. Understand the question types and how questions are ordered.
4. Understand the basic types of distractors.
5. Listen for the information in the questions.
6. Answer each question in your own words before reading the choices.
7. Evaluate the answer choices and mark the answer if you know it.
8. Eliminate answer choices that are wrong and select the best match from what is left.
9. Manage your time and be sure to answer all three questions before the next conversation begins.
10. Read the questions for the next conversation before it starts.

SHORT CONVERSATIONS PRACTICE SET

 **Track 3**

Play Track 3 to hear the Short Conversations

Time Budget: Approximately 15 minutes for 30 questions

Practice 1

1. What are the speakers mainly discussing?

   A. where they go on vacation
   B. when they take time off work
   C. what they do every weekend
   D. how many hours they work each week

2. What about the woman surprised the man?

   A. She seems to have a lot of vacation.
   B. She never works on Mondays.
   C. She never takes days off work.
   D. She works a lot of hours.

3. Look at the graphic. Which company does the woman work at?

	Open During the weekend?	Flexible work?	Vacation days
Company A	Yes	No	30
Company B	No	No	30
Company C	Yes	Yes	25
Company D	No	Yes	25

   A. Company A
   B. Company B
   C. Company C
   D. Company D

Practice 2

4. Who is the man?

   A. an employer
   B. a job applicant
   C. a recruitment officer
   D. a personnel manager

5. What kind of experience are the speakers talking about?

   A. public speaking
   B. project management
   C. organizing events
   D. computer repairs

6. What kind of job is being offered?

   A. computer repair technician
   B. IT project manager
   C. computer programmer
   D. university lecturer

Practice 3

7. Why does the man say, "I can't believe it!"?

   A. He does not think that someone has moved the files.
   B. He is annoyed that someone has moved the files.
   C. He is surprised that the woman is so frustrated.
   D. He doesn't understand why they still use the same filing system.

8. What has the woman changed?

   A. the text of a contract
   B. the furniture
   C. the finance files
   D. the filing system

9. Look at the Graphic. Where is the JDK contract file?

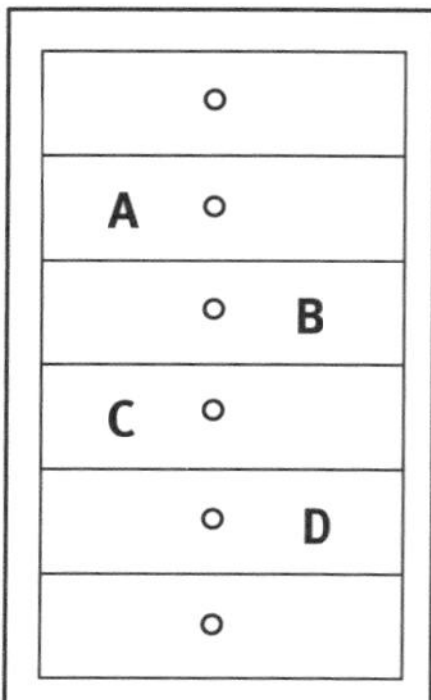

A. [A]
B. [B]
C. [C]
D. [D]

Practice 4

10. What is the woman learning about?
    A. a camera
    B. a projector
    C. a printer
    D. a photocopier

11. Why does the man say, "Don't worry"?
    A. The woman does not need to use the projector.
    B. It is not difficult to use the projector.
    C. The woman will be fully trained next week.
    D. No one in the office knows how to do it.

12. How can users change the size of the image?
    A. by pressing the "resize" button
    B. by pressing the blue arrows
    C. by pressing the red button
    D. by turning the wheel

Practice 5

13. What have the speakers reserved?
    A. a room for an office party
    B. a conference room
    C. a car
    D. tables at a restaurant

14. When was the reservation made?
    A. Monday
    B. Tuesday
    C. Thursday
    D. Friday

15. How long do the speakers need to wait?
    A. half an hour
    B. forty-five minutes
    C. an hour
    D. more than an hour

Practice 6

16. Whom is the woman speaking to?
    A. a policeman
    B. a bus driver
    C. a passenger
    D. a travel agent

17. Where does the woman want to go?
    A. a train station
    B. the airport
    C. the bus station
    D. a subway station

18. How many minutes will the woman need to wait for the next bus?
    A. 3
    B. 5
    C. 8
    D. 15

Practice 7

19. What are the speakers mainly discussing?

    A. new safety rules
    B. rescheduling a meeting
    C. preparing for an inspection
    D. ordering plastic

20. Who will Rory call?

    A. the client
    B. the rest of their team
    C. the safety inspector
    D. the consultant

21. How will Rory contact their team?

    A. by memo
    B. by phone
    C. by email
    D. by text message

Practice 8

22. Where does Tony work?

    A. in the maintenance department
    B. on the shop floor
    C. in the product training department
    D. in the service supplies department

23. What is Tony's problem?

    A. He does not know what to order.
    B. He does not know how to order.
    C. He is not sure if he should order.
    D. He does not know where Mr. Logan's order is.

24. Why are Mr. Logan and Tony not together?

    A. Mr. Logan is ill.
    B. Mr. Logan is in another city.
    C. Tony is on the shop floor.
    D. Tony is in a meeting.

Practice 9

25. Why haven't the contracts been signed?

    A. The man is missing some information.
    B. Aidan has not completed them yet.
    C. The clients do not want to do business.
    D. The lawyers have issues with the content.

26. Why does the man think the clients liked meeting in person?

    A. to make sure they were dealing with the same team
    B. to receive a discount on their services
    C. to make sure no one else was obtaining information
    D. to make sure they got to know the lawyers

27. What does the woman imply about the clients changing their mind?

    A. They did it to reduce costs.
    B. They did it because it was time consuming.
    C. They were not confident in their abilities.
    D. They thought Giulia did a good job.

Practice 10

28. Where are the speakers?

    A. at the office
    B. at the swimming pool
    C. at an art gallery
    D. at a theater

29. What does the woman say about Pedro?

    A. She has missed him.
    B. He is missing his children.
    C. He is glad to have a free evening.
    D. He should have contacted them.

30. What do two of the speakers agree about?

    A. the talent of the female lead
    B. They don't understand what is happening.
    C. They will go for dinner later.
    D. The story is not relevant.

ANSWER KEY

1. B
2. A
3. C
4. B
5. B
6. C
7. B
8. D
9. A
10. B
11. B
12. D
13. D
14. D
15. A
16. A
17. A
18. A
19. B
20. A
21. C
22. D
23. C
24. B
25. D
26. C
27. A
28. D
29. B
30. A

ANSWERS AND EXPLANATIONS

All of the answer choices are included for each question, and in parentheses, there is an explanation of exactly why the wrong answer choices are incorrect. For some questions, we have left the wrong answer explanations blank so that you can fill them in. The more you can analyze and explain the errors in the wrong answer choices, the more skillful and efficient you will become at eliminating incorrect choices and selecting the correct ones.

Sample responses for these Identify the Error answer explanations are included at the end of the Answers and Explanations section.

Practice 1

1. What are the speakers mainly discussing?

   A. where they go on vacation (This repeats the word *vacation*.)

   B. when they take time off work. CORRECT

   C. what they do every weekend (The woman says she works some weekends, but we do not hear what the speakers do every weekend.)

   D. how many hours they work each week (They talk about work, but do not mention this detail.)

2. What about the woman surprised the man?

   A. She seems to have a lot of vacation. CORRECT

   B. She never works on Mondays (She does not take only Mondays off.)

   C. She never takes days off work (In fact, she seems to take more time off than he does.)

   D. She works a lot of hours (They talk about work, but do not mention this detail.)

3. Look at the graphic. Which company does the woman work for?

	Open During the weekend?	Flexible work?	Vacation days
Company A	Yes	No	30
Company B	No	No	30
Company C	Yes	Yes	25
Company D	No	Yes	25

   A. Company A (The woman says she gets 25 vacation days and works flexibly.)
   B. Company B (The woman says she gets 25 vacation days, works flexibly, and sometimes works weekends.)
   C. Company C (The woman says she gets 25 vacation days, works flexibly, and sometimes works weekends.) CORRECT
   D. Company D (The woman says she sometimes works weekends.)

Practice 2

4. Who is the man?
   A. an employer (The woman is a potential employer, but the man is not.)
   B. a job applicant CORRECT
   C. a recruitment officer (This is not mentioned.)
   D. a personnel manager (This repeats the words *project management*.)

5. What kind of experience are the speakers talking about?
   A. public speaking (This repeats the word *speaking*.)
   B. project management CORRECT
   C. organizing events (This repeats the word *organizational*.)
   D. computer repairs (They are talking about programming, not making repairs.)

6. What kind of job is being offered?
   A. computer repair technician (They are talking about programming, not repairs.)
   B. IT project manager (The woman would prefer someone with management potential, but the current job is for a programmer.)
   C. computer programmer CORRECT
   D. university lecturer (This repeats the word *university*.)

Practice 3

7. Why does the man say, "I can't believe it!"?
   A. He does not think that someone has moved the files. (The man is aware that the files had been moved, because he can't find them.)
   B. He is annoyed that someone has moved the files. (CORRECT)
   C. He is surprised that the woman is so frustrated. (The man is frustrated, not the woman.)
   D. He doesn't understand why they still use the same filing system. (He is annoyed because people are not following the current system.)

8. What has the woman changed?
   A. the text of a contract (This repeats the word *contract*.)
   B. the furniture (The files have been moved but not the cabinet.)
   C. the finance files (This repeats the word *files*.)
   D. the filing system CORRECT

9. Look at the graphic. Where is the JDK contract file?

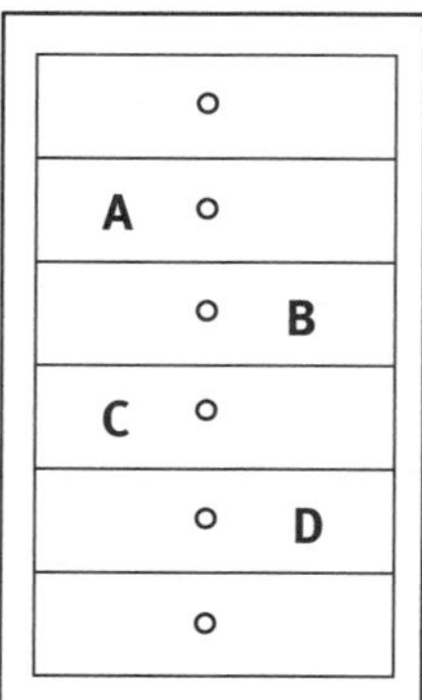

A. [A] (the woman says *It's in the second drawer from the top.*) CORRECT
B. [B] (the woman says *It's in the second drawer from the top.*)
C. [C] (the woman says *It's in the second drawer from the top.*)
D. [D] (the woman says *It's in the second drawer from the top.*)

Practice 4

10. What is the woman learning about?

A. a camera (This repeats the word *camera.*)
B. a projector CORRECT
C. a printer (This is clearly a related technology, but it is not mentioned.)
D. a photocopier (This plays on the words *photo* and *copy.*)

11. Why does the man say, "Don't worry"?

A. The woman does not need to use the projector. (The man shows her how to use it, so she must need to know how to use it.)
B. It is not difficult to use the projector. (CORRECT)
C. The woman will be fully trained next week. (The man shows her immediately.)
D. No one in the office knows how to do it. (The man shows her how the projector works.)

12. How can users change the size of the image?

A. by pressing the "resize" button (This is not mentioned.)
B. by pressing the blue arrows (These control brightness and color.)
C. by pressing the red button (The red button switches the machine on and off.)
D. by turning the wheel CORRECT

Practice 5

13. What do the speakers want to reserve?

A. a room for an office party (This repeats the word *party.*)
B. a conference room (This is not mentioned.)
C. a car (This repeats the word *car.*)
D. a table at a restaurant CORRECT

14. When was the reservation made?

A. Monday (This repeats the word *Monday.*)
B. Tuesday (This repeats the word *Tuesday.*)
C. Thursday (This is not mentioned.)
D. Friday CORRECT

15. How long do the speakers need to wait?

A. half an hour CORRECT
B. forty-five minutes (This is not mentioned.)
C. an hour (This is not mentioned.)
D. more than an hour (This is not mentioned.)

Practice 6

16. Whom is the woman speaking to?
    - A. a policeman CORRECT
    - B. a bus driver (Buses are mentioned, but we do not address a driver as *officer*.)
    - C. a passenger (She is traveling, but we would not address another passenger as *officer*.)
    - D. a travel agent (The topic is travel, but she is clearly in the middle of her journey, not arranging it.)

17. Where does the woman want to go?
    - A. a train station CORRECT
    - B. the airport (She has just come from the airport.)
    - C. the bus station (This repeats the word *bus*.)
    - D. a subway station (This repeats the words *subway station*.)

18. How many minutes will the woman need to wait for the next bus?
    - A. 3 CORRECT
    - B. 5 (This repeats the word *five*.)
    - C. 8 (This repeats the word *eight*.)
    - D. 15 (This repeats the word *fifteen*.)

Practice 7

19. What are the speakers mainly discussing?
    - A. new safety rules ____________________
    - B. rescheduling a meeting CORRECT
    - C. preparing for an inspection ____________________
    - D. ordering plastic ____________________

20. Who will Rory call?
    - A. the client CORRECT
    - B. the rest of their team ____________________
    - C. the safety inspector ____________________
    - D. the consultant ____________________

21. How will Rory contact their team?
    - A. by memo ____________________
    - B. by phone ____________________
    - C. by email CORRECT
    - D. by text message ____________________

Practice 8

22. Where does Tony work?
    - A. in the maintenance department ____________________
    - B. on the shop floor ____________________
    - C. in the product training department ____________________
    - D. in the service supplies department CORRECT

23. What is Tony's problem?
    - A. He does not know what to order. ____________________
    - B. He does not know how to order. ____________________
    - C. He is not sure if he should order. CORRECT
    - D. He does not know where Mr. Logan's order is. ____________________

24. Why are Mr. Logan and Tony not together?
    A. Mr. Logan is ill. ______________________
    ____
    B. Mr. Logan is in another city. CORRECT
    C. Tony is on the shop floor. ______________________
    ____
    D. Tony is in a meeting. ______________________
    ____

Practice 9

25. Why haven't the contracts been signed?
    A. The man is missing some information. (This is not mentioned.)
    B. Aidan has not completed them yet. (The contracts are with the lawyers, so they must have been completed.)
    C. The clients do not want to do business. (This is not mentioned.)
    D. The lawyers have issues with the content. CORRECT

26. Why does the man think the clients liked meeting in person?
    A. to make sure they were dealing with the same team (This is not mentioned.)
    B. to receive a discount on their services (This is not mentioned.)
    C. to make sure no one else was obtaining information CORRECT
    D. to make sure they got to know the lawyers (This is not mentioned.)

27. What does the woman imply about the clients changing their mind?
    A. They did it to reduce costs. CORRECT
    B. They did it because it was time consuming. (It was time consuming for the speakers, not the clients.)
    C. They were not confident in their abilities. (This is not mentioned.)
    D. They thought Giulia did a good job. (This is not mentioned.)

Practice 10

28. Where are the speakers?
    A. at the office (This is not mentioned.)
    B. at the swimming pool (This is not mentioned.)
    C. at an art gallery (This is not mentioned.)
    D. at a theater CORRECT

29. What does the woman say about Pedro?
    A. She has missed him. (Pedro says this about Hlynur.)
    B. He is missing his children. CORRECT
    C. He is glad to have a free evening. (Pedro says this about himself.)
    D. He should have contacted them. (This is not mentioned.)

30. What do two of the speakers agree about?
    A. the talent of the female lead CORRECT
    B. They don't understand what is happening. (Pedro says this, but no one agrees.)
    C. They will go for dinner later. (This is not mentioned.)
    D. the story is not relevant. (The woman says the story **is** relevant.)

Responses for Identify the Error Questions

Practice 7

19. What are the speakers mainly discussing?
    A. new safety rules (*This repeats the word safety.*)
    B. rescheduling a meeting CORRECT
    C. preparing for an inspection (*This repeats the word inspection.*)
    D. ordering plastic (*This repeats the word plastic.*)

20. Who will Rory call?
    - A. the client CORRECT
    - B. the rest of their team (*He will contact them, but not by phone.*)
    - C. the safety inspector (*This repeats the words safety inspection.*)
    - D. the consultant (*She is mentioned, but the man is not asked to contact her.*)

21. How will Rory contact their team?
    - A. by memo (*This is a common method to contact people, but this is not mentioned.*)
    - B. by phone (*He will contact the client by phone, not the team.*)
    - C. by email CORRECT
    - D. by text message (*This repeats the word message.*)

Practice 8

22. Where does Tony work?
    - A. in the maintenance department (*This repeats the words maintenance department.*)
    - B. on the shop floor (*This repeats the words shop floor.*)
    - C. in the product training department (*This repeats the words product training department.*)
    - D. in the service supplies department CORRECT

23. What is Tony's problem?
    - A. He does not know what to order. (*He says what he needs, but does not know if he should order.*)
    - B. He does not know how to order. (*This is not the problem.*)
    - C. He is not sure if he should order. CORRECT
    - D. He does not know where Mr. Logan's order is. (*This is not mentioned.*)

24. Why are Mr. Logan and Tony not together?
    - A. Mr. Logan is ill. (*This is not mentioned.*)
    - B. Mr. Logan is in another city. CORRECT
    - C. Tony is on the shop floor. (*This is true, but that is not the reason why they are not together.*)
    - D. Tony is in a meeting. (*This is not mentioned.*)

CHAPTER 6

Exam Part IV—Short Talks

LEARNING OBJECTIVES

In this section, you'll learn to:

- Use the Kaplan Strategies to recognize the Question types
- Use the Kaplan Strategies to manage your time efficiently
- Identify the 4 main distractors used in Part IV questions

Time Budget for Part IV: Approximately 13 minutes

For this part of the TOEIC exam, you will hear ten short talks. There is only one speaker in each talk. In your exam booklet, you will see three written questions, each with four written responses; you will also hear the question (but not the answer choices). For some questions, you will also be given a graphic to use to answer the question. For each question, you must pick the response that best answers the question. There will be an eight-second pause between questions and an eight-second pause between the end of the last question and the start of the next talk.

TEST-TAKING STRATEGIES

Strategy 1: Know the Directions

It is important to understand what you are being asked to do and to be sure you know the directions *before* you take the test. The directions will look something like this:

> **Directions**: You will now hear short talks given by a single speaker. You will be asked to answer three questions about what the speaker says. Select the best response to each question and mark the letter on your answer sheet. The talks will be spoken only once and will not be printed in your test book.

Please note that for this part of the TOEIC exam, sample questions are not provided, as they were in Parts I and II. However, here is an example illustrating the format of a typical Short Talk, so you can start becoming familiar with it.

You will hear:

Narrator:	*Questions 71 through 73 refer to the following talk.*
Man:	*Good morning, everyone. Today I'd like to discuss our strategy for the New York City area. As I'm sure you're all aware, real estate prices there are among the highest in the nation and are continuing to rise. On the one hand, this is good news in the short term because it means that the company's rental properties there will continue to be profitable. On the other hand, if the trend continues, it means that acquiring and developing new residential and business properties will become more costly; and because rents are so high already, we won't be able to charge what we need to maintain our current return on investment—over time, returns will fall. There are also some signs that the New York market may be turning around—houses and apartments are staying on the market an average of two days longer now than they did six months ago. While sellers are still getting contracts at the prices they want, it's taking longer to get them. This could mean that housing prices and rents are poised to come down soon. The situation is rather mixed and difficult to read. What I'd like us to do is formulate a revised strategy that balances the rewards we now enjoy in the current boom market against the future risks of a soft housing market.*
Narrator:	*Number 71. What does the speaker say could happen if the current trend in real estate prices continues?*

You will be able to read the first question and the four answer choices in your test book:

71. What does the speaker say could happen if the current trend in real estate prices continues?
    A. Return on investment could fall.
    B. Development opportunities could increase.
    C. Fewer residential properties could be available.
    D. Selling commercial properties could become more difficult.

There will be an eight-second pause after the first question. Then you will hear:

Narrator:	*Number 72. What does the speaker claim regarding New York City real estate?*

You will be able to read the second question and the four answer choices in your test book:

72. What does the speaker claim regarding New York City real estate?
    - A. Prices have fallen in the past six months.
    - B. Houses and apartments are taking longer to sell.
    - C. Apartment sales have doubled in the past six months.
    - D. Commercial properties are a good long-term investment.

There will be an eight-second pause after the second question. Then you will hear:

Narrator: *Number 73. What does the speaker want to change?*

You will be able to read the third question and the four answer choices in your test book:

73. What does the speaker want to change?
    - A. a project schedule
    - B. a meeting agenda
    - C. a company strategy
    - D. a real estate contract

Each question is spoken once, followed by an eight-second pause. This means for each question you have only eight seconds to read the question and answer choices, and mark your answer sheet.

Strategy 2: Read the First Few Questions

Because you already know what the directions are, look at the first few questions in your test book while the directions are playing—just as you did for Part III. This will let you know what to expect and what you will need to listen for.

Because the directions for Part IV are short, there is not much time to read ahead. However, try to read as many questions as you can.

Strategy 3: Know the Question Types

The organization of Part IV questions is similar to that for Part III. The questions generally ask for information in the order in which it is presented in the talk: The first question will usually ask about something mentioned near the beginning, the second question will ask about something mentioned in the middle, and the third question will ask about something mentioned near the end.

There are five basic categories of questions for Part IV. (These are essentially the same categories found in Part III).

1. **Gist**—Gist questions will ask what the main topic is, where the talk takes place, or who the intended audience is. Gist questions ask about the overall situation rather than about specific details. For example:

Who is the speaker?

Who is the intended audience?

What is the speaker mainly discussing?

What is the purpose of the announcement?

Where does this talk probably take place?

2. **Detail**—Detail questions ask about information mentioned in the short talk. They can ask about general information or very specific details. Examples include what a speaker has said about something or someone; when an action or event will take place; what role, function, or responsibility people will have; how a problem or situation is being handled; the order in which things are to be done; or what products or services a company provides. For example:

    What does the speaker say about Starboard Enterprises?

    What will happen the next day?

    What will David Johnson's role be?

    Where will the old files be kept?

    When should the first locking nut be removed?

    What service does Travis Consulting provide?

3. **Implication/Inference**—Implication/Inference questions ask about things that are not stated directly by the speaker, such as the speaker's intentions, emotions, expectations, or probable future actions. Common Implication/Inference questions include:

    What does the speaker intend to do next week?

    Why is the speaker surprised?

    What does the speaker expect managers to do?

    What will the speaker probably do next?

    What does the speaker imply about the new rules?

Some Implication/Inference and Gist questions might seem to be similar. For example, a Gist question that asks about who the talk is intended for requires an inference, in that the talk will provide enough information about the location, setting, or situation to make the intended audience obvious, but the identity of the audience will not likely be stated directly. However, while some Gist questions require you to understand an implication or make an inference, they generally focus on the larger picture or the overall situation. Implication/Inference questions tend to deal with implied details about something the speaker is discussing, expecting, planning, or intending to do, or about details that concern the situation or context itself.

4. **Intended Meaning**—Intended Meaning questions ask you to explain the purpose of a part of speech. You will be given a quotation from the talk, usually a phrase, and asked to choose the option that best describes what the speaker means. Here are some examples of Implied meaning questions:

Why does the man say, "Do you know what I mean?"
Why does the woman say "What's up?"
Why does the man say "I don't get it"
Why does the woman say "Crazy, right?"

5. **Graphic Questions**—Graphic questions provide visual data along with the question. To answer the question correctly, you need to use the information in the talk and the information in the visual stimulus. The visual stimulus could be a number of different things. Some possible examples include: a price list, a calendar, a map, a floor plan, a schedule, and a budget. The graphics will be quite short and simple, and it will not be clear from either the graphic on its own, or the talk on its own, what the correct answer is. You must combine both the spoken and printed information to find the correct answer.

Look at the price list. Which item will the woman choose?
Look at the map. Which number shows the position of the speaker?
Look at the calendar. What time will she book the dinner for?
Look at the itinerary. What time will the woman begin her speech?

Strategy 4: Know the Distractors

The distractors for Part IV are essentially the same as those used in Part III. As was the case for Part III, all Part IV distractors will answer the question plausibly; that is, they will be possible answers to the question. When you look at a Part IV question and the answer choices by themselves—without hearing the talk—each choice will answer the question in a logical and realistic way, and no choice can be eliminated using logic or common sense. Each option will be a plausible answer to the question, and there are no impossible answer choices. All TOEIC exam Part IV items are written in this way.

As was described for Part III, none of the Part IV questions are linked in any way; that is, the information contained in a set of question and answer choices will not help you to answer any other questions.

There are four basic types of distractors for Part IV questions:

1. **Not mentioned**—This type of distractor uses words, phrases, and ideas that are not mentioned in the talk, but there is no connection to the language used in the talk. The distractor answers the question plausibly but does not relate to the talk.
2. **Repeated words**—This type of distractor uses words, phrases, and ideas that are mentioned in the talk, but it changes them so that they are not true. The distractor answers the question plausibly but is incorrect.
3. **New words**—This type of distractor introduces new words, phrases, or ideas that may be associated with or implied by language and ideas expressed in the talk, but that are untrue. The distractor answers the question plausibly but is incorrect.
4. **Rephrase/Paraphrase**—This type of distractor takes the original language used in the talk and rephrases or paraphrases it in a way that makes it untrue. The distractor answers the question plausibly but is incorrect.

Note that a set of answer choices may use more than one type of distractor at a time. Not all distractors fit neatly into the categories outlined here; some may seem to belong to more than one category. Note also that each of these distractor types is similar because, in the end, they are incorrect answers to the question. However, it is useful to look at *why* they are incorrect and to understand what you must listen for.

Look at the Part IV directions example again. (Material in *italics* indicates what you will hear; material in **bold** indicates what is printed in your test book.)

Narrator: *Questions 71 through 73 refer to the following talk.*

Man: *Good morning, everyone. Today I'd like to discuss our strategy for the New York City area. As I'm sure you're all aware, real estate prices there are among the highest in the nation and are continuing to rise. On the one hand, this is good news in the short term because it means that the company's rental properties there will continue to be profitable. On the other hand, if the trend continues, it means that acquiring and developing new residential and business properties will become more costly; and because rents are so high already, we won't be able to charge what we need to maintain our current return on investment—over time, returns will fall. There are also some signs that the New York market may be turning around—houses and apartments are staying on the market an average of two days longer now than they did six months ago. While sellers are still getting contracts at the prices they want, it's taking longer to get them. This could mean that housing prices and rents are poised to come down soon. The situation is rather mixed and difficult to read. What I'd like us to do is formulate a revised strategy that balances the rewards we now enjoy in the current boom market against the future risks of a soft housing market.*

Narrator: *Number 71. What does the speaker say could happen if the current trend in real estate prices continues?*

71. What does the speaker say could happen if the current trend in real estate prices continues?

A. Return on investment could fall.

B. Development opportunities could increase.

C. Fewer residential properties could be available.

D. Selling commercial properties could become more difficult.

The correct answer is choice (A). This is a Detail question. Choice (B) uses the word *development* from the talk, but it also introduces the idea of an increase in development opportunities, which is not mentioned, and is therefore a false statement. Choice (C) uses the words *residential properties* from the talk, but the idea that fewer of them will be available is not mentioned and is therefore incorrect. Choice (D) uses words, phrases, and ideas mentioned or implied in the talk (*commercial properties, difficult*), but it rephrases them in a way that is not true.

Narrator: *Number 72. What does the speaker claim regarding New York City real estate?*

72. **What does the speaker claim regarding New York City real estate?**
    - A. **Prices have fallen in the past six months.**
    - B. **Houses and apartments are taking longer to sell.**
    - C. **Apartment sales have doubled in the past six months.**
    - D. **Commercial properties are a good long-term investment.**

The correct answer is (B). This is a Detail question. Choice (A) takes words, phrases, and ideas that are mentioned in the talk (*prices, fall, six months*) and rephrases them to make a false statement. Choice (C) uses words from the talk (*apartment, six months*) but combines them in a way that is incorrect. Choice (D) takes words, phrases, and ideas that are mentioned or implied in the conversation (*commercial properties, long-term investments*) and rephrases them to make a false statement.

Narrator: *Number 73. What does the speaker want to change?*

73. **What does the speaker want to change?**
    - A. **a project schedule**
    - B. **a meeting agenda**
    - C. **a company strategy**
    - D. **a real estate contract**

The correct choice is (C). This is a Detail question. Choice (A) is not mentioned or implied and is an example of a not-mentioned distractor. Choice (B) is not mentioned or implied and is an example of a not-mentioned distractor. Choice (D) repeats words and phrases from the talk (*real estate, contract*), but this is not what the speaker wants to change.

Notice that for each question, all the distractors are plausible answers, and none of the questions or answer choices are of any help in answering other questions.

Strategy 5: Listen for the Information in the Questions

As was described in relation to Part III of the TOEIC exam, by reading the questions in your test book, you will know what information you need to be listening for. For example, if the first question is a Gist question asking about whom the audience is, you should listen carefully for words and phrases that indicate where the talk takes place and who the audience is most likely to be.

The talks will often contain a lot of information that is *not* tested. However, because you are able to read the questions in your test book, you will know what information to be listening for, and you should focus on finding what you need to answer each question.

Note that the questions for Part IV are all *Wh-* information questions—as was the case for Part III. There are no *Yes/No* questions. Go back and review the Question-Response *Wh-* information question material on pages 54–60. Be sure you understand the kinds of information the question types ask for and the format of the expected answers. You should know, for example, that a *When* question deals with time and that you will need to listen for time words (e.g. *today, yesterday, this afternoon, at 10 o'clock*).

You will have to listen carefully to the talk to get information you need. Remember, the question and answer choices used in one question set will *not* help you to answer another question.

Pay attention to the context of the talk. Know who the speaker is and what his or her relationship to the audience is. Listen for clues that tell you where the talk is likely to take place. If a speaker is addressing an audience, the setting and relationship between the speaker and the audience is usually made very clear, and there is often a question that tests whether you have understood this.

Be sure you also understand the purpose of the talk. If, for example, a speaker is addressing an audience, understand why the speaker is addressing this particular audience. If an announcement is being made, listen for clues to its purpose to understand *why* the announcement is being made.

Strategy 6: Answer Each Question in Your Own Words

Read each question and predict the answer in your own words *before* reading the answer choices. If you understand the talk, you should be able to answer each question in your own words. Your predicted answer—or one very closely matching—should be among the answer choices. Remember, there are no trick questions on the TOEIC exam. All the information needed to answer the questions is presented in the talk.

It is much better to have your own idea about the correct answer first, *before* looking at the answer choices. If you look at the answer choices first, you might be attracted to an incorrect choice and wind up listening to the talk for that information, which might not even be mentioned.

Strategy 7: Evaluate the Answer Choices

As you did with Part III, find the answer choice that is a close match to the one you expect and mark your answer sheet. Be sure to fill in the oval completely, as shown in the test directions.

If no answer choice matches your expected answer very well, eliminate as many choices as you can. Remember, because one question and answer choice set will not help you answer another, do not look at answer choices from one question for clues to answer another question.

Often, each answer choice uses words and phrases used in the talk. However, if there is only *one* answer choice that uses words and phrases from the talk, this is very likely the correct one.

Strategy 8: Eliminate Answer Choices

If none of the answer choices matches your expected answer very well, then you must eliminate as many wrong choices as you can. If you find you have to guess, the same guessing strategy used for Part III works for Part IV, too. Eliminate any choices that do not use words and phrases from the talk—the not-mentioned distractor type. (If there is only *one* choice that uses words and phrases from the talk, you should choose this as the correct answer.) The not-mentioned distractors are often the easiest to eliminate.

Strategy 9: Manage Your Time

Remember that there are only eight seconds between questions. There is also an eight-second pause between the end of the last question and the introduction for the next talk. You will need to work quickly to keep up with the test, and you will hear the short talks only once. Do not waste time answering any individual question—you risk missing the beginning of the next talk, which could contain information you need to answer the questions that follow. Select your answer choice and mark it on your answer sheet as quickly as you can.

If you find yourself running out of time, mark your answer sheet with your wild-guess letter. Do not leave any questions unanswered.

Strategy 10: Read the Questions for the Next Talk Before It Starts

Just as each Part III Short Conversations had a brief introduction, each Short Talk in Part IV does, too. For example, you will hear:

Narrator: *Questions 71 through 73 refer to the following talk.*

You should try to answer all three questions for the current talk before you hear the introduction for the next talk. Then, while the introduction is playing, immediately begin reading as many of the next set of questions as you can before the actual talk begins. This will help you focus on what information you need to listen for. When a question includes a graphic, try to understand the information in the graphic, as well as what the question is asking you to find, before you listen to the talk.

Strategy Summary

1. Know the directions.
2. Read the first few questions while the directions are playing.
3. Understand question types and how questions are ordered.
4. Understand the basic types of distractors.
5. Listen for the information in the questions.
6. Answer each question in your own words before reading the answer choices.
7. Evaluate the answer choices and mark the answer if you know it.
8. Eliminate answer choices that are wrong and select the best match from what is left.
9. Manage your time and be sure to answer all three questions before the next talk begins.
10. Read the questions for the next talk before it starts.

SHORT TALKS PRACTICE SET

Now you are ready to do the Short Talks practice, for which you will need to listen to the audio. Choose the best answer from the choices listed and mark it in your book (on Test Day, you will mark your answers on the answer grid). You will find the transcript for the Short Talks in Part Six of this book, but try these first without the transcript so you will be better prepared for the exam.

When you have listened to all of the talks and answered all of the questions, check your answers against the answer key. Then, be sure to read the explanations that follow the answer key.

Track 4

Play Track 4 to hear the Short Talks

Time Budget: Approximately 15 minutes for 30 questions

Practice 1

1. What is the speaker promoting?

   A. international capital
   B. increased imports
   C. foreign investment
   D. increased export

2. Where does this talk take place?

   A. at a trade conference
   B. at a business school
   C. at a corporate board meeting
   D. at a local government meeting

3. According to the speaker, why are foreign buyers interested in Irish products?

   A. They are reasonably priced.
   B. They are high quality.
   C. They are organic.
   D. They are easily available.

Practice 2

4. Why is the SmartShares company in the news?

   A. It has laid off a large part of its workforce.
   B. It has been involved in a criminal court case.
   C. It has expanded into the East Asian market.
   D. It has won an important industry award.

5. According to the report, what is improving for workers in Thailand?

   A. salaries
   B. benefits packages
   C. working conditions
   D. productivity

6. Look at the graphic. What time will the East Asia report begin?

	Presenter
18:00	Mark Francis
18:05	
18:10	
18:20	Jane Withers

   A. 18:00
   B. 18:05
   C. 18:10
   D. 18:20

Practice 3

7. What kind of store is Dunthorps?

   A. clothing
   B. kitchenware
   C. department
   D. furniture

8. Why does the speaker say, "It's crazy!"?

   A. He thinks the items are too expensive.
   B. He believes that the sale is not a good idea.
   C. He thinks the clothes are unusual.
   D. He thinks the reductions are extreme.

9. When does the sale end?

   A. end of June
   B. July 1st
   C. end of July
   D. mid-August

Practice 4

10. Where did the artist get the idea for his piece?

   A. France
   B. The Caribbean
   C. Austria
   D. New Zealand

11. What kind of artwork is being discussed?
    A. sculpture
    B. pencil drawing
    C. painting
    D. photograph

12. Who is the speaker addressing?
    A. buyers at an art sale
    B. an audience at a lecture
    C. artists at a workshop
    D. visitors to a museum

Practice 5

13. Who is Ira Levinson?
    A. the speaker
    B. the building's architect
    C. a new employee
    D. the company founder

14. How many people will work in the building?
    A. 250
    B. 500
    C. 750
    D. 1,000

15. What is the purpose of the talk?
    A. to dedicate a building
    B. to introduce a new employee
    C. to announce plans for a new building
    D. to discuss a change in company policy

Practice 6

16. For how many years have traffic violations been decreasing nationally?
    A. 1
    B. 3
    C. 5
    D. 8

17. Why does the speaker say, "Not according to some?"
    A. Some people think there are more police officers than there used to be.
    B. Some people think that drivers are less likely to break the law.
    C. Some people think that there are fewer reports of traffic violations.
    D. Some people think that drivers are not more law-abiding.

18. What did the police spokesperson say about the figures?
    A. They indicate that drivers are becoming more careful.
    B. They show that policing methods are improving.
    C. They might not say anything about drivers' behavior.
    D. They are probably not very accurate.

Practice 7

19. Which number should a customer press for checking account access?
    A. 1
    B. 2
    C. 3
    D. 4

20. What does pressing 5 allow customers to do?
    A. access their credit card accounts.
    B. speak to a customer service representative.
    C. repeat the menu options.
    D. transfer funds between accounts.

21. What do customers find out?
    A. The menu options will change.
    B. Their calls may be recorded.
    C. They can access their accounts online.
    D. New services have been added.

Practice 8

22. Who is the intended audience for the advertisement?

    A. first-time flyers
    B. commuters
    C. business travelers
    D. students and young people

23. What do Jet Lines executive lounges have?

    A. large-screen TVs
    B. internet access
    C. luggage storage areas
    D. exercise facilities

24. Look at the graphic. Which flight is most likely operated by Jet Lines?

Flight number	Destination	Business class space between seats	Reclining Seats?
345623	Jakarta	1.8 m	Yes
434673	Bangkok	2.2 m	Yes
953423	Kuala Lumpur	2.1 m	No
345563	Hanoi	1.6 m	No

    A. 345623
    B. 434673
    C. 953423
    D. 345563

Practice 9

25. What relationship does Mr. Rushman have with Seiler Logistics?

    A. He is an employee.
    B. He is a customer.
    C. He is a security guard.
    D. He is a driver.

26. Why has Amy Richardson called Mr. Rushman?

    A. to update him about a delivery problem
    B. to apologize for not returning his call earlier
    C. to make a change to her order
    D. to request his help with a problem

27. When has Amy Richardson probably called Mr. Rushman?

    A. in the middle of the afternoon
    B. during his lunch time
    C. early in the morning
    D. at the end of the day

Practice 10

28. How long does it take to get to the airport?

    A. 20 minutes
    B. 25 minutes
    C. 30 minutes
    D. 35 minutes

29. What is true about the single-fare tickets?
    A. They cannot be purchased aboard the train.
    B. They can be paid for with a credit card.
    C. They cost more during rush hour.
    D. They are cheaper if they are bought at the station.

30. What is learned about the advance-purchase discount tickets?
    A. They are available only online.
    B. They are good for three months from the date of purchase.
    C. They discount fares by ten percent.
    D. They cost $25 each.

ANSWER KEY

1. D	11. C	21. C
2. A	12. D	22. C
3. A	13. D	23. B
4. B	14. A	24. B
5. D	15. A	25. B
6. C	16. C	26. A
7. C	17. D	27. D
8. D	18. C	28. D
9. C	19. B	29. B
10. B	20. D	30. C

ANSWERS AND EXPLANATIONS

All of the answer choices are included for each question, and in parentheses, there is an explanation of exactly why the wrong answer choices are incorrect. For some questions, we have left the wrong answer explanations blank so that you can fill them in. The more you can analyze and explain the errors in the wrong answer choices, the more skillful and efficient you will become at eliminating incorrect choices and selecting the correct ones.

Sample responses for these Identify the Error questions are included at the end of the Answers and Explanations section.

Practice 1

1. What is the speaker promoting? (Main idea/ *What*)
   A. international capital (This is not mentioned.)
   B. increased imports (This is not mentioned.)
   C. foreign investment (This is not mentioned.)
   D. increased export CORRECT

2. Where does this talk take place? (Main idea/ *Where*)
   A. at a trade conference CORRECT
   B. at a business school (The speaker welcomes the audience to a trade conference.)
   C. at a corporate board meeting (The speaker welcomes the audience to a trade conference.)
   D. at a local government meeting (The speaker welcomes the audience to a trade conference.)

3. According to the speaker, why are foreign buyers interested in Irish products? (Detail/ *What*)
   A. They are reasonably priced. CORRECT
   B. They are high quality. (This is not mentioned.)
   C. They are organic. (This is not mentioned.)
   D. They are easily available. (This is not mentioned.)

Practice 2

4. Why is the SmartShares company in the news? (Detail/ *Why*)
   A. It has laid off a large part of its workforce. (This is not mentioned.)
   B. It is has been involved in a criminal court case. CORRECT
   C. It has expanded into the East Asian market. (This repeats the words *East Asia*.)
   D. It has won an important industry award. (This is not mentioned.)

5. According to the report, what is improving for workers in Thailand? (Detail/*What*)
   A. salaries (This is not mentioned.)
   B. benefits packages (This is not mentioned.)
   C. working conditions (This is not mentioned.)
   D. productivity CORRECT

6. Look at the graphic. What time will the East Asia report begin? (Graphic)
   A. 18:00 (Mark Francis is reporting on stock markets.)
   B. 18:05 (The SmartShare report will be given next.)
   C. 18:10 (The East Asia report will be given after the SmartShare report.) CORRECT
   D. 18:20 (Jane will give the technology report.)

Practice 3

7. What kind of store is Dunthorps? (Main idea/*What kind*)
   A. clothing (Clothing is mentioned, but the store sells more than clothes.)
   B. kitchenware (This repeats the word *kitchen*.)
   C. department CORRECT
   D. furniture (This is a play on the word *furnishings*.)

8. Why does the speaker say, "It's crazy!"?
   A. He thinks the items are too expensive. (The items are all cheaper than they previously were.)
   B. He believes that the sale is not a good idea. (The speaker is advertising the sale, so he is presenting the sale as a good thing.)
   C. He thinks the clothes are unusual. (He is discussing the price of the clothes, not the style.)
   D. He thinks the reductions are extreme. CORRECT

9. When does the sale end? (Detail/*When*)
   A. end of June (This is not mentioned.)
   B. July 1st (This is when the sale begins.)
   C. end of July CORRECT
   D. Mid-August (This is not mentioned.)

Practice 4

10. Where did the artist get the idea for his piece? (Detail /*Where*)
    A. France (Paris is mentioned, but this is not the answer.)
    B. The Caribbean CORRECT
    C. Austria (Austria is mentioned, but this is not the answer.)
    D. New Zealand (This is not mentioned.)

11. What kind of artwork is being discussed? (Main idea/*What kind*)
    A. sculpture (This is not mentioned.)
    B. pencil drawing (This is not mentioned.)
    C. painting CORRECT
    D. photograph (This is not mentioned.)

12. Who is the speaker addressing? (Main idea/*Who*)
    A. buyers at an art sale (The talk is about art, but the setting is not a sale.)
    B. an audience at a lecture (The speaker says the words *in the next gallery*, suggesting that the group is moving.)
    C. artists at a workshop (The speaker refers to *the museum*.)
    D. visitors to a museum CORRECT

Practice 5

13. Who is Ira Levinson? (Detail/*Who*)
    A. the speaker (The speaker refers to Ira Levinson, and is not talking about himself.)
    B. the building's architect (This is not mentioned.)
    C. a new employee (This is not mentioned.)
    D. the company founder CORRECT

14. How many people will work in the building? (Detail/*How many*)
    A. 250 CORRECT
    B. 500 (This is not mentioned.)
    C. 750 (This is not mentioned.)
    D. 1,000 (This repeats *a thousand*.)

15. What is the purpose of the talk? (Main idea/*What*)
    A. to dedicate a building CORRECT
    B. to introduce a new employee (This is not mentioned.)
    C. to announce plans for a new building (This repeats the words *new building*.)
    D. to discuss a change in company policy (This is not mentioned.)

Practice 6

16. For how many years have traffic violations been decreasing nationally? (Detail/*How many*)
    A. 1 (This is not mentioned.)
    B. 3 (This is not mentioned.)
    C. 5 CORRECT
    D. 8 (This is not mentioned.)

17. Why does the speaker say, "Not according to some?"
    A. Some people think there are more police officers than there used to be. (The speaker says that not everyone believes people are more law-abiding now.)
    B. Some people think that drivers are less likely to break the law. (This is the opposite of what some people think.)
    C. Some people think that there are fewer reports of traffic violations. (The speaker is disputing why there are fewer traffic violations, not if there are fewer violations.)
    D. Some people think that drivers are not more law-abiding. CORRECT

18. What did the police spokesperson say about the figures? (Detail/*What*)
    A. They indicate that drivers are becoming more careful. (The speaker asks if this is the case, but this is not what the police say.)
    B. They show that policing methods are improving. (This is not mentioned.)
    C. They might not say anything about drivers' behavior. CORRECT
    D. They are probably not very accurate. (This is not mentioned.)

Practice 7

19. Which number should a customer press for checking account access? (Detail/*Which*)
    A. 1 (This is to access savings.)
    B. 2 CORRECT
    C. 3 (This is to access credit cards.)
    D. 4 (This is to access retirement and investment accounts.)

20. What does pressing 5 allow customers to do? (Detail/*What*)
    A. access their credit card accounts (Customers must press 3 for this.)
    B. speak to a customer service representative (Customers must press 0 for this.)
    C. repeat the menu options (Customers must press 9 for this.)
    D. transfer funds between accounts. CORRECT

21. What do customers find out? (Detail/*What*)
    A. The menu options will change. (This is not mentioned.)
    B. Their calls may be recorded. (This is not mentioned.)
    C. They can access their accounts online. CORRECT
    D. New services have been added. (This is not mentioned.)

Practice 8

22. Who is the intended audience for the advertisement? (Main idea/*Who*)
    A. first-time flyers (This is not mentioned.)
    B. commuters (This is not mentioned.)
    C. business travelers CORRECT
    D. students and young people (This is not mentioned.)

23. What do Jet Lines executive lounges have? (Detail/*What*)
    A. large-screen TVs (This is not mentioned.)
    B. internet access CORRECT
    C. luggage storage areas (This is not mentioned.)
    D. exercise facilities (This is not mentioned.)

24. Look at the graphic. Which flight is most likely operated by Jet Lines? (Graphic/*What*)
    A. 345623 (Jet Lines offers more leg room, or *space between seats* than any other airline company)
    B. 434673 (Jet Lines offers more leg room, or *space between seats* than any other airline company) CORRECT
    C. 953423 (Jet Lines offers more leg room, or *space between seats* than any other airline company)
    D. 345563 (Jet Lines offers more leg room, or *space between seats* than any other airline company)

Practice 9

25. What relationship does Mr. Rushman have with Seiler Logistics? (Detail/*What*)
    A. He is an employee. (This not logical.)
    B. He is a customer. CORRECT
    C. He is a security guard. (This repeats the words *security guard*.)
    D. He is a driver. (This repeats the word *driver*.)

26. Why has Amy Richardson called Mr. Rushman? (Main idea/*Why*)
    A. to update him about a delivery problem CORRECT
    B. to apologize for not returning his call earlier (She apologizes for missing his call, but that's not why she has called.)
    C. to make a change to her order (This is not logical.)
    D. to request his help with a problem (This is not mentioned.)

27. When has Amy Richardson probably called Mr. Rushman? (Detail/*When*)
    A. in the middle of the afternoon (This repeats the word *afternoon*.)
    B. during his lunch time (This is not mentioned.)
    C. early in the morning (The package was delivered at 7:30 A.M.)
    D. at the end of the day CORRECT

Practice 10

28. How long does it take to get to the airport?
    A. 20 minutes ______________________
    B. 25 minutes ______________________
    C. 30 minutes ______________________
    D. 35 minutes CORRECT

29. What is true about the single-fare tickets?
    A. They cannot be purchased aboard the train. ______________________
    B. They can be paid for with a credit card. CORRECT
    C. They cost more during rush hour. ______________________
    D. They are cheaper if they are bought at the station. ______________________

30. What is learned about the advance-purchase discount tickets?
    A. They are available only online. ______________________
    B. They are good for three months from the date of purchase. ______________________
    C. They discount fares by ten percent. CORRECT
    D. They cost $25 each. ______________________

Answers for the Identify the Error Questions

Practice 10

28. How long does it take to get to the airport? (*Detail/How long*)
    A. 20 minutes (*This is not mentioned.*)
    B. 25 minutes (*This is not mentioned.*)
    C. 30 minutes (*This is not mentioned.*)
    D. 35 minutes CORRECT

29. What is true about the single-fare tickets? (*Detail/What*)
    A. They cannot be purchased aboard the train. (*They can be purchased on board.*)
    B. They can be paid for with a credit card. CORRECT
    C. They cost more during rush hour. (*This is not mentioned.*)
    D. They are cheaper if they are bought at the station. (*This is not mentioned.*)

30. What is learned about the advance-purchase discount tickets? (*Detail/What*)
    A. They are available only online. (*This is not mentioned.*)
    B. They are good for three months from the date of purchase. (*This is not mentioned.*)
    C. They discount fares by ten percent. CORRECT
    D. They cost $25 each. (*This is not mentioned.*)

PART THREE

The Reading Comprehension Section

CHAPTER 7

Exam Part V—Incomplete Sentences

LEARNING OBJECTIVES

In this section, you'll learn to:

- Distinguish between grammar and vocabulary questions
- Use the Kaplan Strategies to Predict the correct answer
- Use the Kaplan Strategies to eliminate wrong answer choices

Time budget for Part V: Approximately 10 minutes

Time management is very important on the Reading Comprehension Section of the TOEIC exam. You are given a total of 75 minutes to work through the 100 questions on these three parts. There will be no indicator on the day you take the exam for when you should move from Part V to Part VI, and from Part VI to Part VII. You do not want to spend too much time on any one part. That is why this practice is very important.

For Part V, you will read 30 incomplete sentences. Beneath each sentence, you will see four words or phrases; you must pick the word or phrase that best completes the sentence.

TEST-TAKING STRATEGIES

Strategy 1: Know the Directions

It is important to understand what you are being asked to do and to be sure you know the directions *before* you take the test.

Unlike the Listening Comprehension Section—where you must keep pace with the recording to avoid falling behind—you must pace yourself in the Reading Comprehension Section. You have 75 minutes to complete Parts V, VI, and VII. When you finish Part V, you can immediately begin Part VI; when you have finished Part VI, you can immediately begin Part VII.

By knowing the Reading Comprehension Section directions and the directions for Part V in advance, you do not need to waste valuable time reading what you already know. As soon as you are told to begin the Reading Comprehension Section, skip the directions and begin working on the Incomplete Sentence questions. The directions will look something like this:

> **READING COMPREHENSION SECTION**
>
> In the Reading Comprehension Section, you will read a variety of texts and answer different types of reading comprehension questions. The Reading Comprehension Section will last 75 minutes. There are three parts, and directions are given for each part. You are encouraged to answer as many questions as possible within the allotted time. Mark your answers on the separate answer sheet. Do not write them in the test book.

Directions: A word or phrase is missing in the following sentences. Four answer choices are given below each of the sentences. Choose the best answer to complete the sentence. Then mark the letter on your answer sheet.

Here is an example illustrating the format of a typical Incomplete Sentence question, so that you can start becoming familiar with it.

101. In the fourth quarter of 2007, Taylor Airlines reported net __________ of $82.5 million.

    A. flights
    B. revenues
    C. services
    D. quantities

The sentence should read: *In the fourth quarter of 2007, Taylor Airlines reported net revenues of $82.5 million.* Therefore, you would mark (B) on your answer sheet.

Strategy 2: Decide Whether the Sentence Tests *Vocabulary* or *Grammar*

The sentences can be divided into two types of questions, based on what the answer choices are.

Vocabulary Questions

All the choices are from different word families but have similar meanings. In the following example sentence, the answer choices are all nouns and are not part of the same word family. They do not share a common root, prefix, or suffix. Each word is different from the others in terms of its form. However, all of the words share a common theme: They are all related to money and payments. This is a classic example of a vocabulary question. To answer a vocabulary question, you must choose the word that completes the sentence *based on its meaning.* These questions test the depth of your vocabulary.

102. A late payment ________ of $25 will be applied to all accounts more than 30 days overdue.

A. fee
B. fare
C. cost
D. price

Grammar Questions

All the word choices are from the same word family. In the following example sentence, the answer choices all contain the same word *open*. This is a classic example of a grammar question. To answer a grammar question, you must choose the word that completes the sentence *based on its form*. These questions test your command of grammar and structure.

103. Trillium Incorporated plans ____________ branch offices in both Seoul and Pusan before the end of the year.

A. open
B. to open
C. opened
D. to be opened

Note that vocabulary and grammar are not always so easily separated; some questions may test vocabulary and grammar at the same time. Pronouns, comparatives, and other kinds of words can have different forms but still be related to each other. However, it is easiest to think in terms of two basic categories.

The ways vocabulary and grammar questions are approached are slightly different.

- **For vocabulary questions**—Look for words and phrases that provide clues to the answer. Often, words or phrases in the sentence will help you eliminate distractors and point you toward the correct choice. In the first example, the words *late* and *overdue* make choices (B) *fare,* (C) *cost,* and (D) *price* less attractive. The words *fares*, *costs,* and *prices* are not usually "late" or "overdue." (A) is correct.
- **For grammar questions**—Focus on the words before and after the blank to determine which part of speech is required. Most often, the words immediately before and after the blank determine which part of speech the correct choice must be. Knowing this helps you to eliminate distractors. In the second example, the word *plans* appears immediately before the blank and *must* be followed by an *to + infinitive*. This eliminates choices (A) *open* and (C) *opened*. As the statement is in active voice, not passive voice, (D) cannot be correct. (B) is therefore the correct answer.

Strategy 3: Predict the Answer

Read each sentence and try to fill the blank with your own word or phrase *before* reading the answer choices. If you understand the sentence, you should be able to correctly predict the word or phrase required to fill the blank. If your predicted answer is among the answer choices, this is likely to be the correct answer.

It is much better to have your own idea about the correct answer *before* looking at the answer choices. If you look at the answer choices first, you might be attracted to an incorrect choice.

Strategy 4: Evaluate the Answer Choices

Find the answer choice that matches the answer you predicted. Before you mark your answer sheet, reread the sentence to make sure the option you are choosing fills the blank the correctly.

If no answer choice matches your expected answer, eliminate as many choices as you can by doing the following:

- For vocabulary questions, read the sentence for context clues that may point to the correct answer or help to eliminate distractors.
- For grammar questions, focus on the words and phrases around the blank to determine the part of speech required, and eliminate distractors that do not fit.

After eliminating as many distractors as possible, select the best choice from what is left.

If you cannot eliminate any distractors, choose one letter—(A), (B), (C), or (D)—and use this for every guessed answer. Using one letter consistently is better than guessing at random.

When you have decided on an answer choice, mark your answer sheet. Be sure to fill in the oval completely, as shown in the test directions.

Strategy 5: Manage Your Time; Answer Every Question

Time management is very important in the Reading Comprehension Section. In the Listening Comprehension Section, the timing is controlled by the audio recording. In the Reading Comprehension Section, you have 75 minutes to complete Parts V, VI, and VII. How quickly you move through each part is up to you. However, because Part VII—the last part of the test—is usually the most difficult and time-consuming, you will want to go through Parts V and VI as quickly as you can so that you will have enough time left to finish Part VII.

Do not waste time working on any individual sentence. Although each sentence is worth the same amount, you should treat them all equally. Select your answer choice and mark it on your answer sheet as quickly as you can so that you can keep up with the timing of this section of the TOEIC exam.

If you find yourself running out of time, mark your answer sheet with your wild-guess letter. Do not leave any questions unanswered.

Strategy Summary

1. Know the directions.
2. Decide whether the sentence tests *vocabulary* or *grammar*.
   a. For vocabulary questions, look for words and phrases that provide clues to the answer.
   b. For grammar questions, focus on the words before and after the blank to determine which part of speech is required.
3. Predict the answer for each sentence in your own words *before* reading the choices.
4. Evaluate the answer choices and mark the answer.
5. Manage your time and be sure to answer every question.

INCOMPLETE SENTENCES PRACTICE SET

Time budget for Incomplete Sentence Practice: 24 minutes for 54 questions

When you have answered all of the questions, check your answers against the answer key. Then read the explanations that follow the answer key.

1. The long-time employee was faithful and ________.

   A. honestly
   B. honest
   C. honor
   D. honesty

2. Next week, a computer trainer will be here to ________ to any questions you may have.

   A. provide
   B. request
   C. respond
   D. answer

3. He was going to meet us ________ at the restaurant or here.

   A. but
   B. yet
   C. neither
   D. either

4. The board of directors tried to think ________ all possible options before reaching a decision.

   A. of
   B. at
   C. by
   D. as

5. If the information is public, ________ is neither unreasonable nor unethical to share it.

   A. his
   B. him
   C. its
   D. it

6. Timing is ________ important when soliciting contributions for political campaigns.

   A. accurately
   B. extremely
   C. quickly
   D. hotly

7. Andrew lives quite a ________ from where he works.

   A. closeness
   B. space
   C. distance
   D. length

8. We are able to ________ your conditions of delivery per your proposal.

   A. accepts
   B. accept
   C. accepting
   D. accepted

9. Next week's seminar ought to provide ________ with a lot of new information.

   A. we
   B. our
   C. ourselves
   D. us

10. The paper division is showing an increased ________.

    A. profit
    B. profiting
    C. profitable
    D. profits

11. Dr. Woo left very early this morning, but ________ because he forgot his briefcase.

    A. revolved
    B. returned
    C. recalled
    D. remembered

12. Payment is due in full within 30 days upon ________ of this invoice.

    A. receipt
    B. receive
    C. reception
    D. receiving

13. Doctors have ________ that stress from work can cause other medical problems.

    A. find
    B. finding
    C. found
    D. finds

14. The warehouse employees have worked overtime every day ________ the last week.

    A. until
    B. along
    C. before
    D. for

15. We do not provide third ________ with biographical information about our clients.

    A. parties
    B. people
    C. impressions
    D. dealings

16. He ________ forgot my name at the company dinner last year.

    A. complete
    B. completed
    C. completely
    D. completeness

17. Attitude is an essential ingredient in finding the ________ possible job.

    A. good
    B. best
    C. higher
    D. easier

18. Ms. Napier chose to travel by bus ________ of taking a taxi.

    A. except
    B. but
    C. besides
    D. instead

19. Mr. Fisher wants us to exchange ideas ________ the proposed reorganization of the Adele Company.

    A. around
    B. between
    C. into
    D. about

20. Realco made _________ offer for the purchase of the Wincorp property.

    A. a grateful
    B. a generous
    C. a wealthy
    D. an attentive

21. The firm was to receive full payment upon _________ of the project.

    A. completion
    B. complexion
    C. complication
    D. commitment

22. After the governor raised taxes, his _________ declined rapidly.

    A. populated
    B. popular
    C. popularity
    D. populate

23. After finishing the week-long seminar, Ms. Beyer packed her suitcase and checked _________ of the hotel.

    A. over
    B. out
    C. in
    D. or

24. Employee handbooks that are _________ written can improve morale and prevent disagreements.

    A. careful
    B. caring
    C. carefulness
    D. carefully

25. When the chairman announced _________ retirement, the board of trustees launched a nationwide search for a replacement.

    A. his
    B. our
    C. its
    D. him

26. Even a company with an excellent image and _________ can fail if it does not meet market standards.

    A. reputedly
    B. reputable
    C. repute
    D. reputation

27. Mr. and Mrs. Kuo are confident that _________ will locate the site themselves.

    A. them
    B. they
    C. themselves
    D. their

28. There are several factors to think about _________ deciding which method of distribution to pursue.

    A. when
    B. what
    C. why
    D. where

29. In an exclusive interview, Mr. Stanowitz _________ that his company would post a loss this quarter.

    A. confided
    B. confidence
    C. confide
    D. confidential

30. The requirements for new food service products were __________ debated at the franchise meeting.

    A. manually
    B. patently
    C. exhaustively
    D. firstly

31. The engineers will all need to stay there __________ the Spanning project is finished.

    A. for
    B. about
    C. until
    D. toward

32. New approaches to mass communication __________ the limits of traditional media channels.

    A. transcend
    B. transcends
    C. transcending
    D. to transcend

33. Airline reservation __________ are being revised to include extensive traveler demographics.

    A. telephones
    B. employees
    C. counters
    D. systems

34. The date for the new product launch has been __________ because of problems in production.

    A. advertised
    B. delayed
    C. produced
    D. mobilized

35. He was asked to testify before the committee __________ his expertise.

    A. since
    B. further
    C. inasmuch as
    D. because of

36. I know we have __________ types of payment plans available for our customers.

    A. much
    B. many
    C. mostly
    D. much more

37. The new shopping mall offers free parking and easy access __________ the highway.

    A. to
    B. with
    C. of
    D. for

38. This brochure provides a brief description of some of the __________ features of the insurance policy.

    A. stately
    B. sporadic
    C. slantwise
    D. salient

39. It is the ability to perform __________ over time that distinguishes great companies.

    A. consistent
    B. consistently
    C. consistency
    D. consisting

40. The growth of the waste disposal industry is being driven by demographics _________ by economic forces.

    A. in order to
    B. as well as
    C. additionally
    D. furthermore

41. The ideal _________ will have a strong sales background and in-country contacts.

    A. position
    B. procedure
    C. expectation
    D. candidate

42. Our consultants can help you _________ employee attitudes and assess training needs.

    A. network
    B. request
    C. survey
    D. volunteer

43. The reports on construction materials, including _________ on cement and ready-mixed concrete, are available in PDF format.

    A. them
    B. that
    C. those
    D. this

44. Sky Travel Air is known for being on time and having few customer _________.

    A. complaints
    B. complain
    C. complaining
    D. complainer

45. Innovative technology _________ by General Car Company debuted in new models last year.

    A. contained
    B. involved
    C. pioneered
    D. performed

46. Good graphic designers can save their clients _________ amounts of money on printing and artwork.

    A. signify
    B. significant
    C. significance
    D. signification

47. The small film company _________ had annual revenues of over four million euros.

    A. previously
    B. someday
    C. along
    D. yet

48. Mergers, takeovers, deregulation, and downsizing have created much _________ in the business world.

    A. uncertain
    B. uncertainly
    C. uncertainties
    D. uncertainty

49. The network will permit communication _________ devices such as a desktop computer and a document retrieval system.

    A. around
    B. between
    C. over
    D. above

50. All directors _________ attend this important board meeting.

    A. must
    B. ought
    C. have been
    D. should be

51. The presentation focuses on the fund's benefit to shareholders _________ than on the company's history.

    A. rather
    B. instead
    C. whereas
    D. although

52. Vendors of security services have reported a sharp increase in demand for video _________ equipment.

    A. negligence
    B. pilot
    C. leakage
    D. surveillance

53. Managers need reference materials that are easy for _________ to understand.

    A. them
    B. they
    C. themselves
    D. theirs

54. Each month, the meat packing plant rewards one employee for _________ the idea that saves the most money.

    A. receiving
    B. submitting
    C. transferring
    D. installing

ANSWER KEY

1. B
2. C
3. D
4. A
5. D
6. B
7. C
8. B
9. D
10. A
11. B
12. A
13. C
14. D
15. A
16. C
17. B
18. D
19. D
20. B
21. A
22. C
23. B
24. D
25. A
26. D
27. B
28. A
29. A
30. C
31. C
32. A
33. D
34. B
35. D
36. B
37. A
38. D
39. B
40. B
41. D
42. C
43. C
44. A
45. C
46. B
47. A
48. D
49. B
50. A
51. A
52. D
53. A
54. B

ANSWERS AND EXPLANATIONS

In the parentheses next to each question, we have identified them as being focused either on vocabulary or grammar with a *V* or a *G*. We have also included the part of speech required by the sentence.

For some of the questions, we have left this blank so that you can fill them in. The better you are at identifying the focus of each question stem, the more skillful and efficient you will become at eliminating incorrect choices and selecting the correct ones.

Sample responses for these Identify the Question Type questions are included at the end of the Answers and Explanations section.

1. The long-time employee was faithful and ____________________. (*G*—adjective)

   A. honestly
   B. honest CORRECT
   C. honor
   D. honesty

2. Next week, a computer trainer will be here to ____________________ to any questions you may have. (*V*—verb)

   A. provide
   B. request
   C. respond CORRECT
   D. answer

3. He was going to meet us ______________________ at the restaurant or here. (*V*—conjunction)
   A. but
   B. yet
   C. neither
   D. either CORRECT

4. The board of directors tried to think ______________________ all possible options before reaching a decision. (*V*—preposition)
   A. of CORRECT
   B. at
   C. by
   D. as

5. If the information is public, ______________________ is neither unreasonable nor unethical to share it. (*G*—pronoun)
   A. his
   B. him
   C. its
   D. it CORRECT

6. Timing is ______________________ important when soliciting contributions for political campaigns. (*V*—adverb)
   A. accurately
   B. extremely CORRECT
   C. quickly
   D. hotly

7. Andrew lives quite a ______________________ from where he works. (*V*—noun)
   A. closeness
   B. space
   C. distance CORRECT
   D. length

8. We are able to ______________________ your conditions of delivery per your proposal. (*G*—verb)
   A. accepts
   B. accept CORRECT
   C. accepting
   D. accepted

9. Next week's seminar ought to provide ______________________ with a lot of new information. (*G*—pronoun)
   A. we
   B. our
   C. ourselves
   D. us CORRECT

10. The paper division is showing an increased ______________________. (*G*—noun)
    A. profit CORRECT
    B. profiting
    C. profitable
    D. profits

11. Dr. Woo left very early this morning, but ______________________ because he forgot his briefcase. (*V*—verb)
    A. revolved
    B. returned CORRECT
    C. recalled
    D. remembered

12. Payment is due in full within 30 days upon ____________________ of this invoice. (*G*—noun)

    A. receipt CORRECT
    B. receive
    C. reception
    D. receiving

13. Doctors have ________________ that stress from work can cause other medical problems. (*G*—verb)

    A. find
    B. finding
    C. found CORRECT
    D. finds

14. The warehouse employees have worked overtime every day ____________________ the last week. (*V*—preposition)

    A. until
    B. along
    C. before
    D. for CORRECT

15. We do not provide third ____________________ with biographical information about our clients. ____________________

    A. parties CORRECT
    B. people
    C. impressions
    D. dealings

16. He ____________________ forgot my name at the company dinner last year. ____________________

    A. complete
    B. completed
    C. completely CORRECT
    D. completeness

17. Attitude is an essential ingredient in finding the ____________________ possible job. ____________________

    A. good
    B. best CORRECT
    C. higher
    D. easier

18. Ms. Napier chose to travel by bus ____________________ of taking a taxi. ____________________

    A. except
    B. but
    C. besides
    D. instead CORRECT

19. Mr. Fisher wants us to exchange ideas ____________________ the proposed reorganization of the Adele Company. (*V*—preposition)

    A. around
    B. between
    C. into
    D. about CORRECT

20. Realco made ____________________ offer for the purchase of the Wincorp property. (*V*—adjective)

    A. a grateful
    B. a generous CORRECT
    C. a wealthy
    D. an attentive

21. The firm was to receive full payment upon ____________________ of the project. (*V*—noun)

    A. completion CORRECT
    B. complexion
    C. complication
    D. commitment

22. After the governor raised taxes, his ____________________ declined rapidly. (*G*—noun)

    A. populated
    B. popular
    C. popularity CORRECT
    D. populate

23. After finishing the week-long seminar, Ms. Beyer packed her suitcase and checked ____________________ of the hotel. (*V*—preposition)

    A. over
    B. out CORRECT
    C. in
    D. for

24. Employee handbooks that are ____________________ written can improve morale and prevent disagreements. (*G*—adverb)

    A. careful
    B. caring
    C. carefulness
    D. carefully CORRECT

25. When the chairman announced ____________________ retirement, the board of trustees launched a nationwide search for a replacement. (*G*—pronoun)

    A. his CORRECT
    B. our
    C. its
    D. him

26. Even a company with an excellent image and ____________________ can fail if it does not meet market standards. (*G*—noun)

    A. reputedly
    B. reputable
    C. repute
    D. reputation CORRECT

27. Mr. and Mrs. Kuo are confident that ____________________ will locate the site themselves. (*G*—pronoun)

    A. them
    B. they CORRECT
    C. themselves
    D. their

28. There are several factors to think about ____________________ deciding which method of distribution to pursue. (*V*—conjunction)

    A. when CORRECT
    B. what
    C. why
    D. where

29. In an exclusive interview, Mr. Stanowitz ____________________ that his company would post a loss this quarter. (*G*—verb)

    A. confided CORRECT
    B. confidence
    C. confide
    D. confidential

30. The requirements for new food service products were ____________________ debated at the franchise meeting. (*V*—adverb)
    A. manually
    B. patently
    C. exhaustively CORRECT
    D. firstly

31. The engineers will all need to stay there ____________________ the Spanning project is finished. (*V*—preposition)
    A. for
    B. about
    C. until CORRECT
    D. toward

32. New approaches to mass communication ____________________ the limits of traditional media channels. (*G*—verb)
    A. transcend CORRECT
    B. transcends
    C. transcending
    D. to transcend

33. Airline reservation ____________________ are being revised to include extensive traveler demographics. ____________________
    A. telephones
    B. employees
    C. counters
    D. systems CORRECT

34. The date for the new product launch has been ____________________ because of problems in production. ____________________
    A. advertised
    B. delayed CORRECT
    C. produced
    D. mobilized

35. He was asked to testify before the committee ____________________ his expertise. ____________________
    A. since
    B. further
    C. inasmuch as
    D. because of CORRECT

36. I know we have ____________________ types of payment plans available for our customers. ____________________
    A. much
    B. many CORRECT
    C. mostly
    D. much more

37. The new shopping center offers free parking and easy access ____________________ the highway. (*V*—preposition)
    A. to CORRECT
    B. with
    C. of
    D. for

38. This brochure provides a brief description of some of the ____________________ features of the insurance policy. (*V*—adjective)
    A. stately
    B. sporadic
    C. slantwise
    D. salient CORRECT

39. It is the ability to perform ____________________ over time that distinguishes great companies. (*G*—adverb)
    A. consistent
    B. consistently CORRECT
    C. consistency
    D. consisting

40. The growth of the waste disposal industry is being driven by demographic ____________________ by economic forces. (*V*—conjunction)

    A. in order to
    B. as well as CORRECT
    C. additionally
    D. furthermore

41. The ideal ____________________ will have a strong sales background and in-country contacts. (*V*—noun)

    A. position
    B. procedure
    C. expectation
    D. candidate CORRECT

42. Our consultants can help you ____________________ employee attitudes and assess training needs. (*V*—verb)

    A. network
    B. request
    C. survey CORRECT
    D. volunteer

43. The reports on construction materials, including ____________________ on cement and ready-mixed concrete, are available in PDF format. (*G*—pronoun)

    A. (A) them
    B. (B) that
    C. (C) those CORRECT
    D. (D) this

44. Sky Travel Air is known for being on time and having few customer ____________________. (*G*—noun)

    A. complaints CORRECT
    B. complain
    C. complaining
    D. complainer

45. Innovative technology ____________________ by General Car Company debuted in new models last year. (*V*—verb)

    A. contained
    B. involved
    C. pioneered CORRECT
    D. performed

46. Good graphic designers can save their clients ____________________ amounts of money on printing and artwork. (*G*—adjective)

    A. signify
    B. significant CORRECT
    C. significance
    D. signification

47. The small film company ____________________ had annual revenues of over four million euros. (*V*—adverb)

    A. previously CORRECT
    B. someday
    C. along
    D. yet

48. Mergers, takeovers, deregulation, and downsizing have created much ______ in the business world. (*G*—noun)

    A. uncertain
    B. uncertainly
    C. uncertainties
    D. uncertainty CORRECT

49. The network will permit communication ____________________ devices such as a desktop computer and a document retrieval system. (*V*—preposition)

    A. around
    B. between CORRECT
    C. over
    D. above

50. All directors ______________________ attend this important board meeting. (*G*—verb)

    A. must CORRECT
    B. ought
    C. have been
    D. should be

51. The presentation focuses on the fund's benefit to shareholders ______________________ than on the company's history.

    ____

    A. rather CORRECT
    B. instead
    C. whereas
    D. although

52. Vendors of security services have reported a sharp increase in demand for video ______________________ equipment.

    ____

    A. negligence
    B. pilot
    C. leakage
    D. surveillance CORRECT

53. Managers need reference materials that are easy for ______________________ to understand. ______________________

    A. them CORRECT
    B. they
    C. themselves
    D. theirs

54. Each month, the meat packing plant rewards one employee for ______________________ the idea that saves the most money.

    ____

    A. receiving
    B. submitting CORRECT
    C. transferring
    D. installing

Answers for the Identify the Question Type Questions

15. We do not provide third ______________________ with biographical information about our clients. (*V—noun*)

    A. parties CORRECT
    B. people
    C. impressions
    D. dealings

16. He ______________________ forgot my name at the company dinner last year. (*G—adverb*)

    A. complete
    B. completed
    C. completely CORRECT
    D. completeness

17. Attitude is an essential ingredient in finding the ______________________ possible job. (*G—adjective*)

    A. good
    B. best CORRECT
    C. profitable
    D. easier

18. Ms. Napier chose to travel by bus ______________________ of taking a taxi. (*V—preposition*)

    A. except
    B. but
    C. besides
    D. instead CORRECT

33. Airline reservation ______________________ are being revised to include extensive traveler demographics. (*V—noun*)

    A. telephones
    B. employees
    C. counters
    D. systems CORRECT

34. The date for the new product launch has been ____________________ because of problems in production. (*V—verb*)

    A. advertised
    B. delayed CORRECT
    C. produced
    D. mobilized

35. He was asked to testify before the committee ____________________ his expertise. (*G—conjunction*)

    A. since
    B. further
    C. inasmuch as
    D. because of CORRECT

36. I know we have ____________________ types of payment plans available for our customers. (*G—adjective*)

    A. much
    B. many CORRECT
    C. mostly
    D. much more

51. The presentation focuses on the fund's benefit to shareholders ____________________ than on the company's history. (*V—conjunction*)

    A. rather CORRECT
    B. instead
    C. whereas
    D. although

52. Vendors of security services have reported a sharp increase in demand for video ____________________ equipment. (*V—noun*)

    A. negligence
    B. pilot
    C. leakage
    D. surveillance CORRECT

53. Managers need reference materials that are easy for ____________________ to understand. (*G—pronoun*)

    A. them CORRECT
    B. they
    C. themselves
    D. theirs

54. Each month, the meat packing plant rewards one employee for ____________________ the idea that saves the most money. (*V—verb*)

    A. receiving
    B. submitting CORRECT
    C. transferring
    D. installing

CHAPTER 8

Exam Part VI—Text Completion

LEARNING OBJECTIVES

In this section, you'll learn to:

- Identify whether the question tests grammar or vocabulary
- Use the Kaplan Strategies to evaluate the answer choices
- Apply the Kaplan Strategies to manage your time effectively

Time Budget for Part VI: Approximately 15 minutes

For this part of the TOEIC exam, you will read four short texts. Each text has four areas which are marked with a numbered line (____________), indicating where a word, phrase or sentence from the text is missing. For each section of missing text, you must choose the correct word phrase or sentence to complete the text from four possible options.

TEST-TAKING STRATEGIES

Strategy 1: Know the Directions

It is important to understand what you are being asked to do and to be sure you know the directions *before* you take the test. The directions will look something like this:

Directions: Read the texts found in the following pages. A word, phrase or sentence is missing in the sentences that follow the texts. Four answer choices are given below each of the sentences. Choose the best answer to complete the sentence. Then mark the letter on your answer sheet.

Here is an example illustrating the format of a typical Part VI passage.

Questions 131–134 refer to the following course description.

Course Description:

Photography 120: Basic Photography for Everyone

Come to class prepared to have fun while learning to use your 35mm SLR film camera.

(We will NOT be ___________ (131.) digital photography in this class. See Course 121: *Basic Digital Imaging for Everyone*, or Course 122: *Turning Your Computer into a Digital Darkroom.*)

The course covers f-stops, shutter speeds, exposure, metering, film types, lenses, filters, flash photography, simple lighting techniques, composition and ways of "seeing," and handheld and tripod shooting techniques.

There will be a different assignment each week. You will shoot both print and slide film, and work in color and black-and-white. You will be encouraged to share your photographs in class to receive feedback from your ___________ (132.).

___________ (133.), you will shoot a minimum of six rolls of film. (The approximate cost for film and processing is $85.)

Bring your 35 mm SLR camera to the first class, as well as your enthusiasm for learning a new skill. No experience necessary!

Required textbook: *Introduction to Photography, 2nd edition* by Don Hasbrook.

(Note: A 35mm camera is the only equipment required for this class. If you do not own a scanner, or have access to one, you may rent one from the school for an additional covering fee. ___________ (134.). Subject to availability.)

131. A. cover
     B. covers
     C. covering
     D. covered

132. A. films
     B. cameras
     C. classmates
     D. photographs

133. A. Your teacher will provide you with
     B. To complete all the assignments
     C. The second level of the course will explain
     D. Most professional photographers

134. A. Talk to your professor about recommended stores
     B. You may be permitted to extend your deadline
     C. Call the main office for details
     D. Look online for a number of providers

Strategy 2: Decide Whether the Sentence Tests *Vocabulary* or *Grammar*

As stated earlier, the main difference between Part V and Part VI of the TOEIC exam is that some of the questions in Part VI need information that is found in other sentences in the passage. This means that, in addition to deciding whether a question tests vocabulary or grammar, you will need to determine *whether the question requires information from other parts of the passage.*

You may be tempted to read each Part VI passage from beginning to end. However, because most of the questions can be answered using only the information in the gapped sentences, you can use your time more effectively by focusing on reading only what you need to read to answer the questions.

You should look at the question sentences first, to determine whether you can answer them without reading the rest of the passage. This will allow you to focus on reading only what you need to read to answer the questions.

Look at the questions in the example passage again.

Question 131

The answer choices are all forms of the word *cover*. This is a grammar question. This question can be answered using only the information in the gapped sentence. None of the surrounding context is required. It is similar to a Part V grammar question.

Question 132

The answer choices are all nouns and are not part of the same word family. They do not share a common root, prefix, or suffix. Each word is different from the others in terms of its form. This is a vocabulary question.

While the answer choices are all words associated with the theme of the passage, this question can be answered using only the information contained in the gapped sentence. It does not require reading any of the surrounding contexts. In this sense, it is really like a Part V vocabulary question.

Question 133

The answer choices are short phrases, and you are given the second part of the sentence. The correct answer will need to make sense when coupled with the sentence ending in the text. This kind of question is unlike the questions found in Part V of the TOEIC. To answer this question correctly, you need to understand the meaning of the sentence as a whole, rather than only identifying the grammar needed, or understanding the vocabulary.

Question 134

The answer choices are complete sentences. You need to understand the topic of the section of the text that is missing the sentence, so that you can find the sentence that matches the topic best. This kind of question is also unlike the questions found in Part V of the test, as you need to understand the gist of the section of the text as a whole.

Once you have determined whether a question tests vocabulary or grammar, you can follow the same steps that you did for Part V:

- **Vocabulary questions**—Look for words and phrases that provide clues to the answer. Often, words or phrases in the sentence will help you eliminate distractors and will point you toward the correct choice. In question 132 from the previous example, the phrase *to receive feedback from* makes choices (A) *films*, (B) *cameras*, and (D) *photographs* less attractive. *Films, cameras,* and *photographs* cannot provide feedback. (C) is the correct answer.
- **Grammar questions**—Focus on the words before and after the blank to determine which part of speech is required. Most often, the words immediately before and after the blank determine which part of speech the correct choice must be. Knowing this helps you to eliminate distractors. In question 131 from the previous example, the words *we will NOT be* immediately before the blank must be followed by a present participle of the verb (with an *ing* ending), *covering*. This eliminates choices (A) *cover,* (B) *covers,* and (D) *covered.* (C) is the correct answer.
- **Questions that require information from other parts of the passage**—First look at the sentences that precede it. The information you need will most often be found near the gap in the text, usually one or two sentences before or after it. If you do not find the information you need there, scan the paragraph of the text as a while, and look at the paragraph in context of the rest of the text. If it appears near the top of a letter or email, it's likely to be a greeting of some kind. If it appears at the bottom of an advertisement, it might direct you to a website, or give you the address of the store that is selling the item. In question 133 from the previous example, we have a sentence that ends *you will shoot a minimum of six rolls of film*, so the first part of the sentence must be related. Only (C) gives an appropriate answer, the students must shoot six rolls of film in order to complete the assignments. In question 134 from the previous example, the missing sentence appears after information about renting a scanner from the school. (C) gives the only appropriate answer—the student can call the main office of the school for more details about renting a scanner. (A) and (D) discuss finding a place to get a scanner from, but the text says that the school can provide them, so they cannot be correct. (B) discusses extending the deadline, but the text talks about getting a scanner, so this cannot be correct either.

Strategy 3: Predict the Answer

Just as you did for Part V, read each question and try to fill the blank with your own word, phrase or sentence *before* reading the answer choices. Because many of the questions do not actually require the surrounding passage text, you will often be able to read the question sentence by itself and correctly predict the word or phrase required to fill the blank. If your predicted answer is among the answer choices, this is likely to be the correct answer.

If the missing text is a longer phrase or sentence, try to predict the type of information that should be there, rather than thinking of your own specific example. Look at the surrounding text, either the remaining part of the sentence for a missing phrase, or the previous and following sentences in a missing sentence. Think about what would be appropriate information to include here, then look at the answer choices and select the sentence or phrase that best matches your ideas.

It is much better to have your own idea about the correct answer *before* looking at the answer choices. If you look at the answer choices first, you might be attracted to an incorrect choice.

Strategy 4: Evaluate the Choices

Find the answer choice that matches the answer you predicted. Before you mark your answer sheet, reread the sentence or section of text to yourself, to make sure the option you are choosing fills the blank the correctly.

If no answer choice matches your expected answer, eliminate as many choices as you can by doing the following:

- For vocabulary questions, read the sentence for context clues that may point to the correct answer or help to eliminate distractors.
- For grammar questions, focus on the words and phrases around the blank to determine the part of speech required and eliminate distractors that do not fit.
- For phrases and sentences, look at the sentences around the gapped sentence to see if there is any additional information you can use.

After eliminating as many distractors as possible, select the best choice from what is left.

If you cannot eliminate any distractors, choose one letter—(A), (B), (C), or (D)—and use this for every wild-guess answer. Using one letter consistently is better than guessing at random.

When you have decided on an answer choice, mark your answer sheet. Be sure to fill in the oval completely, as shown in the test directions.

Strategy 5: Manage Your Time; Answer Every Question

Time management is very important in the Reading Comprehension Section. In the Listening Comprehension Section, the timing is controlled by the audio recording. In the Reading Comprehension Section, you have 75 minutes to complete Parts V, VI, and VII. How quickly you move through each part is up to you. Part VII, the last part of the test, is usually the most difficult and time-consuming, so you will want to leave enough time to finish it.

If you use apply Strategy 2 and determine whether you can answer a question using only the information in the sentence, you should be able to avoid reading too much. This will save you time.

Do not spend too much time working on any individual question. Each question is worth the same amount, so you should treat them all equally. You must not allow yourself to fall behind by laboring too long with any one question. Select your answer choice and mark it on your answer sheet as quickly as you can so that you can keep up with the timing on the TOEIC exam.

If you find yourself running out of time, mark your answer sheet with your chosen guess letter. Do not leave any questions unanswered.

Strategy Summary

1. Know the directions.
2. Look at the sentences for the individual questions first: Decide whether they test *vocabulary* or *grammar* and whether they require information found in other parts of the passage.
   - **Vocabulary questions**—Look for words and phrases that provide clues to the answer.
   - **Grammar questions**—Focus on the words before and after the blank to determine which part of speech is required.
   - **Questions that require information from other parts of the passage**—Look for the information in the sentences that comes immediately *before* or *after* the missing information first.
3. Predict the answer for each question in your own words *before* looking at the choices.
4. Evaluate the answer choices and mark the answer.
5. Manage your time and be sure to answer every question.

TEXT COMPLETION PRACTICE SET

Time Budget: 16 minutes for 21 questions

Practice 1

Questions 1–4 refer to the following email message.

To: Mike Jasper ‹m_jasper@reprographica.com›

From: Jane Willis ‹j_willis@perfectcolor.com›

Date: January 10, 2016 09:28:17 A.M.

Subject: Our meeting

Attachments: meeting summary.doc

Dear Mike,

It was so nice to be able to meet you last week. It's been almost a year now that we have __________ (1.) by email, but meeting face to face always makes a difference. I hope that you found last Friday's meeting as useful as we did. I think it was good for you to be able to see our production processes firsthand. If you need any further __________ (2.) regarding our color calibration system, or any other aspect of the process, please don't hesitate to drop me a line. The __________ (3.) I've included with this message summarizes the key points we agreed on during Friday's discussion. Please take a look and see if you think there need to be any additions or amendments.

__________ (4.).

Kind regards,

Jane

1. A. writing
   B. mailed
   C. messaged
   D. corresponded

2. A. processes
   B. documentation
   C. aspects
   D. indication

3. A. attachment
   B. enclosure
   C. meeting
   D. amendment

4. A. I look forward to hearing from you soon with the details of your proposal.
   B. I'm writing this email to check in about what we discussed in our last meeting.
   C. It will be nice to finally meet you.
   D. You should have had time to look through the documents by now.

Practice 2

Questions 5–8 refer to the following form.

HOW TO COMPLETE YOUR FORMS

All passengers are required to complete the customs declaration form before entering the United States. You should find a copy of this form inside the seat pocket in front of you; ___________ (5.), if there is no form, please ask a member of the cabin crew for one before arrival at your final destination. Passengers who are not U.S. citizens or who are not permanent residents of the United States are required to fill out either a white I-94 form ___________ (6.) a green I-94W form. ___________ (7.).

If you do not require a visa, you must still have a valid machine-readable passport and complete the green I-94 form. All forms must be ___________ (8.) in block capitals using a black or blue pen.

5. A. despite the fact
   B. additionally
   C. however
   D. even though

6. A. either
   B. and
   C. or
   D. also

7. A. Please contact the HR team on the third floor if you require assistance.
   B. Passengers traveling on a visa must complete the white form.
   C. You can book tickets online using your access code
   D. If you are not a US citizen, you do not need to complete these forms.

8. A. completed
   B. completing
   C. complete
   D. being completed

Practice 3

Questions 9–12 refer to the following passage.

MADRID—THE PLACE TO BE

__________ (9.). Many of the continent's most innovative companies and dynamic businesses are already located in this city. __________ (10.), from cutting-edge IT start-ups to well-established corporate finance institutions. In its new role as innovation hub of Europe, Madrid today boasts several world-class conference __________ (11.). Add to this excellent infrastructure and first-class hospitality, and it's easy to see why the city is now host to some of the world's most important trade fairs. In addition to all of this, __________ (12.), Madrid remains one of the world's great cultural cities, offering any and every form of culture and entertainment imaginable. Just one more reason to reconsider Madrid.

9. A. For some years, the number of qualified engineers has been much lower than the global need.
   B. Unfortunately, scientists remain uncertain about the side-effects associated with long term use.
   C. Madrid is fast becoming one of Europe's most important business centers.
   D. A large number of people have expressed interest in making the change, studies have shown.

10. A. Many commuters speak at least one foreign language
    B. Many more are joining them
    C. There are also a large number of jobs
    D. In one recent review

11. A. calls
    B. tools
    C. facilities
    D. localities

12. A. simply
    B. needless
    C. of course
    D. in spite of

Practice 4

Questions 13–16 refer to the following brochure.

BUSINESS OPPORTUNITIES WORLDWIDE

LightWorld was established in the U.K. in 1997 and has ______ (13.) grown into an international franchising network of over 50 stores in eight countries. LightWorld is a market leader in providing lighting solutions for the home and office ______ (14.) are practical, stylishly designed, and economical. We are currently inviting expressions of interest from potential franchisees. LightWorld is interested to hear from you if you would like to open your own ______ (15.) or if you would like to run a LightWorld network within your own country or territory. ______ (16.).

13. A. while
    B. for
    C. then
    D. since

14. A. that
    B. who
    C. these
    D. whose

15. A. opening
    B. light
    C. outlet
    D. setting

16. A. We would like to take this opportunity to thank you for your custom.
    B. To purchase one of our light fittings, visit our store at 1123–1140 Main Road, Omaha.
    C. Thank you for expressing interest in this opportunity.
    D. For more details about this offer or more information about our company, please email info@lightworld.com.eu

Practice 5

Questions 17–20 refer to the following brochure.

MORE AMERICAN HOUSEHOLDS BANKING ONLINE

The number of American households doing their banking online grew by 39.2 percent last year. Experts predict that number to increase by a ________ (17.) 22.5 percent this year, and another 17.6 percent the year after. ________ (18.). Young adults ages 24 to 35 with household incomes of $75,000 or higher are most likely to do their banking online. Today, nearly ________ (19.) that group (48 percent) views bills online, and 46 percent pays bills online. Older adults, those over 65, at all income levels, are the least likely to bank online. A representative for the American Association of Online Bankers says banks ________ (20.) their customers to bank online, "because online banking is much cheaper for banks to provide than traditional in-person teller services."

17. A. more
    B. larger
    C. further
    D. superior

18. A. Older adults are most likely to use banking systems online.
    B. A total of 47.1 million American households are currently banking online.
    C. Please read through these documents carefully before responding.
    D. Our online services are tailored to your needs and easy to use.

19. A. half
    B. twice
    C. double
    D. two times

20. A. to encourage
    B. encouragement
    C. are encouraging
    D. have been encouraged

Practice 6

Questions 21–24 refer to the following memo.

MEMORANDUM

To: All TigerNet employees

From: John Sullivan, CEO

Date: April 4, 2016

Subject: Our Future

The recent collapse of our biggest competitor has many of you wondering whether the same thing could happen here. I would like to set the record straight.

Today, TigerNet is positioned for ______ (21.). We are the market leader with the highest quality, most functionally complete products and proven technology, the strongest balance sheet and financial viability, the most experienced and dedicated workforce, and the most tried, tested, and proven management team in the industry.

While the severe current conditions have weakened many of our competitors—dozens of Internet service providers both small and large have ______ (22.) from the marketplace—we are increasing our market share. As the market continues to consolidate, TigerNet will actually grow. We see enormous business opportunities ahead, and expect ______ (23.) to thrive for at least the next several years.

______ (24.).

-JS-

21. A. success
    B. pleasure
    C. collapse
    D. disappointment

22. A. isolated
    B. decreased
    C. withdrawn
    D. consolidated

23. A. the company
    B. a balance sheet
    C. our competitors
    D. their market share

24. A. Our future is bright.
    B. Please accept my sincere apologies.
    C. Wishing you luck in your future endeavors.
    D. We think you will make a wonderful addition to the team.

Practice 7

Questions 25–28 refer to the following brochure.

TROUBLESHOOTING YOUR DSL MODEM

Most connection problems _____________ by trying one of the following.
25.

Power cycle: Shut off both the modem and the computer and wait for 30 seconds. Turn the modem back on first and then turn on the computer. After the PPPoE light stops blinking and stays on, you can reconnect to the Internet. NOTE: If your modem does not have an on/off switch, _____________ the modem from the electrical wall outlet to turn it off.
26.

Check for line interference: Make sure your modem is not on or _____________ other
27.
electrical devices that may interfere with the signal. This includes your computer monitor, stereo speakers, cordless phone (or its base), or a halogen light.

Call the Peacelink Telephone Support Center _____________. Hours of operation are Monday
28.
through Friday, 7:00 A.M. to midnight, Eastern time, and Saturday and Sunday 9:00 A.M. to 10:00 P.M. Eastern. 800-555-HELP.

25. A. does solve
B. are solving
C. could solve
D. can be solved

26. A. insert
B. depart
C. unplug
D. enclose

27. A. in
B. off
C. near
D. throughout

28. A. and review our current stock of items.
B. before you begin to fill in this form.
C. when your modem stops working.
D. to talk to a technical support representative.

ANSWER KEY

Practice 1

1. D
2. B
3. A
4. A

Practice 2

5. C
6. C
7. B
8. A

Practice 3

9. C
10. B
11. C
12. C

Practice 4

13. D
14. A
15. C
16. D

Practice 5

17. C
18. B
19. A
20. C

Practice 6

21. A
22. C
23. A
24. A

Practice 7

25. D
26. C
27. C
28. D

ANSWERS AND EXPLANATIONS

In the parentheses next to each answer, we have identified them as being focused either on vocabulary (*V*), grammar (G), or a sentence or phrase (S). For some answers, we have left this blank, so that you can fill it in. The more you know about what is going on in the answer choices, the more skillful and efficient you will become at eliminating incorrect choices and selecting the correct ones.

Sample responses for these Identify the Question Type answer explanations are included in the Answers and Explanations section.

Practice 1

1. D ______________________________
2. B ______________________________
3. A ______________________________
4. A ______________________________

Practice 2

5. C (*G*)
6. C (*G*)
7. B (*S*)
8. A (*G*)

Practice 3

9. C (*S*)
10. B (*G*)
11. C (*V*)
12. C (*V*)

Practice 4

13. D (*G*)
14. A (*G*)
15. C (*V*)
16. D (*S*)

Practice 5

17. C (*V*)
18. B (*S*)
19. A (*V*)
20. C (*G*)

Practice 6

21. A (*V*)
22. C (*V*)
23. A (*V*)
24. A (*S*)

Practice 7

25. D (*G*)
26. C (*V*)
27. C (*V*)
28. D (*S*)

Answers for the Identify the Question Type Questions

1. D (*V*)
2. B (*V*)
3. A (*V*)
4. A (*S*)

CHAPTER 9

Exam Part VII—Reading Comprehension

LEARNING OBJECTIVES

In this section, you'll learn to:

- Identify the different types of Reading Passages
- Identify the 6 basic question types in Part VII

Time Budget for Part VII: Approximately 50 minutes

In Part VII of the TOEIC exam, you will read a series of short passages in your test book. Each passage is followed by two to five questions. Each question has four answer choices. You must select the answer choice that best answers the question and mark it on your answer sheet.

Part VII begins with question 147 and ends with question 200. There are a total of 54 questions in Part VII. There are two kinds of reading passages in Part VII:

1. **Single Passage**—In this type of question set, there is one reading passage, followed by two to five questions. There are usually around ten single-question passages. These are questions 147–175. Single passages make up more than half of Part VII (29 of 54 questions).
2. **Multiple Passages**—This type of question set has two or three related reading passages that are always followed by five questions. There are five sets of multiple passages: two sets with two passages each and three sets with three passages each. These are the last passages in Part VII (questions 176–200).

The passages are typically short news articles, advertisements, public notices, memos, email messages, text conversations, letters, faxes and other business correspondence, instructions, and other kinds of everyday texts. They also include graphs, charts, tables, schedules, and other information of this kind.

The questions usually ask about details provided in the passage, inferences that can be made based on the information presented, and about the meaning of words as they are used in the passage. The questions generally ask about information in the order that it is presented in the passage. For the multiple set passages, there is usually at least one question requiring you to use information found in more than one of the passages.

TEST-TAKING STRATEGIES

Strategy 1: Know the Directions

It is important to understand what you are being asked to do and to be sure that you know the directions before taking the test. The directions will look something like this:

> **Directions**: In this part, you will read a selection of text, such as magazine or newspaper articles, letters, or advertisements. Each text is followed by several questions. Select the best answer for each question and mark the letter on your answer sheet.

Here is an example of a Part VII single passage set:

Questions 153–155 refer to the following article.

LOW CROP PRICES HURT FARMERS

Unusually low prices for crops are causing hardships for farmers in Canada. — [1] — Together with a strong Canadian dollar and rising costs, this has led to large-scale losses on many Canadian farms. The Canadian government forecasts net farm income (NFI) this year at $870 million, a significant decline from last year's $1.8 billion NFI.

NFI for the province of Saskatchewan is again likely to be negative this year at an estimated minus $207 million, compared with minus $77 million last year.

— [2] — Manitoba, which is still recovering from floods earlier in the year, is also expected to fall behind expenses and is forecast to have an NFI deficit of $195 million.

Alberta, with its large-scale cattle industry, is generating more income than provinces where farming is based on grains. This year's NFI is forecast at $258 million.

— [3] — Even at the current low prices, farmers in Saskatchewan and Manitoba are having a hard time selling their grains, due to this year's below-average-quality harvest.

— [4] —

153. What is expected for net farm income in Canada?

    A. It will be much lower than the year before.
    B. It will be about the same as the year before.
    C. It will be higher than the original government forecasts.
    D. It will be significantly lower than the original government forecasts.

154. In which of the positions marked [1], [2], [3], and [4] does the following sentence best belong? "Elsewhere, good returns on dairy, eggs, fruit, and poultry have boosted farm income."

   A. [1]
   B. [2]
   C. [3]
   D. [4]

155. Which of the following is *NOT* mentioned as a problem that Canadian farmers are facing?

   A. floods
   B. rising costs
   C. low cattle prices
   D. poor-quality crops

Here is an example of a Part VII multiple passage set:

Questions 181–185 refer to the following advertisement and registration form.

Revolutionize your investment strategies in as little as one hour!

Thursday, February 12 at 7:00 P.M.
Carlton Hotel, St. Morton, LA

We would like to invite you to join renowned investment expert Sandra Gellert for an exclusive free investment seminar.

Sandra Gellert is chief investment officer and portfolio manager of ALC Investments. She recognizes the strong economic environment in Louisiana right now and would like to help YOU with your investment strategy.

Three-time recipient of the coveted national Fund Manager of the Year award, Sandra brings vision as well as everyday good sense to strategic financial planning. She holds a bachelor of commerce degree, a master of business administration degree, and a doctorate in finance and is a chartered financial analyst. This education, combined with a wealth of successful experience in managing financial portfolios, means this seminar is an exciting opportunity for disciplined investment planning.

Topics to be covered:

- Wealth Creation
- Global Investment
- Financial Services
- Oil and Gas
- Pensions and Retirement Funds
- Foreign Exchange Markets
- Specific Company Suggestions

Seating at this event is limited. Please register for this exclusive free session online or fill out the registration form on the back of this flyer and fax it to the number given below.

Register Online: *www.alcinvestments.com/seminar/registration.html*

Register by Fax: (456) 223-1232

This seminar with Sandra Gellert, one of the nation's most sought-after speakers on investments, is sponsored by Synergy Financial, St. Morton City Bank, and Integrated Wealth Services Inc.

(Registration form on back)

REGISTRATION FORM

An Evening with Sandra Gellert

Thursday, February 12 at 7:00 P.M.

Carlton Hotel in St. Morton, LA

Limited Spaces—Register Now!

Name: Paolo Grazzi

Company: Consolidated Investments

Position in Organization: Senior Financial Advisor

Address: 125 67th Street, St. Morton, LA

Tel (work): 456-852-1386 Tel (evening): 456-852-7221

Email: paolog@consolidatedinvestments.com

No. of participants (max 3 per registration): 2

Name of additional participant: Michelle Dubois

Name of additional participant: N/A

Special interests: International investments, oil and gas, retirement funds

181. What is learned about Sandra Gellert?
    - A. She has taught at several universities.
    - B. She has won an award for her latest book.
    - C. She has several business-related degrees.
    - D. She has over 20 years' experience in the financial field.

182. Which of the following will *NOT* be discussed by Sandra Gellert?
    - A. real estate
    - B. currency trading
    - C. retirement planning
    - D. investing internationally

183. Who is said to be one of the seminar's sponsors?
    - A. Michelle Dubois
    - B. Consolidated Investments
    - C. The Morton Chamber of Commerce
    - D. Integrated Wealth Services Inc.

184. What is learned about Paolo Grazzi?

   A. He has charged the registration to a credit card.
   B. He is especially interested in technology stocks.
   C. He will attend the presentation with one other person.
   D. He is the chief investment officer for Consolidated Investments.

185. What will Paolo Grazzi probably do?

   A. fax his registration card.
   B. meet Sandra Gellert for lunch.
   C. go directly to the Carlton Hotel from the airport.
   D. discuss his investment strategy with Michelle Dubois.

Strategy 2: Know the Question Types

The questions usually ask for information in the order that it is presented in the passage.
For example, for a three-question passage, the first question will usually ask about information found near the beginning, the second question will ask about something found in the middle, and the third question will ask about something mentioned near the end.

There are four basic categories of questions for Part VII:

1. **Gist**—Gist questions will ask what the main topic is, why the passage has been written, or what the passage's purpose is. Gist questions ask about the overall situation, rather than about specific details.

   There is usually one Gist question per passage. Following are examples of Gist questions:

   - *What is the article mainly about?*
   - *Why has the bank written this letter?*
   - *What is the main purpose of this email?*
   - *What is learned about the company?*

2. **Detail**—Detail questions ask about information mentioned in the passage. They can ask about general information or very specific details. Examples of what Detail questions might ask about include what products or services a company provides; how much a product or service costs; when or where an action or event will take place; what role, function, or responsibility people will have; how a problem or situation is being handled; and the order or manner in which things are to be done.

   Examples of Detail questions include:

   - *What service does Miller Consulting provide?*
   - *How much are the XJ100s?*
   - *Where will the meeting be held?*
   - *When is the report due?*
   - *What will Rob Dollison be responsible for doing?*
   - *How should the filter be cared for?*

Some Detail questions are asked using *NOT*. For example:

- *What is NOT a service provided by Miller Consulting?*
- *What is NOT included on the meeting agenda?*
- *Which of the following is NOT on sale?*
- *Why will the goods NOT be shipped that day?*

For these questions, you must read the choices carefully. For the first example (*What is NOT a service provided by Miller Consulting?*), three of the four options will be services that *are* provided. You need to pick the one that is *NOT* provided. Be careful!

Detail questions are the most common Part VII questions. There is often more than one per passage.

3. **Implication/Inference questions**—Implication/Inference questions ask about things that are not stated directly in the passage. They often require you to make connections between information that has been presented in different parts of the passage. They may ask about expectations, possibilities, or probable future actions; they can refer to people's emotions or feelings.

   The following are examples of Implication/Inference questions:

   - *Why were analysts surprised by the earnings announcement?*
   - *What does Mr. Davis imply about the price of his products?*
   - *Why does Mrs. Lopez mention April tenth in her email?*
   - *What can be inferred about Tezla Corp.'s annual budget?*

   There is usually one Implication/Inference question per passage.

   At times, Implication/Inference questions and Gist questions may seem to be similar. For example, a Gist question that asks about the purpose of an email message might require drawing an inference; the message might provide enough information to make the purpose obvious, but that information might not be stated directly in the email.

   Although some Gist questions require you to understand an implication or make an inference, their focus is on the larger picture or the overall situation. Implication/Inference questions tend to deal with implied details about the situation or context itself.

4. **Vocabulary**—Vocabulary questions ask you to identify the meaning of a word as it is used in the passage. They will refer to a specific line in a paragraph and will always have the same format. For example:

The word *coveted* in paragraph 2, line 4, is closest in meaning to

A. devoted.

B. desirable.

C. fashionable.

D. advantageous.

Vocabulary questions are not very common. There are usually no more than three on the entire test. They are usually found in the four-question and five-question passages and are usually the last questions in the set.

5. **Sentence Location**—Sentence Location questions give you a sentence that is not currently in the text, and mark the text with 4 possible locations for the sentence to appear. These questions will appear in this format:

In which of the positions marked [1], [2], [3], and [4] does the following sentence best belong?

"If you require special assistance, please notify reception during check in"

A. [1]
B. [2]
C. [3]
D. [4]

To answer Sentence Location questions, first read the sentence to understand the information it contains and think about where you might typically find such a sentence in a text. In the example above, you might expect to find this information in a paragraph about arriving at a hotel. After understanding the sentence, scan the text and look at the four places highlighted. Scan the text around these areas to check whether they contain similar information. If they do not, move onto the next section until you find the appropriate section.

6. **Implied Meaning**—Implied Meaning questions ask you to choose the answer that best describes why something has been written in a text. These questions will appear in this format:

What does Mark mean when he writes "I'm not sure"?

A. He does not know where to find it.
B. He thinks it might not be helpful.
C. He wants to know what to do.
D. He does not understand what he is being asked.

To answer Implied Meaning questions, you need to look at the text where the phrase is located and read the section of text to understand why the phrase has been written. All of the answer choices will most likely give possible definitions for the phrase, so you need to look at the phrase in the context of the rest of the text to understand the meaning.

Strategy 3: Know the Distractors

All Part VII distractors must answer the question plausibly, that is, they must be possible answers to the question. When you read a Part VII question and the answer choices by themselves—without referring to the reading passage—each choice will answer the question in a logical and realistic way, and no choice can be eliminated using logic or common sense. Each answer choice will be a plausible answer to the question. There are no "impossible" answer choices.

Note that none of the Part VII questions is linked in any way—that is, the information contained in a set of question and answer choices will not help you to answer any other questions. Here is an example:

What is enclosed with the letter?

A. a coupon
B. a payment
C. an invoice
D. a brochure

Without reading the passage, none of the answer choices can be eliminated. Each option is a plausible answer to the question. There are no "impossible" answer choices.

The following are the basic types of distractors for Part VII questions:

1. **Not mentioned**—This type of distractor refers to things or ideas commonly associated with the passage content but that are not actually mentioned in the passage. The distractor answers the question plausibly, but it does not relate to the actual passage content.
2. **Repeated words**—This type of distractor uses a key word or phrase from the passage, but it is not true. The distractor answers the question plausibly but is incorrect.
3. **Incorrect paraphrase/misstatement**—This type of distractor uses specific language, facts, or ideas that are mentioned or implied in the passage, but it rephrases, paraphrases, and twists them so that they are not true. The distractor often contradicts or misstates the facts. Sometimes important information is omitted or new information is added. Most of the content of the distractor comes directly from the passage. The distractor answers the question plausibly, but it is incorrect.

   Incorrect choices for Vocabulary questions can all be considered "incorrect paraphrase/ misstatement" distractors because they incorrectly paraphrase the vocabulary word being tested.
4. **Hybrid**—This is not actually a basic distractor type; it is a combination of two or more of the three basic types previously outlined.

A set of answer choices may use more than one type of distractor at a time. Each distractor type is discussed separately here.

Look at the Part VII single passage example again.

Questions 153–155 refer to the following article.

LOW CROP PRICES HURT FARMERS

Unusually low prices for crops are causing hardships for farmers in Canada. — [1] — Together with a strong Canadian dollar and rising costs, this has led to large-scale losses on many Canadian farms. The Canadian government forecasts net farm income (NFI) this year at $870 million, a significant decline from last year's $1.8 billion NFI.

NFI for the province of Saskatchewan is again likely to be negative this year at an estimated minus $207 million, compared with minus $77 million last year. — [2] — Manitoba, which is still recovering from floods earlier in the year, is also expected to fall behind expenses and is forecast to have an NFI deficit of $195 million.

Alberta, with its large-scale cattle industry, is generating more income than provinces where farming is based on grains. This year's NFI is forecast at $258 million.

— [3] — Even at the current low prices, farmers in Saskatchewan and Manitoba are having a hard time selling their grains, due to this year's below-average-quality harvest.

— [4] —

153. What is expected for net farm income in Canada?

A. It will be much lower than the year before.
B. It will be about the same as the year before.
C. It will be higher than the original government forecasts.
D. It will be significantly lower than the original government forecasts.

This is a Detail question. The correct answer is choice (A). Choice (B) misstates the information presented in the first paragraph. This is an example of an incorrect paraphrase/misstatement distractor. Choice (C) contradicts the information in the first paragraph. This is an example of an incorrect paraphrase/misstatement distractor. Choice (D) repeats the words *significantly* and *government forecasts* from the first paragraph, but it twists the facts. It also refers to an "original" forecast that was not mentioned. This is an example of a hybrid distractor.

154. In which of the positions marked [1], [2], [3], and [4] does the following sentence best belong?

"Elsewhere, good returns on dairy, eggs, fruit, and poultry have boosted farm income."

A. [1]
B. [2]
C. [3]
D. [4]

This is a Sentence Location question. The correct answer is choice (D). Choice (A) cannot be correct as the sentences before and after discuss Canada, but the new sentences introduces the topic of 'elsewhere'. (B) must be incorrect, as the sentence discusses that other areas are experiencing good returns, but the following sentence discusses another area that is not experiencing good returns. (C) is incorrect as the following sentence continues to discuss areas that are not doing well. This sentence can only appear at the end of the passage.

155. Which of the following is *NOT* mentioned as a problem Canadian farmers are facing?

    A. floods
    B. rising costs
    C. low cattle prices
    D. poor-quality crops

This is a detail question using the NOT format. The correct answer is choice (C). Choices (A), (B), and (D) are all mentioned as being problems for Canadian farmers. Notice that for each of the questions, all the distractors are plausible answers and that none of the questions or answer choices are of any help in answering other questions.

Strategy 4: Know How to Read Passages

Because you have a limited amount of time to read the passages and answer the questions, you must be an efficient reader. Reading every word of every passage is not reading efficiently. Efficient reading requires *skimming* and *scanning*, described here.

Skim the Passage

Skimming a passage means reading it quickly to understand the main points. When you skim a passage, you are interested in identifying the main idea or main topic. Your goal is to answer the question "What is this passage mainly about?"

For the previous example passage, the answer to the question "What is the passage mainly about?" would be something like this: income from farming in Canada.

For the double passage example previously given, the answer to the question would be something like this: an upcoming investment seminar and the details of someone's registration for the seminar.

To skim a passage, begin at the top of the passage and read only the first few words of each sentence. This should be enough to give you a sense of what the passage is about. Look for and make note of words or phrases that are repeated throughout the passage—these are probably important.

You do not need to read every word of the passage to find the main idea. You are not interested in details—yet. Try underlining or highlighting key points in the text while skimming through the passage. This can help you to predict answers to the questions before looking at the answer choices, making it easier to eliminate the distractors.

Read the Questions

The passages contain more information than you need to answer the questions; there are things mentioned in the passage that are not tested. Your goal is *not* to read the entire passage. Your goal is only to answer the questions. The most efficient way to do this is to know what it is you are looking for *before* you read the passage in depth.

Read the questions—but not the answer choices—so that you know what information you will need to find when you read the passage.

Answer Each Question

Read each question and predict the answer in your own words *before* reading the answer choices. If you understand the passage, you should be able to answer the questions in your own words. For each question, your predicted answer—or one very closely matching your predicted answer—should be among the answer choices.

Remember, there are no trick questions on the TOEIC exam. All the information needed to answer the questions is presented in the passage.

If you read the answer choices first—without answering the question in your own words—you are allowing the TOEIC exam writers to put ideas into your head. You will be tempted to make the answer one of the distractors. It is much better to have your own idea about the correct answer first, *before* looking at the answer choices.

Scan the Passage

Once you know what information you need to find, you should scan the passage to find it. *Scanning* is the process of looking for the key words and phrases you need to answer the questions. Because you have read the questions and know what information to look for, you do not need to read every word in the passage. You only need to find the key words from the questions.

To scan a passage, start at the top and let your eyes go back and forth across the page; look for key words and phrases as you make your way to the bottom of the passage. You are looking only for the answers to the questions.

Strategy 5: Evaluate the Answer Choices; Mark the Answer

After you have scanned the passage to find the information you need, you will need to evaluate the answer choices. Find the answer choice that is the closest match to the answer you have been expecting and mark your answer sheet.

Strategy 6: Eliminate Answer Choices

If none of the choices match your expected answer very well, you must eliminate as many choices as you can. Remember, because one question and answer choice set will not help you answer another, do not look at answer choices from one question for clues to answer another question.

If you must guess, eliminate any choices that do not use words and phrases from the passage—the not mentioned distracter type. The not mentioned distractors are often the easiest to eliminate.

If only one of the answer choices use words and phrases that you recognize from the passage, this is likely to be the correct one.

Strategy 7: Tackle Shorter Passages and Vocabulary Questions First

This strategy is not for everyone. If you are the kind of person who is nervous about "breaking the rules," go ahead and answer the questions in the order in which they occur in your test book. There are some risks in tackling the shorter passages first. These will be explained later in this section.

In the Listening Comprehension Section, the order of the questions is controlled by the audio. In the Reading Comprehension Section, you are free to answer the questions in any order you choose.

There is no rule that says you have to go through the passages in the order in which they are printed in your test book. Test writers would prefer that you answer the questions in the order they appear, but this does not mean you cannot answer them in another order.

The reading passages have between two and five questions each. Generally, passages with fewer questions are shorter and easier than passages with more questions. Therefore, you might consider tackling the short passages first. The basic idea is to answer all the two-question passages first, then the three-question passages, then the four-question passages, and so on.

The advantage to this approach is that you will probably answer more questions in a shorter amount of time, and more questions answered means a potentially higher score. If you answer the questions in the order they are presented, you may be slowed down by harder questions and run out of time, leaving easier questions you might have been able to answer unanswered. If you answer all the easy questions first, you are that much closer to being finished, and you can use your remaining time to work on the more difficult passages.

Some of the reading passages will have a question that asks about how a particular word is used in the passage. These are generally easy questions, and you should try to answer them first. If you are running out of time, look for these questions, scan the passage to find the word, and try to answer the question. Often, if you know the word being tested, you can eliminate one or two answer choices without even reading the passage.

The major disadvantage of answering the questions out of order is that you risk making careless mistakes on your answer sheet—marking the wrong oval or even missing an entire passage. If you make such a mistake, you could wind up with a lower score. If you decide to answer the questions out of order, make absolutely sure you are marking your answer sheet correctly. Double-check to be sure you have not accidentally filled in the wrong oval on your answer sheet. When the end of the test is near, check your answer sheet again to make sure you have not skipped any questions. If you are careful not to make mistakes, this strategy can be very effective.

Strategy 8: Manage Your Time

Everyone makes mistakes, especially when under pressure. If you finish the TOEIC exam before time is called, you should check your answer sheet to make sure you have not missed any questions or marked your answer sheet incorrectly in any way. Check your work for Parts V and VI as well. If you find yourself running out of time, mark your answer sheet with your wild-guess letter. Do not leave any questions unanswered.

Strategy Summary

1. Know the directions.
2. Understand the question types and how the questions are ordered.
3. Understand the basic types of distractors.
4. Know how to read passages.
5. Evaluate the answer choices and mark the answer if you know it.
6. Eliminate answer choices that are wrong and select the best match from what is left.
7. Consider tackling the shorter passages and vocabulary questions first.
8. Manage your time and be sure to answer every question.

READING COMPREHENSION PRACTICE SET

Time budget: 20 minutes for 32 questions

Questions 1–2 refer to the following weather forecast.

This Week's Weather Forecast

The weather forecast for Asia and Australia predicts warm temperatures for the next few days in Beijing; thundershowers on Wednesday could lead to cooler weather Thursday.

Episodes of rain in Shanghai this week, some possibly heavy.

Typically warm and muggy this week in Hong Kong and Singapore.

Windy and cool with showers in Melbourne Wednesday and Thursday, while Brisbane has sunshine every day this week.

1. What is expected for Beijing on Wednesday?
   A. rain
   B. wind
   C. unusual warmth
   D. clear skies

2. What does "Typically warm and muggy" in the forecast mean?
   A. The weather will be mostly hot and damp.
   B. Theft is common in the area.
   C. It will be dry for most of the week.
   D. People should stay inside and keep warm.

Questions 3–4 refer to the following email message.

From: Carlota Fernandez ‹c_fernandez@lgsystems.com›
To: Staff Mailing List ‹staff@lgsystems.com›
Date: May 15th 2016 10:38:42 A.M.
Subject: Visit by Proplan, Inc.

Dear All,

This is to remind you that two representatives from Proplan, Inc. will be here on Friday, May 20, from 9 A.M. to 5 P.M. in the employee lounge. The Proplan representatives will be available to answer all questions regarding your health insurance policy and to discuss how changes may affect you and your families. Please sign up for the 15-minute time slots. The sign-up sheet is in the lounge. I hope this is beneficial to you all.

Regards,
Carlota

3. Why will the Proplan representatives visit?
   A. to discuss health insurance
   B. to provide medical examinations
   C. to distribute health care policies
   D. to sign up participants

4. What should interested employees do?
   A. talk to the benefits department.
   B. read the attached information.
   C. write down questions.
   D. sign up for appointments.

Questions 5–7 refer to the following letter.

Melissa Ketchem
1410 South Walnut Street
Bloomington, IN 47404

28 June 2016

Mr. Donald Baker
Personnel Director
The Asian Plaza Hotel
Tokyo, Japan

Dear Mr. Baker,

I am responding to your recent advertisement for a manager of programs and conventions on the hoteljobs.com website. Enclosed is my résumé, which outlines the considerable experience I have in the hotel management field. — [1] —

My current position as assistant manager at the International Castle Hotel deals almost exclusively with booking and coordinating conventions. — [2] — This, combined with a certificate from the Hotel School in Lausanne, Switzerland, makes me confident that I would be an asset to your staff.

— [3] — I very much appreciate being considered for this position, and I would welcome the opportunity to meet with you at your earliest convenience.

Sincerely yours,
Melissa Ketchem
— [4] —

5. What is Ms. Ketchem sending with this letter?
   - A. a résumé
   - B. a writing sample
   - C. a job description
   - D. a reference letter

6. In which of the positions marked [1], [2], [3], or [4] does the following sentence best belong?
   "P.S. Please feel free to contact my current supervisor for a reference."
   - A. [1]
   - B. [2]
   - C. [3]
   - D. [4]

7. Which task is part of Ms. Ketchem's current job?
   - A. handling conventions
   - B. supervising staff
   - C. coordinating food service
   - D. registering guests

Questions 8–10 refer to the following letter.

Saysee Insurance Company

200 Wilshire Road

London, SW1

May 10, 2016

Mr. Franz Thurman

Polderstraaat 175

Brussels 1050, Belgium

Dear Mr. Thurman,

— [1] — With this letter, we acknowledge receipt of your application materials for the position of claims manager at Saysee Insurance Company. Thank you for your interest. — [2] — Due to the overwhelming response to our advertisement, we will conduct initial interviews over the telephone. Should a follow-up interview then be appropriate, we will ask that you come in to meet with us in person.

To better schedule the initial interview at a mutually convenient time, we are enclosing an Interview Schedule Card. Please complete this card and return it to us as soon as possible. Our schedule permits us to interview only those whose cards we receive prior to June 3rd.

— [3] — You appear to be a strong candidate, and we look forward to hearing from you soon.

Sincerely, — [4] —

Marie Reilly

Personnel Manager

8. Who is Franz Thurman?
   - A. an employee
   - B. an interviewer
   - C. an applicant
   - D. a customer

9. What is the purpose of this letter?
   - A. to schedule an appointment
   - B. to make a job offer
   - C. to reject a candidate
   - D. to request information

10. In which of the positions marked [1], [2], [3], or [4] does the following sentence best belong?
    "Thank you once again for your interest"
    - A. [1]
    - B. [2]
    - C. [3]
    - D. [4]

Questions 11–15 refer to the following article.

HONG KONG—Four of the world's largest container shipping lines announced plans yesterday to form an alliance on routes linking Asia with Europe and North America. Negotiations between the companies are set to begin next month and, if successful, will gradually create an alliance over the next two years.

The four shipping lines, all among the top ten in the world, would share space on each other's vessels, so that maximum use can be made of new, faster ships now being built. This involves customers of one line having their containers put on a ship operated by another line in the alliance. The lines will not take equity stakes in each other.

A spokesperson for one of the companies said the four hoped to agree on the specifics of the plan within the next six to eight months.

11. What is the main idea of the article?

    A. A large trading block will be created.

    B. Cargo shipments are getting bigger.

    C. A transportation coalition will be formed.

    D. Air freight could become cheaper.

12. Who will participate in the alliance?

    A. four large shipping companies

    B. governments in Asia, Europe, and North America

    C. a group of manufacturing companies

    D. several customer protection groups

13. How will members benefit from the alliance?

    A. by sharing space on ships

    B. through reduced competition

    C. by sharing port facilities

    D. through access to larger ships

14. The word *specifics* as used in line 10 is closest in meaning to

    A. members.

    B. costs.

    C. details.

    D. containers.

15. When will the alliance be created?

    A. immediately

    B. at the end of the month

    C. within six to eight months

    D. over a two-year period

Questions 16–20 refer to the following report.

The Chilean Commerce Service

Established to help Chilean firms compete more effectively in the global marketplace, the Chilean Commerce Service has a network of trade specialists located throughout Chile and 67 countries. Commerce Service offices provide information on foreign markets, agent/distributor location services, trade leads, financing aid, and counseling on business opportunities, barriers, and prospects abroad.

There are 15 offices throughout Chile, each headed by a director supported by trade specialists and other staff. Most offices maintain business libraries containing the latest reports from the Department of Commerce. Trade specialists can provide the business community with local export counseling and a variety of export programs and services, including one utilizing a computerized program to help firms determine their readiness to export. Specific recommendations are proposed to help strengthen and enhance a company's exporting ability.

Commercial Officers in the overseas posts gather information about trends and barriers to trade in their areas and seek out trade and investment opportunities to benefit Chile. They also provide a range of services to potential exporters traveling abroad, such as assisting with appointments with key buyers and government officials.

16. Why was the Commerce Service created?
    A. to help Chilean companies import products
    B. to aid Chilean companies working abroad
    C. to educate international specialists
    D. to counsel firms seeking to sell in Chile

17. What is likely to be found at a Commerce Service office?
    A. a currency exchange facility
    B. conference rooms
    C. classrooms
    D. a business library

18. What does the Commerce Service use to evaluate a firm's readiness to export?
    A. a computer program
    B. a questionnaire
    C. an export analysis
    D. a written survey

19. What would a Commercial Service office probably *NOT* do?
    A. introduce businesspeople to government contacts.
    B. look for investment opportunities.
    C. help a Chilean firm write a business plan.
    D. research local market trends.

20. The word *determine* in line 10 is closest in meaning to
    A. evaluate.
    B. improve.
    C. allow.
    D. start.

Questions 21–25 refer to the following invoice and email message.

Sunshine Medical Services

INVOICE No. 322

Date:	August 5th, 2016
Patient:	Barbara Yamada
Address:	26 Whitworth Street, Manchester M24 OPJ
Details:	X-Ray Services
Amount:	£250
Paid:	£100
Payment:	Cash
Balance to pay:	£150

To: Mark Allen ‹m_allen@sunshinemedical.com›
From: David Simpson ‹d_simpson@sunshinemedical.com›
Date: September 30, 2016 - 09:25:18 A.M.
Subject: Barbara Yamada's invoice
Attachments: invoice322.doc

Mark,

Attached is a copy of Mrs. Yamada's invoice. This is still outstanding, so could you contact her please and ask her to settle the account? There's no telephone number on the invoice, but her contact details at home and work are on record. It might be best to call her on her cell phone if we have it, because she is usually out of her office most of the day. If you could you do this sometime today, that would be great.

Many thanks,

David

21. What is the invoice for?
    - A. banking transactions
    - B. clothing purchases
    - C. accounting services
    - D. medical services

22. How was the first payment made?
    - A. by check
    - B. with a credit card
    - C. in cash
    - D. by bank transfer

23. How much is owed on the account?
    - A. £50
    - B. £100
    - C. £150
    - D. £200

24. The word *outstanding* in line 7 of the email is closest in meaning to
    - A. amazing.
    - B. noticeable.
    - C. exceptional.
    - D. overdue.

25. What does David imply about Mrs. Yamada?

    A. Her home number is not on record.
    B. Her cell phone number is not on record.
    C. She may not be in her office.
    D. She has moved to Manchester.

Questions 26–30 refer to the following note and advertisement.

Harriet

I came across this ad in an industry journal last week and immediately thought that it's just what we need. I've been looking through brochures for something similar but haven't found anything that so closely matches what we need. All the others I've found are good for protecting paper files, but they wouldn't provide protection for our work. This one does, though. The only downside is that it's a bit pricier than other ones I've looked at. Still, I think it's worth the extra few dollars. Take a look and see what you think.

Bob

SURESAFE Media Protector

Do not let a fire destroy your business. Protect your priceless media and paper records in one compact unit with SURESAFE. Only 65 centimeters high, this safe fits conveniently under a desk or table. It features a three-number, changeable combination lock with a concealed dial for security.

SURESAFE provides complete fire protection for electronic media. It also offers the extra heat/humidity protection that film records require. Paper records can withstand temperatures up to 175° C and high humidity, but a temperature of 55° C or a combination of 50° C and humidity greater than 85 percent will likely destroy film media. The heat/humidity protection of SURESAFE exceeds industry specifications.

26. How did Bob learn about the SURESAFE Media Protector?

    A. from an advertisement in a journal
    B. from Harriet
    C. from a SURESAFE brochure
    D. from a website review

27. What does Bob imply about the SURESAFE Media Protector?

    A. It is more expensive than similar items.
    B. It will not fit their needs.
    C. It is no longer available.
    D. It will take several weeks to be delivered.

28. What is *NOT* mentioned as being a feature of the SURESAFE Media Protector?
    A. small size
    B. a changeable lock
    C. a hidden dial
    D. all-steel construction

29. The word *withstand* in line 7 of the advertisement is closest in meaning to
    A. burn.
    B. survive.
    C. increase.
    D. change.

30. What is claimed about the SURESAFE Media Protector?
    A. It is guaranteed never to fail.
    B. It is the strongest unit available at any price.
    C. It cannot be opened by thieves or other criminals.
    D. It protects against conditions of high heat and humidity.

Questions 31–32 refer to the following text message chain.

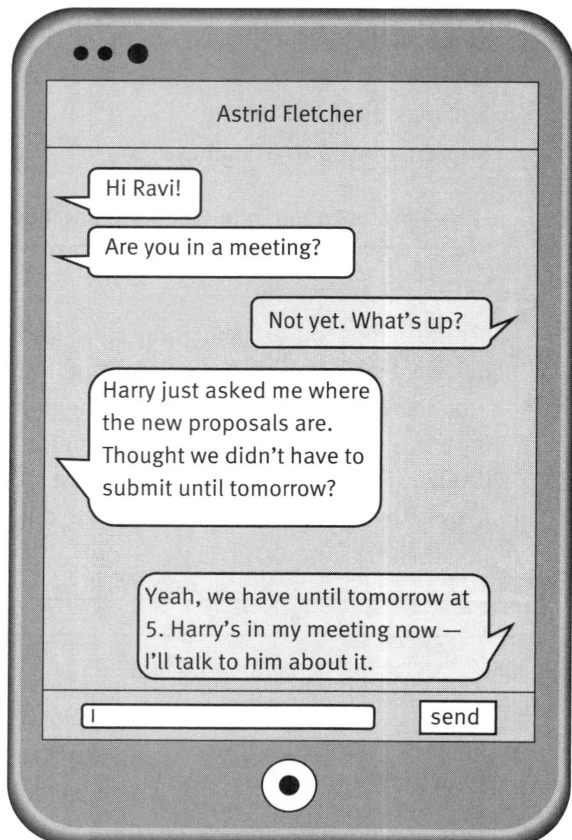

31. What does Ravi mean when he writes "What's up"?
    A. He is asking when the deadline is.
    B. He is asking for an update.
    C. He is asking why Astrid is unhappy.
    D. He is asking what he can do for Astrid.

32. According to Ravi, when do the new proposals need to be submitted?
    A. before Ravi's meeting
    B. before 5 tomorrow
    C. in the afternoon
    D. after 5 tomorrow

Answers and explanations begin on the next page ▶ ▶ ▶

ANSWER KEY

1. A	12. A	23. C
2. A	13. A	24. D
3. A	14. C	25. C
4. D	15. D	26. A
5. A	16. B	27. A
6. D	17. D	28. D
7. A	18. A	29. B
8. C	19. C	30. D
9. A	20. A	31. D
10. C	21. D	32. B
11. C	22. C	

ANSWERS AND EXPLANATIONS

These are the explanations to the Reading Comprehension questions. Next to the answer choices for each question, we have explained in greater detail exactly why the wrong answer choices are incorrect.

For some questions, we have left the wrong answer explanations blank so that you can fill them in. In the blanks next to the question, write the question type. In the blanks next to the answers, write a brief explanation of why the answer is incorrect. The more you can analyze and explain the errors in the wrong answer choices, the more skillful and efficient you will become at identifying, understanding, and eliminating incorrect choices, and selecting the correct ones.

Sample responses for these Identify the Error questions are included at the end of the Answers and Explanations section.

1. What is expected for Beijing on Wednesday? (Detail/*What*)
   - A. rain CORRECT
   - B. wind (Wind is predicted for Melbourne.)
   - C. unusual warmth (This is not mentioned.)
   - D. clear skies (This is not mentioned.)

2. What does "Typically warm and muggy" mean? (Implied Meaning)
   - A. The weather will be mostly hot and damp. CORRECT
   - B. Theft is common in the area. (This is not mentioned, though *mugging* means *stealing*)
   - C. It will be dry for most of the week. (*Muggy* means warm and damp)
   - D. People should stay inside and keep warm. (This repeats the word *warm*.)

3. Why will the Proplan representatives visit? (Gist/*Why*)
   - A. to discuss health insurance CORRECT
   - B. to provide medical examinations (This plays on the health topic.)
   - C. to distribute health care policies (This repeats the words *health care policy*.)
   - D. to sign up participants (This may be a possible reason, but it is not mentioned.)

4. What should interested employees do? (Detail/*What*)
   - A. talk to the benefits department (No, the memo is from the benefits department.)
   - B. read the attached information (This is not mentioned.)
   - C. write down questions (This plays on the words *answer questions*.)
   - D. sign up for appointments. CORRECT

5. What is Ms. Ketchem sending with this letter? (Detail/*What*)

   A. a résumé CORRECT

   B. a writing sample (This is not mentioned.)

   C. a job description (This is not mentioned.)

   D. a reference letter (This is not mentioned.)

6. In which of the positions marked [1], [2], [3], or [4] does the following sentence best belong?
"P.S. Please feel free to contact my current supervisor for a reference." (Sentence Location)

   A. [1] (P.S. means *post script* so this sentence must come at the very end of the letter.)

   B. [2] (P.S. means *post script* so this sentence must come at the very end of the letter.)

   C. [3] (P.S. means *post script* so this sentence must come at the very end of the letter.)

   D. [4] CORRECT

7. Which task is part of Ms. Ketchem's current job? (Detail/*What*)

   A. handling conventions CORRECT

   B. supervising staff (This is not mentioned; it simply repeats the word *staff*.)

   C. coordinating food service (This is not mentioned.)

   D. registering guests (This is not mentioned.)

8. Who is Franz Thurman? (Detail/*Who*)

   A. an employee (No, he would like to be an employee.)

   B. an interviewer (He will be the interviewee.)

   C. an applicant CORRECT

   D. a customer (This is not mentioned.)

9. What is the purpose of this letter? (Gist/*What*)

   A. to schedule an appointment CORRECT

   B. to make a job offer (A job offer would come after the interview.)

   C. to reject a candidate (The company wants to interview the candidate by telephone.)

   D. to request information (No information is being requested.)

10. In which of the positions marked [1], [2], [3], or [4] does the following sentence best belong?
"Thank you once again for your interest" (Sentence Location)

   A. [1] (The sentence says that thanks has already been made, so this sentence must appear after the first thanks)

   B. [2] (This would not appear immediately after the first *thank you*)

   C. [3] CORRECT

   D. [4] (This would not appear after the closing statement *sincerely*)

11. What is the main idea of the article? (Gist/*What*)

   A. A large trading block will be created (A trading block is not being created.)

   B. Cargo shipments are getting bigger (Possibly, but this is not mentioned.)

   C. A transportation coalition will be formed. CORRECT

   D. Air freight could become cheaper (This is not mentioned.)

12. Who will participate in the alliance? (Gist/*Who*)

   A. four large shipping companies CORRECT

   B. governments in Asia, Europe, and North America (These are the shipping routes that will be "linked.")

   C. a group of manufacturing companies (These are not manufacturing companies.)

   D. several customer protection groups (This is not mentioned.)

13. How will members benefit from the alliance? (Detail/*How*)

    A. by sharing space on ships CORRECT
    B. through reduced competition (This is possible, but is not mentioned.)
    C. by sharing port facilities (This is possible, but is not mentioned.)
    D. through access to larger ships (No, the passage says to *maximize use... of faster ships.*)

14. The word *specifics* as used in line 9 is closest in meaning to (Vocabulary)

    A. members.
    B. costs.
    C. details. CORRECT
    D. containers.

15. When will the alliance be created? (Detail/*When*)

    A. immediately (This is not mentioned.)
    B. at the end of the month (Negotiations will begin next month.)
    C. within six to eight months (This is not mentioned.)
    D. over a two-year period CORRECT

16. Why was the Commerce Service created? (Gist/*Why*)

    A. to help Chilean companies import products (The emphasis is on exporting Chilean products.)
    B. to aid Chilean companies working abroad CORRECT
    C. to educate international specialists (Each office already has a trade specialist.)
    D. to counsel firms seeking to sell in Chile (This is not mentioned.)

17. What is likely to be found at a Commerce Service office? (Detail/*What*)

    A. a currency exchange facility (This is not mentioned.)
    B. conference rooms (This is not mentioned.)
    C. classrooms (This is not mentioned.)
    D. a business library CORRECT

18. What does the Commerce Service use to evaluate a firm's readiness to export? (Detail/*What*)

    A. a computer program CORRECT
    B. a questionnaire (This is not mentioned.)
    C. an export analysis (This is not mentioned.)
    D. a written survey (This is not mentioned.)

19. What would a Commercial Service office probably *NOT* do? (Detail/*What*)

    A. introduce businesspeople to government contacts (They assist *with* appointments with key buyers and government officials.)
    B. look for investment opportunities (They seek out trade and investment opportunities.)
    C. help a Chilean firm write a business plan. CORRECT
    D. research local market trends (They gather information about trends.)

20. The word *determine* in line 10 is closest in meaning to (Vocabulary)

    A. evaluate. CORRECT
    B. improve.
    C. allow.
    D. start.

21. What is the invoice for? (Gist/*What*)
    A. banking transactions (This plays on the topic of account information.)
    B. clothing purchases (This is not mentioned.)
    C. accounting services (This plays on the topic of account information.)
    D. medical services CORRECT

22. How was the first payment made? (Detail/*How*)
    A. by check (This is not mentioned.)
    B. with a credit card (This is not mentioned.)
    C. in cash CORRECT
    D. by bank transfer (This is not mentioned.)

23. How much is owed on the account? (Detail/*How*)
    A. £50 (This is not mentioned.)
    B. £100 (This is what has been paid.)
    C. £150 CORRECT
    D. £200 (This is not mentioned.)

24. The word *outstanding* in line 8 of the email is closest in meaning to (Vocabulary)
    A. amazing.
    B. noticeable.
    C. exceptional.
    D. overdue. CORRECT

25. What does David imply about Mrs. Yamanda? (Detail/*What*)
    A. Her home number is not on record (It is on record.)
    B. Her cell phone number is not on record (It is on record.)
    C. She may not be in her office. CORRECT
    D. She has moved to Manchester (This uses Manchester from the address on the invoice.)

26. How did Bob learn about the SURESAFE Media Protector? ______________________________
    A. from an advertisement in a journal CORRECT
    B. from Harriet ______________________________
    C. from a SURESAFE brochure ______________________________
    D. from a website review ______________________________

27. What does Bob imply about the SURESAFE Media Protector? ______________________________
    A. It is more expensive than similar items. CORRECT
    B. It will not fit their needs. ______________________________
    C. It is no longer available. ______________________________
    D. It will take several weeks to be delivered. ______________________________

28. What is NOT mentioned as being a feature of the SURESAFE Media Protector? ______________________________
    A. small size ______________________________
    B. a changeable lock ______________________________
    C. a hidden dial ______________________________
    D. all-steel construction CORRECT

29. The word *withstand* in line 7 of the advertisement is closest in meaning to (Vocabulary)

    A. burn.

    B. survive. CORRECT

    C. increase.

    D. change.

30. What is claimed about the SURESAFE Media Protector? (Detail/ *What*)

    A. It is guaranteed never to fail. (This is not mentioned.)

    B. It is the strongest unit available at any price. (This is not mentioned.)

    C. It cannot be opened by thieves or other criminals. (This is not mentioned.)

    D. It protects against conditions of high heat and humidity. CORRECT

31. What does Ravi mean when he writes "What's up"? (Intended Meaning/ *What*)

    A. He is asking when the deadline is. (This has not been introduced yet.)

    B. He is asking for an update. (This is not mentioned.)

    C. He is asking why Astrid is unhappy. (There is no indication that Astrid is upset.)

    D. He is asking what he can do for Astrid. CORRECT

32. According to Ravi, when do the new proposals need to be submitted?

    A. before Ravi's meeting (Ravi writes *We have tomorrow until 5*)

    B. before 5 tomorrow CORRECT

    C. in the afternoon (Ravi writes *We have tomorrow until 5*)

    D. after 5 tomorrow (Ravi writes *We have tomorrow until 5*)

Answers for the Identify the Error Questions

26. How did Bob learn about the SURESAFE Media Protector? (*Detail/How*)

    A. from an advertisement in a journal CORRECT

    B. from Harriet (*Bob is informing Harriet about the product.*)

    C. from a SURESAFE brochure (*Brochures are mentioned, but this is not how Bob learns about the product.*)

    D. from a website review (*This is not mentioned.*)

27. What does Bob imply about the SURESAFE Media Protector? (*Detail/What*)

    A. It is more expensive than similar items. CORRECT

    B. It will not fit their needs. (*He says it's just what we need.*)

    C. It is no longer available. (*This is not mentioned.*)

    D. It will take several weeks to be delivered. (*This is not mentioned.*)

28. What is *NOT* mentioned as being a feature of the SURESAFE Media Protector? (Detail/ *What*)

    A. small size (*An entire sentence describes the advantages of its small size.*)

    B. a changeable lock (*It has a three-number changeable combination lock.*)

    C. a hidden dial (*The dial is concealed for security.*)

    D. all-steel construction CORRECT

PART FOUR

Vocabulary Builders

CHAPTER 10

Vocabulary-Building Exercises

LEARNING OBJECTIVES

In this section, you'll learn to:

- Identify the 10 most common word families
- Use the vocabulary lists to remember words more effectively

There is no better way to improve your TOEIC exam score than to broaden your vocabulary. Therefore, in addition to learning Kaplan's test-taking strategies and practicing the different types of TOEIC exam questions, review the list of words included in this chapter. It is not enough to know a word's meaning; you have to be able to understand the word when you hear or see it in different contexts and know how to use the word yourself. That is where the vocabulary exercises come in. They will help you put your newly acquired vocabulary into action.

The five word lists that follow each include ten of the most common word families you will find on the TOEIC exam. They are grouped in word families because we have found that students learn more words more efficiently when the words are grouped together. In fact, anytime you come across a new word—in this book or any reading material—it is a good idea to study the other words within the same family.

You will find this especially helpful for Part V (Incomplete Sentences) because you must often distinguish between the different forms of a particular word. The vocabulary and grammar exercises also provide additional focused review for the types of questions you'll encounter in Part V.

For even more vocabulary-building, read as much material in English as you can. Many English-language newspapers and magazines are available for free online; for example, you can read the *Washington Post* daily newspaper online at *www.washingtonpost.com*.

In addition, write each new word you encounter and its sentence in a notebook. Writing down new words helps you to remember them. You should also make note of new uses of words you already know, and review your notebook often.

Remember: You cannot learn all these words in a day—or even in a week for that matter! Instead, work with the lists and exercises little by little each day that you study.

1. Look up all the words on a list in the glossary on page 207.
2. Listen to the list on the audio CD.
3. Try the exercises for that list.
4. Check your answers using the answer key at the end of this chapter.

WORDS YOU NEED TO KNOW

The words in these lists appear frequently on the TOEIC exam—and they are commonly used in business situations. Mastering these words can help you on the TOEIC exam and in your career.

Track 5

Play Track 5 to help you learn the correct pronunciation of these words.

VOCABULARY LISTS

List 1	List 2
ad *noun*	accept *verb*
advertise *verb*	acceptable *adjective*
advertisement *noun*	acceptance *noun*
applicant *noun*	accepting *adjective*
application *noun*	attend *verb*
apply *verb*	attendance *noun*
beneficent *adjective*	attendant *noun*
beneficial *adjective*	attention *noun*
beneficially *adverb*	develop *verb*
beneficiary *noun*	developers *noun*
benefit *noun, verb*	development *noun*
confide *verb*	expect *verb*
confidence *noun*	expectation *noun*
confident *adjective*	expecting *verb*
confidential *adjective*	facilitate *verb*
employ *verb*	facility/facilities *noun*
employee *noun*	form/forms *noun*
employer *noun*	form/forms *verb*
employment *noun*	format *noun*
experience *noun, verb*	network *noun, verb*
interview *noun, verb*	networking *noun, adjective*
interviewee *noun*	procedure/procedures *noun*

interviewer *noun*	proceed *verb*
person *noun*	proceeding *noun*
personal *adjective*	process *noun, verb*
personalized *adjective*	processing *noun*
personnel *noun*	specific *adjective*
position *noun, verb*	specifically *adverb*
train *verb*	specification *noun*
trainee *noun*	specifics *noun*
trainer *noun*	specify *verb*
training *noun*	

List 3	**List 4**
account *noun, verb*	arrange *verb*
accountant *noun*	arrangement *noun*
accounting *noun*	brochure *noun*
budget *noun, verb*	complete *adjective, verb*
consult *verb*	completion *noun*
consultant *noun*	manage *verb*
consulting *adjective*	management *noun*
document *noun, verb*	manager *noun*
documentation *noun*	managerial *adjective*
firm *adjective, noun*	operate *verb*
interest *noun, verb*	operation *noun*
interested *adjective*	operational *adjective*
interesting *adjective*	operator *noun*
inventory *noun*	policy *noun*
organization *noun*	post *verb*
organize *verb*	postage *noun*
pay *noun, verb*	postal *adjective*
payable *adjective*	postmaster *noun*
payment *noun*	present *adjective*
profit *noun, verb*	present *noun*
profitability *noun*	present *verb*
profitable *adjective*	presentation *noun*
proposal *noun*	propose *verb*
supervise *verb*	supervisor *noun*

List 5	
commerce *noun*	industry *noun*
commercial *adjective, noun*	international *adjective*
compete *verb*	internationalize *verb*
competent *adjective*	market *noun, verb*
competition *noun*	marketing plan *noun*
competitive *adjective*	negotiate *verb*
competitor *noun*	negotiations *noun*
export *noun, verb*	negotiator *noun*
exporter *noun*	promote *verb*
global *adjective*	promotion *noun*
industrial *adjective*	promotional *adjective*
industrialize *verb*	trade *noun, verb*

VOCABULARY EXERCISES FOR LIST 1

Exercise 1

Directions: Give the verb form for each of the following nouns in the space provided.

Noun	Verb
1. ad	
2. application	
3. beneficiary	
4. confidence	
5. employer	
6. trainee	

Exercise 2

Directions: Replace the underlined words or phrases with a word from the following list that has a similar meaning. Use each word only once.

question
beneficiary
position

trainee
personal
profit
experience
employ
advertisement
confidential

1. George did not know about the concert until he saw the poster about it. ________________
2. The company expects to benefit a great deal from the new trade agreement between the United States and Mexico. ________________
3. I would like for these discussions regarding our dealings with Cedar Industries to be secret. ________________
4. Jorge's grandmother named him in her will as the recipient of her home and all its furnishings. ________________
5. Mariko's background in the publishing industry was rather limited, but the manager liked her enthusiasm and willingness to learn. ________________
6. During the busy holiday season, many retailers use temporary help. ________________
7. Martha received a promotion and she now has a new job in the international marketing department. ________________
8. Everyone passed the course, except one new employee. ________________
9. The reporter wanted to interview the company president about his plans to expand operations to Vietnam. ________________
10. I considered some of the employer's questions private and answered them reluctantly. ________________

Exercise 3

Directions: Complete the sentences with the correct form of the underlined word.

1. If you are interested in applying for the job, you should fill out an __________.
2. The interviewee seemed uncomfortable during the __________ and only responded in short answers.
3. An advertising campaign is being developed to __________ our new soft drink to teenagers.
4. The message was very _________, so I decided to deliver it in person.
5. Per the terms of the new labor agreement, the company needs to employ ten new ________ by the end of the month.
6. The benefit for the Children's Food Bank raised a lot of money, proving once again how ______ these types of events are.

Exercise 4

Directions: Match the word in column A with its definition in column B.

Column A	Column B
1. trainee	a. a person who gives a job to someone
2. applicant	b. a person who receives money or property when somebody dies
3. employer	c. someone learning a new trade
4. interviewer	d. a candidate for a job
5. person	e. someone asking another person questions
6. beneficiary	f. an individual

Exercise 5

Directions: Complete the sentences by filling the blank with the correct word from the list. Use each word only once.

beneficially
confided
personalized
positions
employment
training

1. Many graduates will be seeking permanent __________ in July.
2. If Joyce loses any of her __________ pens, she knows someone will recognize her initials.
3. Very few people lost their __________ despite the company's restructuring program.
4. I have two weeks of __________ before I actually start my new job.
5. Mr. LaRue __________ in his employees that the company was seeking bankruptcy.
6. Her experience was felt __________ by her colleagues.

VOCABULARY EXERCISES FOR LIST 2

Exercise 1

Directions: Form nouns from these verbs by adding *-ance, -ation,* or *-ment. Make any other necessary spelling changes.*

Verb Form	Noun Form
1. to develop	__________________
2. to specify	__________________
3. to accept	__________________
4. to attend	__________________
5. to expect	__________________

Exercise 2

Directions: Fill the blanks with the correct preposition in parentheses.

1. Attendance __________ (at, in) the play had dropped, so they decided to cancel the remaining shows.
2. The speaker was frustrated because no one seemed to be paying attention __________ (with, to) him.
3. The process __________ (for, to) recycling many of our household items is not as difficult as many people think.
4. Putting all computers on the same network would help the sales team __________ (on, with) their work.
5. The president wanted a status report on the development __________ (of, for) the new software program.
6. The attendant was very polite and helpful __________ (to, at) the customers and received many compliments.
7. Thomas was unable to attend the awards banquet, so Mark accepted the award __________ (for, with) him.
8. The workers formed a circle __________ (around, through) Mr. Martini's desk and sang "Happy Birthday" to him.

Exercise 3

Directions: Complete these sentences by filling the blanks with the correct word in parentheses.

1. Because they did not __________ (specific, specifically) say the meeting would start at noon, no one knew when to arrive.
2. The food __________ (process, processing) plant had to close down because of a labor dispute.

3. Some wealthy __________ (developers, developing) are hoping to build a resort along the coast.
4. David is not very __________ (acceptable, accepting) of changes in the office.
5. __________ (Attendance, Attending) at today's staff meeting is required.
6. The __________ (attendant, attending) physician had to call a specialist to help with this case.
7. Many professionals join organizations because they are often a good __________ (network, networking) source.
8. Two workers were fined for not following the correct __________ (procedures, proceedings).

Exercise 4

Directions: Complete this paragraph by filling the blanks with the correct word from the list. Use each word once.

form	acceptable	networks
format	processing	specifications
attendance	developing	forms
expected	facilitate	

At the beginning of the new season, the television (1) __________ mailed out viewer response (2) __________ to get feedback on their new shows. After (3) __________ and evaluating the completed cards, it became apparent that most viewers did not like the violent (4) __________ of many shows. Violent TV shows were no longer (5) __________ to most viewers. The television producers had not (6) __________ such a negative response to their shows. They decided to (7) __________ a committee of viewers and writers to establish some (8) __________ for (9) __________ a new television show. One producer was selected to (10) __________ the meetings, and all those in (11) __________ said that much was accomplished.

VOCABULARY EXERCISES FOR LIST 3

Exercise 1

Directions: Complete these sentences by filling in the blanks with the correct form of the underlined word.

1. I have hired an __________ to take care of all my <u>accounts</u>.
2. We probably won't use those <u>consultants</u> again, because their __________ fee was very high.
3. Sally had to get the original <u>documents</u> from the shipping company, because customs would not release the package without proper __________.
4. A smart consumer should <u>be interested</u> in the __________ rates that banks charge on credit cards.

5. Those in the advertising field are organizing an advertising __________ that would cater to new graduates.
6. The department store claimed that he had failed to pay his last bill, but according to his records, he had sent a __________ three weeks ago.
7. Peter was convinced that his new venture would be __________, and he predicted that they would see profits within the year.
8. The law __________ stood firmly behind its decision to represent the oil company.

Exercise 2

Directions: Underline the two words in column B that are associated with the word in column A.

Column A	Column B
1. payable	due, free, owing, trade
2. payment	crime, service, cash, check
3. budget	economize, unorganized, plan, start
4. interest	savings, loan, loss, purchase
5. organization	business, individual, profit, foundation
6. document	verbal, painting, paper, birth certificate
7. consultant	advisor, conference, mentor, distributor

Exercise 3

Directions: Fill the blanks with the correct word from the list. Use each word once.

paid	documented	budget	inventory	organize
firm	profitable	account	consult	interests

1. The company appeared to be __________, so the business community was surprised when it filed for bankruptcy.
2. The invoice had been incorrectly marked __________, so a past due notice was never mailed to the customer.
3. The union tried to __________ its members to vote against the new contract.
4. Our __________ of women's shoes needs to be updated with new styles.
5. The idea __________ me, but I need about a week to think it over.
6. Management was __________ about its decision to penalize employees for being late.
7. The police officer __________ what each witness had to say about the accident.
8. Unsure of the import-export laws of Brazil, Auto Components, Inc. decided to __________ with a trade expert.
9. Peggy finds that she needs to __________ her time if she wants to get everything done.
10. The witness gave a detailed __________ of the accident to the police officer.

Exercise 4

Directions: Fill the blanks with the correct form of the word in parentheses.

1. That idea sounds __________ (interested, interesting) to me; I'd like to see some further research.
2. The bill was marked __________ (paid, payable), so I mailed a check the next day.
3. After several years of struggling, the company is finally showing signs of __________ (profitable, profitability).
4. Edward goes to all the shareholders' meetings because he has an __________ (interest, interesting) in the company.
5. International travelers should be careful to keep all __________ (document, documentation) of items purchased on a trip.
6. The hotel manager was unable to __________ (account, accounting) for the drop in hotel guests.
7. I'm thinking of leaving the company and becoming an independent __________ (consulting, consultant).

VOCABULARY EXERCISES FOR LIST 4

Exercise 1

Directions: Underline the word in the sentence that is closest in meaning to the word in parentheses.

1. (placement)	The president did not like the arrangement of the chairs at the head table of the banquet.
2. (booklet)	The museum decided to add colored photos to its brochure, and everyone seemed to be pleased with the result.
3. (fully)	Ms. Abrams was not completely convinced of the need to hire a part-time receptionist.
4. (completion)	The fulfillment of this contract certainly calls for a celebration, as everyone worked so hard on it.
5. (governing)	Carlos was hired for his excellent managerial skills, and the board is counting on him to organize the various departments.
6. (operating)	The company decided to lower its overhead expenses and move to a less expensive building.
7. (policy)	Many companies have initiated a no-smoking rule inside the office; smokers now have to go outside.
8. (postage)	I didn't put enough stamps on my letter, so it was returned to me.

9. (present)	The board of directors awarded the retiring vice president with a commemorative gift for his 35 years of service to the company.
10. (suggest)	I propose that we discuss this matter over lunch.

Exercise 2

Directions: Match the words in column B that have the opposite meaning to the words in column A.

Column A	Column B
1. arrange	a. out of order
2. complete	b. absent
3. operational	c. subordinate
4. to post	d. partial
5. present	e. disorganize
6. supervisor	f. to remove

Exercise 3

Directions: Complete the sentences with the correct word from the list. Use each word once.

policy	management	supervises
operating	arranged	posted
brochure	complete	managerial

1. Anyone __________ heavy machinery should not take medications.
2. The homeowner __________ a sign warning trespassers to stay off his property.
3. The trading partners of the developing country have complained about what they consider to be an overly restrictive trade __________.
4. The company will be laying off some employees, and some of those positions are in _______.
5. Alice wanted to purchase the __________ works of her husband's favorite composer for his birthday.
6. Shawn looked through the Help Wanted ads for any __________ positions, but he only found a few entry-level positions in the fields that interested him.
7. According to this __________, there is a scenic highway that goes all the way to the coast.
8. The receptionist did not like the way the temporary help had __________ her desk.
9. David received a promotion, and now he __________ four other employees.

Exercise 4

Directions: Match each sentence part in column A with its correct completion in column B.

Column A	Column B
1. Once the fan belt had been fixed,	a. after two accidents in one year.
2. A complete audit was requested	b. for organizing the next day's operations.
3. The cruise line had trouble renewing its insurance policy	c. the machine was operational.
4. The proposal to raise room rates	d. but only a partial one was approved.
5. The evening supervisor is responsible	e. was approved by hotel management.

VOCABULARY EXERCISES FOR LIST 5

Exercise 1

Directions: Match the words in column B that have the opposite meaning to the words in column A.

Column A	Column B
1. export	a. closed to debate
2. competitor	b. internal
3. global	c. import
4. negotiable	d. colleague
5. promote	e. downplay

Exercise 2

Directions: Circle the word in the list that does not belong with the others.

1. international, foreign, domestic, global, intercontinental
2. market, farm, shop, retail store, bazaar
3. bargain, stall, negotiate, compromise, talk over
4. criticize, promote, advertise, market, build up
5. competitor, challenger, rival, adversary, loser

Exercise 3

Directions: Match each sentence part in column A with its correct completion in column B.

Column A	Column B
1. Dan received a promotion	a. because the exchange rate is much higher.
2. Some people change currency	b. because it is unable to compete on the black market with the international firms.
3. The negotiations to lease the building	c. after being with the company for seven years.
4. I'm sure that Mary is a competent worker	d. apply for a job at an ad agency.
5. After graduating in marketing, Elaine decided to	e. because her references say that she is capable of handling most situations.
6. The clothing industry is not doing well here	f. came to a halt when one of the attorneys became ill.

Exercise 4

Directions: Complete the dialogue by filling in the blanks with the correct word from the list. Use each word once.

industrial	promotional	compete
promoting	industries	internationally
market	commercials	negotiated

A: How did the viewers like the new movie?

B: It hasn't come out yet. We have just started (1) __________ it.

A: What's the movie about again?

B: It takes place during the (2) __________ Revolution and features workers in various (3) __________.

A: How do you plan to (4) __________ it?

B: Well, we have (5) __________ with several theaters around the country, and they'll all begin showing it next month. We also hope it will be shown (6) __________.

A: Do you think it will (7) __________ well with the action movies?

B: It should. We need to run some (8) __________ on television and develop more (9) _______ materials.

Exercise 5

Directions: Complete each sentence with the correct form of the verb in parentheses.

1. Two local companies __________ (compete) last year for the government contract to build a federal building.
2. The company is planning on __________ (export) its laser printers to Europe next year.

3. Developing countries are working hard to become __________ (industrialize) in order to improve their economies.
4. Rolf should be a good addition to the sales team; his experience is extensive and he _______ (market) automobile parts for five years now.
5. William _________ (negotiate) the sale of timber products to a foreign country and received a promotion from his employer in the timber industry.
6. Once the trade ban is lifted, our company will be free __________ (trade) with that country again.

VOCABULARY AND GRAMMAR EXERCISES FOR PART V

For Vocabulary questions in Part V, all four possible answers will be the same part of speech. That is, they will all either be verbs, nouns, modifiers (adjectives and adverbs), conjunctions (*and, but, either*, etc.), or prepositions. Focus on the context of the sentence and your knowledge of vocabulary to identify the correct answer. Make sure you read the entire sentence so that you get the full context of the sentence before trying to complete it.

For the Grammar questions in Part V, all four possible answers share a common root but are different parts of speech. The possible answers will be a variety of verbs, nouns, modifiers (adjectives and adverbs), and pronouns. Because the answer choices are usually different forms of the same word, your task is to select the form of the word that is grammatically correct. To start, read the entire sentence to get its full context; then, focus on the words on either side of the missing word. These often provide clues as to which part of speech is required. For example, the article *the* or *a* in front of the blank tells you a noun is missing.

The vocabulary tested on the TOEIC exam is the kind that you would expect to see in business reports, newspaper or magazine articles, advertisements, public notices, and other types of everyday written contexts. The TOEIC exam tests a wide variety of grammar points. At a minimum, you should be familiar with the following:

- **PRONOUNS**
  - Possessive pronouns (*mine, yours, his, hers, its, ours, theirs*)
  - Subject pronouns (*I, you, he, she, it, we, they*)
  - Object pronouns (*me, you, him, her, it, us, them*)
  - Reflexive pronouns (*myself, yourself, himself, herself, itself, ourselves, yourselves, themselves*)
  - Relative pronouns (*who, which, what, that*)
  - Interrogative pronouns (*who, which, what*)
  - Demonstrative pronouns (*this, that, these, those*)
- **VERBS**
  - Tenses and their usage
  - When to use *-ing* forms

    - Infinitives with and without *to*
    - Common irregular verbs and their forms
    - Irregular past participles
    - Subject-verb agreement

- **ADJECTIVES and ADVERBS**
    - Differences between adjectives and adverbs
    - Use of adjectives, including nouns as adjectives
    - Use and forms of comparatives and superlatives
    - Use of adverbs

- **PREPOSITIONS and PHRASAL VERBS**
    - Common prepositions (*to, on, in, at, from...*)
    - Common prepositional phrases (*look up, go over, turn on...*)

- **CONJUNCTIONS**
    - Common conjunctions and their uses (*but, however, although, yet, so, despite...*)

Vocabulary and Grammar Practice Exercises

1. We ________ credit cards, checks, or money orders for payment.

   A. accept
   B. exist
   C. pay
   D. are

2. Due to decreasing sales, major automobile manufacturers are ________ customer rebates.

   A. asking
   B. offering
   C. showing
   D. taking

3. Sales have improved since we changed the way ________ is displayed in the window.

   A. mechanic
   B. management
   C. merchandise
   D. mask

4. Susan went ________ early on Friday because she was ill.

   A. town
   B. home
   C. house
   D. place

5. We have arranged for an ________ flight on Tuesday.

   A. early
   B. angry
   C. ugly
   D. eager

6. Passengers are able to travel ________ and inexpensively by train.

   A. frankly
   B. perfectly
   C. shortly
   D. comfortably

7. Both President Scarpati ________ Chairman Green spoke at the national meeting.

   A. or
   B. and
   C. but
   D. yet

8. Mr. Lipton was in good spirits and reported that he was neither tired ________ hungry after his flight from Sydney.

   A. nor
   B. either
   C. and
   D. but

9. Please have the attached documents sent out ________ express mail service.

   A. of
   B. at
   C. to
   D. by

10. Ms. Roswell was transferred from Mexico City ________ Los Angeles in April.

    A. by
    B. to
    C. through
    D. with

11. They ________ the brochure before we could make the changes.

    A. printed
    B. printing
    C. printers
    D. prints

12. The memorandum was ________ through via mail.

    A. sending
    B. sends
    C. sender
    D. sent

13. Because the ________ was broken, the equipment had to be brought up the stairs.

    A. elevation
    B. elevator
    C. elevate
    D. elevated

14. If full payment is not received within 30 days, ________ will be charged on the amount due.

    A. interesting
    B. interest
    C. interested
    D. interests

15. After months of negotiations, we were ________ awarded the Gibbson account.

    A. final
    B. finalized
    C. finally
    D. finality

16. The convention provides a chance to meet ________ distributors and representatives without leaving the country.

    A. international
    B. internationalize
    C. internationally
    D. internationalized

17. On behalf of the social services committee, ________ have the honor of inviting you to the Annual Spring Fashion Show.

    A. you
    B. our
    C. we
    D. me

18. Ms. Wilson says the hardest part of ________ job is setting priorities.

    A. she
    B. herself
    C. hers
    D. her

ANSWER KEY

1. A
2. B
3. C
4. B
5. A
6. D
7. B
8. A
9. D
10. B
11. A
12. D
13. B
14. B
15. C
16. A
17. C
18. D

VOCABULARY AND GRAMMAR REVIEW FOR PART VI

On Part VI of the TOEIC exam, you will be making use of strategies very similar to those you used for Part V. This is because, essentially, Part VI is a variation of Part V that uses whole texts instead of individual sentences. The missing words and phrases fall into the categories we discussed in chapter 7: those that test your knowledge of vocabulary, those that test your knowledge of grammar and those that test your understanding of the text. Your first strategy, therefore, is to identify which type of incomplete sentence you are completing.

There is one more important difference between the Part V and Part VI. In Part VI, you are given full texts, not single sentences, so some of the missing words are cohesive devices. These are words that hold the text together, or organize it. Examples of cohesive devices are:

- Pronouns (*he, she, him, them*)
- Possessive adjectives (*his, her, your*)
- Conjunctions (*because, but, however, whereas*)

Sometimes these are used to refer back or forward to things mentioned in the text. Other times they are used to join thoughts or ideas together.

Practice 1

Questions 1–4 refer to the following letter.

Dear Mr. Jones,

As a valued __________ (1.) to *Coffee Aficionado* magazine, we thought you ought to be the first to know of a very special offer we are making beginning next month. Now that you've been receiving *Coffee Aficionado* for some time, you'll no doubt have gotten used to our first-class reporting of all the latest industry news. You'll also have realized that there is no other __________ (2.) currently available that gives the depth and __________ (3.) of information you expect to find on all things coffee. And certainly you'll have understood that from our team of experts and specialists in the field, you are getting the most informed opinions available. And things just got better! __________ (4.) a two-year subscription to *Coffee Aficionado* for only $32.95.

1. A. subscriber
   B. buyer
   C. member
   D. associate

2. A. reporter
   B. coffee
   C. pamphlet
   D. publication

3. A. size
   B. width
   C. breadth
   D. height

4. A. We're making you this very special offer:
   B. We'd like to apologize for our mistake by offering
   C. Unfortunately, we will no longer be able to offer
   D. We'd like to request to buy

Practice 2

Questions 5–8 refer to the following passage.

White Noise Is Good Noise

We live in an __________ (5.) noisy world. Heavy traffic, barking dogs, and loud music from our neighbors are all examples of the kind of noise pollution that many people find unbearable. Doctors now cite noise disturbance as one of the most common causes of anxiety and depression in their patients. One way to reduce __________ (6.) impact is the use of a white noise generator in the home or office. __________ (7.) White noise actually occurs often in nature: pouring rain, waterfalls, or surf crashing on the beach are all examples. Some units simply reproduce recordings of these sounds, __________ (8.) other more sophisticated units generate white noise electronically.

5. A. increase
   B. increased
   C. increasingly
   D. increasing

6. A. its
   B. their
   C. your
   D. our

7. A. This tea set can be yours for only $24.99.
   B. White noise is sound at a certain frequency that effectively blocks out or neutralizes other sounds.
   C. How often have you been interrupted from sleep by unwelcome noises outside?
   D. Visit our website to learn more!

8. A. when
   B. nevertheless
   C. likewise
   D. whereas

ANSWER KEY

1. A
2. D
3. C
4. A
5. C
6. A
7. B
8. D

GLOSSARY

The following is a glossary for the words in all five lists.

List 1

ad *noun*	advertisement
advertise *verb*	to show that something is for sale/that you want something
advertisement *noun*	a notice which shows that something is for sale/that you want something
applicant *noun*	a person who applies, as for employment
application *noun*	asking for a job; a request, or a form filled out in making one; any thing applied, as a remedy
apply *verb*	to ask for a job; to refer to; to make a request; to put or spread on
beneficent *adjective*	doing or resulting in good
beneficial *adjective*	producing benefits; advantageous; favorable
beneficially *adverb*	producing benefits; advantageous; favorable
beneficiary *noun*	anyone receiving or to receive benefit, as funds from a will, an insurance policy, etc.
benefit *noun*	anything contributing to improvement; advantage; payments made by an insurance company or public agency; a public performance, bazaar, etc. with the proceeds going to help some person or cause
benefit *verb*	to receive advantage; to profit
confide *verb*	to trust (in someone), especially by sharing secrets
confidence *noun*	trust; assurance; belief in one's ability
confident *adjective*	full of confidence; certain; sure of oneself
confidential *adjective*	secret; entrusted with private matters
employ *verb*	to give work to someone, usually for payment; to use
employee *noun*	a person who is employed by an employer; one who works for another
employer *noun*	a person who hires workers and pays them for their work
employment *noun*	working; a job
experience *noun*	something that happens to you; knowledge of something because you have seen it or done it
experience *verb*	to have experience of; to undergo
interview *noun*	a talk with someone, often broadcast or reported in a newspaper
interview *verb*	to talk with someone; to ask questions of someone
interviewee *noun*	the person being interviewed
interviewer *noun*	the person conducting the interview; a person asking someone questions
person *noun*	a human being

personal *adjective* — private, individual; belonging to one person
personalized *adjective* — made personal; marked with one's name, etc.
personnel *noun* — persons employed in any work, enterprise, service, etc.; a department for hiring employees, etc.
position *noun* — the way in which a person or thing is placed or arranged; one's attitude or opinion; rank; employment, job
position *verb* — to put in a certain position
train *verb* — to teach someone or an animal how to do something; to practice for a sport
trainee *noun* — a person being trained
trainer *noun* — a person who trains others
training *noun* — instruction, practice

List 2

accept *verb* — to agree to receive something; to agree to something
acceptable *adjective* — worth accepting; satisfactory
acceptance *noun* — the act of receiving something; an approval
accepting *adjective* — a willingness to accept
attend *verb* — to take care of; to go with; to be present at
attendance *noun* — the number of persons attending
attendant *noun* — one who attends or serves
attention *noun* — mental concentration or readiness; notice or observation; care or consideration
develop *verb* — to grow or make grow; to use for a better purpose; to start to get
developers *noun* — those who develop things, especially real estate and projects
development *noun* — thing that develops; being developed; area where new houses are built
expect *verb* — to think/to hope that something is going to happen or is true
expectation *noun* — anticipation; a thing looked forward to
expecting *verb* — anticipating
facilitate *verb* — to make easy or easier, to assist
facility/facilities *noun* — skill; dexterity; a building that facilitates some activity
form/forms *noun* — shape; paper with blank spaces that you have to write in; state/condition
format *noun* — the shape, size, and arrangement of something such as a book; the arrangement or plan of a presentation
form *verb* — to shape, to make
network *noun* — an arrangement of parallel wires; a system of interconnected roads, individuals; a chain of transmitting radio and TV stations
network *verb* — to connect; to interconnect wires, roads, individuals
networking *noun* — the making of contacts and trading of information; the interconnection of computer systems

procedure/procedures *noun*	the act or method of proceeding in an action; a series of steps taken to accomplish an end; a guideline
proceed *verb*	to go on; to carry on some action; to take legal action
proceeding *noun*	a going on with what one has been doing; a course of action; a record of transactions
process *noun*	the course of being done; course of time, etc.; method of doing something, with all the steps involved
process *verb*	to prepare by or subject to a special process
processing *noun*	preparation by a special process
specific *adjective*	definite; peculiar to or characteristic of something; of a particular kind
specifically *adverb*	definite, peculiar with respect to a particular action
specification *noun*	a list of particulars, as to size, quality, etc.; something specified
specifics *noun*	specified details, particulars
specify *verb*	to describe details

List 3

account *noun*	a counting; a record of business transactions, bank/charge account; a credit customer; an explanation, report
account *verb*	to give a financial reckoning; to give reasons
accountant *noun*	one whose work is accounting
accounting *noun*	the figuring and recording of financial accounts
budget *noun*	a stock of items; a plan adjusting expenses to income; estimated cost of living, operating
budget *verb*	to put on a budget; to plan (your time)
consult *verb*	to talk things over; to seek information or instruction from; to consider
consultant *noun*	a person who consults another; a person who gives professional or technical advice
consulting *adjective*	advising
document *noun*	anything printed, written, etc. that may be used to record or prove something
document *verb*	to provide with or support by documents
documentation *noun*	being documented or having documents
firm *adjective*	solid, hard; showing determination; strong, certain
firm *noun*	a business company
interest *noun*	a right to, or share in something; advantage; a feeling of curiosity, concern about something; money paid for the use of money
interest *verb*	to involve or excite the interest or attention of; to cause to have an interest, share in
interested *adjective*	having an interest or share; feeling or showing interest
interesting *adjective*	exciting curiosity or attention; of interest
inventory *noun*	an itemized list of goods, property, etc., as of business; the store of goods for such listing, stock

organization *noun* — an organizing or being organized; any organized group, as a club
organize *verb* — to arrange for; to establish; to persuade to join a cause, group
pay *noun* — money paid, wages, salary
pay *verb* — to give what is due; to settle; to give (a compliment, attention, etc.); to be profitable
payable *adjective* — that can be paid; due to be paid
payment *noun* — a paying or being paid; something paid
profit *noun* — advantage, gain; financial gain, the sum remaining after deducting costs
profit *verb* — to gain financially; to benefit; to be of advantage
profitability *noun* — having profit, capability to gain profit
profitable *adjective* — having profit, advantageous

List 4

arrange *verb* — to put in the correct order; to classify; to prepare or plan
arrangement *noun* — an arranging; a plan; a settlement
brochure *noun* — a short printed document for informational or promotional purposes, a pamphlet
complete *adjective* — whole; entire; thorough
complete *verb* — to finish; to make whole or perfect
completion *noun* — the finishing/end of something
manage *verb* — to control the movement or behavior of; to have charge of; direct
management *noun* — a managing or being managed; the person managing a business, institution, etc.
manager *noun* — one who manages
managerial *adjective* — of a manager or management
operate *verb* — to be in action; act; work
operation *noun* — the act or method of operating; any of a series of procedures in some work or plan as in industry or warfare; any surgical procedure
operational *adjective* — having to do with the operation of a device, system; that can be used; in use
operator *noun* — a person who operates a machine (a telephone operator); a person engaged in business or industrial operations
policy *noun* — wise management; principle, plan; a written insurance contract
post *verb* — to put up; to announce/warn by posting notices; to mail
postage *noun* — the amount charged for mailing something
postal *adjective* — of mail or post offices
postmaster *noun* — a manager of a post office
present *adjective* — being at a specified place; the present time or occasion
present *noun* — the present time or occasion; a gift
present *verb* — to introduce (a person); to exhibit, show; to give a gift

presentation *noun*	a presenting or being presented; something presented
proposal *noun*	a proposing; a proposed plan; an offer of marriage
propose *verb*	to put forth for consideration, approval; to plan or intend
supervise *verb*	to oversee or direct
supervisor *noun*	one who oversees or directs

List 5

commerce *noun*	trade on a large scale, as between countries
commercial *adjective*	of commerce or business; made or done for profit
commercial *noun*	a paid advertisement, often on television or radio
compete *verb*	to be in rivalry; contend
competent *adjective*	capable, fit; sufficient
competition *noun*	a contest, match
competitive *adjective*	liking competition
competitor *noun*	one who competes
export *noun*	anything exported
export *verb*	to send to another country or region for sale
exporter *noun*	one who exports
global *adjective*	worldwide
industrial *adjective*	having to do with industries or with the people working in industries
industrialize *verb*	to establish or develop industrialism; organize as an industry
industry *noun*	steady effort; any branch of productive, manufacturing enterprise; any large-scale business activity; the owners and managers of industry
international *adjective*	between or among nations; concerned with the relations between nations; of or for people in various nations
internationalize *verb*	to become international, develop international relations
market *noun*	a gathering of people for buying and selling things; a place where goods are sold; trade; demand (for goods, etc.)
market *verb*	to offer for sale; to sell
marketing plan *noun*	a plan to sell/promote goods
negotiate *verb*	to settle a transaction; to discuss with view a to reaching an agreement
negotiations *noun*	discussions toward an agreement
negotiator *noun*	one who negotiates agreements
promote *verb*	to raise to a higher rank or position; to further growth
promotion *noun*	a raise; increase in rank or position
promotional *adjective*	of or for growth in sales
trade *noun*	an occupation, skilled work; buying and selling; commerce
trade *verb*	to carry on a business; to exchange; barter

VOCABULARY EXERCISES ANSWERS

List 1

Exercise 1

1. advertise
2. apply
3. benefit
4. confide
5. employ
6. train

Exercise 2

1. advertisement
2. profit
3. confidential
4. beneficiary
5. experience
6. employ
7. position
8. trainee
9. question
10. personal

Exercise 3

1. application
2. interview
3. advertise
4. personal
5. employees
6. beneficial

Exercise 4

1. c
2. d
3. a
4. e
5. f
6. b

Exercise 5

1. employment
2. personalized
3. positions
4. training
5. confided
6. beneficially

List 2

Exercise 1

1. development
2. specification
3. acceptance
4. attendance
5. expectation

Exercise 2

1. at
2. to
3. for
4. with
5. of
6. to
7. for
8. around

Exercise 3

1. specifically
2. processing
3. developers
4. accepting
5. attendance
6. attending
7. networking
8. procedures

Exercise 4

1. networks
2. forms
3. processing
4. format
5. acceptable
6. expected
7. form
8. specifications
9. developing
10. facilitate
11. attendance

List 3

Exercise 1

1. accountant
2. consulting
3. documentation
4. interest
5. organization
6. payment
7. profitable
8. firm

Exercise 2

1. due/owing
2. cash/check
3. economize/plan
4. savings/loan
5. business/foundation
6. paper/birth certificate
7. advisor/mentor

Exercise 3

1. profitable
2. paid
3. organize
4. inventory
5. interests
6. firm
7. documented
8. consult
9. budget
10. account

Exercise 4

1. interesting
2. payable
3. profitability
4. interest
5. documentation
6. account
7. consultant

List 4

Exercise 1

1. arrangement
2. brochure
3. completely
4. fulfillment
5. managerial
6. overhead
7. rule
8. stamps
9. gift
10. propose

Exercise 2

1. e
2. d
3. a
4. f
5. b
6. c

Exercise 3

1. operating
2. posted
3. policy
4. management
5. complete
6. managerial
7. brochure
8. arranged
9. supervises

Exercise 4

1. c
2. d
3. a
4. e
5. b

List 5

Exercise 1

1. c
2. d
3. b
4. a
5. e

Exercise 2

1. domestic
2. farm
3. stall
4. criticize
5. loser

Exercise 3

1. c
2. a
3. f
4. e
5. d
6. b

Exercise 4

1. promoting
2. Industrial
3. industries
4. market
5. negotiated
6. internationally
7. compete
8. commercials
9. promotional

Exercise 5

1. competed
2. exporting
3. industrialized
4. has marketed
5. negotiated
6. to trade

PART FIVE

Practice Tests

PRACTICE TEST 1

 **Track 6**

Play Track 6 to hear the audio for Part I

SECTION 1—LISTENING COMPREHENSION

In the Listening Comprehension Section, you will have the chance to demonstrate how well you understand spoken English. The Listening Comprehension Section will take approximately 45 minutes. There are four parts, and directions are given for each part. You must mark your answers on the answer sheet. Do not write them in the test book.

PART I: PHOTOGRAPHS

Directions: For each question, you will hear four statements about the photograph in your test book. When you hear the statements, choose the one statement that best describes what you see in the photograph. Then, find the number of the question on your answer sheet and mark your answer. The statements will not be written in your test book and will be spoken just once.

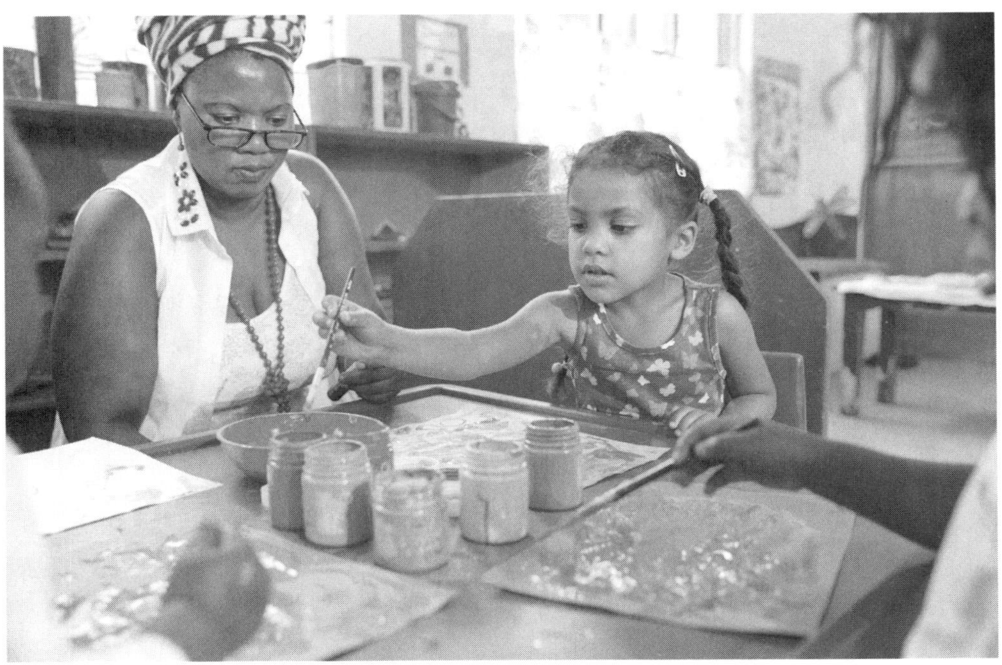

Now listen to the four statements.  

Choice (C), "She's painting a picture," best describes what you see in the picture. Therefore, you should fill in choice (C) in your answer sheet.

1. 

2. 

3. 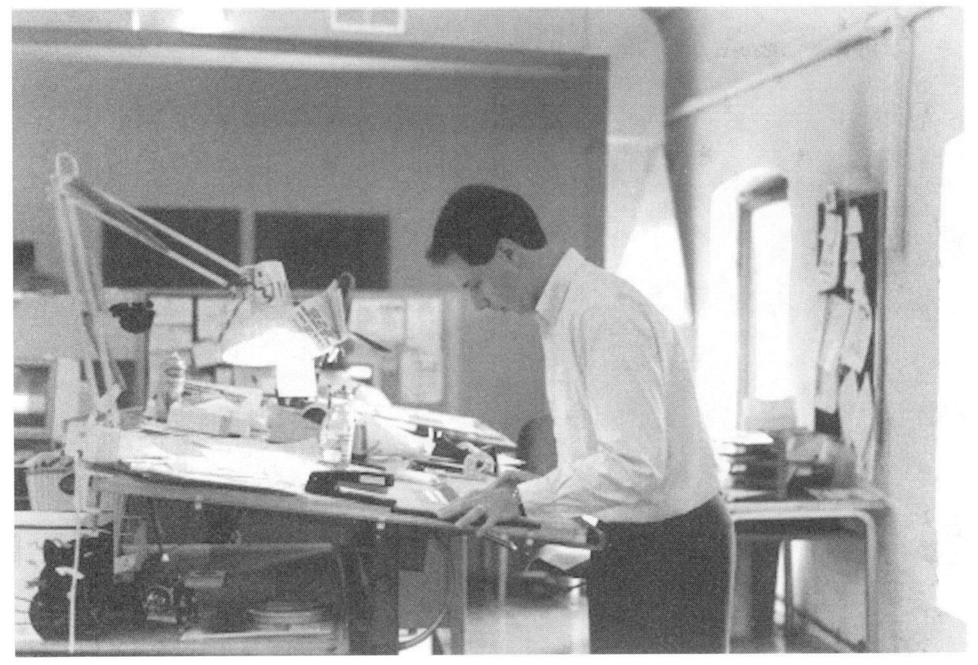

4. 

5.

6.

 **Track 7**

Play Track 7 to hear the audio for Part II

PART II: QUESTION-RESPONSE

Directions: You will hear a question or statement and three responses spoken in English. They will be spoken only once and will not be printed in your test book. Choose the best response to the question or statement and mark the letter on your answer sheet.

Listen to a sample question:

Sample Answer

Choice (B), "It's the second room on the left," best answers the question. Therefore, you should fill in choice (B) on your answer sheet.

7. Mark your answer on your answer sheet.

8. Mark your answer on your answer sheet.

9. Mark your answer on your answer sheet.

10. Mark your answer on your answer sheet.

11. Mark your answer on your answer sheet.

12. Mark your answer on your answer sheet.

13. Mark your answer on your answer sheet.

14. Mark your answer on your answer sheet.

15. Mark your answer on your answer sheet.

16. Mark your answer on your answer sheet.

17. Mark your answer on your answer sheet.

18. Mark your answer on your answer sheet.

19. Mark your answer on your answer sheet.

20. Mark your answer on your answer sheet.

21. Mark your answer on your answer sheet.

22. Mark your answer on your answer sheet.

23. Mark your answer on your answer sheet.

24. Mark your answer on your answer sheet.

25. Mark your answer on your answer sheet.

26. Mark your answer on your answer sheet.

27. Mark your answer on your answer sheet.

28. Mark your answer on your answer sheet.

29. Mark your answer on your answer sheet.

30. Mark your answer on your answer sheet.

31. Mark your answer on your answer sheet.

 **Track 8**

Play Track 8 to hear the audio for Part III

PART III: SHORT CONVERSATIONS

Directions: You will now hear a number of conversations between two or more people. You will be asked to answer three questions about what the speakers say. Select the best response to each question and mark the letter on your answer sheet. The conversations will be spoken only once and will not be printed in your test book.

32. What are the speakers planning?

A. a luncheon
B. a conference
C. a seminar
D. a dinner

33. How many people are expected to attend?

A. 50
B. 55
C. 60
D. 65

34. What has changed?

A. the time
B. the number of people
C. the venue
D. the catering company

---

35. What is described as a nightmare?

A. public transport
B. traffic
C. taxes
D. snow

36. Why is the woman angry?

A. She spent three hours getting to work.
B. She's late for a meeting.
C. One of her colleagues started work three weeks ago.
D. Mr. Wells is late again.

37. Where are the speakers?

A. at breakfast
B. in a meeting
C. in a cab
D. on an office trip

---

38. What has Mr. Jansen called about?

A. air tickets
B. travel insurance
C. a meeting confirmation
D. a hotel reservation

39. Where is Ms. Brody?

A. traveling abroad
B. at the travel agency
C. at home
D. in a meeting

40. What does Mr. Jansen need to know regarding Ms. Brody's trip?

A. where she plans to travel to
B. when she will arrive
C. which airline she is traveling with
D. what she will be presenting

---

41. Why has Serena been working late?

A. Her department is being audited.
B. She's been going to the gym.
C. They're preparing for a party.
D. She's accounting for the busy period.

42. What does Ahmed want the memory stick for?

- **A.** to store video testimonials
- **B.** to move files
- **C.** to increase his computer storage
- **D.** to backup files

43. Where is the memory stick?

- **A.** next to Ahmed
- **B.** on Serena's desk
- **C.** in Greta's office
- **D.** in a filing cabinet

---

44. Who are the speakers talking about?

- **A.** a painter
- **B.** a writer
- **C.** a sculptor
- **D.** an actor

45. Where are the speakers?

- **A.** New York
- **B.** London
- **C.** Paris
- **D.** Glasgow

46. What event do the speakers refer to?

- **A.** an exhibition
- **B.** a dinner
- **C.** a conference
- **D.** a play

---

47. Who are the men?

- **A.** electricians
- **B.** plumbers
- **C.** movers
- **D.** decorators

48. Where is the blue box?

- **A.** in the office
- **B.** in the kitchen
- **C.** in the bedroom
- **D.** in the truck

49. Where are the men working?

- **A.** in an office block
- **B.** in a factory
- **C.** in a house
- **D.** in a school

---

50. What are the speakers discussing?

- **A.** how they get to work
- **B.** which floors they work on
- **C.** where the main elevator is
- **D.** when the elevator will be fixed

51. Why is the lift out of order?

- **A.** The button panel is broken.
- **B.** They are building a new one.
- **C.** The machinery needs replacing.
- **D.** They're adding an 11th floor.

52. What will the man do?

- **A.** show the woman an alternative elevator
- **B.** help the woman take the crates up the stairs
- **C.** unpack the crates for the woman
- **D.** find someone from maintenance to fix the elevator

---

53. Why is Colleen Rankin in Australia?

- **A.** She works there.
- **B.** She is on vacation there.
- **C.** She is on a business trip here.
- **D.** She has retired there.

GO ON TO THE NEXT PAGE.

54. When will the woman return from Australia?

A. Thursday
B. Friday
C. Saturday
D. Sunday

55. Who is the man in relation to the woman?

A. her boss
B. her employee
C. her customer
D. her travel agent

---

56. What goods are the speakers talking about?

A. newspapers
B. office equipment
C. clothes
D. electrical appliances

57. Where has the shipment come from?

A. Shanghai
B. Dublin
C. Dubai
D. Hong Kong

58. What has caused the delay?

A. payment problems
B. bad weather
C. customs issues
D. manufacturing problems

---

59. What are the speakers talking about?

A. a desktop computer
B. a printer
C. a laptop computer
D. a scanner

60. What does the special offer include?

A. a rebate
B. extra user support
C. an extended warranty
D. extra equipment

61. What does the man ask for?

A. a reduction in price
B. a catalog
C. a product demonstration
D. a business card

---

62. What do the speakers imply about the current furniture?

A. It should be replaced.
B. They don't want it to change.
C. They are not fashionable anymore.
D. The time to buy new chairs has passed.

63. Look at the graphic below. Which area does the man think the kitchen should be in?

A. 1
B. 2
C. 3
D. 4

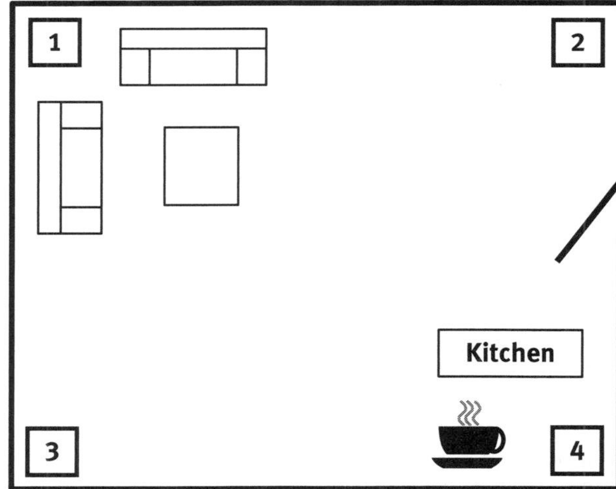

64. What does the woman suggest?

A. She should talk to Ricardo.
B. The feedback given by the man will not be helpful.
C. The redesign team should be more open to ideas.
D. The man should discuss an alteration with the redesign team.

65. What does the woman ask the man?

A. how much they can spend
B. when to have the staff party
C. if he's checked the prices
D. where to hold the party

66. Why does the woman say, "That's annoying"?

A. He hasn't chosen a date.
B. His team can't make Saturday.
C. She strongly disagrees.
D. The prices vary for each night.

67. Look at the graphic below. Which night will they book the venue for?

A. Monday
B. Thursday
C. Friday
D. Saturday

Booking Fees		
Monday - Wednesday	Thursday - Friday	Saturday - Sunday
$650	$750	$950

68. What are the speakers most likely to be doing?

A. scheduling a staff party
B. interviewing potential staff
C. planning to work overtime
D. arranging a presentation with investors

69. Why does the man say "Of course"?

A. He is confirming that he likes work on Sunday.
B. He forgot that it would be inappropriate to schedule the call at the weekend.
C. He already knew that the call should be over the weekend.
D. He forgot that Vikesh likes to work on Saturday and Sunday

70. Look at the graphic below. On which day will they schedule the meeting?

A. Tuesday
B. Thursday
C. Friday
D. Saturday

	Leroy	Rhonda
Monday		
Tuesday		
Wednesday		
Thursday		
Friday		
Saturday		
Sunday		

 **Track 9**

Play Track 9 to hear the audio for Part IV

PART IV: SHORT TALKS

Directions: You will now hear some short talks given by a single speaker. You will be asked to answer three questions about what the speaker says in each talk. Select the best response to each question and mark the letter (A), (B), (C), or (D) on your answer sheet. The talks will be spoken only once and will not be printed in your test book.

71. What event will occur on May 28th?

- **A.** a speech
- **B.** a play
- **C.** a ballet
- **D.** a concert

72. How much is the cheapest ticket without the discount?

- **A.** $3
- **B.** $8
- **C.** $13
- **D.** $18

73. Where can people buy tickets?

- **A.** in local stores
- **B.** at the student union office
- **C.** on the internet
- **D.** from the speaker

---

74. What is Mr. Park's title?

- **A.** head chef
- **B.** head waiter
- **C.** vice president
- **D.** customer service representative

75. What will Mr. Park mainly focus on this year?

- **A.** food presentation
- **B.** waiters
- **C.** menu items
- **D.** customer service

76. What does the speaker want the employees to do?

- **A.** Contact Mr. Park directly.
- **B.** Ask questions after the talk.
- **C.** Wear their uniforms.
- **D.** Continue to treat customers well.

---

77. Where is this introduction taking place?

- **A.** at a board of directors meeting
- **B.** at a store managers meeting
- **C.** at a retirement dinner
- **D.** at a shareholders meeting

78. What is one of Mr. Nazar's accomplishments?

- **A.** strengthening domestic sales
- **B.** directing company policy
- **C.** increasing production
- **D.** reducing overhead

79. What is one of Mr. Nazar's goals in his new role?

- **A.** merging operations
- **B.** retraining staff
- **C.** reducing expenses
- **D.** expanding international sales

---

80. Where is it expected to rain?

- **A.** Zurich
- **B.** southeastern Switzerland
- **C.** the northern valleys
- **D.** Geneva

81. Look at the graphic. Which area shows the weather forecast for the Central Valley?

A. Area A
B. Area B
C. Area C
D. Area D

	A.M.	P.M.	Temperatures
Area A			9–12°C
Area B			2–5°C
Area C			12–18°C
Area D			5–9°C

82. Where has snow already been reported?

A. the suburbs of Zurich
B. along the Italian-Austrian border
C. in the southern mountains
D. along the French border

83. What did Mr. Hausman do?

A. published a book
B. wrote the speech
C. opened a bank
D. introduced the speaker

84. What does the woman mean when she says, "As we are aware"?

A. The changes have been happening for a long time.
B. The presenters all knew about the changes before they happened.
C. The audience is listening carefully to the talk.
D. The audience is familiar with the changes.

85. What is this talk mainly about?

A. regulating capital markets
B. the history of industry management
C. financial services and business planning
D. banking changes in the past 20 years

86. What kind of company does the speaker work for?

A. travel agency
B. construction company
C. hotel chain
D. customer service company

87. Why does the speaker say, "Very briefly"?

A. He wants to talk through something quickly.
B. They will have a short break.
C. He wants to keep questions to a minimum.
D. The improvements will not take long.

88. What does the speaker ask the board of directors to make available?

A. a team of interior designers
B. new furniture for the lobbies
C. money to upgrade the facilities
D. customer service goals

89. What is the purpose of this announcement?

A. to conclude the evening's program
B. to introduce an guest
C. to advertise a product
D. to begin the evening's program

90. Who will be the guest next week?

A. a corporate vice president
B. Dr. McDermott
C. an employee motivation expert
D. Peter Thompson

91. What topic was probably discussed on the program?

A. crisis management
B. managing change
C. inspiring workers
D. contemporary technology

---

92. What is the speaker doing?

A. announcing a meeting
B. summarizing a previous meeting
C. beginning a meeting
D. interrupting a meeting

93. How many agenda items are there?

A. 3
B. 4
C. 5
D. 6

94. Look at the graphic. When will they discuss policy changes?

A. 13:05
B. 13:15
C. 13:35
D. 13:50

Time	Topic
13:00–13:05	summary
13:05–13:15	
13:15–13:35	
13:35–13:50	project planning
13:50–14:00	

---

95. Who is speaking?

A. captain of the flight
B. lead flight attendant
C. member of the ground staff
D. copilot

96. Where is the flight going?

A. Edinburgh
B. Manchester
C. Liverpool
D. London

97. What delayed the flight?

A. a mechanical problem
B. a late arriving flight
C. weather conditions
D. a security alert

---

98. What is the talk mainly about?

A. a piece of research
B. annual sales figures
C. a proposal for a new hotel
D. management techniques

99. What is the speaker's main interest?

A. The effects of tourism
B. The cost of vacation packages
C. How to organize hotels
D. The demand for tourism

100. What was measured?

A. money spent
B. pollution
C. tourist numbers
D. money earned

Stop! This is the end of the Listening Comprehension Section of the exam. Turn to Part V.

You will have one hour and 15 minutes to complete Parts V, VI, and VII of the exam.

SECTION 2—READING COMPREHENSION

In the Reading Comprehension Section, you will read a variety of texts and answer different types of questions. The Reading Comprehension Section will last 75 minutes. There are three parts, and directions are given for each part. You are encouraged to answer as many questions as possible within the allotted time. Mark your answers on the separate answer sheet. Do no write them in the test book.

PART V: INCOMPLETE SENTENCES

Directions: A word or phrase is missing in the following sentences. Four answer choices are given below each of the sentences. Choose the best answer to complete the sentence. Then mark the letter on your answer sheet.

101. Mr Griffin is well known for saying ________ comes to his mind.

A. anything
B. everyone
C. whatever
D. anymore

102. All visitors must be ________ by a security officer while they are on-site.

A. detected
B. accompanied
C. revised
D. arrested

103. The factory shuts down every August for ________.

A. maintenance
B. maintain
C. maintained
D. maintainer

104. Mr. Masuyama has excelled in his new position as senior account executive;________, he deserves a raise.

A. yet
B. or
C. although
D. thus

105. Though Mr. Ramirez is not a citizen of the United States, he has had to pay U.S. income taxes ________.

A. moreover
B. anyway
C. anyhow
D. since

106. Suzko Industries has hired additional inspectors to ensure that the highest production quality is ________.

A. achieve
B. achiever
C. achievement
D. achieved

107. For questions concerning any of the policies in this handbook, please consult ________ the head of your department.

A. at
B. with
C. about
D. for

108. During the seminar, Ms. Williams taught ________ how to calculate the annual return on an investment.

A. they
B. their
C. them
D. themselves

109. Customers have three weeks ________ report a credit dispute.

A. to
B. until
C. before
D. so

110. Dr. Allan forecasts that world demand for ________ ceramics will increase by 8 percent next year.

A. advance
B. advanced
C. advancing
D. advancement

111. Though he received the fax early Monday morning, Mr. Medina waited until Friday to ________.

A. rely
B. delay
C. relay
D. reply

112. The directors will go ________ the street to the main office to meet the department managers.

A. across
B. by
C. of
D. against

113. As economic links between the two regions ________, the flexibility of the international banking sector will be tested.

A. strong
B. strength
C. strengthen
D. stronger

114. Please send the ________ documents instead of photocopies.

A. original
B. originate
C. origin
D. originality

115. To comply with the new environmental regulations, the power plant design will need to be drastically ________.

A. alternated
B. avoided
C. altered
D. attached

116. The one ________ that sets the company apart is its self-directed team approach to management of operations.

A. element
B. elemental
C. elements
D. elementary

117. The luncheon was held to honor the senior employees who will be retiring ________ June.

A. at
B. in
C. among
D. on

118. The annual percentage rate for purchases may ________ from month to month.

A. vary
B. variety
C. various
D. varied

119. Mr. Teska ________ the weaknesses in the proposal.

A. entered into
B. joined with
C. signed up
D. pointed out

120. I support Mr. Lin's goals of more efficient management, but I object to the methods proposed to achieve ________ goals.

A. those
B. there
C. them
D. their

121. Applicants must submit two letters ________.

A. refer
B. of reference
C. refers to
D. a referred

122. Parking is limited to hotel guests, and ________ will be towed.

A. violated
B. violate
C. violating
D. violators

123. Mr. Loder was able to hand out most of the ________ items that we brought to the trade show.

A. promotional
B. promoted
C. promote
D. promotes

124. If you are late for the meeting, please enter the boardroom________.

A. quieter
B. quietly
C. quietest
D. quiet

125. Architect Jon Rushmore ________ a huge foyer with a large marble staircase.

A. enlightens
B. entrusts
C. envisions
D. enlists

126. When facing challenges in the workplace, it is often best to prioritize tasks to put them in________.

A. confirmation
B. perspective
C. satisfaction
D. reinforcement

127. Mr. Hamilton received a promotion ________ he developed the most successful advertising campaign of the year.

A. though

B. while

C. because

D. due

128. The designers are coming on Friday morning ________ the floors for new carpeting.

A. to measure

B. is measured

C. a measurement

D. for measurable

129. The human resources team has decided on a new ________ to hiring staff in the sales department.

A. access

B. arrival

C. commitment

D. approach

130. Many workers report that they prefer being alone at the office because they can ________ more work done.

A. get

B. be

C. do

D. go

PART VI: TEXT COMPLETION

Directions: Read the texts found in the following pages. A word or phrase is missing in the sentences below the text. Four answer choices are given below each of the sentences. Choose the best answer to complete the sentence. Then mark the letter on your answer sheet.

Questions 131–134 refer to the following stimulus.

From:	Margaret Kim <m.kim@kr_consulting.com.
To:	Susan Parker <s_parker@parkerdesigns.com>
CC:	Kevin Rutland <k.rtuland@kr_consulting.com>
Date:	October 10th, 2016 11:14:21 A.M.
Subject:	Finally getting back to you...

Dear Susan,

So sorry that I have not been able to reply to your message earlier, but this really is the first ________ (131) I've had in a week to sit down and respond to emails. I don't know if I told you, but last week we had the auditors visit the office, and so I'm sure you can imagine how busy we were. Anyway, I've had a look at the plans you sent and I'm really excited by them. You really seem to have understood what we are looking for. Kevin Rutland has also taken a look at them and is ________ (132) impressed. There are a number of things that we'd like to discuss with you, and we think it's best if you come to our office here in Vermont. Please let us know the most ________ (133) date for you. Obviously we will cover travel and accommodation. ________ (134)

Regards,

Margaret

131. **A.** opening
B. opportunity
C. prospect
D. occurrence

132. **A.** just as
B. the same
C. identically
D. alike

133. **A.** suited
B. convenient
C. nicely
D. fitted

134. **A.** Looking forward to hearing from you soon.
B. Thanks for getting back to me so quickly.
C. See you in Vermont next Thursday.
D. Please do not contact me again.

Questions 135–138 refer to the following stimulus.

> **PhotoMatic**
>
> Specialists in professional quality pre-owned and refurbished photographic equipment.
>
> **WANTED**
>
> We urgently ______ (135) your cameras, lenses, cases, and other accessories. We have customers all over North America, Europe, and beyond searching for secondhand professional equipment ______ (136) good condition. We are also interested in telescopes, binoculars, and collectable vintage cameras.
>
> **Top Prices Paid**
>
> We will buy for cash directly but are also happy to sell on your behalf on a commission ______ (137). We can arrange to collect from you, or you can send directly to your nearest PhotoMatic outlet with shipping and handling charges covered by us. For more details, please contact us at (212) 333-4444, call your nearest PhotoMatic outlet, ______ (138)

135. **A.** ask
B. require
C. demand
D. invite

136. **A.** on
B. at
C. of
D. in

137. **A.** way
B. basis
C. kind
D. means

138. **A.** thank you for responding to the survey.
B. or visit us online at www.photomatic.com.
C. as we are not contactable by phone during the weekdays.
D. which can be purchased from our store.

Questions 139–142 refer to the following stimulus.

NINDO LIMITED WARRANTY

THIS WARRANTY IS VALID ONLY FOR PRODUCTS PURCHASED IN EUROPE

______
139

This product is warranted to the original ______ (140) to be free from defects of quality at the time of purchase and for a period of 12 months after the date of purchase. If, during the warranty period, your product is found to be defective, the product will be repaired using NINDO replacement parts, ______ (141) the product will be replaced with the same or similar model within a reasonable period of time. To obtain these warranty services, you must produce this card and proof of purchase in the form of a ______ (142) sales receipt.

139. **A.** For further warranty information, visit www.nindotech.com/fr/warranty.
B. Once you have submitted your claim, please allow 4–5 working days for us to ship your replacement.
C. For other countries, please contact the store where purchased.
D. This is your final warning before eviction.

140. **A.** purchaser
B. card
C. seller
D. store

141. **A.** so
B. and
C. or
D. too

142. **A.** buying
B. repaired
C. defective
D. valid

Questions 143–146 refer to the following stimulus.

> With this classic text, Bob Bingley has done more to alter views in *Change Management* than any other author before or since. He explains the main concepts behind the management of change with clarity, originality, and humor. ___(143)___ deals with change in all its aspects and from the viewpoint of all those that ___(144)___ by change. The book looks at what change means for both large-scale and small-scale organizations. Bingley successfully shows that, ___(145)___ the right techniques and a logical approach, even the most sweeping changes can be implemented without disruption. ___(146)___ and several new chapters on the impact of technology on the management of change.

143. **A.** She
B. He
C. This
D. That

144. **A.** are affected
B. affected
C. is affected
D. have affected

145. **A.** gives
B. he gave
C. to give
D. given

146. **A.** For further information, contact us weekdays 9:00 A.M.–5:00 P.M. on (020) 4423 3456
B. Bob Bingley lives in Oxford with his wife, fellow writer,
C. *The Glorina Standard* called it 'an unforgettable read'
D. This new edition includes a preface by the author

PART VII: READING COMPREHENSION

Directions: In this part, you will read a selection of text, such as magazine or newspaper articles, letters, or advertisements. Each text is followed by several questions. Select the best answer for each question and mark the letter on your answer sheet.

Questions 147–148 refer to the following stimulus.

Abarcorporation Performance Record

	Year 3	Year 2	Year 1
Sales	$679,823	$379,722	$489,357
Net Income	$14,805	$19,977	$35,465
Earnings per Share	$0.75	$1.04	$1.89
Shareholders Equity	$275,242	$257,515	$245,006
Return on Equity (1)	5.3%	7.8%	14.5%

(1) Defined as net income divided by shareholder equity, minus extraordinary items. (Periods listed are years ending Dec. 31.)

147. How much money did each share make in Year 2?

- **A.** $1.04
- **B.** $14.50
- **C.** $14,805
- **D.** $379,722

148. What must be subtracted to determine Return on Equity?

- **A.** extraordinary items
- **B.** net income
- **C.** shareholders equity
- **D.** earnings per share

Questions 149–151 refer to the following stimulus.

Laser Printers

— [1] — Laser printers use xerographic technology similar to that used in photocopiers. They can reproduce an almost limitless variety of type forms and sizes, as well as complex graphics. — [2] — Images are electronically created on a light-sensitive drum, usually with a scanning laser. Powdered toner adheres to areas where light touches the drum and then transfers to a sheet of paper, which is briefly heated to fuse the toner to the paper permanently. — [3] — A typical laser printer can print 20 color pages a minute, compared to 12 for an ink-jet printer; older dot-matrix printers can take 45 seconds to print a single page. When they were first introduced, laser printers typically cost over a thousand dollars. Now prices have dropped to only a few hundred, at most. — [4] —

149. What is implied as an advantage of laser printers?

A. speed
B. ease of use
C. low ink costs
D. superior printing quality

150. According to the passage, how much did early laser printers cost?

A. a few hundred dollars
B. approximately $500
C. $500–$700
D. over $1,000

151. In which of the positions marked [1], [2], [3], or [4] does the following sentence best belong?
"They operate very quickly"

A. [1]
B. [2]
C. [3]
D. [4]

Questions 152–153 refer to the following stimulus.

The Growing Economy Fund

May 12, 2016

Dear Investor:

Last week, the Board of Trustees of The Growing Economy Fund declared a 100% share dividend. This has the same effect as a 2-for-1 share split. This transaction will occur Thursday, May 24, to shareholders of record at the close of business on Wednesday, May 23.

As a result of this transaction, the number of shares you owned before the transaction will be doubled, while the net asset value will be reduced by half. The reduced net asset value makes it easier financially for people who prefer to purchase shares of the fund in 100-share increments. This does not alter the total value of your Growing Economy Fund investment. It simply means that you will own twice the number of shares at half the price per share.

If you have any questions, please avail yourself our toll-free information number. Registered brokers are available 24 hours a day.

Yours truly,

Alexandria Gadbois

Alexandria Gadbois

Secretary for the Board of Trustees

The Growing Economy Fund

152. When will the transaction take effect?

- **A.** May 23
- **B.** May 24
- **C.** December 31
- **D.** January 1

153. What will happen to shares of the fund?

- **A.** They will be reduced to half their original number.
- **B.** They will double in number.
- **C.** They will be offered for sale at a lower price.
- **D.** They will be available to the public for the first time.

Questions 154–156 refer to the following stimulus.

SALES FORECASTS

— [1] — Sales forecasts should be based on prices that adequately consider the market for the product, and its value to the customer versus competitive products in the marketplace.

— [2] — Investors sense a serious danger signal when an entrepreneur suggests there is no competition for his or her product or service. — [3] — The product may be unique but there are probably other products that function similarly.

If so, the pricing has to be evaluated in light of those products.

— [4] — The price should produce a return sufficient to cover the level of expenses typical for a company in that industry. In high-technology businesses, for example, higher gross margins generally are needed to provide for the higher costs of research and development, as well as marketing and distribution.

154. In which of the positions marked [1], [2], [3], or [4] does the following sentence best belong?
"Pricing should also reflect these considerations."

- **A.** [1]
- **B.** [2]
- **C.** [3]
- **D.** [4]

155. The term a *return* as used in line 9 of the passage is closest in meaning to

- **A.** a profit.
- **B.** come back.
- **C.** an expense.
- **D.** departure.

156. What is implied about high-technology businesses?

- **A.** Their value to customers is difficult to measure.
- **B.** Their product prices are more competitive.
- **C.** Their sales are lower than other industries.
- **D.** Their research and development costs are high.

Questions 157–159 refer to the following stimulus.

CREDIT APPLICATION FORM

1. Background

Name: Sarah P. Taylor **Date of Birth:** Feb. 25, 1985

Highest Educational Degree: Master's **# of Dependents/Ages:** 2 (Ages 3 & 5)

2. Employment and Income

Name of Company: Binational Commission **Position:** Director **Years at Job:** 4

Address: 5 Ahmed El-Ali Street, Alexandria, EGYPT **Years at Present Address:** 2

Telephone: 842-5001 **Monthly Wage Income:** $3,500

Other Monthly Income: $1,500 **Source of other Income:** Trust Annuity

3. Credit References

Bank: National Bank of Egypt **Account Number:** 34-55090

Account Type: Checking **Balance:** $12,000 **Credit Card(s):** None

Account Number(s): N/A **Balance:** N/A

Other Debt: (Type) Car Loan **Loan Institution:** National Bank of Egypt

Balance: $5,500

157. How many years has the applicant worked for the Binational Commission?

A. 1
B. 2
C. 3
D. 4

158. How many sources of income does the applicant have?

A. 1
B. 2
C. 3
D. 4

159. How much money does the applicant owe?

A. $1,500
B. $3,500
C. $5,500
D. $12,000

Questions 160–162 refer to the following stimulus.

WARRANTY INFORMATION

For coverage under this limited warranty, proof of the date and place of purchase must be submitted. The easiest way to do this is to complete the attached warranty card and mail it now.

If warranty service is needed, contact our customer service department at the address or phone number below. If defects appear under normal use, Umbrellas Unlimited will replace the product free of charge.

This warranty does not apply to damage that has been caused by customer abuse. Also, present color technology does not enable us to warrant against color fading over time. We suggest that the golf umbrella be stored away from direct sunlight when not in use.

This warranty is good for three years. Umbrellas Unlimited will not, under any circumstances, be liable for damage caused by misuse of any product. This warranty is not applicable outside the USA.

160. What must a customer do to activate the warranty?

- **A.** complete the attached warranty card
- **B.** provide proof of purchase
- **C.** register online
- **D.** call the customer service department

161. What is meant by the phrase *liable for damage* in the text?

- **A.** intentional damage
- **B.** guaranteed to fix
- **C.** likely to stop working
- **D.** responsible for breaking

162. What is NOT true about the company's warranty?

- **A.** It does not cover damage due to customer abuse.
- **B.** It is in effect for three years.
- **C.** It is honored worldwide.
- **D.** It promises replacement of defective products.

Questions 163–166 refer to the following stimulus.

Subjective Prices Versus and Objective Prices

There are two ways to price items: subjectively and objectively.

A subjectively priced item is based either on what the seller perceives it is worth or what the seller thinks someone will pay for it. Generally these items have an aesthetic, rather than a utilitarian, value. Retailers of subjectively priced items include artists, some highly skilled craftspeople, and sellers of antiques and collectibles. An objectively priced item, on the other hand, is priced according to some concrete formula based on its actual cost to produce.

Almost all traditional retailers, from the corner grocer to the new car dealer, sell objectively priced items.

When buying a subjectively priced item, first analyze your needs and weigh your options. This is accomplished by answering three questions: *What do I want? Is it worth my money?* and *Is it important to me?*

163. According to the passage, how do subjectively and objectively priced items differ?

- **A.** Objectively priced items are usually more expensive.
- **B.** Subjectively priced items have an aesthetic value.
- **C.** Objectively priced items are less utilitarian.
- **D.** Subjectively priced items are more common.

164. What is implied about antiques?

- **A.** They are priced subjectively.
- **B.** They were probably made by skilled craftspeople.
- **C.** They are sometimes overpriced.
- **D.** Their prices go up and down.

165. What can be inferred about most traditional retailers?

- **A.** They set their prices based on what they perceive consumers will pay.
- **B.** They set prices using a formula based on the cost to produce their goods.
- **C.** They tend to make higher profits than nontraditional retailers.
- **D.** They tend to analyze the needs of their customers.

166. The word *weigh* as used in line 10 of the passage is closest in meaning to the word

- **A.** decide.
- **B.** count.
- **C.** evaluate.
- **D.** reduce.

Questions 167–170 refer to the following stimulus.

High pressure moving across northern Mexico will funnel cooler air down the Northwest Coast. Temperatures will be at least 3 to 6 degrees lower throughout Baja California, and Sonora. The cooler air will not reach the Southwest, where temperatures will soar past 32, some 6 degrees above normal. Because of low humidity and a stable atmosphere, afternoon thunderstorms are unlikely. Dry conditions will also persist across Durango.

A low-pressure system will move slowly east through the northeastern region of Mexico today, spreading showers and heavy thunderstorms across Coahuila and Nuevo Leon. Winds from the north behind this system will dislodge a pool of cold air over Texas. The leading edge of this chilled air will reach Monterrey later today, but the core of the cold air will not arrive until midweek. A cold front trailing this low-pressure system will push showers and thunderstorms across the Chihuahua and Durango later today. Showers may form as far west as the eastern slopes of the Sierra Madre.

167. What conditions will northwestern Mexico experience?

A. cool air

B. rain

C. low humidity

D. dry conditions

168. Where will temperatures be higher than usual?

A. Baja California

B. Sonora

C. the Southwest

D. the northeastern region

169. When will the majority of the cold air from Texas reach Monterrey?

A. that morning

B. later that afternoon

C. the next day

D. midweek

170. What will the cold front cause?

A. dry air

B. strong winds

C. rainstorms

D. snow

Questions 171–175 refer to the following stimulus.

> **Company Profile: Synco Corporation**
>
> The Synco Corporation ranks among the leading international manufacturers of tires and industrial products made from rubber and plastics. Last year, it was first in tire sales in Germany, second in Europe, and fourth worldwide.
>
> Despite last year's severe recession, lower exchange rates, and steep drops in automotive sales, Synco recorded a net income of 50 million euros on sales of 10 billion euros, an all-time high. A dividend of 3 million euros is planned.
>
> Extensive measures to streamline production resources, cut costs, and create new products have substantially enhanced Synco earnings potential for next year and beyond. A public offering of new stock will be made July 1.

171. Who is the report probably written for?

- **A.** Synco administrators
- **B.** prospective investors
- **C.** potential suppliers
- **D.** Synco competitors

172. What is NOT mentioned about Synco?

- **A.** Its position for plastics sales
- **B.** Its rankings for tire sales
- **C.** Its measures to improve performance
- **D.** Its plans for paying dividends

173. What were Synco's total sales in the previous year?

- **A.** 3 million euros
- **B.** 50 million euros
- **C.** 1 billion euros
- **D.** 10 billion euros

174. What is implied about automotive sales in the previous year?

- **A.** Their decline should have decreased Synco's revenues.
- **B.** Their increase is responsible for Synco's record sales.
- **C.** They reached an all-time high.
- **D.** They were lower than expected.

175. What is expected for Synco?

- **A.** Its new products will be cheaper.
- **B.** Its earnings will grow.
- **C.** It will expand its market share.
- **D.** Its stock price will remain high.

Questions 176–180 refer to the following stimulus.

The International Employment Newsletter

No matter where your career is headed, we can help to identify the best direction for you. The International Employment Newsletter is written for all professionally minded people seeking a new position or hoping to improve their current status. Each issue contains hundreds of regional, national, and international job opportunities. In addition, we offer expert career advice, such as letter and résumé writing for beginning job seekers, and negotiating and networking strategies for experienced professionals.

Regardless of where you are with your career, The International Employment Newsletter can help you.

Look for us at your local newsstand or subscribe today for convenient home delivery.

The International Employment Newsletter
1644 Madison Avenue
New York, NY 10017

December 3rd, 2016

Elizabeth Ralls

245 5th Avenue

New York, NY 10001

Dear Ms. Ralls,

Thank you for your subscription to *The International Employment Newsletter*. Your subscription is for the period January to June. However, should you be interested in extending your subscription to a full 12 months, bear in mind that we are currently making the following special offer: take out a 12-month subscription before the end of January and you will receive a 10 percent discount. If you are interested, please complete the form on the reverse of this letter and return it in the enclosed postage-paid envelope.

Remember that you can cancel your subscription at any time and we will be happy to refund your remaining balance. You'll only pay for copies of *The International Employment Newsletter* that you have actually received—no more.

Sincerely,
Heinrich Gill
Sales Manager

176. What service is offered by *The International Employment Newsletter*?

A. translation and interpretation
B. preparation for job interviews
C. résumé preparation
D. work visa applications

177. What is learned about *The International Employment Newsletter*?

A. It is available only by subscription.
B. It is published every two weeks.
C. It can be read on the Internet.
D. It can be purchased at newsstands.

178. How long is Ms. Ralls's current subscription?

A. 3 months
B. 6 months
C. 1 year
D. 2 years

179. What is available to Ms. Ralls until the end of January?

A. a book
B. a discount
C. a special edition
D. a class

180. What has been included with the letter?

A. a coupon
B. a survey form
C. a sample issue
D. an envelope

GO ON TO THE NEXT PAGE.

Questions 181–185 refer to the following poster and email.

The Piano Tuners' Guild of Northern Ireland invites you to

The 10th PTGNI Convention

Friday 17th to Saturday 18th March 2017

Bay View Hotel, Portrush, County Antrim

Registration forms and further details available from:

www.ptgni.org/resgistration.html

Highlights

Opening plenary session: Friday 9:00 A.M.
Derrick Gill, UK

As chairperson of the PTGNI, Derrick opens the 10th convention and welcomes delegates to what promises to be a stimulating and enjoyable weekend.

Keynote presentation: The Apprenticeship Crisis Friday 11:00 A.M.
James Townsend, USA

We're proud to be able to welcome Mr. Townsend, president of the North American Association of Piano Technicians, on his second appearance at a PTGNI convention. Mr. Townsend's thought-provoking talk concentrates on the key problems facing the profession worldwide: the lack of trainee technicians entering the field and on what can be done to halt the drain.

Hybrid Tuning Saturday 10:30 A.M.
Randy Wilson, USA

Once thought of as mutually exclusive, traditional aural tuning and high-tech digital tuning techniques can in fact be used together. Mr. Wilson will show how tradition and technology can come to the aid of the modern tuner. The session will be full of useful tips on how the two techniques can complement each other, and on how to avoid common pitfalls.

RayTone RT50—Next-generation Tuning Saturday 3:00 P.M.
Gunter Kliebermann, Germany

We are very happy to welcome Mr. Kliebermann to this year's convention. His presentation introduces the long-awaited RayTone RT50. He will discuss the key improvements of the RT50 over its predecessor, the RT40—now standard equipment for many technicians. Mr. Kliebermann's session also includes demonstrations of many of the "hidden" features of the RT series. We are grateful to RayTone for their support in making this presentation possible.

Note: Rooms for attendees are available at the Bay View Hotel and at the Clear Sands Hotel. Contact them directly to make reservations.

To: Mike Stern <m_stern@ptgni.org>

From: Greg Watts <g_watts@ptgni.org>

Date: Friday, January 27th, 2017

Subject: Convention Posters

Mike

Just a quick note to say that the posters for the convention have come from the printers. They look great, but the problem is that in the title it says this is our tenth convention, when in fact it's our eleventh. It's too late to do anything about it now—it will take a week to have them reprinted, and we don't have time—we're already running late on distributing these. Besides, I'm sure most people won't even notice. If they do, we'll just have to joke about it. What else can we do?

The posters have been delivered to our office, so we'll need to organize distribution. Speak to you on Monday.

Greg

181. What is NOT mentioned in the notice?

A. which hotels attendees can stay at
B. what time the talks are scheduled
C. how much the convention costs to attend
D. how to get further information about the convention

182. Whose presentation is about a new piece of equipment?

A. Gunter Kliebermann's
B. Randy Wilson's
C. James Townsend's
D. Derrick Gill's

183. What is the keynote presentation about?

A. how to train new technicians
B. the difficulties of being an apprentice
C. the future of the piano technician profession
D. how the tuning profession is different in the United States

184. What can be inferred about Greg and Mike?

A. They are training to be piano tuners.
B. They will present at the convention.
C. They organize the convention.
D. They are printers.

185. What is wrong with the posters?

A. the dates
B. the size
C. the colors
D. the title

Questions 186–190 refer to the following two emails and price list.

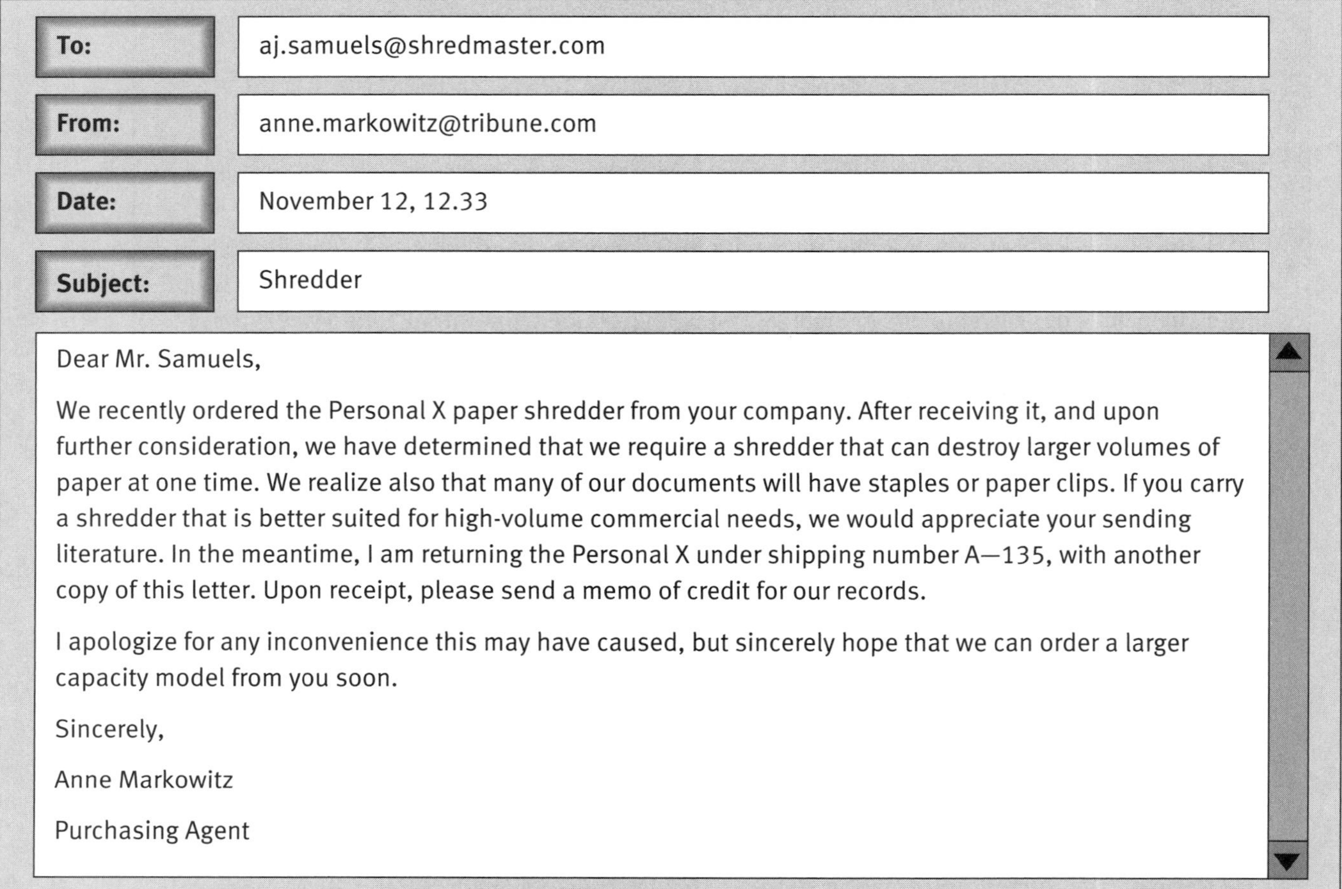

To:	aj.samuels@shredmaster.com
From:	anne.markowitz@tribune.com
Date:	November 12, 12.33
Subject:	Shredder

Dear Mr. Samuels,

We recently ordered the Personal X paper shredder from your company. After receiving it, and upon further consideration, we have determined that we require a shredder that can destroy larger volumes of paper at one time. We realize also that many of our documents will have staples or paper clips. If you carry a shredder that is better suited for high-volume commercial needs, we would appreciate your sending literature. In the meantime, I am returning the Personal X under shipping number A—135, with another copy of this letter. Upon receipt, please send a memo of credit for our records.

I apologize for any inconvenience this may have caused, but sincerely hope that we can order a larger capacity model from you soon.

Sincerely,

Anne Markowitz

Purchasing Agent

To:	k.wheeler@tibs.com
From:	d.scrivner@tibs.com
Date:	April 15th, 2017 2:24:18 P.M.
Subject:	profit sharing

Paul,

A customer has just returned a Personal X shredder because it's not heavy duty enough for their needs.

They've asked if we have another model that can cope with larger volumes of paper and with staples as well. I think what they really need is the Office X, but I'm not sure if we have any in stock. Could you check? Also, can you please send her a brochure and give a quote stating our current price for the Office X?

I've scanned the original message and attached it to this email.

Thanks

Gina

Product	Price	Description
Personal X	$35.00	for occasional use at home
Office X	$65.00	for office use, can shred thick card and up to 50 sheets of paper in one go. Suitable for 24/7 use
Heavy X	$120.00	for plastics, metals and woods. Shreds heavy duty items for warehouse security and recycling
Solar X	$82.00	solar paneled shredder with capacities comparable to the Personal X model.

186. Why has the paper shredder been returned?

A. It does not suit the customer's needs.

B. It is too expensive.

C. It is broken.

D. It is not what the customer ordered.

187. Which of the following is probably one of Anne Markowitz's duties?

A. researching industry trends

B. handling customer complaints

C. buying supplies for her company

D. preparing her company's brochures

188. What can be inferred about the Personal X?

A. It cannot handle documents with staples.

B. It is no longer in stock.

C. It can shred credit cards and CDs.

D. It can shed up to seven pages at one time.

189. What does Gina Andrews want to know?

A. which replacement model to recommend

B. which models are currently in stock

C. where to send the Office X

D. where the invoice should be sent

190. How much does the shredder Gina recommends cost?

A. $35.00

B. $65.00

C. $82.00

D. $120.00

Questions 191–195 refer to the following notice, plan, and email.

CORPORATE NOTICE

Congratulations to all employees! Our third-quarter report has just been completed, and shows a profit increase of 15% over the same quarter a year ago. With the current growing market, we anticipate an even greater increase in net profits by the end of our fiscal year this June. As you know, a profit-sharing plan is being developed and should be ready for implementation in July. Please see the table below for further details. Keep up the good work!

TIBS PROFIT SHATING PLAN

Please note that contribution to a profit sharing plan is available to all employees but not mandatory.

- Maximum Contribution: 25% of employees salary
- Minimum Contribution: None

Payment can be issued in cash or stock. Proportion of profit is predetermined.

To:	k.wheeler@tibs.com
From:	d.scrivner@tibs.com
Date:	April 15th, 2017 2:24:18 P.M.
Subject:	Profit Sharing

Hi Kate,

Just wondering if you've heard the news about the profit-sharing plan. There was a notice up on our department board announcing that profits are up 15% from the same time last year, and that the profit-sharing plan will be ready by July. Where have we heard that before! Was the notice sent to your department, too? I'll be very surprised if the plan starts in July. They've been promising it for the last two years and nothing's happened. Have you heard anything?

David

191. What had been completed?

A. a quarterly report
B. a profit-sharing plan
C. employee evaluations
D. a market analysis

192. What is the maximum amount an employee can pay into their plan?

A. one tenth of their taxes
B. 15% of their salary
C. 25% of their taxes
D. one quarter of their salary

193. How did David learn about the news?

A. An email was sent to all employees.
B. A notice was posted in his department.
C. A colleague told him.
D. He read it in a newspaper.

194. What can be inferred about Kate and David?

A. They work in different companies.
B. They are not pleased about the news.
C. They are pleased about the news.
D. They work in different departments.

195. When did the company first suggest a profit-sharing plan?

A. three years ago
B. two years ago
C. a year ago
D. six months ago

Questions 196–200 refer to the following email, attachment, and letter.

To:	ALL STAFF
From:	harriet.bingley@kreighton.com
Date:	December 9th, 2018
Subject:	Internal Opportunities

Dear all

A number of positions in our offices have recently become available. Please see the attached document for more information about the various roles.

Kreighton Software is looking to fill the vacant posts with driven, results-oriented employees. To apply, submit your C.V., cover letter and reference to the Human Resources Department (2nd floor, room 265, email: applications.hr@kreightonsoft.com). Please remember to note the position code on the first page of your application if submitting a hardcopy, or in the subject bar if applying by email.

Eligible employees must:

- have worked for Kreighton Software full time for at least one year.
- obtain written authorization to apply for the role from their direct manager.
- demonstrate a passion for Kreighton Software, and a detailed knowledge of the business (including an awareness of aspects of the business which fall outside the general duties of their role).

We're looking forward to your submissions. Any questions just ask.

Harriet

HR and Headhunting

Kreighton Software

Internal Opportunities

Position Title and Band	Required Qualifications and Experience	Position Code
Senior Developer *(Band 4)*	BSc degree qualification. Must have knowledge of the range of online assets and 2 years' experience as a Developer.	1205
Senior Software Engineer *(Band 4)*	BSc degree qualification. Must have a working knowledge of relevant platform building technologies.	1206
Product Manager *(Band 6)*	MA/MSc degree. At least 3 years working on projects with Kreighton. In-depth knowledge of entire production process necessary.	1207
Human Resources Administrator *(Band 2)*	Demonstrable interest in working in HR, and an awareness of the department's roles. Employees qualified in First Aid training preferred.	1411
Head of Finance *(Band 8)*	Band 6 or higher with at least 2 years' experience in current role, and at least 5 years' experience working in Finance.	1502
Sales Manager *(Band 5)*	Employees must have attained above average sales in at least 3 of the past 6 months, and demonstrate leadership qualities.	1801

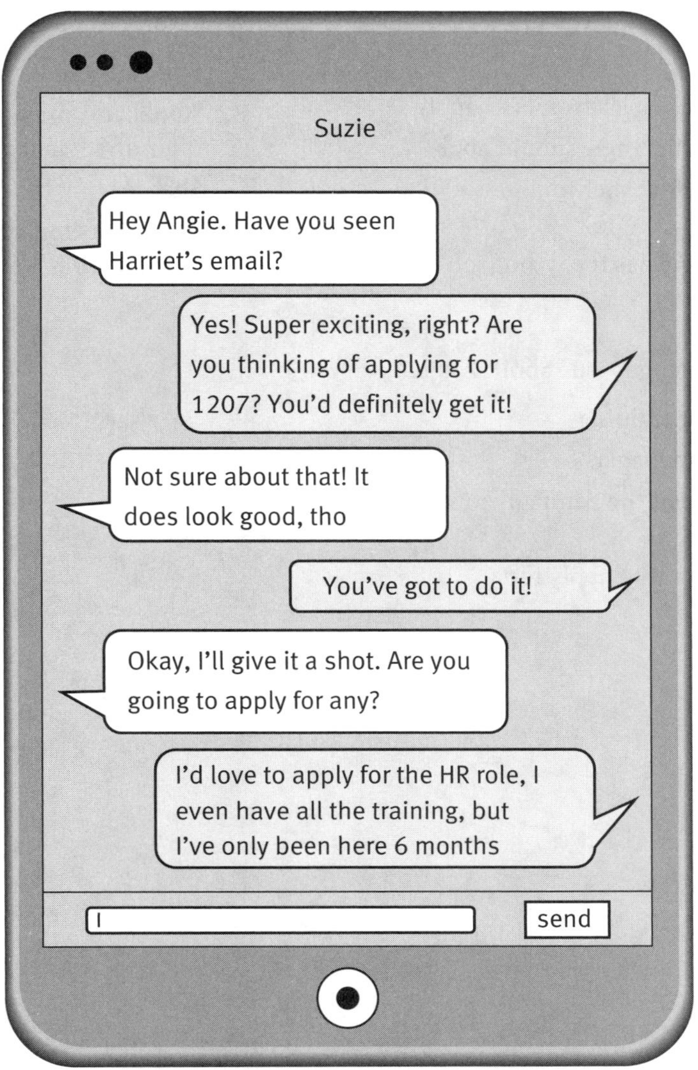

196. Which of the following does NOT need to be included in the application?

A. a cover letter written by the applicant

B. a letter of reference from their current manager

C. a C.V.

D. the job code for the role applied for

197. Which position does Angie recommend Suzie apply for?

A. Product Manager

B. Human Resources Administrator

C. Head of Finance

D. Sales Manager

198. In the text message chain, why does Suzie write "Not sure about that"?

A. She doesn't know if she wants to apply.

B. She doesn't think Angie should apply.

C. She is not sure that she would be successful.

D. She thinks Angie has the wrong job information.

199. Which of the following is true about Angie?

A. She has first aid training

B. She is the HR manager.

C. She has worked at the company longer than Suzie.

D. She does not want to apply for a different job.

200. Why won't Angie apply for the role?

A. She's waiting for a different position.

B. Applicants must obtain permission from their direct managers.

C. She's leaving the company in half a year.

D. Applicants must have worked at the company for over a year.

Stop! This is the end of the exam. If you finish before time is called, you may go back to Parts V, VI, and VII and check your work.

PRACTICE TEST 1 ANSWER KEY

Part I	Part II	Part III	Part IV	Part V	Part VI	Part VII
1. A	7. C	32. A	71. D	101. C	131. B	147. A
2. C	8. A	33. D	72. D	102. B	132. A	148. A
3. B	9. C	34. B	73. C	103. A	133. B	149. A
4. A	10. B	35. A	74. C	104. D	134. A	150. D
5. D	11. A	36. D	75. D	105. B	135. B	151. C
6. A	12. A	37. B	76. D	106. D	136. D	152. B
	13. C	38. B	77. B	107. B	137. B	153. B
	14. B	39. D	78. A	108. C	138. B	154. D
	15. C	40. A	79. C	109. A	139. C	155. A
	16. A	41. A	80. A	110. B	140. A	156. D
	17. C	42. B	81. D	111. D	141. C	157. D
	18. C	43. D	82. B	112. A	142. D	158. B
	19. A	44. C	83. D	113. C	143. B	159. C
	20. B	45. D	84. D	114. A	144. A	160. B
	21. B	46. B	85. C	115. C	145. D	161. D
	22. A	47. A	86. C	116. A	146. D	162. C
	23. C	48. D	87. A	117. B		163. B
	24. B	49. C	88. A	118. A		164. A
	25. A	50. D	89. A	119. D		165. B
	26. B	51. C	90. D	120. A		166. C
	27. A	52. A	91. C	121. B		167. A
	28. C	53. A	92. C	122. D		168. C
	29. B	54. D	93. D	123. A		169. D
	30. A	55. A	94. B	124. B		170. C
	31. B	56. C	95. B	125. C		171. B
		57. A	96. A	126. B		172. A
		58. C	97. C	127. C		173. D
		59. C	98. A	128. A		174. A
		60. D	99. A	129. D		175. B
		61. A	100. B	130. A		176. C
		62. A				177. D
		63. C				178. B
		64. D				179. B
		65. B				180. D
		66. D				181. C
		67. C				182. A
		68. D				183. C
		69. B				184. C
		70. C				185. D
						186. A
						187. C
						188. A
						189. B
						190. B
						191. A
						192. D
						193. B
						194. D
						195. B
						196. B
						197. A
						198. C
						199. A
						200. D

PRACTICE TEST 1 ANSWERS AND EXPLANATIONS

Section 1—Listening Comprehension

Part I: Photographs

1. (A)

The photograph shows a technician using a machine. **(A)** describes the photograph. **(B)** plays on *wires*—what we see—and *unwired*. **(C)** plays on *watching over* and *writing over*. **(D)** cannot be correct; there are no *cars* in the picture.

2. (C)

The photograph shows a plant on a stool, in front of patio doors leading outside. The doors are *closed*, not *open* **(A)**. The plant is on a *stool*, not on a *table* **(B)**. **(C)** correctly identifies that the plant is on top of the *stool*. The object is a *stool*, not a *chair* **(D)**.

3. (B)

The photograph shows a man leaning over a desk to work. **(B)** correctly describes the photograph. The man is *standing*, not *getting up*. The man is *working*, not *cleaning*. The light is already turned on.

4. (A)

The photograph shows a truck parked next to the wall of a building. **(A)** correctly describes the photograph. It is not *raining*, and no one is *loading*. There is no *man* in the photograph. This plays on *house* and *warehouse*, but there are no people in the photograph and the building is not a house.

5. (D)

The photograph shows a man taking a photograph. **(D)** correctly describes what is happening. He is taking a photograph, not *loading a* film. It is a *camera* not a pair of *binoculars*. There is no *woman* in the photograph.

6. (A)

The photograph shows two open drawers in a cabinet, the top one filled with cutlery, and the bottom one filled with plates. **(A)** correctly describes the photograph. The plates are in the *bottom* drawer, not the *top* one. There is no table in the photograph. It is a *cabinet* not a dishwasher.

Part II: Question-Response

7. (C)

The questions asks *Do you have an additional pair of bookends?* **(C)** correctly answers the question in a yes/no format, and responds appropriately (*I have an extra pair*). **(A)** confuses pair with the fruit pear. **(B)** confuses *pair* with the similar sounding *spare*.

8. (A)

The question asks *Are gratuities already added in, or are they separate?* **(A)** correctly identifies that the question is asking whether the cost (*price*) includes the tip (*gratuities*). **(B)** fails to identify that the sentence is about the price of something. **(C)** talks about *meals* instead of *gratuities*, and as the answer offers two options, the correct answer will not start with yes/no.

9. (C)

The question asks *Why do you want to advertise in the trade publications?* **(C)** offers the appropriate explanation. **(A)** and **(B)** repeat *trade*, but do not answer the question.

10. (B)

The question asks *What are the arrangements for publicizing the general's visit?* **(B)** responds with a publicity event. **(A)** plays on the word *arrangements*. **(C)** plays on the word *visit*.

11. (A)

The question asks *You've had experience with this particular software, haven't you?* The question requires a yes/no response, so eliminate **(B)**, which plays on *software* and *menswear*. **(A)** offers the correct response. **(C)** confuses *experience* and *expensive*.

12. (A)

The question asks *Why didn't she attend the medical conference yesterday?* **(A)** provides an appropriate response. **(B)** confuses the meaning of *attend* in the sentence. **(C)** uses the similar sounding word *medicine*, but does not relate to the question.

13. (C)

The question asks *When will the payroll be finished?* The answer requires a date in the future, **(C)** is correct. **(A)** answers in the present continuous tense. **(B)** confuses *payroll* with *roll.*

14. (B)

The question asks *Did you send an invitation to Mr. Maxwell?* **(B)** gives the appropriate response. **(A)** and **(C)** do not relate to the question.

15. (C)

The question asks *Who will be taking notes at the meeting?* The answer will give a person, so **(C)** is correct. **(A)** gives a person, but confuses *notes* to be taken in the future, with a *note* taken in the past. **(B)** repeats *taking* but does not answer the question.

16. (A)

The question asks *What would you like to drink with your meal?* **(A)** is the only response which provides a *drink*. **(B)** discusses *dessert*, not *drinks*. **(C)** discusses *tables*, not *drinks*.

17. (C)

The question asks *How is your new assistant working out?* **(C)** correctly describes an employee's performance. **(A)** confuses *working out* with *workout*. **(B)** confuses *assistant* with *assistance*.

18. (C)

The question asks *The uniforms have been ordered already, haven't they?* **(A)** and **(B)** discuss ordering food not *uniforms*. **(C)** gives the correct response.

19. (A)

The question asks *Who should I contact to get the sink repaired?* **(A)** provides an appropriate person to call. **(B)** is irrelevant as it discusses *car mechanics* and does not answer the question. **(C)** offers an irrelevant opinion about apartments, and the question asks about a *broken sink*.

20. (B)

The question asks *Where is your office in New York?* The answer will give a location, **(B)** is correct. **(A)** answers a *When* question. **(C)** offers irrelevant information.

21. (B)

The question asks *When's a good time to telephone Mr. Boros?* The answer will give a time in the future, **(B)** is correct. **(A)** does not relate to the question. **(C)** gives a time in the past.

22. (A)

The question asks *Are you going to print new business cards or keep your old ones?* **(A)** correctly answer the question. **(B)** confuses *business card* and *printer's card*. **(C)** confuses *print* with *printer*.

23. (C)

The question asks *Where did you leave the Zurich invoices?* The answer will give a location, so **(C)** is correct. **(A)** confuses *invoices* with *voices*. **(B)** repeats the words *leave* and *you*, but does not answer the question.

24. (B)

The question asks *How did you get here so quickly?* The correct answer will give an explanation, **(B)** is correct. **(A)** would explain why someone's journey was *slow* not *quick*. **(C)** confuses *here* with *hear/heard*.

25. (A)

The question asks *You have a computer at home, don't you?* **(A)** offers an appropriate answer to the question. **(B)** does not make sense. A laptop wouldn't fit into a wallet. **(C)** discusses a *phone*, not a *laptop*.

26. (B)

The question asks *Would you like the lunch special, or will you stick with your regular order today?* **(B)** gives an appropriate response to the question. **(A)** discusses food (*delicious*), but does not answer the question. **(C)** repeats the word *lunch*, but answers a *When* question.

27. (A)

The question asks *How much do we have left in our mailing budget?* The response will discuss a monetary figure, so **(A)** is correct. **(B)** repeats *left* and *budget*, but does not answer the question. **(C)** repeats *mailing* and *budget*, but does not answer the question.

28. (C)

The question asks *How much vacation do you get this year?* **(C)** gives an appropriate amount of time. **(A)** answers a *When* question. **(B)** answers a *Where* question.

29. (B)

The question asks *I think they're going to finish before the deadline, don't you?* **(B)** correctly answers in terms of the speed of the work being done. **(A)** plays on the words *deadline* and *line*. **(C)** plays on the words *deadline* and *dead end*.

30. (A)

The question asks *When is the tour group from Brazil due to arrive?* **(A)** gives an appropriate time. **(B)** repeats *Brazil* but discusses a plane landing, not a *tour group* arriving. **(C)** repeats the word *tour*, but discusses the speaker returning, not a *tour group* arriving.

31. (B)

The question asks *What's at the top of our agenda this morning?* **(B)** correctly provides a topic to be discussed. **(A)** confuses the meaning of *top* in the sentence. **(C)** plays on the words *agenda* and *agent*, as well as *morning* and *noon*.

Part III: Short Conversations

32. (A)

The woman says *Mrs Colby also invited the instructors to lunch*, so the speakers are planning a luncheon **(A)**. **(B)** and **(C)** are not mentioned in the conversation, and the meal must be lunch, not dinner **(D)**, as the time given for the meal is *midday.*

33. (D)

When the man asks how many people will be attending, the woman replies *It's sixty-five*; **(D)** is correct. **(B)** and **(C)** are not mentioned in the conversation, and **(A)**, *fifty*, is the original number of people planned for.

34. (B)

The man says *originally, we were supposed to have fifty, but I know the number has gone up since last week*, so **(B)** is correct. The time **(A)** and the *catering company* **(D)** are mentioned but do not change. The venue **(C)** is not mentioned.

35. (A)

Mr. Wells says *the subway service is a nightmare too*, so **(A)** is the correct answer. He says *Traffic is pretty bad*, so **(B)** is not possible. The other man talks about the taxes but he doesn't use the word *nightmare*, so **(C)** is also wrong. **(D)** is incorrect because Mr. Wells says *Traffic is pretty bad with all the snow.*

36. (D)

The woman says *I get that Mr. Wells, but this has gone too far. This is not the first time you're late for a meeting*, so **(D)** is the correct answer. It doesn't say how long it took her to get to work, so **(A)** is not possible. **(B)** is incorrect because she says *you're late for a meeting*. **(C)** is also wrong; she is angry because he is late, not because he is new.

37. (B)

The woman says *who has the agenda?* and the man says *let's review our notes from last week*. The speakers are in a meeting, so **(B)** is correct. The speakers discuss traveling to work, but they are not traveling now, or on an office trip. It is also not mentioned that they are having breakfast.

38. (B)

The man (Eric Janson), *says she's covered for her trip to China next week*; the call is about *travel insurance* **(B)**. *Air tickets* **(A)** and *hotel reservations* **(D)** are related to the travel topic, but are not mentioned in the conversation. It is mentioned that Ms Brody is in a meeting **(C)**, but this is not the purpose of Mr Janson's call.

39. (D)

The woman says *I'm sorry but Ms Brody's in a meeting right now*; **(D)** is correct. Ms Brody is about to travel **(A)**, but has not set off yet. **(B)** and **(C)** are not mentioned in the text.

40. (A)

Mr Janson says *she needs to send me the details of her trip—I mean the cities she'll be visiting*; he needs to know where she plans to travel **(A)**. **(B)** and **(C)** relate to travel but are not mentioned in the conversation. **(D)** relates to meetings, but is not mentioned in the conversation.

41. (A)

(A) is the correct answer, as Serena says *we're slammed in accounting at the moment, making sure everything's okay for our audit*. The *gym* is not mentioned, nor is a *party*, and she is not in a busy period, but getting ready for an audit.

42. (B)

Ahmed says *I need it to move some files from the cloud* so **(B)** is correct. Serena has been using the memory stick for video testimonials, not Ahmed. Ahmed has run out of computer storage, but he's not using the memory stick to increase his storage. He's not backing up files, he is moving the files.

43. (D)

Serena says *it's in our filing cabinet, you know, the one by Greta's office?* **(D)** is correct. It's near Greta's office, not in her office, and the first woman thought it was on Serena's desk, but it's not. Ahmed wants to borrow the memory stick, so he doesn't currently have it.

44. (C)

The woman says *until a week ago I'd never heard of her*, and the man responds *me neither, but then I don't know much about sculpture*; they are talking about a sculptor **(C)**. *Painting* is mentioned but a *painter* **(A)** is not. **(B)** and **(D)** are not mentioned in the text.

45. (D)

(A), **(B)** and **(C)** are locations which exhibit the sculptor's work.

46. (B)

The woman says *I really think it will make a big difference to the dinner*, so **(B)** is correct. **(A)**, **(C)** and **(D)** are not mentioned in the conversation.

47. (A)

The first man says *I'm going to need ten more feet of wire to install these overhead lights*; the men are electricians **(A)**. **(B)**, **(C)**, and **(D)** are not mentioned in the conversation.

48. (D)

The first man says *we've got some more in a blue box in the truck;* the *blue box* is in the *truck* **(D)**. The *office* **(A)** and *bedroom* **(B)** are mentioned in the conversation, but neither are the location of the box. **(C)** is not mentioned in the conversation.

49. (C)

The first man mentions *the bedrooms and the kitchen*, the men must be working in a house **(C)**. **(A)**, **(B)**, and **(D)** are not mentioned.

50. (D)

The woman says *can you tell me when the elevator will be working?* The speakers are discussing when the elevator will be fixed. The man says he takes the stairs to his office, but the speakers are not discussing how they get to work. The woman mentions that she works on the 11th floor, but they are not discussing this as the main topic. The speakers all already know where the main elevator is, they are not discussing this.

51. (C)

The woman says *they were planning to do a routine check-up...Then they found that some of the machinery is a bit worn, so they need to replace those parts now.* **(C)** is correct. The *button panel* and the *11th floor* are mentioned, but they are not the reason the elevator is out of order. The speakers do not say that a new elevator is being built.

52. (A)

The man says *it's round the back, by the cafeteria. Here, it'll be easier if I just show you, come with me*, when talking about the *service elevator*, so **(A)** is correct. The man does not offer to get maintenance, take the crates upstairs, or unpack the crates.

53. (A)

The man says *after all those years working out there, I'm sure that Colleen has some useful contacts*, Colleen works in Australia, **(A)**. The female speaker is going to Australia for a business trip **(C)**, but Colleen has worked there for *years*. **(B)** and **(D)** are not mentioned in the text.

54. (D)

The man says *why don't you stay an extra night and fly back on Sunday*; **(D)** is correct. *Friday* **(B)** and *Saturday* **(C)** are mentioned but are not the day the woman will return. *Thursday* **(A)** is not mentioned in the conversation.

55. (A)

The man says *As your boss, I can approve the cost of another night's accommodation*, so the man is the woman's boss **(A)**.

56. (C)

The woman says *have you heard any news on that shipment of sportswear from Shanghai?* They are discussing clothes. *News* is mentioned in the conversation, but *newspapers* **(A)** are not. **(B)** and **(D)** are not mentioned in the conversation.

57. (A)

The woman says *have you heard any news on that shipment of sportswear from Shanghai?* **(A)** is correct. **(D)**, *Hong Kong* is mentioned but is not where the shipment has come from. **(B)** is the location of the speakers and **(C)** is not mentioned in the conversation.

58. (C)

The man says *there's been a problem in customs*, so **(C)** is correct. **(A)**, **(B)** and **(D)** are not mentioned in the text.

59. (C)

The woman says *this is already a great price on a quality laptop*, so **(C)** is correct. **(A)** cannot be correct because the computer is a laptop, **(B)** and **(D)** are not mentioned in the conversation.

60. (D)

The woman says *we'll throw in a free carrying case and a choice between a memory upgrade or a graphics software package*; the special offer includes *extra equipment* **(D)**. **(A)**, **(B)** and **(C)** are not mentioned in the conversation.

61. (A)

The man asks *can't I just get a reduction in the price instead of the software of the memory upgrade?* **(A)** is correct. **(B)**, **(C)** and **(D)** are not mentioned in the conversation.

62. (A)

The man says *it's about time we got some new chairs and tables* and the woman says *I know, the old ones are so worn,* so the speakers agree that the furniture should be replaced. They do want the furniture to change, so **(B)** and **(D)** are incorrect. They want the furniture to change because it's *worn*, which means damaged, not because it's unfashionable. **(C)** is incorrect.

63. (C)

The man says *I'm not sure about this, see, the kitchen's right next to the door*, so eliminate **(D)** as he doesn't think the kitchen should remain where it currently is. We can also eliminate **(B)**, as he doesn't think the kitchen should be near the door. The man says *I think we should move it so that it's on the opposite side of the room from the door, next to the sofas*. He thinks it should be in position **3**, so **(C)** is the correct answer.

64. (D)

The woman says *You should suggest that to Ricardo. He's in charge of the redesign*. **(D)** is correct. **(A)** is incorrect because she suggests that the man talk to Ricardo, not that she talks to him herself. **(B)** and **(C)** are incorrect, she says the team *was asking for feedback.*

65. (B)

This Detail question asks what the woman asks the man. The woman says *Larry, we need to choose which evening to have the staff party on in the last week of the month. When's best for your team?* **(B)** is correct. **(A)** and **(D)** have already been decided, and **(C)** is what the man asks the woman.

66. (D)

This Detail questions asks why the woman says *that's annoying*, so you should be actively listening out for this phrase and the surrounding conversation. Before the woman says *that's annoying*, the man says *Sofia was looking at their website yesterday*. Apparently some nights are more popular, so they charge more. The woman is annoyed because the prices for the venue vary for each night.

67. (C)

This question includes a graphic. You need to use the information in the conversation and the graphic to decide which night the venue will be booked for. In the conversation, the woman says Damien said we couldn't spend more than $800 on the venue, and if possible, it would be better to have the party after we submit the new client's contract on Friday morning. Looking at the graphic, Saturday–Sunday is too expensive for them, and they should have the party after the contract is submitted on Friday morning, so Friday is the best night to book the venue. **(C)** is correct.

68. (D)

The man says *Okay, we've got our pitch sorted, so now we just need to schedule a time with the investors to present it.* Investors is a synonym for financiers, so **(D)** is the answer. They are planning to meet with people who are not part of their company, so **(A)** and **(B)** are incorrect. They do not mention any *overtime*, so **(C)** is incorrect.

69. (B)

The woman says *we can't schedule it for the weekend, not everyone's as fond of work as you* before the man says *Of course, okay, that narrows it down*, so the man says *of course* because he has just realized that the call should not be scheduled during the weekend. **(B)** is correct.

70. (C)

The graphic shows that Leroy and Rhonda are both free only on Tuesday, Friday and Saturday, so they cannot meet on Thursday. The woman says that they can't schedule the call on the weekend, and the man says he can't do the first two days in the week, so they can only meet on Friday. **(C)** is correct.

Part IV: Short Talks

71. (D)

The speaker says *we hope you will come and help us welcome the Colombia National Symphony for the first time to Seattle on Saturday, May 28th*. The event will be a concert **(D)**. **(A)**, **(B)** and **(C)** are not mentioned in the talk.

72. (D)

The speaker says tickets are eighteen, twenty-four and thirty dollars. The cheapest ticket is $18 **(D)**. **(A)**, **(B)** and **(C)** are not mentioned in the talk.

73. (C)

The speaker says *you can also buy seats for all our events online, at www.seattlearts.com*, tickets can be bought on the internet **(C)**. **(B)** repeats the words *student union*, but tickets cannot be bought here. **(A)** and **(D)** are not mentioned in the talk.

74. (C)

The speaker says *John Park, the vice president*, so **(C)** is correct. **(B)** repeats the word *waiter*, and **(D)** repeats the word *customer*, but do not describe Mr. Park's title. **(A)** relates to the food industry but is not mentioned in the talk.

75. (D)

The speaker says *this year he will be concentrating on customer service*; **(D)** is correct. **(A)** *food presentation* is only one aspect of customer service. **(B)** repeats the word *waiter*. **(C)** *menu items* were focused on last year.

76. (D)

The speaker says *I hope you will work hard, smile, and demonstrate how well we treat our customers*; **(D)** is correct. **(A)**, **(B)** and **(C)** are not mentioned in the talk.

77. (B)

The speaker says *I'm sure all of the store managers will join me in welcoming Mr Nazar*, so **(B)** is the most likely answer. **(A)** is not mentioned in the talk, and as *managers* are present, it is unlikely to be a board of directors meeting. **(C)** does not relate to the talk, which is welcoming a new member, not saying goodbye to a retired worker. **(D)** is unlikely to be correct as only managers are present at the meeting.

78. (A)

The speaker says *under his direction domestic sales have increased by 30 percent*. **(A)** is correct. **(B)**, **(C)** and **(D)** are not mentioned in the talk.

79. (C)

The speaker says *Mr. Nazar will be looking at new ways to lower expenses*. **(C)** is correct. **(A)**, **(B)** and **(D)** are not mentioned in the talk.

80. (A)

The speaker says *The weather in Zurich today, rain at times*. **(A)** is correct. **(B)** repeats the word *Switzerland*. **(D)** and **(C)** are not mentioned in the talk.

81. (D)

The speaker says that Central Valley will have a *mostly cloudy day with some areas of mixed rain and snow . . . highs around 9 degrees*. The only area to show highs of 9 degrees is Area D, so the answer must be **(D)**.

82. (B)

The speaker says *Italian-Austrian border*, so **(B)** is correct. **(A)**, **(C)** and **(D)** are not mentioned in the talk.

83. (D)

The speaker says *thank you for your introduction, Mr. Hausman*. Mr. Hausman introduced the speaker **(D)**. **(A)**, **(B)** and **(C)** are not mentioned in the talk.

84. (D)

The woman says *As we are aware, tremendous changes have been made in the financial services sector over the past decade, and they are set to continue*. The woman is commenting on the fact that the audience is already familiar with this information. The answer is **(D)**.

85. (C)

The speaker says *I would like to speak about financial services and how they affect planning processes for business and industry*; **(C)** is correct. **(D)**, **(A)** and **(B)** are not mentioned in the talk.

86. (C)

The speaker says *I spent two months visiting our hotel units. The* speaker works for a hotel chain **(C)**. **(A)**, **(C)** and **(D)** are about travel, buildings, and customer service, but are not mentioned in the talk.

87. (A)

The man says *My goal was to evaluate the architectural structure of both the interiors and exteriors. Very briefly, we surpass the competition in customer service, but many of our units need structural updating.* The man is giving a quick overview. **(A)** is the answer.

88. (A)

The speaker says *I feel we should have a team of interior designers redecorate the lobbies and rooms. I'd like to suggest to the board that they make these improvements a priority.* **(A)** is correct. **(B)** repeats the word *lobbies.* **(C)** and **(D)** are not mentioned in the talk.

89. (A)

The speaker says *well folks, that concludes our show for this evening.* **(A)** is correct. **(B)** cannot be correct as the program is over. **(C)** and **(D)** are not mentioned in the talk.

90. (D)

The speaker says *please listen again next week when we will visit with Mr. Peter Thompson.* **(D)** is correct. The employee motivation expert, Dr. McDermott **(B)** and **(C)** is the current guest. **(A)** is not mentioned in the talk.

91. (C)

The speaker says *we have been talking with Dr. Julia McDermott, the renowned management consultant and expert in the field of employee motivation* the topic discussed on the program was most likely about inspiring workers. **(C)** is correct. **(B)**, managing change, is the topic to be discussed next week. **(A)** and **(D)** are not mentioned in the talk.

92. (C)

The speaker says *I'm going to begin by briefly summarizing what we'll try to cover over the next hour.* The speaker is starting a meeting **(C)**. The meeting is currently happening **(A)**. The speaker is discussing what will be covered in the current meeting **(B)**. The speaker is *conducting*, not *interrupting* the meeting **(D)**.

93. (D)

The speaker says *you can see that there are five agenda items on the meeting invitation I sent out, but there's also another important item to add to the list.*There are 6 agenda items to discuss; **(D)** is correct. There are originally 5 items to discuss **(C)**, but another item has been added. **(A)** and **(B)** are not mentioned in the talk.

94. (B)

The speaker says *after this summary, we'll do a quick update of what everyone's been working on, then I've reserved 20 minutes for us to talk about changes to our policy. Once we've covered that, we'll discuss project planning*. The discussions about changes to the policy must begin at 13.15.

95. (B)

The speaker says *My name is James Watts and I'm your lead flight attendant on today's flight.* **(B)** is correct. **(A)** repeats the word *captain*. **(C)** and **(D)** are not mentioned in the talk.

96. (A)

The speaker says from *London Gatwick to Edinburgh.* **(A)** is correct. The flight is *departing* from London **(D)**. **(B)** and **(C)** are not mentioned in the talk.

97. (C)

The speaker says *we'd like to apologize for the slight delay this morning, which has been due to fog grounding flights most of the morning up in Edinburgh.* **(C)** is correct, as the weather is responsible for the delays. **(A)**, **(B)** and **(D)** are not mentioned in the talk.

98. (A)

The speaker says *this next slide shows how the different elements of our research fit together.* **(A)** is correct. **(B)** is not mentioned in the talk. **(C)** repeats *hotel* and **(D)** repeats *manager*.

99. (A)

The speaker says *the impact visitors have on the local environment*; the speaker's main interest is the effect of tourism **(A)**. **(B)**, **(C)** and **(D)** are related to travel and tourism, but are not the primary focus of the speaker's talk.

100. (B)

The speaker says *data came from measurements of erosion on pathways and increases in pollution of various kinds.* **(B)** is correct. **(A)** and **(D)** are not mentioned in the talk. The talk is about tourism, but tourist numbers **(C)** are not measured.

Section 2—Reading Comprehension

Part V: Incomplete Sentences

101. (C)

Only **(C)**, *whatever*, completes the sentence fully; it is the correct pronoun. *Anything* would need to be followed by a specific noun (which/that). *Everyone* relates to people, not speech. *Anymore* would be used to refer to something in the past.

102. (B)

(B), *accompanied*, is the only logical choice in the sentence. Visitors would not be *arrested* or *revised* while on site. *Detected* would also be illogical in the sentence.

103. (A)

Maintenance is a noun and is logical within the sentence. *Maintain* gives the word in present tense verb form. **(C)** gives the word in past tense verb form. *Maintainer* relates to a person or object which *maintains*.

104. (D)

The missing word will connect the two clauses positively; only **(D)** can be correct. **(A)** and **(C)** are used to connect opposing clauses. **(B)** is used to present two different options.

105. (B)

The missing word will modify the sentence by connecting the two opposing clauses; *anyway* means regardless, so completes the sentence logically. *Moreover* would be used for complementary clauses. *Anyhow* means carelessly or by one means or another, so would not fit the meaning of the sentence. *Since* would need to be followed by an explanation.

106. (D)

This is a grammar question. The second clause of the sentence is in the present perfect tense; *achieved* **(D)** is correct. *Achieve* **(A)** gives the present singular. **(B)** and **(C)** are nouns.

107. (B)

This is a vocabulary question; *which* gives a preposition which logically completes the sentence. *At* would not be used for a consultation, or two-way conversation. *About* needs to apply to an object, but none is given after the missing word in the sentence. *For* does not work in the sentence, as a discussion needs to take place *between* the addressed and the head of the department.

108. (C)

This is a grammar question; the missing word will be a plural pronoun, *them*, is correct. *They*, would be used to refer to the subject of a clause, and the missing word refers to the object. *Their* would be used to refer to a group of people who possess or own the subject. *Themselves* is a reflexive plural pronoun.

109. (A)

This is a vocabulary question; the missing word is a conjunction which joins a time frame (*three weeks*) with an action (*report a credit dispute*), **(A)** is correct. Customers should report their dispute within three weeks; they do not have to wait three weeks *until* or *before* reporting their dispute. *So* would be used if the first clause caused the second, which is not the case in the sentence.

110. (B)

This is a grammar question. The missing word describes an attribute of the noun ceramics, so the missing word must be an adjective. *Advanced* is the only answer choice that is an adjective, so **(B)** is the correct answer.

111. (D)

This is a vocabulary question. The sentence needs a noun which means respond. *Reply* is correct. *Rely* sounds similar but means to depend on. *Delay* would mean Mr. Medina waited until Friday to *not respond*, which does not make sense. *Relay* sounds similar to *reply*, but means to repeat information, and Mr. Medina needs to reply with new information.

112. (A)

This is a vocabulary question. The missing word must be a preposition which compliments *go*, and describes an action with a street; *across* must be correct; the directors crossed the street. *By* is incorrect, the directors could not go alongside the street, they would have to be on the street. *Of* and *against* are not actions which can be done with streets.

113. (C)

This is a grammar question. The missing word must be a verb which modifies the *economic links* in the sentence. *Strengthen* is correct, as it means to make strong, whereas *strength* is simply the quality of being *strong*, neither of which are logical in the sentence. *Stronger* would be used to highlight a difference between the strength of the two regions, but the sentence describes the strength of the regions collectively.

114. (A)

This is a grammar question. The missing word is an adjective which modifies the following word, *documents*. *Original* gives the word in adjective form. **(B)** is a verb. **(C)** and **(D)** are nouns.

115. (C)

This is a vocabulary question, as the power plant needs to comply with *new* regulations, the existing design will need to be changed. *Altered* means changed. *Alternated* means to change back and forth between two specific conditions. *Avoided* and *attached* do not discuss changing the plan.

116. (A)

This is a grammar question. The missing word must be a noun in the singular because of the pronoun *one* which appears before the missing word. **(A)** gives a noun in the singular. **(B)** and **(D)** are adjectives which mean fundamental/basic. **(C)** gives a noun in the plural.

117. (B)

This is a vocabulary question. The missing word is a preposition which compliments the month, *June*. A person would retire *in* June. *At* would be used to refer to a specific time of day, and *on* would be used for a specific day, neither are suitable for use with an entire month. *Among* would be used for physical objects, not time in a month.

118. (A)

This is a grammar question. The missing word is a verb which will apply to *month to month*. *Vary* gives the correct verb form. *Variety* is a noun. *Various* is an adjective. *Varied* gives a verb in the past tense, but the percentage rate will continue to change, so the verb must be in the future tense.

119. (D)

This is a vocabulary question. A prepositional phrase which applies to *the weaknesses* of the proposal will complete the sentence. *Pointed out* is correct. *Entered into* would be used for a discussion. *Joined with* would be used if Mr. Teska united/collaborated with another person. *Signed up* would be used for joining an activity, not highlighting weaknesses.

120. (A)

This is a grammar question. The missing word is a pronoun which must compliment the noun *goals*. *Those* is correct because the pronoun refers to a specific noun. *There* is an adverb. *Them* would only be used if it was not followed by the specific noun. *There is* a determiner, and would be used if we knew whose goals they were.

121. (B)

(B), *of reference,* gives the verb in its correct form. *Refer* gives the verb in present tense. *Refers to* is a modifier. *A referred* is singular, and the sentence requires a plural (*two letters*).

122. (D)

Violators gives the logical noun. *Violated* gives the verb in the past tense. *Violate* gives a verb in the infinitive. *Violating* gives a verb in the present continuous.

123. (A)

Promotional logically modifies the noun *items* in the sentence. *Promoted* gives a verb in the past tense. *Promote* gives a verb in the infinitive. *Promotes* gives a verb in the present tense.

124. (B)

The sentence requires an adverb; *quietly* is logical. *Quieter* and *quietest* are comparative adjectives, which are used to compare multiple things. *Quiet* is an adjective, and the sentence needs an adverb.

125. (C)

The sentence needs a verb in the present tense; *envisions* is logically correct, as the architect imagines a foyer with a marble staircase. **(A)**, **(B)** and **(D)** give words in the present tense, but *enlightens*, *entrusts* and *enlists* do not make sense in the sentence.

126. (B)

This is a vocabulary question, and *perspective* is logically correct; prioritising work tasks helps to understand and approach the tasks logically. The work needs to be ordered, not *confirmed. Satisfaction* does not make sense in the sentence. The work needs to be ordered, not *reinforced*.

127. (C)

The conjunction needs to be causal, as the first clause is the result of the second clause; *because* is correct. *Though* and *while* would be used for opposing clauses. *Due* should modify a noun or a pronoun, and the sentence modifies a verb (*developed*).

128. (A)

This is a grammar question. The sentence needs a verb in the infinitive as the sentence is in the future tense; *to measure* is correct. *Is measured* gives the past tense. *A measurement* gives a noun. *For measurable* gives an adjective.

129. (D)

This is a vocabulary question. The missing word must apply to hiring staff in a new way. The noun *approach* is correct. *Access* and *arrive* would mean to enter something or somewhere. *Commitment* would mean an obligation or dedication to a cause, which is not logical in the sentence.

130. (A)

Get gives the correct verb for the sentence. *Be* is the wrong vocabulary for the sentence. *Do* is already given in the correct tense (*done*) in the sentence. *Go* is not logical in the sentence.

Part VI: Text Completion

131. (B)

This is a vocabulary question. The missing word is a noun; *opportunity* correctly completes the sentence. *Opening* suggests a beginning, whereas the email conversation is already begun. *Prospect* applies to the possibility of a future event. *Occurrence* simply means event, and the sentence needs a word which means chance.

132. (A)

This is a vocabulary question. The missing word is an adverb or modifier. *Just as* is correct. *The same* and *alike* are adjectives, and we need an adverb. *Identically* would not be means exactly alike, but the sentence wants to express that Keith Rutland equally impressed.

133. (B)

This is a vocabulary question. The missing word is an adjective or modifier. *Convenient* logically pairs with *for* in the sentence. *Suited* and *fitted* would need to pair with *to* not *for*. *Nicely* is an adverb and would modify the missing word.

134. (A)

The gap needs a concluding sentence. **(B)** is an introductory sentence, so it is not the answer. **(C)** cannot be correct as the email asks Susan to choose a date, so it is not clear when they will meet in Vermont. **(D)** cannot be correct as Margaret wants to hear from Susan again about when they will meet. **(A)** must be the answer.

135. (B)

This is a vocabulary question. The missing word is a verb. *Require* is correct, as it logically completes the sentence. *Demand* is too forceful and would not be used in a polite letter. *Ask* would need for be followed by a preposition, such as *for*. A person would be *invited*, but items would need to be *requested*.

136. (D)

This is a vocabulary question. The missing word is a preposition. The equipment would need to be *in* good condition. **(A)**, **(B)**, and **(C)** are all inappropriate prepositions for the condition of equipment.

137. (B)

This is a vocabulary question. The missing word is a noun which will pair with commission. *Basis* is correct, as it describes the commission payment as a foundation. *Way* and *means* do not pair with commission. *Kind* would mean type.

138. (B)

The sentence begins by saying *For more details, please contact us at (212) 333-4444, call your nearest PhotoMatic outlet*. The sentence is providing contact information, so the gap is likely to provide another method of contact. **(B)** must be the answer.

139. (C)

The missing sentence comes after the sentence *THIS WARRANTY IS VALID ONLY FOR PRODUCTS PURCHASED IN EUROPE*; only **(C)** continues this information, by directing those who purchased the product outside of Europe. **(A)** is a concluding sentence, **(B)** would occur later in the text, and **(D)** does not relate to the information in the text.

140. (A)

This is a vocabulary question. The missing word is a noun and must be a person, not a *card* or a *store*. From the sentence, we can tell that the product must be warranted at the time of purchase to the person who **bought** the item, not the person who **sold** it, so the *purchaser* is correct, and the *seller* is incorrect.

141. (C)

This is a vocabulary question. The missing word is a conjunction which needs to join up two different choices. *Or* must be correct. *So* would be used if the first clause caused the second. *And* or *too* would be used if both clauses would occur, but the sentence offers two separate choices.

142. (D)

This is a vocabulary question. The missing word is an adjective or modifier of the noun *receipt*. *Valid* is correct, as a *defective* or *repaired* receipt would not be likely to be accepted. *Buying* would not modify *receipt*.

143. (B)

This is a vocabulary question. The missing word is a pronoun which describes a man, Bob Bingley. *He* must be correct. **(A)**, **(C)**, and **(D)** are all inappropriate pronouns to describe one man.

144. (A)

This is a grammar question. The missing word is a verb which applies to multiple people in the present tense (*all those*). *Are affected* is correct. *Affected* needs to include *are* to give the correct voice. *Is affected* gives the singular. *Have affected* gives the past tense.

145. (D)

This is a grammar question. The missing word is a verb and needs the participle *given*. *Gives* would be used for the immediate present tense. *He gave* would be used for the past. *To give* is the infinitive.

146. (D)

The gap begins the sentence that ends with *and several new chapters on the impact of technology on the management of change*. The sentence ending is discussing the contents of the book, so **(D)** must be the correct answer. **(A)** gives contact information, **(B)** discusses the author of the book and **(C)** quotes a review of the book.

Part VII: Reading Comprehension

147. (A)

This is a Detail question. To find out how much money each share made in Year 2, look at the row Earnings Per Share in the column Year 2. $1.04 is the answer. **(B)** uses information of Return on Equity from Year 3. **(C)** gives the Net Income in Year 2. **(D)** gives the Sales in Year 2.

148. (A)

This is a Detail question. In the information under the table, we are told that Return on Equity is *defined as net income divided by shareholder equity, minus extraordinary items*. **(A)** is correct. **(B)** repeats the words Net Income. **(C)** repeats the words Shareholder Equity. **(D)** repeats the words Earnings Per Share.

149. (A)

This is a Gist question. The text says this about laser printers: *they operate very quickly. A typical laser printer can print 20 color pages a minute, compared to 12 for an ink-jet printer*. The *speed* is the implied advantage of laser printers. **(B)**, **(C)**, and **(D)** are not mentioned in the text.

150. (D)

This is a Detail question. The text says: *when they were first introduced, laser printers typically cost over a thousand dollars*. **(D)** is correct. **(A)** repeats the words *a few hundred dollars*. **(B)** and **(C)** are not mentioned in the text.

151. (C)

The sentence talks about speed. **(A)** cannot be correct, as we don't know what *they* are yet. **(B)** cannot be correct, as this section of the text is discussing the complexity of these printers. **(C)** could be correct, as the following sentence discusses how quickly these printers can work. **(D)** cannot be correct, as the previous sentence discusses the cost, not the speed.

152. (B)

This is a Detail question. The text says *this transaction will occur Thursday, May 24*. **(B)** is correct. **(A)** gives the day they must be shareholders. **(C)** and **(D)** are not mentioned in the text.

153. (B)

This is a Gist question. The text says *as a result of this transaction, the shares you owned before the transaction will be doubled, while the net asset value will be reduced by half*. **(B)** is correct. **(A)** repeats the word *half*, but it is the asset value, not the original number which will be halved. **(C)** and **(D)** are not mentioned.

154. (D)

The sentence discusses another thing that pricing must take into account, which is cost considerations. We know from this that the sentence must appear after discussing one consideration about pricing and before going into more detail about cost considerations. The sentence must appear in location 4; **(D)** is correct.

155. (A)

This is a vocabulary question. The text says *the price should produce a return sufficient to cover the level of expenses... higher gross margins generally are needed.* In the sentence, *a return* means *a profit,* **(A)** is correct. **(B)**, **(C)**, and **(D)** do not give the correct meaning.

156. (D)

This is a Gist question. The text says *In high-technology businesses, for example, higher gross margins generally are needed to provide for the higher costs of research and development, as well as marketing and distribution.* It is implied in the text that research and development costs for high-technology businesses are high, **(D)**. **(A)**, **(B)**, and **(C)** are not mentioned in the text.

157. (D)

This is a Detail question, asking how many years the applicant has worked for Binational Commission. As the applicant lists it as his current job, look at the number given for Years at Job, which is 4. **(D)** is correct. **(A)**, **(B)**, and **(C)** are not mentioned in the text.

158. (B)

This is a Detail question which asks how many sources of income the applicant has. The income from their job (monthly wage income) is one, and the additional income (Source of other Income) lists one extra source of income, a Trust Annuity. The applicant therefore has two sources of income. **(B)** is correct. **(A)**, **(C)**, and **(D)** must all therefore be incorrect.

159. (C)

This is a Detail question asking how much money the applicant currently owes. The applicant only has one type of debt, a loan for a car. The total loan is given in the final Balance section: *$5,500.* **(C)** is correct. **(A)** gives the applicant's monthly income from her *Trust Annuity.* **(B)** gives the applicant's monthly income from her *wages.* **(D)** gives her *bank balance.*

160. (B)

This is a Detail question, asking what a customer must do to activate the warranty. The text says *For coverage under this limited warranty, proof of the date and place of purchase must be submitted.* The correct answer is **(B)**. **(A)** repeats *warranty,* but the text does not mention a *warranty card.* **(D)** is only if service is needed, not to activate the warranty. **(C)** is not mentioned in the text.

161. (D)

The phrase comes from the sentence *Umbrellas Unlimited will not, under any circumstances, be liable for damage caused by misuse of any product,* which means that if a product is broken while being used incorrectly, the company is not responsible for replacing the product. *Liable for damage* means *responsible for breaking*; **(D)** is correct.

162. (C)

This is a Detail question, asking for the statement which is not true about the company's warranty. **(A)** is true; the text says *the warranty does not cover damage that has been caused by customer abuse.* **(B)** is true; the text says *this warranty is good for three years.* **(C)** is incorrect and is therefore the correct answer; the text says *this warranty is not applicable outside the USA.* **(D)** is true; the text says *if defects appear under normal use, Umbrellas Unlimited will replace the product free of charge.*

163. (B)

This is a Gist question, asking how subjectively and objectively pried items differ. The text says *a subjectively priced item is based either on what the seller perceives it is worth or what the seller thinks someone will pay for it. Generally, these items have an aesthetic rather than a utilitarian value*. The correct answer in **(B)**. **(A)** and **(D)** are not mentioned in the text. **(C)** repeats the word utilitarian.

164. (A)

This is a Detail question, asking what is implied about antiques. the text says *Retailers of subjectively priced items include artists, some highly skilled craftspeople, and sellers of antiques and collectibles.* **(A)** is correct. **(B)** repeats the words *skilled craftspeople.* **(C)** and **(D)** are not mentioned in the text.

165. (B)

This is a Gist question, asking what can be inferred about traditional retailers. We know from the text that *almost all traditional retailers... sell objectively priced items*. We also know from the text that *an objectively priced item... is priced according to some concrete formula based on its actual cost to produce*. We can infer that most traditional retailers *set prices using a formula based on the cost to produce their goods*. **(B)** is correct. **(C)** and **(D)** are not mentioned in the text, and **(A)** describes objectively, not subjectively, priced goods.

166. (C)

This is a vocabulary question, asking for the meaning of *weigh* in the sentence. The text says *first analyze your needs and weigh your options*. In the sentence, *weigh* means *evaluate*. **(A)**, **(B)**, and **(D)** are all inappropriate definitions for *weigh*.

167. (A)

This is a Detail question, asking about the conditions in northwestern Mexico. The text says *high pressure moving across northern Mexico will funnel cooler air down the Northwest coast.* **(A)** is correct. **(B)**, **(C)**, and **(D)** all repeat words from the text, but do not give the correct answer.

168. (C)

This is a Detail question, asking where the temperatures will be higher than usual. The text says *the cooler air will not reach the Southwest, where temperatures will soar past 32, some 6 degrees above normal.* **(C)** is correct. **(A)**, **(B)**, and **(D)** all repeat words from the text, but do not give the correct answer.

169. (D)

This is a Detail question, asking when the majority of cold air from Texas will reach Monterrey. The text says *Winds from the north... will dislodge a pool of cold air over Texas. The leading edge of this chilled air will reach Monterrey later today, but the core of cold air will not arrive until midweek.* **(D)** is correct. **(B)** refers to the initial *leading edge* of cold, not the majority. **(A)** and **(C)** are not mentioned in the text.

170. (C)

This is a Detail question, asking what the cold front will cause. The text says *a cold front trailing this low-pressure system will push showers and thunderstorms across the Chihuahua and Durango later today.* **(C)** is correct. **(A)** repeats the words *air* and *dry*, but does not give the correct answer. **(B)** and **(D)** are not mentioned in the text.

171. (B)

This is a Gist question, asking who the report is likely to be written for. The final sentence of the passage says *a public offering of new stock will be made July 1*. The report is most likely to be written for *prospective investors*. **(A)**, **(C)**, and **(D)** are not mentioned in the text.

172. (A)

This is a negative Detail question, asking what is not mentioned about Synco. **(A)** is not mentioned in the text, so it is the answer. **(B)** is mentioned in the text: *last year, it was first in tire sales in Germany....* **(C)** is mentioned in the text: *extensive measures to streamline production resources, cut costs, and create new products have enhanced Synco's earning potential.* **(D)** is mentioned: *a high dividend of 3 million euros is planned.*

173. (D)

This is a Detail question, asking for Synco's total sales in the previous year. The text says *Synco recorded a net income of 50 million euros on sales of 10 billion euros*. **(D)** is correct. **(A)** gives the planned dividend. **(B)** gives the net income. **(C)** is not mentioned in the text.

174. (A)

This is a Gist question, asking what is implied about automotive sales in the previous year. The text says *despite last year's severe recession, lower exchange rates, and steep drops in automotive sales, Synco recorded a net income of 50 million euros... an all-time high*. This suggests that the decline in automotive sales *should have decreased Synco's revenues*. **(B)** states that automobile sales rose, but they fell. **(C)** and **(D)** do not refer to automotive sales.

175. (B)

This is a Detail question, asking what is expected for Synco. The text says *extensive measures... have substantially enhanced Synco's earning potential for next year and beyond*. **(B)** is correct. **(D)** repeats *stock*. **(A)** and **(C)** are not mentioned in the text.

176. (C)

This is a Detail question, asking about the services offered by the newsletter. The text says *we offer expert career advice, such as letter and résumé writing for beginning job seekers*. **(C)** is correct. **(A)**, **(B)**, and **(D)** are not mentioned in the text.

177. (D)

This is a Detail question, asking what is learned about the newsletter. The text says *look for us at your local newsstand or subscribe today*. **(D)** is correct. **(A)** repeats *subscribe*, but the newsletter is also available at newsstands. **(B)** and **(C)** are not mentioned in the text.

178. (B)

This is a Detail question, asking for the length of Mr. Ralls's current subscription. The text says *your subscription is for the period January to June*. **(B)** is correct; Mr. Ralls's subscription is for 6 months. **(C)** plays on the 12-month subscription Mr. Ralls is offered. **(A)** and **(D)** are not mentioned.

179. (B)

This is a Gist question, asking what is available to Mr. Ralls until the end of January. The text says *take out a 12-month subscription before the end of January and you will receive a 10 percent discount*. **(B)** is correct. **(A)**, **(C)**, and **(D)** are not mentioned in the text.

180. (D)

This is a Detail question, asking what has been included in the letter. The text says *please complete the form on the reverse of this letter and return it in the enclosed postage-paid envelope*. **(D)** is correct. **(A)**, **(B)**, and **(C)** are not mentioned in the text.

181. (C)

This is a negative (NOT) Detail question, asking what is not mentioned in the notice. **(A)** is mentioned: *rooms for attendees are available at the Bay View Hotel and the Clear Sands Hotel*. **(B)** is mentioned: *Opening plenary session: Friday 9.00am*. **(C)** is not mentioned, so it is the answer. **(D)** is mentioned: *registration forms and further details available from: www.ptgni.org*.

182. (A)

This is a Detail question, asking whose presentation is about new equipment. The text says *we are very happy to welcome Mr. Kliebermann to this year's convention. His presentation includes the long-awaited RayTone RT50*. **(A)** is correct. None of the other speakers are discussing new equipment, **(B)**, **(C)**, and **(D)** are all incorrect.

183. (C)

This is a Detail question, asking what the keynotes presentation will be about. Looking at the text, James Townsend is scheduled to give the *Keynote presentation*. His talk will focus on *the key problems facing the profession worldwide... and on what can be done to halt the drain*. **(C)** is correct. **(A)** repeats the word *technicians*. **(B)** repeats the word *apprentice*. **(D)** is not mentioned in the text.

184. (C)

This is a Gist question, asking what can be inferred about Greg and Mike. Looking at Greg's email to Mike, they discuss the production of posters for the convention and talk about the distribution. We can infer that Mike and Greg *organize the convention.* **(D)** *printers* are mentioned, but Mike and Greg are not the printers. **(A)** and **(B)** are not mentioned in the email.

185. (D)

This is a Detail question, asking what is wrong with the posters. The email says *the problem is that in the title it says this is our tenth convention, when in fact it's our eleventh.* **(D)** is correct. **(A)**, **(B)**, and **(C)** are not mentioned in the text.

186. (A)

This is a Gist question, asking why the paper shredder has been returned. The text says *we have determined that we require a shredder that can destroy larger volumes of paper at one time.* **(A)** is correct. **(B)**, **(C)**, and **(D)** are not mentioned in the text.

187. (C)

This is a Detail question. The email says *Anne Markowitz, Purchasing Agent.* **(C)** is correct. **(B)** is incorrect; she is making a complaint, not handling one. **(A)** is not mentioned. **(D)** repeats the word *brochures.*

188. (A)

This is a Gist question, asking what can be inferred about the Personal X. The text says *we require a shredder that can destroy larger volumes of paper at one time. We realize also that many of our documents will have staples or paper clips.* **(A)** is correct. **(B)**, **(C)**, and **(D)** are not mentioned in the text.

189. (B)

This is a Gist question, asking what Gina Andrews wants to know. Gina writes in her email *I'm not sure if we have any in stock. Could you check?* **(B)** is correct. **(A)**, **(C)**, and **(D)** are not mentioned in the text.

190. (B)

Gina recommends the Office X model, looking at the price list, this model costs $65.00. The answer is **(B)**.

191. (A)

This is a Gist question, asking for what had been completed. The test says *our third-quarter report has just been completed.* **(A)** is correct. **(B)** repeats the words *profit-sharing plan*, but this has not yet been completed. **(C)** and **(D)** are not mentioned in the text.

192. (D)

The second text states that employees can pay a maximum of 25%, or one quarter, of their salary. **(D)** is correct.

193. (B)

This is a Gist question, asking how David learned about the news. In his email to Kate, he writes *there was a notice up on our department board.* **(B)** is correct. **(A)**, **(C)**, and **(D)** are not mentioned in the text.

194. (D)

This is a Detail question, asking what can be inferred about Kate and David. The email says *was the notice sent to your department, too?* Kate and David must be in different departments. **(D)** is correct. Kate and David appear to work in the same company, not different ones. There is no indication that Kate and David are pleased or not pleased about the news.

195. (B)

This is a Detail question, asking when the company first suggested a profit-sharing plan. in his email, David writes *they've been promising it for the last two years.* **(B)** is correct. **(A)**, **(C)**, and **(D)** are not mentioned in the text.

196. (B)

The email states that a cover letter, C.V. and the job code need to be included, so the correct answer is **(B)**; employees needs to ask their managers for permission, but they do not need a written referral from them.

197. (A)

Angie says *Are you thinking of applying for 1207? You'd definitely get it!* Looking at the table, position 1207 is the role Product Manager, so the answer must be **(A)**.

198. (C)

After Angie writes *you'd definitely get it* Suzie replies *not sure about that!* Suzie is not sure that she would get the role if she applied. The answer is **(C)**.

199. (A)

Angie says *I'd love to apply for the HR role, I even have all the training, but I've only been here 6 months* looking at the HR role, this role asks for First Aid training, so this must be what Angie has. The correct answer is **(A).**

200. (D)

Angie says *I'd love to apply for the HR role, I even have all the training, but I've only been here 6 months*; the email specifies that employees can only apply for the roles if they have worked at the company for more than one year. **(D)** is correct.

PRACTICE TEST 2

 **Track 10**

Play Track 10 to hear the audio for Part I.

SECTION 1—LISTENING COMPREHENSION

In the Listening Comprehension Section, you will have the chance to demonstrate how well you understand spoken English. The Listening Comprehension Section will take approximately 45 minutes. There are four parts, and directions are given for each part. You must mark your answers on the answer sheet. Do not write them in the test book.

PART I: PHOTOGRAPHS

Directions: For each question, you will hear four statements about the photograph in your test book. When you hear the statements, choose the one statement that best describes what you see in the photograph. Then, find the number of the question on your answer sheet and mark your answer. The statements will not be written in your test book and will be spoken just once.

Now listen to the four statements.

Choice (C), "The mechanic is under the car," best describes what you see in the picture. Therefore, you should fill in choice (C) on your answer sheet.

1. 

2. 

3.

4.

5.

6.

 **Track 11**

Play Track 11 to hear the audio for Part II.

PART II: QUESTION-RESPONSE

Directions: You will hear a question or statement and three responses spoken in English. They will be spoken only once and will not be printed in your test book. Choose the best response to the question or statement and mark the letter on your answer sheet.

Listen to a sample question:

Sample Answer

Choice (B), "Yes, what can I help you with?" best answers the question. Therefore, you should fill in choice (B) in your answer sheet.

7. Mark your answer on your answer sheet.

8. Mark your answer on your answer sheet.

9. Mark your answer on your answer sheet.

10. Mark your answer on your answer sheet.

11. Mark your answer on your answer sheet.

12. Mark your answer on your answer sheet.

13. Mark your answer on your answer sheet.

14. Mark your answer on your answer sheet.

15. Mark your answer on your answer sheet.

16. Mark your answer on your answer sheet.

17. Mark your answer on your answer sheet.

18. Mark your answer on your answer sheet.

19. Mark your answer on your answer sheet.

20. Mark your answer on your answer sheet.

21. Mark your answer on your answer sheet.

22. Mark your answer on your answer sheet.

23. Mark your answer on your answer sheet.

24. Mark your answer on your answer sheet.

25. Mark your answer on your answer sheet.

26. Mark your answer on your answer sheet.

27. Mark your answer on your answer sheet.

28. Mark your answer on your answer sheet.

29. Mark your answer on your answer sheet.

30. Mark your answer on your answer sheet.

31. Mark your answer on your answer sheet.

GO ON TO THE NEXT PAGE.

Track 12

Play Track 12 to hear the audio for Part III.

PART III: SHORT CONVERSATIONS

Directions: You will now hear a number of conversations between two people. You will have to answer three questions about what the speakers say in each conversation. Select the best response and mark the letter on your answer sheet. The conversations will be spoken only once and will not be printed in your test book.

32. What does Mufasta say about Los Angeles?

A. He applied for a job there.
B. He's going to move there.
C. His cousin lives there.
D. He's going there for the weekend.

33. Who is Stuart?

A. Thandie's boss
B. Thandie's assistant
C. Mufasta's partner
D. Mustafa's boss

34. What do we know Mr. Albright?

A. He offered Mustafa a job.
B. He wants to live in Los Angeles.
C. He told Thandie she could take Stuart to LA with her.
D. He interviewed Stuart for a position in LA.

---

35. What is the man looking for?

A. his desk
B. Mrs. Silva
C. staples
D. boxes

36. Where is what he is looking for?

A. on his desk
B. in the closet
C. in Mrs. Silva's office
D. in the top drawer

37. What does the woman offer to do?

A. to take him out for a run
B. to check the top drawer
C. to get what the man needs
D. to order four boxes

---

38. What is the problem with the lecture?

A. It starts too late.
B. Professor Turan is sick.
C. Professor Turan might not be able to give the lecture.
D. It was canceled.

39. What suggestion does the woman make?

A. going out in the snow
B. showing a video
C. coming to the building through an alternative route
D. looking for the professor in his office

40. Why does the man disagree with the woman?

A. He thinks they shouldn't cancel the lecture.
B. He doesn't like videos.
C. He doesn't want to be involved in her latest projects.
D. He wants to invite the professor to a different lecture.

---

41. What do the man and woman tell the other woman about?
   - **A.** a promotion
   - **B.** a new company
   - **C.** a new office at their company
   - **D.** a new position that is available in their building

42. What does Michel say about New Zealand?
   - **A.** It'd be amazing to live there.
   - **B.** He's going to move there.
   - **C.** His family lives there.
   - **D.** There are many job opportunities in his field.

43. What does Louise NOT say about New Zealand?
   - **A.** The food is amazing.
   - **B.** The weather's incredible.
   - **C.** It's a good place to live.
   - **D.** Her sister loves New Zealand.

---

44. Whose job application was unsuccessful?
   - **A.** Malik
   - **B.** Oliver
   - **C.** Monika
   - **D.** Peter

45. What does the woman say about Peter?
   - **A.** His behavior is justified.
   - **B.** He's not qualified.
   - **C.** His father helps him out a lot.
   - **D.** He probably thought he was too good for his job.

46. What does the man say about the recruitment decision at the end?
   - **A.** It was stupid.
   - **B.** It was unsurprising.
   - **C.** It stinks.
   - **D.** It hasn't been received well.

---

47. Who recommended the film to the woman?
   - **A.** Abdullah
   - **B.** her sister
   - **C.** a colleague
   - **D.** the man

48. What does the man say about DVDs?
   - **A.** He thinks they're better than streaming.
   - **B.** He thinks they're better than nothing.
   - **C.** He says Abdullah rents them.
   - **D.** He doesn't like renting them.

49. What does the man want to do?
   - **A.** finish the film they're watching
   - **B.** download a film
   - **C.** call her sister
   - **D.** hire a streaming service

---

50. What does the man say about his jacket?
   - **A.** He's had it for years.
   - **B.** He doesn't like wearing it.
   - **C.** It's too tight.
   - **D.** He couldn't find it.

51. Where are they going?
   - **A.** to a clothes store
   - **B.** to the theater
   - **C.** to the movies
   - **D.** to a restaurant

52. What is the woman's opinion of the jacket?
   - **A.** She thinks it's too tight.
   - **B.** She doesn't like the color.
   - **C.** She thinks it's beautiful.
   - **D.** She doesn't want the man to wear it.

GO ON TO THE NEXT PAGE.

53. What do the man and woman disagree about?

A. how cold the office is
B. whether or not it's winter
C. the office dress code
D. work productivity

54. What does the woman think their bosses would prefer?

A. that the central heating costs were kept low
B. that the man was warm enough
C. that employees always arrived on time
D. that the man always followed the dress code

55. What does the woman suggest?

A. to check the lost and found for a sweater
B. to go home now and get changed
C. to ask to borrow a colleague's jumper
D. to go shopping at lunch and buy a coat

---

56. Why didn't the woman have a good weekend?

A. She saw a lot of bugs during her trip.
B. Her husband was sick.
C. She had a problem with her toilet.
D. She fell off a rock during her hiking trip.

57. Where did the man go at the weekend?

A. to a party
B. on a hiking trip
C. he thought it was better not to tell her
D. to a meeting

58. Who is Pedro?

A. their boss
B. the woman's boss
C. the man's brother
D. the woman's husband

---

59. What does the man suggest they order for lunch?

A. fried chicken
B. Chinese
C. Japanese
D. anything as long as it's good

60. Why doesn't the woman accept the man's suggestion?

A. She thinks it has too much cholesterol.
B. She doesn't like rice.
C. She loves Chinese.
D. She wants to eat something with mayo.

61. What does the man decide to have for lunch?

A. Japanese
B. a sandwich
C. tuna pasta
D. avocado salad

---

62. What is the woman doing?

A. waiting at the Madison Building
B. giving directions
C. looking for her friend
D. going to her meeting

63. Why does the man say "the good news is"?

A. The man is at the Madison Building.
B. The woman is close to where her meeting is taking place.
C. The woman followed the right directions.
D. The man is not going to the Madison Building.

64. Look at the graphic below. Which number shows the location of the Madison Building?

- **A.** 1
- **B.** 2
- **C.** 3
- **D.** 4

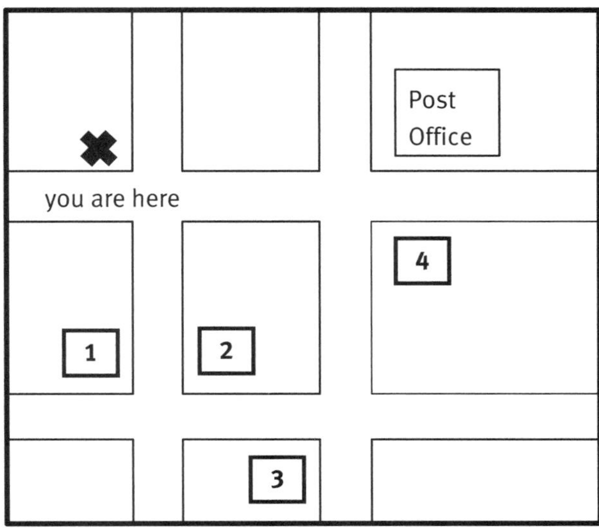

65. What is this conversation mainly about?

- **A.** the yearly profits
- **B.** last quarter's expenses
- **C.** product rebranding
- **D.** the quarterly sales

66. What does the man say is doing well?

- **A.** last quarter's profits
- **B.** laptop sales
- **C.** product rebranding
- **D.** yearly sales

67. Look at the graphic below. Which product does the man think should be discontinued?

- **A.** printers
- **B.** software
- **C.** laptops
- **D.** cell phones

Quarterly Profit Report

	This Quarter	Last Quarter
Laptop Sales	$45,000	$23,000
Cell Phone Sales	$3,500	$2,500
Software Sales	$4,500	$6,000
Printer Sales	$2,500	$4,000
Other	$10,000	$11,000

68. What does the woman imply about WhisperTech?

- **A.** They are the speakers' most valuable clients.
- **B.** It provides a similar service to the company the speakers work at.
- **C.** The company has not been very successful in recent years.
- **D.** It makes more money than the company the speakers work at.

69. Why are the speakers meeting Ramona?

- **A.** to discuss buying a company
- **B.** to strategize plans to close WhisperTech
- **C.** to interview the CEO about her career
- **D.** to plan a retirement party

70. Look at the graphic below. When will they schedule the meeting?

- **A.** Monday
- **B.** Tuesday
- **C.** Thursday
- **D.** Friday

Cherry's Calendar

	Monday	Tuesday	Wednesday	Thursday	Friday
AM	Project Scoping		Annual Leave	Budgeting	
PM		Finance Meeting			Interviews

 **Track 13**

Play Track 13 to hear the audio for Part IV.

PART IV: SHORT TALKS

Directions: In this part of the test you will hear some talks given by a single speaker. You will have to answer 3 questions about each talk. Choose the correct option and mark the answer (A), (B), (C), or (D) on your answer sheet.

71. Why did Mr. Ginola call?

- **A.** To provide information about a meeting
- **B.** To hire a video maker
- **C.** To confirm a telephone number
- **D.** To check an email address

72. What is the video conference about?

- **A.** the schedule for Thursday
- **B.** the new business agenda
- **C.** an acquisition
- **D.** new business opportunities in Boston

73. Why does Mr. Ginola give his office number?

- **A.** so people can reach him for the conference
- **B.** in case people might want to contact him before Thursday
- **C.** so staff can help him decide the agenda
- **D.** to confirm the video conference

---

74. Where are you most likely to hear this announcement?

- **A.** on a plane
- **B.** on a train
- **C.** at the train station
- **D.** at the airport

75. Why is there a delay?

- **A.** There are too many passengers.
- **B.** It's raining in New York.
- **C.** There is bad weather in Seattle.
- **D.** The system's being updated.

76. Look at the table. Which flight is the speaker discussing?

- **A.** Flight 1
- **B.** Flight 2
- **C.** Flight 3
- **D.** Flight 4

Flights

	Airline	Status	Boarding Time
Flight 1	American Airways	delayed	3:55
Flight 2	Seattle Airline	on time	3:55
Flight 3	American Airways	on time	2:00
Flight 4	Seattle Airline	delayed	2:00

---

77. What was Mrs. Takeda's speech about?

- **A.** contributing to the society
- **B.** dealing with questions
- **C.** innovations
- **D.** current market affairs

78. What does the speaker mean when she says, "please show her some Brazilian courtesy"?

- **A.** She is asking the audience to show her around and help her find her way.
- **B.** She is looking for a language translator to help with answering questions.
- **C.** She is asking the audience not to interrupt the guest while she eats.
- **D.** She is looking for a volunteer to help the guest with her bags.

79. When's the next presentation?

A. in 10 minutes
B. at lunchtime
C. after lunchtime
D. at the end of the day

---

80. What is the recording mainly about?

A. guided tours
B. restaurants in Las Vegas
C. a service interruption
D. hotel reservations

81. How can callers make a theater reservation?

A. by using their website
B. only after 27 November
C. by sending an email
D. by calling an agency

82. What service do they NOT offer?

A. hotel information
B. theater reservations
C. restaurant reservations
D. guided tours

---

83. What is the event?

A. A dinner event for human resources professionals
B. The grand opening of Chef Lafayette's dining experience
C. Harold Clipton's professional development program
D. A dining experience with Michael Lucas

84. Who has worked in professional development for more than 30 years?

A. the speaker
B. Harrold Clipton
C. Michelle Lucas
D. Chef Lafayette

85. Why does the speaker say, "that's enough from me"?

A. He is admonishing the audience.
B. He is introducing the next speaker
C. He is drawing the event to a close.
D. He has had enough food.

---

86. Where would you be most likely to hear this talk?

A. a TV ad
B. a lecture
C. an opening speech
D. a radio soap opera

87. What requirement is NOT mentioned?

A. replying to emails
B. speaking on the phone
C. being good with people
D. expertise in finance

88. What's the name of the company responsible for the recording?

A. Wall Street
B. Office Wizards
C. Work For You
D. No Magic

---

89. Who is giving this announcement?

A. the master of ceremony
B. a member of staff
C. a student
D. Ms. Bilal

90. What is the event?

A. a breakfast get-together
B. a luncheon
C. a dinner party
D. a seminar

91. What can be found in the welcome pack?

A. Ms. Bilal's speech, her notes and the course schedule

B. a training manual, the course schedule, and a notepad

C. a training manual, Ms. Bilal's schedule, and her notes

D. a map, the course schedule, and a notepad

---

92. Where is this speech taking place?

A. on a TV commercial

B. in a company meeting

C. on a radio show

D. at a press conference

93. What was the survey about?

A. TV channels

B. boxes

C. product assessment

D. convenience stores

94. What were the survey's main findings?

A. People are using streaming services more than ever.

B. People prefer watching TV shows at fixed times.

C. The quality of the image provided is better than before.

D. People would like more "box sets."

---

95. What is the recording about?

A. a weather forecast

B. vacation plans

C. beach report

D. local news

96. What does the speaker expect to happen throughout the weekend?

A. a good shower

B. 10 different things

C. blue skies

D. people will listen to the local news

97. When does the recording take place?

A. Sunday

B. Friday

C. Saturday

D. Tuesday

---

98. What kind of sale is the store having?

A. holiday

B. going out of business

C. end of summer

D. back to school

99. Which products are discounted 50%?

A. CDs

B. LPs

C. MDs

D. electronics

100. Look at the table. Which store is being discussed?

A. Store 1

B. Store 2

C. Store 3

D. Store 4

	Location	**Hours of Operation**	**Type of Store**
Store 1	52nd and Broadway	10:00 until 21:00	fashion
Store 2	number 52, Broadway	10:00 until 21:00	stationery
Store 3	number 52, Broadway	9:00 until 22:00	shoes
Store 4	52nd and Broadway	9:00 until 22:00	tech

Stop! This is the end of the Listening Comprehension Section of the exam. Turn to Part V.

You will have one hour and 15 minutes to complete Parts V, VI, and VII of the exam.

SECTION 2—READING COMPREHENSION

In the Reading Comprehension Section, you will read a variety of texts and answer different types of questions. The Reading Comprehension Section will last 75 minutes. There are three parts, and directions are given for each part. You are encouraged to answer as many questions as possible within the allotted time. Mark your answers on the separate answer sheet. Do no write them in the test book.

PART V: INCOMPLETE SENTENCES

Directions: There are 30 incomplete sentences below (questions 101–130). Four words or phrases are given below each one of them. You are to select the best answer (A), (B), (C), or (D) to complete the sentence. Then mark the letters on your answer sheet.

101. You can ________ me to take you to the airport.

A. count on
B. count in
C. count down
D. count up

102. If money was the issue, she ________ hesitate over signing the new contract.

A. can't
B. wouldn't
C. mustn't
D. may not

103. Profits soared during the last semester; ________, the board was extremely happy with the new management.

A. nevertheless
B. however
C. therefore
D. having said that

104. Sales usually fall drastically ________ January. It's the post-Christmas effect.

A. on
B. in
C. at
D. last

105. The owners will allow neither management ________ staff to work overtime due to budget constraints.

A. and
B. or
C. but
D. nor

106. The new ________ starts on Tuesday. I heard she's really tough.

A. consultant
B. consult
C. consultation
D. consulting

107. Mr. Passos handed in his resignation only ________ that his new job had fallen through.

- **A.** find out
- **B.** found out
- **C.** had found out
- **D.** to find out

108. The new client wants his merchandising ________ by Monday morning, so back to work and no excuses.

- **A.** deliver
- **B.** delivered
- **C.** to deliver
- **D.** delivering

109. ________ the European crisis, the euro has fallen by 10%.

- **A.** After
- **B.** Because of
- **C.** Although
- **D.** When

110. The market is so volatile that prices ________.

- **A.** have daily been readjusted
- **B.** daily have been readjusted
- **C.** have been readjusted daily
- **D.** have been daily readjusted

111. UPW announced that a German group is expected to ________ its South American plants.

- **A.** acquire
- **B.** acquired
- **C.** acquiring
- **D.** will acquire

112. Investors should be made aware that Mr. Simpson has a very ________ way of doing business.

- **A.** parallel
- **B.** direct
- **C.** perpendicular
- **D.** adjacent

113. In order to increase productivity, staff must be ________ motivated.

- **A.** frequent
- **B.** frequented
- **C.** frequently
- **D.** frequency

114. Bonuses may be awarded at the ________ of the board.

- **A.** discretion
- **B.** discrete
- **C.** discretely
- **D.** discretionary

115. ________ by the quarterly numbers, the board granted a hefty bonus to all management and staff.

- **A.** Impressive
- **B.** Impress
- **C.** Impressing
- **D.** Impressed

116. Employees who lose faith in their bosses ________ question most decisions taken by management.

- **A.** approximately
- **B.** specially
- **C.** typically
- **D.** exactly

117. Mrs. Youssef has submitted a redevelopment ________ to convert her house into three apartments.

A. permission
B. allowance
C. statement
D. proposal

118. Jack Wilkins will be replacing Salvatore Datolo, ________ is being transferred to our new branch in Montreal.

A. which
B. that
C. who
D. it

119. Duncan Media has not launched a successful software ________ its operational system *Adios* came out five years ago.

A. for
B. from
C. since
D. when

120. For more than a decade, Halford Kitchens has helped people ________ their dreams into reality.

A. adapt
B. transform
C. replace
D. inspire

121. If banks ________ the number of mortgages, house prices would have to fall.

A. restricted
B. restrict
C. will restrict
D. restricting

122. The landlord will want the deposit ________ before giving the keys.

A. be paid
B. paid
C. pay
D. paying

123. There is no ________ body to fight for workers in many developing countries.

A. represent
B. representation
C. representing
D. representative

124. There has been an increase in local ________ national violence.

A. but
B. however
C. nevertheless
D. and

125. The local politicians will meet ________ Seattle next week.

A. on
B. at
C. in
D. from

126. The company will collaborate ________ the police investigation.

A. of
B. in
C. with
D. from

127. Our recommendation was to ________ interest rates.

A. raise

B. raised

C. have raised

D. raising

128. ________ the new manager refuses to praise his staff, people are still doing their best for the company.

A. Therefore

B. Although

C. However

D. Because of

129. Memos ________.

A. are once distributed a week.

B. once are distributed a week.

C. are distributed a week once.

D. are distributed once a week.

130. ________ Mr. King was giving his speech, people were looking at their phones.

A. During

B. So

C. Why

D. While

PART VI: TEXT COMPLETION

Directions: Read the texts below. A word is missing in some of the sentences. You are to choose the best answer (A), (B), (C), or (D) to complete the text. Then mark the letters on your answer sheet.

Questions 131–134 refer to the following letter.

PWF S/A

Alameda Araguaia, 614

Barueri, SP 06487-370

Tel: (55) 11 5553129 Fax: (55) 11 5553198

www.pwf.com

November 14, 2016

Ms. Paula Lampard

Supervisor of Product Development

Target Solutions

Boston, MA 03276

Dear Ms. Lampard,

It was a pleasure __________ (131) you at the conference in Moscow last month.

As we discussed, I sincerely believe that our cables and wires can not only save you a lot of money, but also improve the quality of your services. If you are still willing, I would like to ship you some __________ (132) of our premium copper, gold, and platinum series for your evaluation.

I am sure you will find them to be of the highest standard. Should you decide to opt for us as one of your suppliers, I believe meeting in person would allow us to __________ (133) evaluate your wants and needs.

Please let me know, at your earliest convenience, __________ (134).

Cordially,

Henrique Farias

CEO

(55) 11 5553128

hfarias@pwf.com

131. **A.** meet
B. met
C. will meet
D. meeting

132. **A.** samples
B. tastings
C. demonstrations
D. shows

133. **A.** fully
B. full
C. fill
D. filling

134. **A.** when we are likely to receive your samples.
B. the price list for our items can be found on our website at www.pwf.com.br.
C. see you at the conference next year!
D. if and when you would like us to ship the samples.

Questions 135–138 refer to the email that follows.

From: Giovanni
To: Mohammad
Re: Rome

Hi Mohammad,

Julie just told me you're moving to Rome! I was so sad to learn that you will be leaving us but I know that you have always wanted to live in Europe. It seems like all my friends are ___(135)___ Chicago for one reason or another.

If you need any help with the preparations, please let me know. Also, I have a very good friend from University who lives in Rome if you need a place to stay for a short time ___(136)___ you are looking for a new home.

___(137)___. It has been a pleasure working with you all these years and I can only wish you the best in the world. I know you will probably be very busy in the coming weeks, but I'd love to meet for dinner or drinks before you embark on this new adventure. Fridays are always good ___(138)___ me. If you can't make it, I'll understand.

Talk to you soon,

Giovanni

135. **A.** leave
B. leaving
C. left
D. having left

136. **A.** after
B. before
C. during
D. while

137. **A.** Her email is sancharez@email.com
B. The office really won't be the same without you.
C. I regret to inform you that I will be terminating my contract with this company.
D. Since you've been gone, things have really changed here.

138. **A.** at
B. on
C. in
D. for

Questions 139–142 refer to the following brochure.

Checklist for being successful

Any ambitious person on the road to fame and success should keep a checklist close by.

____
139

☐ **1. Always a professional**

Whatever you do, you have to be professional. Remember to be fair and remain polite at _________ (140), because tables can turn at any moment in professional life.

☐ **2. Think about the future**

Today's decisions will dictate your future tomorrow. Manage relationships in a courteous manner and acting out decisions in the best fashion. Too many people fail to see _________ (141) the tip of their nose and then wake up wondering what happened to the rest of their face.

☐ **3. Understand your mistakes**

We all make mistakes. Learn _________ (142) your mistakes because no one is infallible. Avoid arrogance and remember: the key, when all is said and done, is how you bounce back.

Want to learn more?

Call us at 0800 555 7124 and speak to one of our counselors.

Your future starts today!

139. **A.** Discuss these policy changes with your line manager.
B. Check out our website for an example.
C. Here's a handy one for you to use:
D. Try to remain calm while you practice.

140. **A.** the time
B. all times
C. all the times
D. sometimes

141. **A.** behind
B. between
C. behalf
D. beyond

142. **A.** from
B. of
C. by
D. in

Questions 143–146 refer to the email that follows.

From: hannah@abol.com
To: moorek@wells.com
Subject: Application for post IT2976–Hannah Black

Dear Mr. Moore,

Please find enclosed my résumé in application for the post ______ (143) in the *Scranton Times* on February 16.

The nature of my degree course has prepared me for this post. It involved a great deal of independent research, requiring initiative, self-motivation, and a ______ (144) range of skills. For one course, Marketing Tools, an understanding of the internet industry was essential. I found this subject to be very stimulating. I am a fast and accurate writer who thrives when working ______ (145) pressure. I have a keen eye for detail and I should be very grateful for the opportunity to progress to market reporting. I believe I am able to take on the responsibility of this position immediately, and have the enthusiasm and determination to ensure that I make a success of it.

______ (146)

I look forward to hearing from you soon,

Hannah Black

143. **A.** advert
B. advertisement
C. advertising
D. advertised

144. **A.** big
B. wide
C. deep
D. long

145. **A.** under
B. with
C. on
D. in

146. **A.** Thank you for taking the time to consider this application.
B. Yours sincerely,
C. Thank you for taking the time to apply to this position.
D. Send my regards to Jane and the kids.

PART VII: READING COMPREHENSION

Directions: Read the selection of texts below. Each text is followed by a group of questions. Select the correct option and mark the letter (A), (B), (C), or (D) on your answer sheet.

Questions 147–149 refer to the following fax.

FAX

From: Divit Sai

To: Shipping, Upton Textile

Fax Number: 613-555-1975

Date: January 12, 2017

Order:

15 red canopies (ref. CA91) @ $50.00 = $750.00

30 red umbrellas (ref. UM08) @ $5.50 = $165.00

10 blue display booths (ref. DB03) @ $140.00 = $1,400.00

Total Order = $2,315.00

Bill to:

BBX Ltd

Box 14776

Ottawa, Ontario, Canada K1A 0A1

Ship to:

Unique Hotel

205 Ste-Catherine St. West

Montreal, Quebec, Canada H3B 5L1

1-514-555-2561

147. How many total items are being ordered?

A. 10

B. 15

C. 30

D. 55

148. Where are the items to be shipped?

A. Upton Textile

B. Ottawa

C. Montreal

D. Divit Sai

149. What is the total price for the blue items?

A. $165.00

B. $750.00

C. $1,400.00

D. $2,315.00

GO ON TO THE NEXT PAGE.

Questions 150–153 refer to the following notice.

> ***Investing in Properties?***
>
> Learn the ins and outs of property investment at this informational webinar. This dynamic, info-packed webinar will all cover all the basics of property investment. It will cover town planning, redevelopment proposals, buy-to-let mortgages, bidding in auctions, and much, much more. The webinar will be led by a group of property experts with vast experience in North America, Asia, and Europe. There is no fee for this webinar so what are you waiting for?
>
> Join us on Saturday, March 22
>
> 3–4 P.M.
>
> ***www.dlcproperties.com/webinar***
>
> Registration required. Limited places!

150. Where would this notice most likely be found?

A. in a glossy magazine
B. in a department store catalog
C. on a news website
D. in the movies

151. Who is conducting the webinar?

A. a property investor
B. a town planner
C. a group of experts
D. an IT technician

152. How much does the webinar cost?

A. nothing
B. it doesn't say
C. $22
D. you can find out on their website

153. Which is NOT mentioned in the notice?

A. the different topics the webinar will cover
B. the date and time
C. the number of places
D. the speakers

Questions 154–156 refer to the table that follows.

REFRESHER 2016

Group 1:	**Group 2:**
From June 12 to August 21 2 to 5 P.M. Workload: 24 hours	From June 13 to August 22 1:30 to 4:30 P.M. Workload: 24 hours
SCHEDULE:	SCHEDULE:
26/06	**27/06**
CLT (Communicative Language Teaching)	CLT (Communicative Language Teaching)
03/07	**11/07**
Classroom Management & Dynamics	Classroom Management & Dynamics
17/07	**18/07**
Teaching Grammar	Teaching Grammar
24/07	**25/07**
Teaching Vocabulary	Teaching Vocabulary
31/07	**01/08**
Teacher Roles + Learner Roles	Teacher Roles + Learner Roles
07/08	**08/08**
Productive Skills	Productive Skills
14/08	**15/08**
Receptive Skills	Receptive Skills
21/08	**22/08**
Visual Aids in EFL + Blended Learning	Visual Aids in EFL + Blended Learning

PLACE OF EVENT: Bournemouth University
Fern Barrow, Talbot Campus, Poole, Dorset, BH12 5BB

154. How many workshops is the course made of?

- **A.** 2
- **B.** 3
- **C.** 8
- **D.** 16

155. Who is this refresher aimed at?

- **A.** teachers
- **B.** managers
- **C.** producers
- **D.** doctors

156. How long is each workshop?

- **A.** 3 hours
- **B.** 24 hours
- **C.** 2 months
- **D.** a year

Questions 157–159 refer to the following announcement.

> As the market leader with over sixty years of experience making people's lives easier with durable easy-to-use products, LW can offer you exciting career opportunities. — [1] —
>
> LW is constantly growing and looking for energetic and innovative professionals who are not afraid to think outside the box. — [2] — If you are looking for a position in a modern and stimulating work environment with plenty of opportunities to hone your skills and grow professionally, then we want you!
>
> We are currently receiving applications for more than 20 posts in areas that range from product development to human resources. — [3] — LW offers an exciting financial package including competitive salary, cycling scheme, health club, health insurance and much more. — [4] —
>
> Please visit our website www.lwcareers.com or call us on 1-800-555-2012 to find out about the exciting job opportunities awaiting for you.

157. What is this announcement about?

- **A.** career opportunities
- **B.** a TV listing
- **C.** a cycling scheme
- **D.** a new range of products

158. In which of the positions marked [1], [2], [3], and [4] does the following sentence best belong?
"Does this sound like you?"

- **A.** [1]
- **B.** [2]
- **C.** [3]
- **D.** [4]

159. What is the name of the company that made the announcement?

- **A.** LW
- **B.** Health Club
- **C.** Outside the Box
- **D.** The Range

Questions 160–163 refer to the following letter.

Mr. Park
3 Middle River Drive
Fort Lauderdale, FL 33305

Abia Abu
TV World
19 22nd Avenue
Miami, FL 33136

October 15 2016

Dear Ms. Abu,

On October 7, I ordered the following: Innovations 4K Ultra HD Smart TV 60'. — [1] —. However, I have now noticed that the product above is outdated and does not live up to the standards of most similar products in the market. In fact, this TV offers poorer image quality than my old television, which I bought more than 5 years ago. I am very disappointed with the product and would like to cancel the order and ask you to confirm that you will not be claiming any further payment. Please contact me as soon as possible and let me know how to return the product and cancel my payment plan. — [2] — You can reach me by phone at 954-555-6256.

— [3] —Enclosed is a copy of the invoice and payment plan contract. I look forward to hearing from you soon — [4] —.

Sincerely,

Johnathan Park

160. Why does the author of the email write "in fact"?

A. to provide statistics
B. to emphasize his previous point
C. to state his emotional reaction
D. to outline his requests

161. What information is NOT mentioned in the letter?

A. the delivery date
B. the product model
C. the problem with the product
D. the form of payment for the product

162. What is enclosed with the letter?

A. TV instructions
B. a photo ID
C. a financing contract
D. an image of the product

163. In which of the positions marked [1], [2], [3], and [4] does the following sentence best belong?

"I had seen the product on television and I had very high expectations."

A. [1]
B. [2]
C. [3]
D. [4]

Questions 164–166 refer to the article that follows.

The Best in VENICE Entertainment

Nestled beneath a magnificent cliff line, the bay enjoys its own micro-climate, some of the warmest sea temperatures in California, and stunning views of the mountains. Whatever you want from a day at the seaside, you'll find it all here. Whether it's chilling on a deckchair, strolling along the beach, enjoying tasty food, or just admiring miles of breath-taking coast line—Venice is the ideal location whatever the weather or time of year. Every section offers a different experience, so why not try out one of many superb water sports or enjoy plenty of family attractions? There is a bit of sand with your name on it!

Explore new places, visit your favorite family attraction, try a different activity, or embark on an exciting adventure. Make the most of the great outdoors in Venice by jumping in the water and experiencing one of our many water sports, such as surfing, kayaking, and jet-skiing, to name a few. If you prefer to stay dry, why not hire a bike, go on foot, or enjoy a guided tour and discover hidden gems and must-see locations.

Whether you're visiting Venice for a day or staying for the whole summer, be sure to check out **Info Venice** for great activities and unique attractions!

www.infovenice.com

164. What is the main topic of the article?

A. water sports
B. summer vacations
C. family entertainment
D. things to do in Venice

165. The word *strolling* in paragraph 1, line 4, is closest in meaning to

A. walk
B. run
C. cycle
D. ride

166. According to the article, where can you find more information about Venice?

A. outdoors
B. on a website
C. tourist information
D. different locations

Questions 167–170 refer to the following chart.

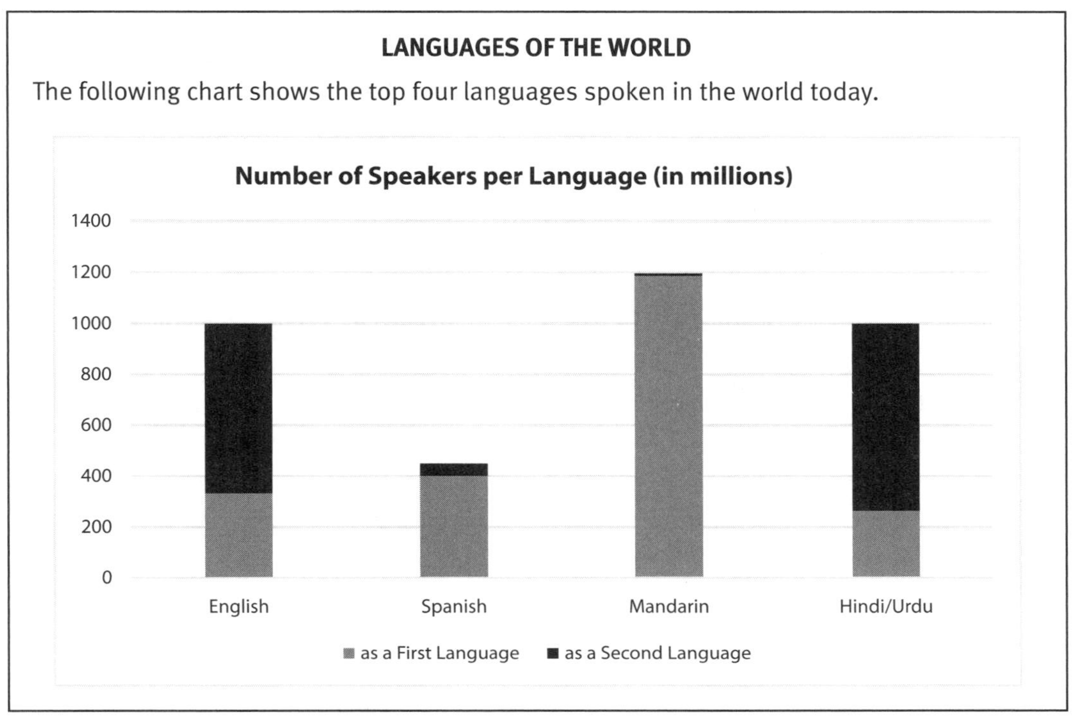

167. Which language has approximately 400 million native speakers?

- **A.** English
- **B.** Spanish
- **C.** Mandarin
- **D.** Hindi/Urdu

168. How many people speak English as a second language?

- **A.** approximately 350 million
- **B.** approximately 450 million
- **C.** approximately 650 million
- **D.** approximately 1 billion

169. How many speakers of Hindi/Urdu are there in total?

- **A.** approximately 250 million
- **B.** approximately 750 million
- **C.** approximately 1 billion
- **D.** approximately 1.2 billion

170. Which language has the fewest non-native speakers?

- **A.** English
- **B.** Spanish
- **C.** Mandarin
- **D.** Hindi/Urdu

Questions 171–173 refer to the advertisement below.

> **ITab 2**
>
> Enjoy greater flexibility than ever before with the ITab 2. Remarkably slim and lightweight, use it to take your e-books, photos, videos, and work-related files with you everywhere you go.
>
> The ITab 2's high definition display provides you with the perfect environment for performing office tasks. Use the enhanced ITab S2's power keyboard for a desktop experience and work on a range of documents and files.
>
> Get top security with the ITab 2's accurate fingerprint system. Activate the fingerprint lock by pressing the home button.
>
> Order online from www.itab2.com and get a free name engraving or hard cover for your ITab 2.
>
> ITab 2 available in black, silver and gold. From $399.00.

171. Which of the following adjectives CANNOT be used to describe the product?

- **A.** thin
- **B.** light
- **C.** flexible
- **D.** free

172. What is the fingerprint functionality for?

- **A.** unlocking the tablet
- **B.** making the system accurate
- **C.** using it at home
- **D.** using the power keyboard

173. Which is a benefit of buying the product online?

- **A.** You pay only $399.00.
- **B.** You get to choose the color.
- **C.** You can get your name engraved on the tablet at no extra cost.
- **D.** You get the latest model.

Questions 174–175 refer to the notice that follows.

Daily Specials

Monday

Cream of broccoli soup served with garlic croutons and mascarpone cheese. Served with a cheese twist.

Tuesday

Gluten-free enchiladas with sweet and sour pulled pork, shredded chicken breast, and jalapeno cheese. Served with a green salad.

Wednesday

Homemade mac and cheese made with fresh spinach pasta, gruyere cheese, and parmesan shavings. Served with garlic bread.

Thursday

Giant sweet potato topped with Greek-style cheese, cherry tomatoes, and black olives. Served with a green salad.

Friday

Grilled mini eggplant with halloumi cheese and Portobello mushrooms. Served with a tomato salad.

174. Which daily special is NOT suitable for vegetarians?

- **A.** Monday
- **B.** Tuesday
- **C.** Wednesday
- **D.** Thursday

175. What ingredient do all the specials have in common?

- **A.** bread
- **B.** green salad
- **C.** cheese
- **D.** tomatoes

Questions 176–180 refer to the following advertisement and email.

HAKANO'S INN

Your four-star choice in the center of Tokyo.

Room includes:

- *1 double bed or two single beds*
- *Free Wi-Fi*
- *Cable TV and Pay Per View*
- *Mini bar*

Hotel facilities:

- *24/7 room service*
- *Bistro bar and wine cellar*
- *Game room*
- *Indoor pool and sauna*

Location:

Downtown Tokyo 5 minutes from Shinjuku train station. Free shuttle bus available from major airports and train stations.

Book now** on www.hakanosinn.com and get **a discount rate!

From: Sue Wallace
To: Akihiro Nomoto
Re: Itinerary

Hi Mr. Nomoto,

Attached you will find my travel itinerary. I arrive at Tokyo airport on Sunday, January 19 at 9 A.M. I believe you have arranged for someone to pick me up from the airport with a sign. Can you please confirm that? This is my first time in Tokyo, and since I don't speak the language, I would rather not hire a taxi or use a shuttle service to the hotel. Also, I find 5-star hotels too impersonal so I downgraded my reservation and will be staying at Hakano's Inn in the center of town. Now I can also walk to the office every day, keep fit, and save some precious time.

I look forward to meeting your team so we can start negotiations early on Monday morning.

Thank you,

Sue Wallace

176. Which hotel service does Sue prefer not to use?

A. room service
B. free shuttle bus
C. Wi-Fi
D. hot food

177. What type of hotel was Sue initially going to stay in?

A. a hostel
B. a three-star hotel
C. a four-star hotel
D. a five-star hotel

178. How does Sue intend to go to work?

A. by train
B. by bus
C. by taxi
D. on foot

179. Which reason does Sue NOT give for changing her reservation?

A. She thinks big hotels are too impersonal.
B. She doesn't like 5-star hotels.
C. She can do some exercise.
D. She can save time.

180. When is Sue going to meet Akihiro's colleagues?

A. January 19
B. Sunday
C. Monday
D. 9 A.M.

GO ON TO THE NEXT PAGE.

Questions 181–185 refer to the following two emails.

From: lisat@bmail.com
To: monteiro@dxrecruitment.com
Subject: Referred by Yasmin Patwari

Dear Ms. Monteiro,

My former colleague Yasmin Patwari recommended that I contact you to find out if you had any recommendations regarding employment in the IT industry in New York. I am currently employed at Fast Systems as a Java developer, but I believe it is the right time for a professional challenge.

I would be thankful for any advice you have regarding my job search. I would greatly appreciate it if you would review my résumé, and I would welcome the opportunity to meet with you at your convenience.

Thank you for your consideration. I look forward to hearing from you.

Sincerely,

Lisa Tripura

From: monteiro@dxrecruitment.com
To: lisat@bmail.com
Subject: Re: Referred by Yasmin Patwari

Hi Lisa,

First of all, thanks for choosing us to help you with your next career move. I had a quick look at your résumé and I am sure we will be able to find you a suitable position in no time. The first step would be to meet in person so we can discuss your credentials and experience. How about Thursday, October 27 at 11 A.M.? If it's too soon for you, just let me know and we can rearrange that. On that day, I will need you to bring some form of identification, proof of address, and a copy of your MBA certificate. If you want to bring the original, we can make the copies here.

In the meantime, please get in touch if you have any questions.

Best,

Paola Monteiro

DX Recruitment Solutions

29 3rd Avenue

New York, NY 10011

212-555-3986

181. Why is Lisa contacting Ms. Monteiro?

A. He's Yasmin's boss.
B. She's unemployed.
C. She's looking for a new job.
D. She wants to challenge her.

182. What does Paola recommend?

A. meeting in person
B. getting an MBA
C. reviewing her résumé
D. wearing a suit

183. Which of the following does Paola NOT ask Lisa to bring?

A. a certificate
B. a proof of residence
C. identification
D. a bank statement

184. What do we know about Lisa?

A. She's Yasmin's best friend.
B. She doesn't like her job.
C. She works with computers.
D. She lives in New York.

185. Who does Paola work for?

A. Yasmin
B. a recruitment agency
C. an IT company
D. she's self-employed

GO ON TO THE NEXT PAGE.

Questions 186–190 refer to the following notice, email, and course list.

PERSONAL MARKETING WORKSHOP

All employees are invited to attend a special in-house workshop on personal marketing. The workshop consists of 3 two-hour weekly sessions and will cover basic topics such as body language, writing styles, and language grading. The workshop will be held for three Wednesdays, 5:30–7:30 P.M., starting on March 12. Space is limited. To attend, please call Pietro Bonucci at extension 3241.

From: bonuccihr@newworld.com
To: Undisclosed-Recipient;
Subject: Professional Development Program

Dear all,

We are extremely proud to announce the first workshop part of our continuous professional development program. This first workshop will start next Wednesday, March 12, and will cover basic aspects of personal marketing. For those of you who do not understand the term, personal marketing is the concept of selling your image as a professional through conventional marketing strategies that are used for marketing products. This first workshop will be divided into 3 sessions, always on Wednesday from 5:30–7:30 P.M.

There are 50 spaces available, and if demand is too high, we might consider opening extra sessions on Thursdays. If you have any questions about the workshop contents, you can contact me directly at extension 3241. I would rather answer any questions over the phone so I will not be replying to emails on this subject. Hope you enjoy this new era in Human Resources here at New World and take advantage of all the development opportunities we are about to offer.

Sincerely,

Pietro Bonucci
Head of Human Resources
New World Software
305-555-8851

Title	Start Date	Description
Personal Marketing	March 12	Improve your professional image
Writing Styles	April 12	Develop your linguistic skills
Language Learning	May 12	A beginner's, course in French or Spanish
Body Language	June 12	What is your body saying about you?

186. What is the topic of the workshop discussed in the email?

A. Marketing

B. Personal Marketing

C. Professional Development

D. Human Resources

187. What is the workshop part of?

A. a software training course

B. marketing strategies

C. a professional development program

D. extra sessions

188. Where will the workshops be held?

A. at home

B. at New World

C. over the phone

D. at a hotel

189. How often does a new workshop begin?

A. every week

B. every second Wednesday

C. every 3 weeks

D. once a month

190. If an employees would like more information about the course, how should they contact Mr. Bonucci?

A. over the phone

B. in person

C. by email

D. at the workshop next Wednesday

Questions 191–195 refer to the following agenda, email, and text message chain.

AFRICA UNITE

CHARITY DINNER 2016

THURSDAY, SEPTEMBER 11, 6:30 P.M.

PLACE: REGINALD'S

AGENDA

1. Welcome Cocktail with Cristiano Lopez
2. Slideshow–Previous Years' Projects 2013–15 with Charlotte Johnson
3. Fundraising Auction with Miss Universe Jennifer Cato
4. Date Auction with Patricia Anniston
5. Dance Performance by Yuri Popov

Tickets: $2,000.00

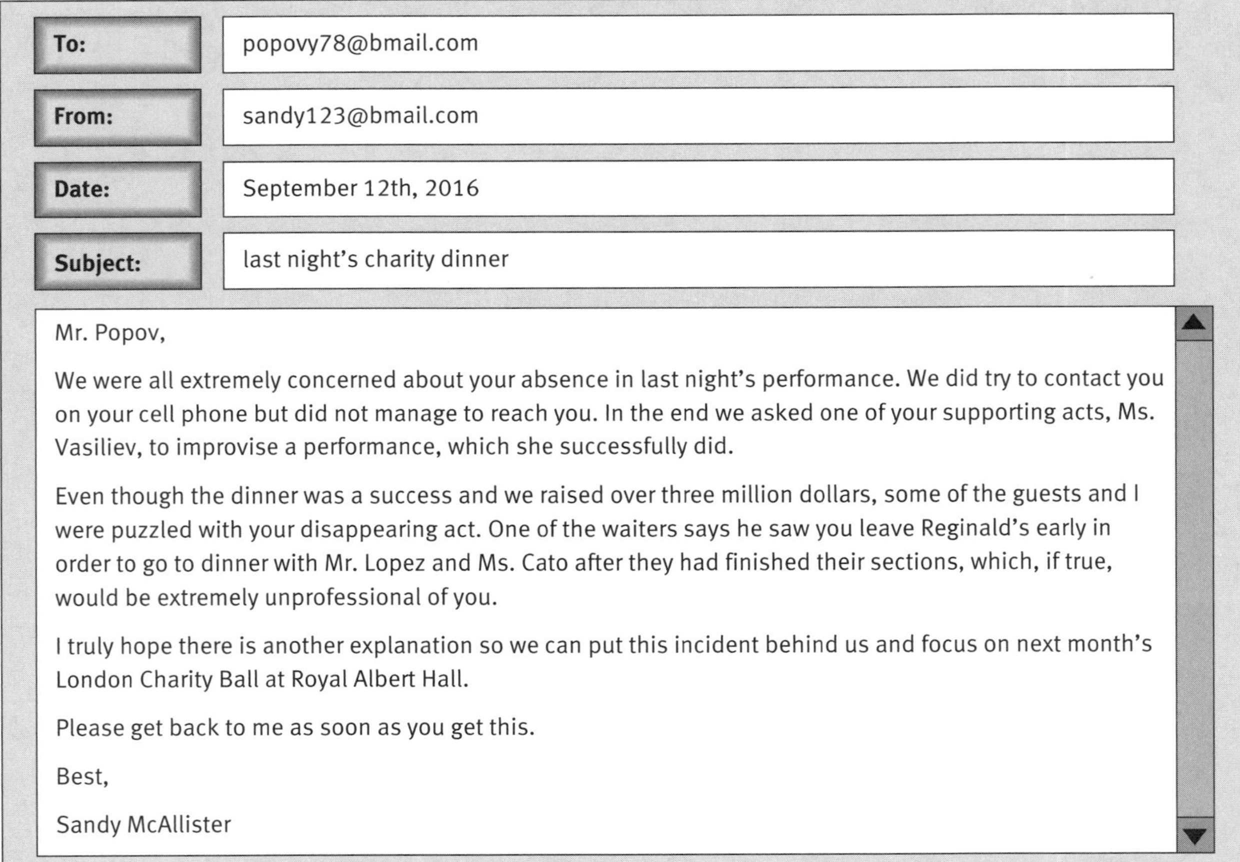

To: popovy78@bmail.com

From: sandy123@bmail.com

Date: September 12th, 2016

Subject: last night's charity dinner

Mr. Popov,

We were all extremely concerned about your absence in last night's performance. We did try to contact you on your cell phone but did not manage to reach you. In the end we asked one of your supporting acts, Ms. Vasiliev, to improvise a performance, which she successfully did.

Even though the dinner was a success and we raised over three million dollars, some of the guests and I were puzzled with your disappearing act. One of the waiters says he saw you leave Reginald's early in order to go to dinner with Mr. Lopez and Ms. Cato after they had finished their sections, which, if true, would be extremely unprofessional of you.

I truly hope there is another explanation so we can put this incident behind us and focus on next month's London Charity Ball at Royal Albert Hall.

Please get back to me as soon as you get this.

Best,

Sandy McAllister

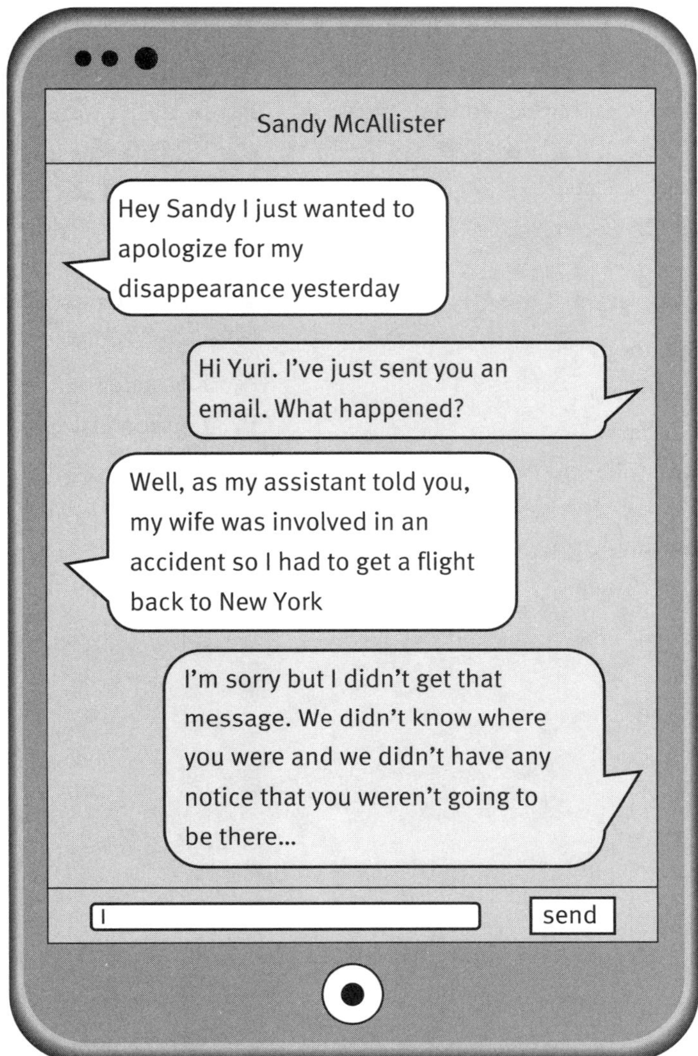
Sandy McAllister
Hey Sandy I just wanted to apologize for my disappearance yesterday
Hi Yuri. I've just sent you an email. What happened?
Well, as my assistant told you, my wife was involved in an accident so I had to get a flight back to New York
I'm sorry but I didn't get that message. We didn't know where you were and we didn't have any notice that you weren't going to be there...
send

191. Why does Sandy send the email?

A. She is worried about Mr. Popov's wife.
B. She wants to know what happened the night before.
C. She couldn't find Ms. Cato.
D. She's looking for Mr. Lopez.

192. How much money was raised at the event?

A. two thousand dollars
B. over two million dollars
C. three thousand dollars
D. over three million dollars

193. Who spoke about charitable projects?

A. Cristiano Lopez
B. Charlotte Johnson
C. Jennifer Cato
D. Patricia Anniston

194. Why does Mr. Popov say he left early?

A. he finished his affairs early
B. he didn't want to make his speech
C. his wife was injured
D. he joined Ms. Cato and Mr. Lopez for dinner

195. Where is the next event organized by Mrs. McAllister?

A. Reginald's
B. London Tower
C. Royal Albert Hall
D. Africa

Questions 196–200 refer to the following email, attachment, and letter.

To:	javier.gg67@email.com
From:	autoconfirm@bookhotels.com
Date:	December 9th, 2018
Subject:	Booking Confirmation: Teddy's Hotel

Thank you for your booking, Javier!

Your booking reference is **AW8131441**

You will receive an email shortly, confirming receipt of your reservation. Please take a moment to check through the details provided below. You should contact one our customer service department immediately should there be any discrepancies in this information. Rooms are available from 2:00 P.M. for check-in and must be vacated at or before 10:00 A.M. on the day of your departure.

Teddy's Hotel San Antonio

Hotel and Park ticket price:	£959.00
Arrival date:	Sunday 03 September 2017
Departure date:	Wednesday 06 September 2017
Length of stay:	3 Nights
Park days:	4 Days
Room type:	Luxury Room with 2 double beds and balcony (for arrivals before 29th March 2017: breakfast not included due to refurbishment)
Adults: 2 Child: 2	
Package:	20% off Hotel and Park Tickets + FREE Full Board Meal Plan, including quick service breakfast in Teddy's Happy World, or full continental breakfast in the hotel dining room. Lunch and dinner provided at your chosen hotel!
Special requests:	Special requests are noted in your reservation, but can only be confirmed when you check in to the hotel.

Teddy's Hotel
125 Sunny Heights
San Antonio, TX 78201

Bill to | **Invoice Date:** 06/12/19

Javier Garcia
109 St Peter's Road
BH1 2LU
Bournemouth, UK

Description	Unit Price	Amount
Hotel & Park	N/A	£959.00
Charges for vegan options × 6	$5.00	$30.00
Room upgrade × 2 nights	$44.00	$88.00
Priority Passes × 4	$15.00	$60.00
	TOTAL	**$1,137.00**

12:21	*Javier*	Hi there, I wonder if you could help me with an issue at a hotel I recently stayed with
12:22	*Customer Service Advisor*	I can do my best. Can you give me the booking reference and let me know what the problem was?
12:25	*Javier*	Sure, here's the number: AW8131441. I was charged extra for something in my invoice
12:26	*Customer Service Advisor*	Okay, thanks for sharing. I'm going to need to transfer you to the sales representative for this particular hotel. To confirm, you stayed at Teddy's hotel for 3 nights last month?
12:30	*Javier*	That's it.
12:32	*Customer Service Advisor*	Thanks, just transferring you now.
12:34	*Sales Rep*	Hi Javier, looks like you have a query about your bill?
12:36	*Javier*	Yes, I've been charged extra for some meals, but your website said that these would be included in the price. I followed the process outlined in the confirmation email, and let them know our requirements, but we still were billed extra.
12:37	*Sales Rep*	Thanks for bringing this to our attention. Are you able to hold on while I contact the hotel on your behalf?
12:38	*Javier*	Sure.
12:39	*Sales Rep*	Great—won't be a moment.

196. How many people is the booking for?

A. 1
B. 2
C. 3
D. 4

197. How much does one priority pass cost?

A. $5.00
B. $15.00
C. $30.00
D. $60.00

198. How many nights did Javier and his family stay at the hotel?

A. 1 night
B. 2 nights
C. 3 nights
D. 4 nights

199. In the instant messaging chat at 12:30, why does Javier write "that's it"?

A. He's verifying the information.
B. He's frustrated by the mistake.
C. He's accepting the problem.
D. He's showing the employee the issue.

200. What will most likely happen next?

A. The sales representative will contact Teddy's Hotel.
B. Javier will cancel his booking.
C. The customer service advisor will request a refund.
D. Javier will complain about the booking company's service.

Stop! If you finish before time is called, you may check your work on this section only. Do not turn to any other section in the test.

PRACTICE TEST 2 ANSWER KEY

Part I	Part II	Part III	Part IV	Part V	Part VI	Part VII
1. D	7. C	32. C	71. A	101. A	131. D	147. D
2. C	8. C	33. B	72. C	102. B	132. A	148. C
3. A	9. C	34. C	73. B	103. C	133. A	149. C
4. B	10. B	35. C	74. D	104. B	134. D	150. C
5. C	11. B	36. B	75. C	105. D	135. B	151. C
6. D	12. C	37. C	76. A	106. A	136. D	152. A
	13. A	38. C	77. D	107. D	137. B	153. C
	14. A	39. B	78. C	108. B	138. D	154. C
	15. A	40. A	79. A	109. B	139. C	155. A
	16. B	41. C	80. C	110. C	140. B	156. A
	17. A	42. A	81. D	111. A	141. D	157. A
	18. C	43. A	82. C	112. B	142. A	158. B
	19. A	44. C	83. A	113. C	143. D	159. A
	20. C	45. D	84. C	114. A	144. B	160. B
	21. A	46. B	85. B	115. D	145. A	161. A
	22. C	47. C	86. A	116. C	146. A	162. C
	23. A	48. D	87. D	117. D		163. A
	24. B	49. D	88. B	118. C		164. D
	25. B	50. A	89. B	119. C		165. A
	26. B	51. B	90. A	120. B		166. B
	27. A	52. C	91. B	121. A		167. B
	28. B	53. A	92. B	122. B		168. C
	29. A	54. B	93. C	123. D		169. C
	30. C	55. A	94. A	124. D		170. C
	31. B	56. B	95. A	125. C		171. D
		57. A	96. C	126. C		172. A
		58. D	97. B	127. A		173. C
		59. B	98. B	128. B		174. B
		60. A	99. D	129. D		175. C
		61. D	100. D	130. D		176. B
		62. D				177. D
		63. B				178. D
		64. C				179. A
		65. D				180. C
		66. B				181. C
		67. A				182. A
		68. B				183. D
		69. A				184. C
		70. C				185. B
						186. B
						187. C
						188. B
						189. D
						190. A
						191. B
						192. D
						193. B
						194. C
						195. C
						196. D
						197. B
						198. C
						199. A
						200. A

PRACTICE TEST 2 ANSWERS AND EXPLANATIONS

Section 1—Listening Comprehension

Part I: Photographs

1. (D)

The photograph shows a man looking at an orange in a grocery store. **(A)** claims he's looking for *apples*, but he's holding an *orange*. There's no indication that the man is *counting* anything **(B)**, he's only holding one item. The man is holding but not *eating* **(C)** an orange. **(D)** is correct; the man is *checking* (looking at) the fruit he is holding.

2. (C)

The photograph shows three screws, with a screwdriver turning the middle one. **(C)** correctly describes the image. **(A)** is a trap; there are *three screws* but the screw doesn't necessarily need *three turns*. **(B)** mentions hammers and nails, which are not present in the image. **(D)** is incorrect; we cannot tell whether the wood is secure.

3. (A)

The photograph shows a library with shelves (or bookcases) filled with books. **(A)** correctly describes the scene; the books are stacked on the *shelves*. **(B)** confuses *crates* with *shelves*. The man is reading, not buying **(C)**, the book. **(D)** claims the library is open all day, but this is not shown in the picture.

4. (B)

The photograph shows two chefs with vegetables being instructed by their teacher. **(B)** is correct; the chefs are *preparing* the *vegetables*. No one is *counting* the vegetables. The teacher is directing, not *listening to,* his students. The food is still being chopped, so has not yet been cooked, or *over-cooked*.

5. (C)

The photograph shows a real estate agent showing a couple around an empty property. **(C)** correctly describes the photograph. The house is empty, and none of the characters live there, so they are not *coming home* **(A)**. The building is an empty house, not a *hotel* **(B)**. The real estate agent is showing the couple around; they are not visiting a friend (*acquaintance*) **(D)**.

6. (D)

The photograph shows two men talking over coffee. Their notepads suggest they are discussing a work project; **(D)** correctly describes this. **(A)** confuses *giving a speech* with *speaking to each other*. They are not eating, so the cannot be having lunch **(B)**. Neither of the men are writing **(C)**.

Part II: Question-Response

7. (C)

The statement says *this is a great hotel*, and expects a response in agreement or disagreement. **(C)** correctly agrees by saying *it is*. **(B)** responds in agreement but to a different topic (being *hungry*). **(A)** talks about *time* not the *hotel*.

8. (C)

The question asks *who sent the email?* The answer must contain the person responsible for the action. **(C)** correctly names the person when it says *my secretary did*. **(A)** does not mention an *email*, but a phone *call*. **(B)** does not mention *emails*, but talks about *files*.

9. (C)

The question asks *have the contracts arrived yet?* This requires a yes/no answer and possibly a past time expression in the case of a positive response. **(C)** correctly provides both (*yes, yesterday*). **(A)** is a yes/no answer but talks about *people*, not *contracts*. **(B)** is not a yes/no answer.

10. (B)

The question asks *who did you think would come?* **(B)** correctly answers *who* by saying *my partner*. **(A)** repeats the verb *come* but does not answer *who*. **(C)** uses the verb *think* in the past but does not answer *who*.

11. (B)

The question asks *how many candidates are there in the group dynamics?* **(B)** correctly provides the number of candidates by saying *there are about 20.* **(A)** provides a number but it is related to telling the time (*... starts at 5*). **(C)** uses the word *candidates* but fails to answer *how many.*

12. (C)

The question asks *where shall we go*? This requires an answer with a place, a destination. **(C)** correctly provides this when it suggests *that small Indian restaurant in the square.* **(B)** talks about a preference and does not relate to the question. **(A)** uses the verb *go* but does not answer the question *where.*

13. (A)

The question asks *how much does this TV cost?*, so it requires a monetary value in its answer. **(A)** correctly does that (*it's 500 dollars*). **(B)** uses the word *TV* but does not give a value. **(C)** says *how many* TVs but does not answer the question *how much.*

14. (A)

The question asks *what time are you leaving today?*, and this requires an answer with a future time expression. **(A)** provides that (*I'll leave at about 4.30...*). **(B)** uses a past tense expression instead of future. **(C)** uses the word *leave* as a noun and not a verb.

15. (A)

The question asks *how busy is the lecture theater today?* **(A)** correctly replies by describing it as *crowded.* **(B)** gives a yes/no answer about a woman (*she*). **(C)** uses the word *lecture* as a verb and not a noun like in the original statement.

16. (B)

The question asks *where's the supervisor's office?* and requires an answer with a place/location. **(B)** correctly provides this (*it's on the 5th floor*). **(A)** uses the word *supervisor* but does not answer *where.* **(C)** uses the noun *supervision* but does not address an office's location. It talks about *crime* and *punishment.*

17. (A)

The question asks *what color shirt would you like to buy?* **(A)** correctly answers it by mentioning possible colors (*black* and *white*) and design (*patterned*) of a shirt. **(B)** talks about buying a shirt, but in the past and not in the future as required by the question (*would you like to buy?*). Also, it does not mention any colors. **(C)** mentions a color (*green*) but refers to a park, not a shirt.

18. (C)

The question asks *did the new assistant order more black toners?* And this requires a yes or no answer. **(C)** is the only alternative to do that. **(A)** uses the word *black* but refers to a color preference. **(B)** uses the word *tone* which sounds like *toner* but has different meaning color.

19. (A)

The question asks *would you like to play basketball after work?*. It is an invitation and **(A)** gives an appropriate response (*I'm sorry but...*). **(B)** uses the word *basketball,* but does accept or refuse an invitation. **(C)** uses the word *basket* as part of the compound noun *shopping basket.*

20. (C)

The question asks *where should I file this report?* **(C)** correctly provides a location for the reports (*in the filing cabinet...*). **(A)** uses the word *report* as a verb and not a noun like in the original question. **(B)** uses the word *should* but does not answer *where.*

21. (A)

The question asks *where did you buy those shoes?* **(A)** correctly provides a place (*at the new shopping mall*). **(B)** is a yes/no answer and requires an open answer. **(C)** uses both the words *where* and *shoes* but does not mention the place where the shoes were bought.

22. (C)

The question asks *what did Mrs. Nomoto email you about?* This requires a reason in the answer. **(C)** gives the correct answer by refusing to give a reason (*I was asked not to tell anyone...*). **(A)** talks about the *mail*, but not an *email*. **(B)** provides Mrs. Nomoto's email address but not the reason for her email.

23. (A)

The question asks *why isn't Mr. Amorim here yet?* **(A)** gives the correct answer by giving a possible reason (*he might be stuck in the traffic*). **(B)** mentions his *new* position, not a possible reason for being late. **(C)** uses the word *here* but refers to a woman (*she's not...*) and not a man (*Mr. Amorim*).

24. (B)

The question asks *who won the tender?* This refers to a process of selling assets or services at a stated fixed price. **(B)** correctly answers who by giving people as a response: *we did*. **(A)** repeats *tender* but uses the word as an adjective with the meaning of soft. **(C)** uses the verb *won* but does not answer *who*.

25. (B)

The question asks *where do you keep the spare keys?* A location/place is required. **(B)** correctly answers the question by saying *under the purple vase...* **(A)** uses the verb *keep* but does not mention a location for the keys. **(C)** is a yes/no answer and the question requires an open answer.

26. (B)

The question asks *what did you think of the play?* This requires an opinion. **(B)** correctly gives one by saying *I thought it was excellent*. **(A)** uses the word *play* as a verb and not a noun like in the original question. **(C)** uses both *think* and *play* but do not express an opinion or talk about the *play*.

27. (A)

The statement says *I can help you do the typing if you need help with the invitation letters*. This is an offer and **(A)** gives an appropriate reply (*Thank you, but...*). **(B)** talks about a skill (*I can type pretty fast*) but does not accept or refuse help. **(C)** talks about a *party* which is not mentioned in the original statement.

28. (B)

The question asks *what kind of workshops are they planning for the conference?* **(B)** correctly answers the question by mentioning different kinds of workshops (*team development, presentation skills, and personal marketing*). **(A)** uses the words *work* and *shop* but not as compound noun so the meaning is different. **(C)** uses the word *kind* as an adjective with the meaning of *generous*.

29. (A)

The question asks *how many candidates responded to our newspaper ad?* **(A)** correctly provides a number of candidates (*more than a hundred*). **(B)** uses the word *newspapers* but does not mention a number of candidates. **(C)** uses the word *candidate* but does not answer *how many*.

30. (C)

The question asks *can you show me how to use the new system?* This is a request. **(C)** correctly gives a positive response (*Of course*). **(A)** does not reply to a request, it merely confirms information (possibly a phone *call*). **(B)** repeats the word *show* but uses it as a noun and not a verb.

31. (B)

The question asks *Will you be in Florida this time next year?* **(B)** gives an appropriate response by agreeing with the original statement (*I will*) and providing extra information (*we're moving there after I retire*). **(A)** uses the time expression *next year* but does not talk about *Florida*. **(C)** talks about a vacation *next week*, but the question asks about *next year*.

Part III: Short Conversations

32. (C)

Mustafa says *My cousin lives in Los Angeles*, so **(C)** is the correct answer. **(A)** and **(B)** are wrong because they talk about *Thandie*, not *Mustafa*. **(D)** is wrong because Thandie says *I only have this weekend to pack*.

33. (B)

Thandie says *I would only go if they could find a place for Stuart* and so Stuart is the second male speaker. Stuart says *Thandie's asked me to keep working as her assistant.* **(B)** is correct.

34. (C)

Thandie says *I told Mr. Albright that I would only take the job if I could take Stuart with me*, so **(C)** is the correct alternative.

35. (C)

The man says *Could you tell me where you keep the staples?* **(C)** is correct. The woman says *There must be one in your desk,* but she is referring to a stapler, so **(A)** is incorrect. **(B)** is also wrong because the man says *what I'll do is ask Mrs. Silva to order some more*, but there is no indication that he doesn't know where she is. **(D)** is not possible, because when the man says *Three boxes, maybe four?* he's talking about the staples, not the boxes themselves.

36. (B)

The woman says *I'm sure there are at least 2 boxes in the supply closet.* **(B)** is correct. **(A)** is wrong because, when the woman says *There must be one in your desk,* she's referring to a *stapler*, not *staples*. **(C)** is also incorrect because the man says *what I'll do is ask Mrs. Silva to order some more* but there is nothing indicating that there are staples in her office. **(D)** is wrong because when the woman asks *Did you check the top drawer?*, she's talking about a stapler, not staples.

37. (C)

The woman says *let me get them for you*. **(C)** is correct. **(B)** is incorrect because she asks if the man checked the top drawer (*Did you check the top drawer?*). **(A)** is not correct either, because the man is the one who uses the word *run*, as part of a phrasal verb (*run out of*) which has a different meaning. **(D)** is wrong because the woman offers to get the boxes (*Let me get them for you*), not order them.

38. (C)

The man says *we'd better come up with an alternative if Professor Turan can't make it here.* He's worried that the professor might not be able to give the lecture. **(C)** is the answer. The man uses the word *late*, but not in reference to the lecturer; eliminate **(A)**. **(B)** is not mentioned in the conversation. **(D)** repeats *cancel*, but the woman says *we should consider canceling* so the lecture has not been cancelled yet.

39. (B)

The woman says *why don't we show them that video about some of his latest projects?*, so **(B)** is correct. **(A)** repeats *snow*, but *going out* into the snow is not mentioned in the conversation. **(C)** confuses the meaning of *alternative* in the sentence; it applies to *plans,* not *routes*. **(D)** is not mentioned in the conversation.

40. (A)

The woman says *we should consider canceling the lecture,* and the man says *I think it's too late to cancel it.* **(A)** is correct. **(B)**, **(C)**, and **(D)** are not mentioned in the conversation.

41. (C)

The man says *have you heard about the new project? The one in Auckland?*, and the woman says *Are you talking about the new office in New Zealand?*, so **(C)** must be correct.

42. (A)

Michel says *Wouldn't it be amazing to live in New Zealand?* This is rhetorical question, so **(A)** is the right answer. *Louise* says she'd like to live there, not *Michel*. This means **(B)** is wrong. Louise also says *My sister lives there*, so it's not Michel who has family there and **(C)** is incorrect. Michel says *They'll let us apply for the positions as soon as they become available*, but doesn't say anything about *his field.* This means **(D)** is not possible either.

43. (A)

Louise says *My sister's there, the weather's amazing*, so **(B)** is incorrect. She also says *it's one the best places to live in the world*, so **(C)** is also wrong. **(D)** is not possible because she says *My sister lives there with her husband and kids and they love it*. This means **(A)** is the only possible answer.

44. (C)

The woman says *Monika's been doing such a great job and she would've been perfect in the role*. This suggests she *applied* but was *unsuccessful*, so **(C)** is correct. **(A)** is incorrect because *Malik made* the *decision*, which means he was the recruiter. **(B)** is wrong because the man says *Oliver's son applied*, not *Oliver* himself. **(D)** is wrong because the man says *Peter's going to fail* in *his new role*, which means his *application* was successful.

45. (D)

The woman says *Peter might've thought it was beneath him*, which means he *thought* he was *too good* for it, so **(D)** is the correct answer. **(A)** is wrong because the woman then says *not that this justifies his behavior*, which means it doesn't. **(B)** and **(C)** are incorrect because it's the man who says that *Peter* has *no qualifications* and his *dad*, not the woman, is *pulling the strings*, i.e. *helping*.

46. (B)

The man says everyone *anticipated the recruitment decision*, which means it was *unsurprising*, so **(B)** is correct. **(A)** is incorrect because the man says *Monika* is *not stupid*—he never calls the *decision stupid*. **(C)** is incorrect because he says the *decision stings*, i.e. hurts, not *stinks*, i.e. is terrible. **(D)** is incorrect because the woman says she *hopes* that *Monika* has *taken it well*, but the man never comments on how everyone else has *taken it*.

47. (C)

The woman says *it was definitely someone from work*. **(C)** is the correct answer. It can't be **(A)** because when the man asks *Probably Abdullah, am I right?*, the woman doesn't give a positive response. **(B)** is also incorrect because the woman says *I'll ask my sister which one they use...* when she talks about a streaming service, not the film they're watching. The man says *This is the worst film I've ever seen* so **(D)** is also wrong.

48. (D)

The man says *we should get one of those streaming services. Then we wouldn't have to rent DVDs*. **(D)** is the correct answer. The man uses the word 'nothing' to say they don't have a film to watch, not that a DVD is better than nothing. **(A)** and **(C)** are not mentioned in the conversation.

49. (D)

The man says *we should get one of those streaming services*. **(D)** is correct. Neither the man nor the woman uses the word *download* during the conversation, so **(B)** is not possible. **(C)** is wrong because the woman is the one to mention her sister when she says *I'll ask my sister which one they use...*, not the man. **(A)**is not mentioned in the conversation.

50. (A)

The man says *I've had it for years* so **(A)** is the correct option. The man says *you probably haven't seen me wearing it because it was too tight*, not the he does not like wearing the jacket. The jacket *was* too tight, but is not anymore. **(D)** is not mentioned in the conversation.

51. (B)

The woman says *we should get going now or we'll miss the play*. A play is something you see in a theater so **(B)** is the correct answer. **(A)**, **(C)**, and **(D)** are not mentioned in the conversation.

52. (C)

The woman says *what a beautiful jacket*, so **(C)** is the correct answer. **(B)** The man is the one to use the word *tight*, not the woman. The woman says *the color goes really well with your eyes*, not that she doesn't like the color. The woman says the man should *wear it more often*, not stop wearing it.

53. (A)

The man says *it sure is cold today*, and the woman replies *You really think so? It is winter, you know. I'm toasty*. **(A)** is correct; the man thinks the office is cold but the woman doesn't. **(B)** repeats *winter*, but they do not disagree about the season. **(C)** repeats *dress code*, but the man tells the woman he doesn't understand the dress code, not that he disagrees with her. **(D)** repeats *productivity*, but they do not dispute work productivity.

54. (B)

The woman says *I'm sure our bosses would rather you were warm enough*. **(B)** is correct. **(A)** repeats *central heating*, but this does not relate to their bosses. **(C)** is not mentioned in the text. **(D)** repeats *dress code*, but the woman says she thinks their bosses would prefer for the man to be warm than to strictly follow the dress code.

55. (A)

The woman says *Why don't you check the lost and found? There might be a spare jumper you can wear for today*. **(A)** is the answer. **(B) (C)** and **(D)** are not mentioned in the text.

56. (B)

The woman says *my husband had a stomach bug and couldn't leave the toilet for the whole weekend*. **(B)** is the correct answer. The woman uses the word *bug* with the meaning of *bacteria* or *virus* so **(A)** is incorrect. **(C)** repeats *toilet*, but an issue with the toilet itself is not mentioned. **(D)** plays on *Rockies* (a mountain range) and the similar sounding *rock*.

57. (A)

The woman asks *did you go to that party in the end?* and the man replies *I must say the party wasn't that good*, so **(A)** is the correct option. The woman mentions the hiking trip, not the man, so **(B)** is wrong. The man uses the word *better* when he asks the woman about her husband, so **(C)** is also wrong. **(D)** is happening later o, not during the weekend.

58. (D)

When the man asks about the woman's husband she replies *Oh, Pedro?*, so **(D)** is the correct answer. **(A)**, **(B)**, and **(C)** are not mentioned in the conversation.

59. (B)

When the woman suggests Japanese the man says *I had Japanese yesterday, Susan. How about Chinese?*, so **(B)** is the correct answer. The man says *fried rice* and not *fried chicken* so **(A)** is not possible. **(C)** is wrong because the woman suggests Japanese (*I was thinking about Japanese here*). **(D)** is also incorrect because the man uses the adjective *good* to describe *fried rice*, not any food.

60. (A)

The woman says *I'm really trying to cut down on cholesterol* so **(A)** is the correct option. The woman doesn't say anything about rice so **(B)** is not possible. **(C)** repeats *I love Chinese*, but this is not a reason to reject the suggestion. **(D)** is mentioned by the man, not the woman.

61. (D)

At the end of the conversation, the man says *I didn't know they made an avocado salad. It sounds nice, can you order one for me too, instead of the sandwich?*, so **(D)** is the correct answer. The man says *I had Japanese yesterday, Susan. How about Chinese?* **(A)** is incorrect. **(B)** and **(C)** are incorrect because the man initially wants a *tuna sandwich* but later changes his mind.

62. (D)

The man says *You've got your meeting in 15 minutes, right?* and the woman responds by saying *that's why I'm calling... am I in the wrong place*? The woman is making her way to the meeting. The answer is **(D)**.

63. (B)

The man says *so, I'm really sorry about this, Niko, but we gave you the wrong address... the good news is you're not far away from where you need to be...* The woman's meeting is not too far away, so the answer is **(B)**.

64. (C)

The man says *so you want to go down Bleacher street, and when you get to the Post Office... don't cross the road to it, turn right and walk down the road, then keep straight and cross the road once, and that should get you to the Madison Building, it will be on your right, on the corner once you've crossed the road.* Following these directions on the map, beginning at the cross, the Madison Building must be in position 3, so **(C)** must be correct.

65. (D)

This question asks for the gist of the conversation. The man says 'Head Office has just sent out our profits for the last quarter,' and the speakers discuss this throughout the conversation. **(D)** is correct.

66. (B)

This question asks what the man says is doing well. The man says 'we're doing really well with laptop sales'; **(B)** is correct. **(A)**, **(C)**, and **(D)** are all mentioned in the conversation, but the man does not say these areas are doing well.

67. (A)

This question includes a graphic. You need to use the information in the conversation and the graphic to decide which product the man thinks will be discontinued. The man says *I think if anything's making less than $3,000 at this point we should just scrap it entirely.* Looking at the graphic, the only product making less than $3,000 in this quarter is printer sales, so the man thinks that this product should be discontinued. **(A)** is correct. **(B)** and **(C)** made more than $3,000 in both quarters, and **(D)** only made less than $3,000 in the previous quarter, but made more than $3,000 in the current quarter.

68. (B)

The woman says *WhisperTech?! They're our biggest competitors!* so WhisperTech must provide a similar service to that provided by the company that the man and woman work for. **(B)** is correct.

69. (A)

The man says *he's going to try and sell* and the woman says *And you think we can buy? Wow!* The speakers will schedule a meeting to look into buying WhisperTech. The answer is **(A)**.

70. (C)

The man says he *can't do any mornings next week* which means they must meet in the afternoon, so they can only meet on Monday or Thursday. The woman says *let's take the later day* so they must decide to schedule the meeting on Thursday.

Part IV: Short Talks

71. (A)

The man says *I'm calling about the video conference that is scheduled for Thursday morning. My assistant is going to email you the agenda.* **(A)** is correct. The man says *video conference* but does not mention a *video maker.* **(B)** is incorrect. **(C)** is also incorrect as the man says *you can reach me in my Boston office at 310-555-6106.* **(D)** The man uses the word *email* twice, but doesn't talk about checking one.

72. (C)

The man says *it is a very important meeting and I just want to make sure that all those involved in the acquisition have a say.* **(C)** is correct. **(A)** gives the day the video conference is being held. When the man says *my assistant is going to email you the agenda*, he means the agenda for the *meeting*; the meeting is not *about* an agenda. **(D)** repeats *Boston*, but the man doesn't discuss *business opportunities* in Boston.

73. (B)

The man says *if there is anything you would like to discuss with me before the video conference, you can reach me in my Boston office at 310-555-6106.* **(B)** is the correct answer. It's a *video conference*, so **(A)** is incorrect. The man says *if there is anything you would like to discuss*; this is not an invitation to discuss an agenda. The video conference has already been confirmed (*I'm calling about the video conference that is schedule for Thursday morning*).

74. (D)

The announcement says *passengers waiting to board flight AA178 to Seattle*, so it must be at an airport. **(D)** is correct. Since passengers are still waiting to board the flight, the announcement can't have been made on the plane; **(A)** is not possible. **(B)** and **(C)** are wrong because the announcement says *flight* so trains or train stations are not an option.

75. (C)

The announcement says *because of bad weather conditions, the aircraft left Seattle two hours late*, so **(C)** is the correct answer. The announcement says *passengers waiting to board flight* but doesn't say that there are *too many* of them, so **(A)** is incorrect. **(B)** is also wrong because the *heavy rain* is in Seattle, not New York. The word *updated* is used with the meaning of *keeping passengers informed*, so **(D)** is also incorrect.

76. (A)

The speaker says *Passengers waiting to board American Airways flight to Seattle*, so the flight is going to Seattle but the airline is American Airways, so we can eliminate **(B)** and **(D)** as the table says the airline for these flights is *Seattle Airline*. The flight is described as *delayed* and the *boarding time will not take place before 3:45* so **(A)** must be the correct answer.

77. (D)

The woman says *it is always good to hear such an innovative insight on the current market situation*, so **(D)** is the correct answer. The woman uses the word *contribution* but doesn't say anything about *society*, so **(A)** is wrong. **(C)** is also incorrect because the woman uses the word *innovative* to talk about the Mrs. Takeda's ideas, not speech topic. The woman says *I'm sure you must have hundreds of questions you would like to ask her* but not that the topic of the speech was answering questions, so **(B)** is not possible.

78. (C)

The speaker says *I believe Mrs. Takeda won't mind answering some of your questions during lunchtime. However, when I say lunchtime, please show her some Brazilian courtesy and let our guest finish her lunch before you approach her.* The speaker is asking guests not to interrupt her when she's eating; the answer is **(C)**.

79. (A)

The woman says *it's time to move on to our next presentation, which is due to start in 10 minutes*. **(A)** is correct. **(B)** and **(C)** repeat *lunchtime*, but this is when Mrs. Takeda will answer questions, not when the next presentation starts. **(D)** is not mentioned in the talk.

80. (C)

The recording says *we are sorry to inform that our office is closed until 27 November due to very unlikely circumstances*, so **(C)** is the correct option. The recording mentions some of the services they offer: *we're doing the best we can to get our lines open again, and provide out-of-town visitors with local hotel information, theater reservations and guided tours* but these services are not the main reason for the recording, since they are not being offered. **(A)**, **(B)**, and **(D)** are all incorrect.

81. (D)

The recording says *if you would like to make a theater reservation you can contact our partner agency Vegas Shows on 702-555-0410.* **(D)** is correct. **(A)** gives the website, which customers should use for *hotel information*, not *theater reservations*. **(C)** is not mentioned in the conversation. **(B)** repeats *27 November*, but it is possible to make reservations before this date.

82. (C)

The question asks for the services NOT offered. The recording says *we're doing the best we can to get our lines open again, and provide out-of-town visitors with local hotel information, theater reservations and guided tours. Restaurants* are not mentioned. **(C)** is the correct answer. **(A)**, **(B)**, and **(D)** are all mentioned in the conversation.

83. (A)

The man says *I would like to welcome you all to our professionals of Human Resources dinner party.* **(A)** is correct. **(B)** repeats *Chef Lafayette*, who provided the food, but this is not the event. **(C)** is also wrong because even though the man announces Harold Clipton as a *guest of honor*, he doesn't say anything about a program. **(D)** is not possible because the man refers to Michelle Lucas as *our first speaker*.

84. (C)

The man says *she has given seminars all over the world and worked in professional development for 30 years before she retired* when presenting the first speaker. Then the man introduces the first speaker: *Ladies and gentlemen, I give you Michelle Lucas*. **(C)** is the correct answer. The man doesn't say anything about himself, so **(A)** is not possible. **(B)** refers to Harold Clipton as a *guest of honor*, but doesn't talk about his experience, so **(B)** is incorrect. **(D)** repeats *Chef Lafayette*, but a chef does not have 30 years' experience in professional development.

85. (B)

The speaker says *But that's enough from me. Ladies and gentlemen, I give you Michelle Lucas*. The man is welcoming the next speaker to the stage, so the answer is **(B)**.

86. (A)

The man says *pick up your phone right now and call us at 1 800 555 3667 to speak to one of our agents*, which means the audience he's trying to reach is listening to him remotely. The language is typical of a TV advertisement. **(A)** is the correct answer. It is very unlikely that a speaker would try to sell a service during a lecture so **(B)** is not possible. The same applies to **(C)**. **(D)** is not mentioned in the talk.

87. (D)

The question asks for the requirement which is not mentioned. The ad says *if you know how to check and reply to emails, answer a telephone, and build a good rapport with people, we have some more work for you*. **(D)** is the only answer choice not mentioned as a requirement.

88. (B)

The man says *Office Wizards has hundreds of available positions*. so **(B)** is correct. **(A)** repeats *Wall Street*, but *well-established Wall Street firms* are an example of the positions offered, not the name of the company. **(C)** repeats *work for you*, but this is not given as the name of the company. **(D)** is part of the slogan (*Office Wizards. No magic, just work*) but is not the name of the company.

89. (B)

The man says *now that our bring and share breakfast is nearly finished, please go back to your seats for a final word from our master of ceremonies, Noor Bilal*. The use of the pronoun *our* indicates that the speaker is part of the staff. **(B)** is correct. **(A)** and **(D)** refer to Ms. Bilal, the master of ceremonies, who is not the speaker. **(C)** repeats *students*, but this is mentioned as an instruction by the speaker, not given as the speaker's profession.

90. (A)

The man says *now that our bring and share breakfast is nearly finished*. **(A)** is correct. Since **(B)** and **(C)** are other meal times they can't be correct. **(D)** is not mentioned in the talk.

91. (B)

The speaker says *you will find the course schedule, notepad, and training manual inside your welcome packs*. **(B)** is correct. **(A)** and **(C)** are mentioned in the talk, but *Ms. Bilal's speech* or *schedule* is not included in the welcome pack. **(D)** is not mentioned in the talk.

92. (B)

The woman says *dear colleagues*. **(B)** must be correct, as *colleagues* suggests a business environment, and **(B)** is the only suitable answer choice. TV commercials, radio shows, and press conferences would not address their audience as *colleagues*.

93. (C)

The woman says *during the past 3 months we conducted a comprehensive survey to assess our products*. **(C)** is correct. **(A)** is incorrect because even though the speaker mentions TV programs, the survey was about their products (*to assess our products*). **(B)** confuses *boxes* with *box sets*. **(D)** confuses the adjective *convenient* with the noun *convenience store*.

94. (A)

The woman says *people are getting more and more interested in using streaming services.* **(A)** is correct. **(B)** refers to a previous survey. **(C)** refers to the streaming services, not their findings. **(D)** repeats *box sets*, but does not explain the new findings.

95. (A)

The man says *this is your local weather report with Javier Poole.* **(A)** is correct. **(C)** repeats *beach*, but this is not the main topic of the talk. **(D)** discusses upcoming talks. **(B)** is not mentioned in the talk.

96. (C)

The man says *we're also expecting blue skies throughout the entire weekend.* **(C)** is correct. **(A)** repeats *shower*, but *there is only a ten percent chance of showers*. **(B)** and **(D)** are not mentioned in the talk.

97. (B)

The man says *we can expect temperatures to rise above thirty-five for tomorrow and Sunday, so the next two days will be boiling hot people*. If the next two days are Saturday and Sunday, then the recording must take place on a Friday. **(B)** is correct. **(D)** is mentioned elsewhere in the text as a *future* time, not the current day.

98. (B)

The man says *Dixon Records is going out of business.* **(B)** is correct. **(A)**, **(C)**, and **(D)** are not mentioned in the talk.

99. (D)

The man says *half off throughout our entire electronics department.* **(D)** is correct. The man mentions *CDs, LPs,* and *MPs* but doesn't say that they are 50% off. **(A)**, **(B)**, and **(C)** cannot be correct.

100. (D)

The speaker says *our electronics department*, so the store sells *tech* or technology. The store opens at 9:00 A.M. and shuts at 10:00 P.M., or 22:00 so **(A)** and **(B)** can be eliminated. Finally, the speaker says the store is on the corner of 52nd and Broadway, not number 52 on Broadway, so the answer must be **(D)**.

Section 2—Reading Comprehension

Part V: Incomplete Sentences

101. (A)

(A) is correct because it means *depend on*. **(B)** means *include*, **(C)** means *count to zero*, and **(D)** means *start counting at a particular number*.

102. (B)

This is an *unreal conditional* and **(B)** is the only possible modal. **(A)**, **(C)**, and **(D)** are only possible in real conditionals.

103. (C)

(C) is correct because *therefore* indicates a consequence. **(A)**, **(B)**, and **(D)** indicate contrast.

104. (B)

In is the preposition used for months of the year so **(B)** is correct. **(A)** can be used with dates and **(C)** can only be used with festivals and special dates. **(D)** can be used with months, but to indicate past.

105. (D)

(D) is the correct answer because it is usually paired with *neither*. **(A)** is usually used in positive sentences to join them equally. **(B)** can't be paired with *neither*, and **(C)** indicates contrast.

106. (A)

(A) is the correct answer because a *consultant* is a person. **(B)** and **(D)** are verbs. **(C)** is a noun referring to a thing or service.

107. (D)

When *only* is used with the meaning of a negative or unfortunate result, it is followed by an infinitive with *to*. **(D)** is the correct answer. **(A)** is gives the infinitive, but does not include *to*. **(B)** and **(C)** are conjugated.

108. (B)

(B) is the correct answer because someone else will deliver the merchandising and the past participle is required to form the passive. **(A)** and **(C)** are infinitive. **(D)** is a participle, but a present participle.

109. (B)

(B) indicates a reason and is followed by a noun phrase. **(A)** could be used for the first clause, but the second clause is in the present tense and *after* would need to be followed by a clause in the past tense. **(C)** indicates contrast, and **(D)** indicates the time something starts and both should also be followed by a clause.

110. (C)

Frequency adverbs can appear in different parts of a sentence. *Daily* can only appear at the end of a sentence, so **(C)** is the correct answer. The positions in **(A)**, **(B)**, and **(D)** could be correct for other adverbs, but not *daily*.

111. (A)

The verb *expect* is usually followed by an infinitive with *to*, so **(A)** is the correct answer. **(B)** is a past participle, **(C)** is a gerund, and **(D)** contains the modal verb *will*.

112. (B)

A *direct* manner of *doing* something means people might do what they want or say exactly what they want to save time. *Direct* is the only adjective that collocates with *manner*, so **(B)** is the correct answer. **(A)** means *side by side* and does not collocate with *manner*. **(C)** means *at an angle of 90°*. **(D)** means *next to*.

113. (C)

Motivated is an adjective, so it can only be modified through an adverb. *Frequently* is an adverb, so **(C)** is correct. **(A)** is an adjective, **(B)** is a past participle, and **(D)** is a noun.

114. (A)

At the discretion is a fixed expression which means *the freedom to decide what needs to be done,* so **(A)** is the correct answer. **(B)** means *individually separate*, **(C)** means *separately*, and **(D)** means *available for use*.

115. (D)

The preposition *by* usually follows a past participle in passive sentences. **(D)** is correct because it is a past participle. **(A)** is an adjective, **(B)** is a noun, and **(C)** is a gerund.

116. (C)

We need an adverb with the meaning of *generally* or *frequently*, so **(C)** is the correct option. **(A)** means *almost*, **(B)** means *for a special purpose*, and **(D)** is used to emphasize *accuracy* or express *agreement*.

117. (D)

Proposal is the only noun to collocate with both the verb *submit* and the noun *redevelopment*, so **(D)** is the correct answer. A *redevelopment proposal* means a plan to change the structure of a building. **(A)** can collocate with *redevelopment* but not with the verb *submit*. **(B)** and **(C)** cannot be used with either *submit* or *redevelopment*.

118. (C)

A relative pronoun referring to a person is required, so **(C)** is the only possible answer. **(A)** refers to things, **(B)** can refer to people but cannot follow a comma, and **(D)** is not a relative pronoun.

119. (C)

(C) is correct because this is a sentence in the present perfect tense which mentions when the action started (*five years ago*), so the conjunction *since* is required. **(A)** is also commonly used with the present perfect but to indicate a period of time. **(B)** and **(D)** cannot be used with the present perfect to say *how long*.

120. (B)

Transform is the only verb that indicates a process of change and can be followed by the preposition *into*, so **(B)** is the correct answer. **(A)** and **(C)** can be used for changes but don't take the preposition *into*. **(D)** neither talks about change nor takes the preposition *into*.

121. (A)

This is a second conditional and the if clause needs a verb in the past simple or continuous, so **(A)** is the only possible answer. **(B)** is present simple and would be correct in a first conditional sentence. **(C)** is future and can only be used in the main clause of a first conditional. **(D)** is gerund.

122. (B)

This is a passive structure because it is not the landlord who has to pay the deposit, it's the tenant. Passive structures need the past participle so **(B)** is the correct answer. **(A)** is a passive structure but the verb *be* is not used with the causative verb *want*. **(C)** is infinitive and **(D)** is gerund.

123. (D)

Body is a noun so what we need in the gap is an adjective. **(D)** is the only adjective. **(A)** is a verb in the infinitive, **(B)** is a noun, and **(C)** is a gerund.

124. (D)

The gap asks for a conjunction which describes an *addition*. **(D)** is correct. **(A)**, **(B)**, and **(C)** indicate a contrast.

125. (C)

In is the correct preposition for a city so **(C)** is the correct answer. **(A)** is not commonly used for places. **(B)** can be used for some places in town (at the movies, at church, etc.), but not for a city. **(D)** is a preposition of movement.

126. (C)

The verb *collaborate* collocates with the preposition *with* so **(C)** is the only possible answer. **(A)** and **(D)** are never possible with the verb *collaborate*. **(B)** could be used with the verb *collaborate* to talk about a place, but not with the idea of an association which is given in the sentence.

127. (A)

The preposition *to*, with some exceptions (phrasal verbs, be/get used to, etc.), is usually followed by an infinitive. **(A)** is the correct answer. **(B)** is past, **(C)** is present perfect, and **(D)** is gerund.

128. (B)

We need a conjunction that expresses a contrast. **(B)** is correct. **(C)** also expresses contrast but would only be correct if it appeared in between the two clauses, but the missing word begins at the beginning of the first clause in the sentence. **(A)** expresses cause and effect and **(D)** expresses a reason.

129. (D)

Adverbs of frequency can appear in different places in a sentence. However, *once a week* can only be used at the beginning or the end of a sentence, so **(D)** is the only possible answer. **(A), (B)** and **(C)** have the wrong word order.

130. (D)

The sentence requires a word that means *during* which can be followed by a clause (subject + verb), so **(D)** is the correct answer. **(A)** can only be followed by a noun phrase. **(B)** is used to talk about consequences. **(C)** would only be used if the sentence were a question.

Part VI: Text Completion

131. (D)

The clause 'It's a/an + noun' should be followed either by a gerund (–ing) or infinitive with to. **(D)** is the correct option because it's a gerund. **(A)** is an infinitive but without *to*. **(B)** is past and **(C)** has a modal verb for future meaning.

132. (A)

The sentence requires a plural noun with the meaning of *a small quantity intended to show what the whole is like*, so **(A)** is the only possible answer. **(B)** would be used for food samples, **(C)** means *to illustrate*, and **(D)** means a *spectacle* or *display*.

133. (A)

The gap asks for an adverb and **(A)** is the only adverb among the options. **(B)** is an adjective, **(C)** is an infinitive, and **(D)** is a gerund.

134. (D)

The sentence begins by asking the reader of the email to provide some information (*Please let me know*), so the sentence must end with some information that the recipient can provide. **(B)** and **(C)** can be eliminated as they do not ask for information. **(A)** asks for a timeline for the writer to receive samples, but earlier in the letter he offers to send samples, so **(A)** cannot be correct. **(D)** relates to the information earlier in the letter, so it is the correct choice.

135. (B)

The gap follows the verb *be* in sentence which indicates a process of change. This means the gerund is required to form a present continuous sentence and **(B)** is the correct alternative. **(A)** is infinitive, **(C)** is past, and **(D)** is perfect gerund.

136. (D)

A conjunction with meaning of *during the time that* is required here, so **(D)** is the correct answer. **(A)** and **(B)** cannot be used to indicate that two things are happening at the same time. **(C)** needs to be followed by a noun.

137. (B)

The previous paragraph mentions a friend whom Giovanni can put Mohammad in touch with, but this paragraph talks about Giovanni's feelings about Mohammad leaving, so **(A)** is incorrect. **(B)** introduces the content of the paragraph appropriately, so is correct. **(C)** is a formal resignation, and **(D)** suggests that Mohammad has already left, so cannot be the answer.

138. (D)

(B) and **(C)** do not collocate with the adjective *good*. **(A)** could be used with the adjective *good* with the meaning of *having the required qualities*. **(D)**, when combined with *good*, can have the meaning of *valid* or *possible*, so **(D)** is the correct answer.

139. (C)

The paragraph is introducing the checklist below, so **(C)** must be correct, as it is the only option to introduce the list that follows. **(A)** mentions *policy changes* not a checklist for success. **(B)** says the example is online, but it's actually on the page. **(D)** mentions practicing something, but the article is about following a checklist.

140. (B)

The sentence requires an idiom which means *continuously*, so **(B)** is the correct option. **(A)** means *a specific time in the past*. **(C)** and **(D)** can't go with the preposition *at*.

141. (D)

The sentence asks for a preposition with the meaning of *at the further side of*, so **(D)** is the only possible answer. **(A)** has the meaning of *at the far side of something so as to be hidden by it*. **(B)** means *into the space separating two things*, and **(C)** is not a preposition of place.

142. (A)

When the verb *to learn* has the meaning of *to acquire knowledge or skill*, it requires the preposition from. **(A)** is the correct answer. **(B)** would change the meaning of the verb to *to become aware of*. **(C)** would say *how* something was learned (by practicing a lot). **(D)** would mention the place where something was learned.

143. (D)

The gap asks for a past participle to form a relative clause in which the pronoun *which* and auxiliary *was* has been omitted. **(D)** is the past participle and correct answer. **(A)** is an infinitive, **(B)** is a noun, and **(C)** is a gerund.

144. (B)

The adjective *wide* is the only option that collocates with the noun *range*, so **(B)** is the correct answer. Even though **(A)**, **(C)**, and **(D)** might express similar meanings when isolated from the noun, they do not go with the phrase *range of skills*.

145. (A)

When the noun *pressure* has the meaning of *a sense of urgencies*, it requires the preposition *under*. **(A)** is the correct answer. **(B)**, **(C)**, and **(D)** are seldom used with the noun *pressure* and would be inappropriate here.

146. (A)

All of the options are closing sentences for letters, so check the information in the text to find the most appropriate option. **(B)** is a final sign off, but the text follows this gap with *I look forward to hearing from you soon*, so *yours sincerely* is not needed above this statement. **(C)** thanks the recipient for the application, but it is the writer of the email that is applying. **(D)** suggests a familiar relationship between the writer and the recipient of the email, but the content of the text does not. **(A)** is correct.

Part VII: Reading Comprehension

147. (D)

The order says *15 red canopies, 30 red umbrellas, and 10 blue display booths*, so the total number of items is 55. **(D)** is the correct answer. **(A)** refers to the number of *blue display booths only*. **(B)** refers to the number of *red canopies* only. **(C)** refers to the number of *red umbrellas* only.

148. (C)

The fax says *ship to: Montreal, Quebec, Canada H3B 5L1*. **(C)** is the correct answer. **(A)** is the name of a company, **(B)** is the location of the company to be billed, and **(D)** is the name of the person placing the order.

149. (C)

The only blue items in the order are the *blue display booths* and the fax says *10 blue display booths (ref. DB03) @ $140.00 = $1,400.00*, so **(C)** is the correct answer.

150. (C)

The notice is aimed at *investors* and **(C)** is the most likely place to find it, since it's the only alternative where business information can be found. **(A)** is known for talking about *gossip*, not *business*. **(B)** would usually contain ads for products sold at the store. **(D)** is likely to offer *posters* and *ads*, but not business opportunities.

151. (C)

The notice says *The webinar will be led by a group of property experts...*, so **(C)** is the correct option. **(A)** is who the notice aims at. The notice says *It will cover town planning...*, but nothing about the speakers being *town planners*. There's no mention of *IT*, so **(D)** is not possible.

152. (A)

The notice says *There is no fee for this webinar*, so **(A)** is the correct option. **(B)** is incorrect because the notice does say that the webinar is free. **(C)** is wrong because 22 is the date of the webinar (March 22). The notice includes the website but does not say anything about checking the fee there, so **(D)** is also incorrect.

153. (C)

The notice says *It will cover town planning, redevelopment proposals, buy-to-let mortgages, bidding in auctions, and much, much more*, so **(A)** is mentioned. It also says *Join us on Saturday, March 22 3–4 P.M.*, so **(B)** is mentioned in the notice as well. **(D)** can also be found in the notice (*The webinar will be led by a group of property experts with vast experience in North America, Asia and Europe*), so **(C)** is the correct answer.

154. (C)

The table mention eight different dates for each group, so **(C)** is the correct answer. **(A)** is the number of groups, **(B)** is the number of hours for each sessions, and **(D)** is the number of sessions for both groups.

155. (A)

The table lists various workshops whose topics include the word *teaching*, so **(A)** is the correct answer. The table says *classroom management*, but that's a teaching skill, so **(B)** is incorrect. One of the workshops addresses *productive skills*, which means writing and speaking a language, so **(C)** is also wrong. There's no mention of *doctors* or medicine, so **(D)** is not possible.

156. (A)

The table says *2 to 5 PM* and *1:30 to 4:30 PM*, so **(A)** is the correct option. **(B)** is the total number of hours for each group, **(C)** is the period of time in which the refresher will be held, and there's no mention of *years* in the schedule, so **(D)** is also wrong.

157. (A)

The announcement says *LW can offer you exciting career opportunities*, so **(A)** is the correct answer. There's no mention of *TVs*, so **(B)** is not possible. The announcement mentions a *cycling scheme* as a benefit, but not the main topic addressed by it so **(C)** is also incorrect. The announcement says *making people's lives easier with durable easy-to-use products* as part of the company's description, so **(D)** is wrong.

158. (B)

The sentence asks *Does this sound like you?* So the text before this sentence must describe the attributes of a person; only [2] does this, so **(B)** must be the answer.

159. (A)

The announcement says *LW can offer you exciting career opportunities* and *LW is constantly growing*. **(A)** is correct. **(B)** is one of the benefits offered by the company, not the company name. *Think outside the box* is an idiom, not the name of the company. The word *range* appears in the text as a verb which indicate a variety of options, it is not the name of the company.

160. (B)

The author of the email writes *I have now noticed that the product above is outdated and does not live up to the standards of most similar products in the market. In fact, this TV offers poorer image quality than my old television, which I bought more than 5 years ago.* The speaker says *in fact* in order to give evidence for his previous claim, so **(B)** must be correct.

161. (A)

The letters says *Innovations 4K Ultra HD Smart TV 60*, so **(B)** is mentioned. The letter says *this TV offers poorer image quality than my old television*, so **(C)** is mentioned as well. **(D)** is mentioned when the letter says *payment plan contract*, so **(A)** is the only choice not mentioned in the letter.

162. (C)

The letter says *enclosed is a copy of the invoice and payment plan contract.* If there is a payment plan contract, it means the product was *financed.* **(C)** correct. The letter doesn't say anything about *instructions*. There's no mention of an *ID* document. **(D)** repeats *image*, but this is used in the text to refer to the poor quality of the TV.

163. (A)

The sentence introduces the item bought, before the writer discusses their issues with the product. The correct placement of the sentence must be [1]. **(A)** is correct.

164. (D)

The article mentions different things that can be done in Venice (*chilling on a deckchair, strolling along the beach, enjoying tasty food*). **(D)** is correct. The article mentions *water sports* and *staying for the whole summer* only as among the many things that can be done in Venice. **(C)** repeats *family* but this is not the main topic of the article.

165. (A)

strolling means *walking casually* so **(A)** is the correct option. Even though **(B), (C),** and **(D)** are verbs of movement, they do not have similar meanings to 'stroll'.

166. (B)

The article says *be sure to check out Info Venice for great activities and unique attractions! www.infovenice.com.* **(B)** is the correct answer. **(A)** is incorrect because the article says that there are many *outdoor activities* in Venice, but not that information about the city can be found outdoors. There's no mention of a tourist information office so **(C)** is also wrong. **(D)** is incorrect because the article says *discover hidden gems and must-see locations*, but this does not mean that information about Venice can be found in different locations.

167. (B)

The lighter color represents native speakers and it is around the 400 million mark in the bar representing the Spanish language, so **(B)** is the correct option. The numbers for the other languages are: **(A)** English–approximately 350 million, **(C)** Mandarin–approximately 1,150 million, and **(D)** Hindi/Urdu–approximately 250 million.

168. (C)

The darker color represents non-native speakers and the chart shows that English is the language which is around the 650 million mark, so **(C)** is the correct language. 350 million is the number of speakers of English as a first language, so **(A)** is incorrect. 450 million is the approximate number of Spanish speakers, so **(B)** is also incorrect. **(D)** is also incorrect because 1 billion is the approximate total number of speakers of both English and Hindi/Urdu.

169. (C)

The chart shows that when numbers for native and non-native speakers are combined, both English and Hindi have approximately 1 billion speakers, so **(C)** is the correct answer. 250 million is the number of speakers of Hindi as a first language, so **(A)** is incorrect. 750 million is the number of speakers of

Hindi as a second language, so **(B)** is also incorrect. **(D)** is wrong because 450 million is the total number of Spanish speakers.

170. (C)

The darker bars represent *non-native speakers* and Mandarin has the shortest darker bar. **(C)** is the correct answer. Hindi **(D)** has the highest number of non-native speakers followed by English **(A).** Spanish **(B)** also has more non-native speakers than Mandarin **(C)**.

171. (D)

The advert says *remarkably slim* **(A)** and *lightweight* **(B)**. It also says *enjoy greater flexibility* **(C)** so **(D)** is the only adjective not used to describe the product.

172. (A)

The advert says *activate fingerprint lock by pressing the home button*, so **(A)** is the correct answer. The advert uses the adjective *accurate* to describe the system, but this is not the main function. **(C)** repeats *home*, but the ad talks about a *home button*, not using the product at home. The ad says *use the enhanced ITab S2's power keyboard for a desktop experience,* but there's no connection between the keyboard and the fingerprint functionality.

173. (C)

The advert says *order online from www.itab2.com and get a free name engraving*, so **(C)** is the correct answer. The article says *from $399.00* but it doesn't say the offer is only valid online, so **(A)** is not possible. The ad says *ITab 2 available in black, silver, and gold* but doesn't say these colors are only available online. **(D)** is not mentioned in the text.

174. (B)

Tuesday's special is made with *pulled pork* and *chicken breast*, so it's not suitable for vegetarians. **(B)** is correct. **(A)**, **(C)**, and **(D)** do not contain any meat.

175. (C)

All the specials contain cheese (Monday–*mascarpone cheese*, Tuesday–*jalapeno cheese*, Wednesday–*gruyere* and *parmesan*, Thursday–*Greek-style cheese*, and Friday–*halloumi*), so **(C)** is the correct answer.

176. (B)

The email says *I would rather not hire a taxi or use a shuttle service to the hotel*, and the advert mentions a free shuttle bus as one of the services provided by the hotel, so **(B)** is the correct answer. The email doesn't say anything about *room service*. The ad mentions *free Wi-Fi* as one of the services, but it is not mentioned in the email; **(C)** must be incorrect. **(D)** is not mentioned in the text.

177. (D)

The email says *also, I find 5-star hotels too impersonal so I downgraded my reservation.* **(D)** is correct. **(C)** is not possible because *Hakano's Inn* is a 4-star hotel. Neither the ad nor the email talk about 2 or 3-star hotels, so **(A)** and **(B)** are not possible.

178. (D)

Sue says in the email *now I can also walk to the office every day*, so **(D)** is the correct alternative. The ad says the hotel is near the train station but there is no mention of Sue using the train, so **(A)** is not possible. **(B)** is also wrong because the word *bus* is only used in the ad when talking about one of the services offered by the hotel (*free shuttle bus*). **(C)** is wrong because Sue says she would not like to take a taxi from the airport to the hotel.

179. (A)

The question asks for the reason not mentioned in the text. In the email Sue says *I find 5-star hotels too impersonal*, which eliminates choice **(B)**. **(C)** is also mentioned in the email when Sue says *Now I can also walk to the office every day*. **(D)** is mentioned when Sue says she can *save some precious time* so **(A)** is the only reason not to be mentioned in the text. Sue says she finds *5-star hotels* impersonal, not big hotels. **(A)** is correct.

180. (C)

Sue says *I look forward to meeting your team so we can start negotiations early on Monday morning.* **(C)** is correct. *Sunday, January 19* is the date Sue arrives in Tokyo. *09:00 A.M.* is the time Sue arrives at Tokyo airport.

181. (C)

Lisa says in her email *my former colleague Yasmin Patwari recommended that I contact you to find out if you had any recommendations regarding employment.* **(C)** is the correct answer. There's no mention of a *boss*, so **(A)** is not possible. Lisa says *I am currently employed.* **(D)** repeats *challenge*, but Lisa wants to challenge herself, not Ms. Monteiro.

182. (A)

Ms. Monteiro says *the first step would be to meet in person.* **(A)** is the correct answer. **(B)** repeats *MBA*, but Lisa already has an MBA, so she would not need to get one. **(C)** and **(D)** are not mentioned in the email.

183. (D)

Paola asks Lisa to bring *a copy of your MBA certificate* **(A)**, *proof of address* **(B)**, and *some form of identification* **(C).** There's no mention of a bank statement so **(D)** is the correct answer.

184. (C)

Lisa says she is looking for *employment in the IT industry* and is currently employed *as a Java developer.* **(C)** is correct. Lisa uses Yasmin as a reference but doesn't say they are *best friends*, so **(A)** is not possible. **(B)** is not mentioned in the text; Lisa says she is simply *looking for a new challenge*. Lisa says she's looking for a job in New York, but she doesn't say *she lives in New York*, so **(D)** is wrong.

185. (B)

At the end of Paola's email we can read *DX Recruitment Solutions*, so **(B)** is the correct answer. Yasmin is Lisa's reference so **(A)** is not possible. **(C)** is also wrong because Lisa says *I contact you to find out if you had any recommendations regarding employment in the IT industry*, but there's no information to show that Paola works for an IT company. **(D)** is not mentioned in either email.

186. (B)

The heading of the notice is *personal marketing workshop*, so **(B)** is the correct answer. The word *marketing* is present only as part of the topic of the workshop, so **(A)** is wrong. **(C)** is incorrect because the workshop is part of a professional development program, but *professional development* is not the topic of the workshop. **(D)** is also wrong because *Human Resources* is the company department responsible for organizing the workshop.

187. (C)

The email says *we are extremely proud to announce the first workshop part of our continuous professional development program*, so **(C)** is the correct answer. **(A)** is incorrect because New World Software is the name of the company, but there's no mention of a *software training course*. **(B)** is also wrong because the word *marketing* is part of the workshop *topic*, not a training program. **(D)** repeats *extra sessions* from the text but does not answer the question.

188. (B)

The notice says *a special in-house workshop*, so **(B)** is the correct answer. The word *house* is used in the notice but it doesn't mean the workshop can be attended from home, so **(A)** is incorrect. **(C)** is also wrong because the only mention of using a phone is when Pietro asks employees to contact him over the phone. **(D)** is not mentioned in the text.

189. (D)

The table shows the start date for new courses as every month on the 12th. The new courses start each month. **(D)** is correct.

190. (A)

Pietro says *I would rather answer any questions over the phone so I will not be replying to emails on this subject.* **(A)** is correct. **(C)** is also wrong because Mr.Bonucci says *I will not be replying to emails on this subject.* **(B)** and **(D)** are not mentioned in the text.

191. (B)

Sandy says *we were all extremely concerned about your absence in last night's performance*, so **(B)** is the correct answer. **(A)** is not mentioned in the text. **(C)** is incorrect as Sandy says *one of the waiters says he saw you leave Reginald's early, in order to go to dinner with Mr. Lopez and Ms. Cato.* **(D)** is also incorrect because Sandy says *In the end we asked one of your supporting acts, Mrs.Vasiliev, to improvise a performance.*

192. (D)

Sue says *we raised over three million dollars ...*, so **(D)** is the correct answer. **(A)** is wrong because two thousand dollars is the ticket price. **(B)** and **(C)** are not mentioned.

193. (B)

The agenda says *Slideshow–Previous Years' Projects 2013–15 with Charlotte Johnson.* **(B)** is correct. Cristiano Lopez is hosting the *welcome cocktails*. Jennifer Cato is hosting the *fundraising*. Patricia Anniston is hosting the *date auction*.

194. (C)

In the text chain, Mr. Popov writes *Well, as my assistant told you, my wife was involved in an accident so I had to get a flight back to New York.* The answer is **(C)**.

195. (C)

Mrs. McAllister says *I truly hope there is an explanation so we can put this incident behind us and focus on next month's London Charity Ball at Royal Albert Hall.* **(C)** is the correct answer. *Reginald's* is the location of the current event. **(B)** is not mentioned in the text. *Africa Unite* is the name of the current charity event, so **(D)** is incorrect.

196. (D)

The email says the booking is for 2 adults and 2 children, so the booking is for 4 people. **(D)** is correct.

197. (B)

The invoice states that each individual pass costs $15.00. **(B)** is the answer.

198. (C)

The email states that Javier booked the hotel for 3 nights. **(C)** is correct.

199. (A)

Looking at the conversation, Javier writes after the customer service advisor writes *To confirm, you stayed at Teddy's hotel for 3 nights last month?* The advisor is asking is the information they have is correct, and Javier is confirming this, so **(A)** is correct.

200. (A)

The sales rep writes *Are you able to hold on while I contact the hotel on your behalf?* so the answer must be **(A)**.

PRACTICE TEST 3

 **Track 14**

Play Track 14 to hear the audio for Part I.

SECTION 1—LISTENING COMPREHENSION

In the Listening Comprehension Section, you will have the chance to demonstrate how well you understand spoken English. The Listening Comprehension Section will take approximately 45 minutes. There are four parts, and directions are given for each part. You must mark your answers on the answer sheet. Do not write them in the test book.

PART I: PHOTOGRAPHS

Directions: For each question, you will hear four statements about the photograph in your test book. When you hear the statements, choose the one statement that best describes what you see in the photograph. Then, find the number of the question on your answer sheet and mark your answer. The statements will not be written in your test book and will be spoken just once.

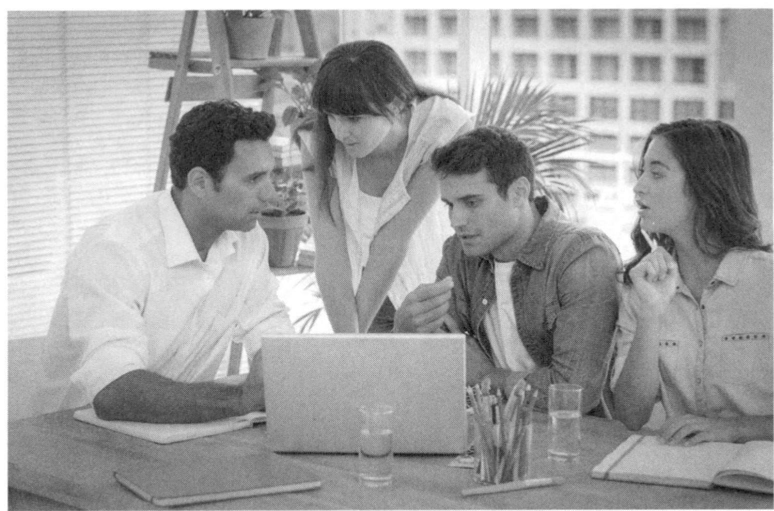

Now listen to the four statements.

Choice (B), "They're gathered around the table," best describes what you see in the picture. Therefore, you should fill in choice (B) in your answer sheet.

1. 

2. 

3.

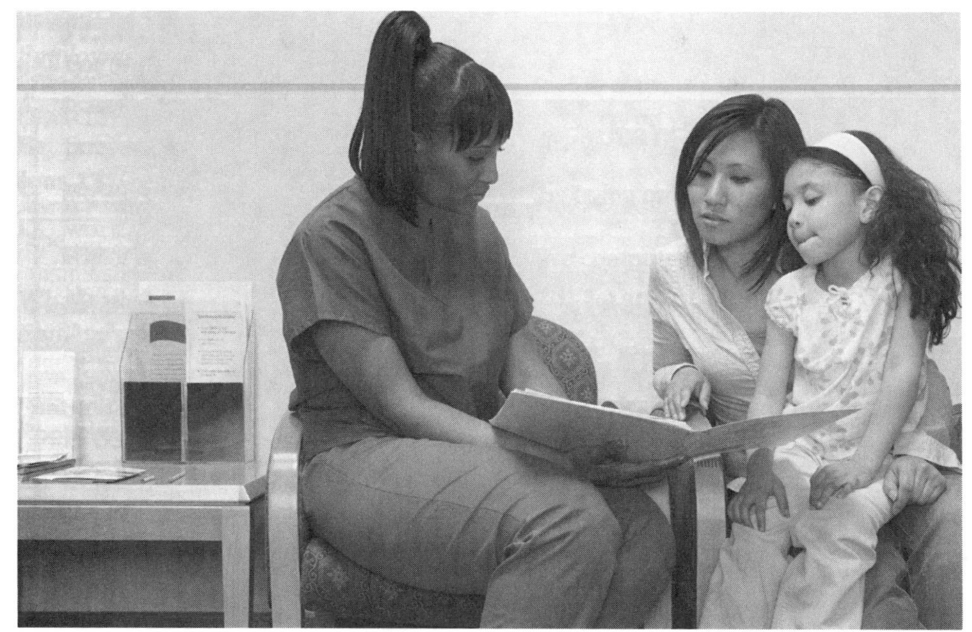

4.

GO ON TO THE NEXT PAGE.

5.

6.

 **Track 15**

Play Track 15 to hear the audio for Part II.

PART II: QUESTION-RESPONSE

Directions: You will hear a question or statement and three responses spoken in English. They will be spoken only once and will not be printed in your test book. Choose the best response to the question or statement and mark the letter on your answer sheet.

Listen to a sample question:

Sample Answer

Choice (A), "It's this afternoon; at two," best answers the question. Therefore, you should fill in choice (A) in your answer sheet.

7. Mark your answer on your answer sheet.

8. Mark your answer on your answer sheet.

9. Mark your answer on your answer sheet.

10. Mark your answer on your answer sheet.

11. Mark your answer on your answer sheet.

12. Mark your answer on your answer sheet.

13. Mark your answer on your answer sheet.

14. Mark your answer on your answer sheet.

15. Mark your answer on your answer sheet.

16. Mark your answer on your answer sheet.

17. Mark your answer on your answer sheet.

18. Mark your answer on your answer sheet.

19. Mark your answer on your answer sheet.

20. Mark your answer on your answer sheet.

21. Mark your answer on your answer sheet.

22. Mark your answer on your answer sheet.

23. Mark your answer on your answer sheet.

24. Mark your answer on your answer sheet.

25. Mark your answer on your answer sheet.

26. Mark your answer on your answer sheet.

27. Mark your answer on your answer sheet.

28. Mark your answer on your answer sheet.

29. Mark your answer on your answer sheet.

30. Mark your answer on your answer sheet.

31. Mark your answer on your answer sheet.

 **Track 16**

Play Track 16 to hear the audio for Part III.

PART III: SHORT CONVERSATIONS

Directions: You will now hear a number of conversations between two people. You will be asked to answer three questions about what the speakers say in each conversation. Select the best response and mark the letter on your answer sheet. The conversations will be spoken only once and will not be printed in your test book.

32. Where is this conversation likely to take place?

A. a business conference
B. a job interview
C. a client meeting
D. a performance review

33. Which of the following reasons does the man NOT give for his career progression?

A. his performance
B. his experience
C. the transferable skills he acquired
D. his education

34. What happened to the senior project manager the man worked with?

A. She died.
B. She was laid off.
C. She closed her business.
D. She moved to Central America.

---

35. Where is the conversation taking place?

A. in a supermarket
B. in an office
C. in hotel reception
D. in a restaurant

36. What do we learn about the couple's vacations?

A. They went to a resort.
B. They went to many different places.
C. They visited vineyards.
D. They spent a lot of time by the pool.

37. What do we learn about the couple?

A. They're about to acquire a new business.
B. They opened a hotel in the Andes.
C. They always go to the same place on their vacations.
D. They want Arnold to work for them.

---

38. What's the man looking for?

A. his cell phone
B. his briefcase
C. theater tickets
D. Andy's brown coat

39. What do we learn about the woman?

A. She doesn't like the theater.
B. She doesn't like the new director of operations.
C. She has a new role in the company.
D. She doesn't want to see Andy.

40. What does the woman mean when she says "I'll probably take a hot bath and hit the sack"?

A. She wants to take a bath before going to the theater.
B. She wants to take a bath and go straight to bed.
C. She wants to take a bath and then decide if she's going to the theater.
D. She wants to take a bath and watch a movie on her sofa.

---

41. Why won't the number 52 bus stop at Central Square?

    A. Some of the roads are under repair.
    B. It is early in the morning.
    C. The buses have a new route.
    D. There's a street market at Central Square.

42. According to the woman, how can the man get to Central Square?

    A. There's another bus on Grand Street.
    B. He can use the subway.
    C. He can take the bus on Mulholland Avenue.
    D. You can't get to Central Square on Saturdays and Sundays.

43. Why shouldn't the man worry?

    A. The street market is only held at weekends.
    B. There is an east bound train.
    C. There are street signs to help him get to Central Square.
    D. Grand Street is only five miles away from where he is.

---

44. Who is Mr. Garcia?

    A. a regular patient
    B. a pharmaceutical sales rep
    C. Dr. Walker's husband
    D. Dr. Walker's business partner

45. Why is Mr. Garcia calling?

    A. He thinks the antibiotics aren't working.
    B. He's been sick for 10 days.
    C. He feels a lot stronger.
    D. He can't find her prescription.

46. What does the woman offer to do?

    A. call Dr. Walker straightaway
    B. ask Dr. Walker to call her back in 2 or 3 hours
    C. ask Dr. Walker for another copy of the prescription
    D. ask Dr. Walker to prescribe something stronger

---

47. What is affecting customer's service lines?

    A. They are short staffed in Tokyo.
    B. Too many customers are having problems in Kyoto.
    C. Some of the staff is being relocated to Kyoto.
    D. Some of the staff have to commute from Tokyo to Kyoto.

48. When does Sally expect things to get back to normal?

    A. after the weekend
    B. before the end of the week
    C. after her trip to Michigan
    D. after her trip to Kyoto

49. What does the man say about Sally?

    A. She's been doing a great job.
    B. She's an excellent clerk.
    C. She should be doing her job.
    D. She should be proud of Michigan.

GO ON TO THE NEXT PAGE.

50. Where are the store signs?

A. in Chicago
B. next to the furniture
C. at the printer
D. downstairs

51. Why does the woman want to call an architect?

A. to let her know the opening is on Monday.
B. to tell her that the signs and furniture have arrived.
C. to tell her to work next weekend.
D. to open the brown boxes.

52. When does the store open?

A. on Friday
B. at the weekend
C. on Monday
D. in two weeks

---

53. In which direction does the man want to go?

A. left
B. right
C. forward
D. backward

54. What time is it now?

A. 4:15
B. 4:45
C. 5:15
D. 5:45

55. Where are the speakers going?

A. a basketball game
B. a conference
C. a meeting
D. an old office

---

56. What time did the man go to bed?

A. at 4:00
B. after 4:00
C. before 4:00
D. He doesn't know.

57. How many hours of sleep does the woman need?

A. less than 7
B. 7 or more
C. 10
D. more than 8 on Saturdays

58. Why did the man get up early?

A. He had to go to the office to finish a presentation.
B. He had to do some work in his house.
C. He usually wakes up early on Saturdays.
D. He had a party to go to.

---

59. Where does the woman live?

A. near the new supermarket
B. just outside Manhattan
C. next to a bagel store
D. opposite her children's school

60. How does the man get to work?

A. on foot
B. by car
C. by bus
D. by train

61. What time will the woman meet the man tomorrow?

A. 7:15
B. 7:45
C. 8:15
D. 8:45

---

62. What does the woman say about the Bernard Building?

  A. It's a building for fashion designers.
  B. She's meeting a client there.
  C. It's a space for legal advice.
  D. It's used by people working in artistic professions.

63. What is the man's profession?

  A. Fashion Designer
  B. Artist
  C. Lawyer
  D. Clothes Manager

64. Look at the graphic below. Which number shows the location of the Bernard Building?

  A. 1
  B. 2
  C. 3
  D. 4

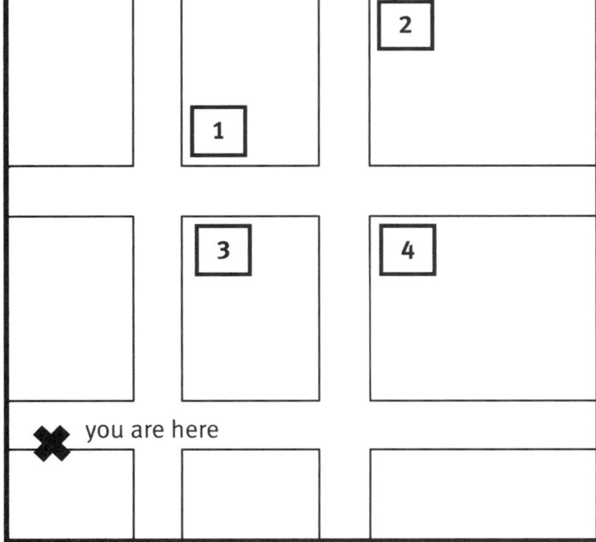

65. Why has the budget increased?

  A. They need to increase their online presence.
  B. They need to improve their products.
  C. They are creating more products this year than in the previous year.
  D. Their feedback was negative.

66. Why does the man say "Right?"?

  A. He also thinks they should have done something sooner.
  B. He's checking that he understands.
  C. He's identifying an issue with the budget.
  D. He's making sure that the woman is familiar with the plan.

67. Look at the graphic. Which budget does the woman think should change?

  A. Research
  B. Production
  C. Editing
  D. Tech

Spring Budget, 2019	
Research	$5,000
Production	$10,000
Editing	$7,500
Tech	$22,250
TOTAL	$45,000

68. What is most likely the relationship between the two speakers?

  A. acquaintances
  B. mother and son
  C. husband and wife
  D. colleagues

69. Who are the speakers visiting next week?

A. the realtors
B. the owner of the amusement park
C. their children
D. her mother

70. Look at the graphic below. When will they go to the amusement park?

A. Tuesday
B. Wednesday
C. Thursday
D. Friday

Tuesday		85 °F
Wednesday		95 °F
Thursday		78 °F
Friday		79 °F

 **Track 17**

Play Track 17 to hear the audio for Part IV.

PART IV: SHORT TALKS

Directions: You will hear some talks given by a single speaker. You will be asked to answer three questions about each talk. Select the best response to each question and mark the letter (A), (B), (C), or (D) on your answer sheet. The talks will be spoken only once and will not be printed in your test book.

71. Where would this announcement most likely be heard?

- **A.** on a plane
- **B.** at an airport
- **C.** at a bus stop
- **D.** at a train station

72. Who is speaking?

- **A.** a waitress
- **B.** a bus driver
- **C.** a pilot
- **D.** a flight attendant

73. When is the announcement being made?

- **A.** before take-off
- **B.** after take-off
- **C.** before landing
- **D.** after landing

---

74. When is the annual conference?

- **A.** November 14
- **B.** November 16
- **C.** next week
- **D.** on Saturday

75. When should the employees confirm their presence?

- **A.** November 14
- **B.** November 16
- **C.** by the end of next week
- **D.** on Saturday

76. What is the speaker talking about when he says, "maybe next year"?

- **A.** allowing kids to attend the event
- **B.** increasing the budget for the party
- **C.** inviting employees' partners to the conference
- **D.** allowing questions at the event.

---

77. Where is the speaker?

- **A.** in a computer factory
- **B.** in a food factory
- **C.** in a restaurant
- **D.** in a laboratory

78. What is the speaker discussing?

- **A.** company research plans
- **B.** machine operating instructions
- **C.** a new line of products
- **D.** a traditional recipe

79. What is the name of the company?

- **A.** Finest Ingredients
- **B.** Nutritional Values
- **C.** Mouth-watering Foods
- **D.** Richmond Foods

---

80. What is the recording mainly about?

- **A.** order information
- **B.** emergency procedures
- **C.** hours of operation
- **D.** account information

81. How can the listener contact the company in case of an emergency?

- **A.** by mail
- **B.** by phone
- **C.** using their website
- **D.** by phone or their website

82. What time are the offices open on Saturday?

- **A.** 8:00 A.M.–7:00 P.M.
- **B.** 8:00 A.M.–3:00 P.M.
- **C.** 9:00 A.M.–7:00 P.M.
- **D.** 9:00 A.M.–3:00 P.M.

---

83. What should workers do if equipment is damaged or lost?

- **A.** report to their supervisors
- **B.** report to Health and Safety
- **C.** borrow visitors' equipment
- **D.** leave the building

84. What are the requirements for visitors entering the building?

- **A.** to be accompanied at all times
- **B.** to wear appropriate gear
- **C.** to be accompanied at all times and wear appropriate gear
- **D.** to wear temporary equipment

85. Who might ask visitors to leave the building?

- **A.** all workers
- **B.** Mr. Lyndon
- **C.** supervisors
- **D.** security personnel

---

86. What is opening?

- **A.** a new family resort
- **B.** a new leisure center
- **C.** a new spa
- **D.** a new restaurant chain

87. What is not mentioned by the speaker?

- **A.** laundry services
- **B.** water parks
- **C.** room service
- **D.** contact information

88. Look at the table. What is the opening date for the hotel being discussed?

- **A.** May 12
- **B.** June 16
- **C.** July 4
- **D.** July 25

New Hotels in Acapulco

Hotel Chain	Family Friendly?	Swimming Pool?	Opening Date
Resort to Us	Yes	Yes	May 12
Sundown	Yes	Yes	June 16
Resort To Us	No	Yes	July 4
Sundown	No	Yes	July 25

---

89. Who is listening to this announcement?

- **A.** tourists
- **B.** football players
- **C.** latecomers
- **D.** employees

90. How is the group traveling?

- **A.** by bus
- **B.** by train
- **C.** by taxi
- **D.** by van

91. Look at the itinerary. What time will they start playing football?

A. 12:00
B. 13:30
C. 14:30
D. 16:00

Itinerary	
12:00–12:30	
12:30–13:30	lunch
13:30–14:30	
14:30–15:50	
15:50–16:00	return to the bus
16:00–17:00	

92. How many levels are reserved for visitor parking?

A. one
B. two
C. three
D. four

93. Who may park in the red spaces?

A. employees
B. visitors
C. management
D. trucks

94. What will happen to employees who park in wrong spaces?

A. They will lose their spaces.
B. They will lose their jobs.
C. They will have their cars clamped.
D. They will have their cars ticketed and towed.

95. Who are most likely to be the listeners?

A. secretaries
B. managers
C. software developers
D. lawyers

96. How many hours do employees work a week?

A. 30
B. 35
C. 40
D. 45

97. When is the office closed?

A. on Sundays
B. at weekends
C. between 7:00 A.M. and 9:00 P.M.
D. four weeks a year

98. Where is the talk probably being given?

A. on a tour bus
B. at the zoo's entrance hall
C. in a university lecture
D. in a conference room

99. What will the listeners have the opportunity to do?

A. learn what caused the major ice ages
B. learn more about the animals who lived before and after the major ice ages
C. learn more about the new animals at the zoo
D. learn more about the origin of life

100. Why does the speaker say "find out for yourself"?

A. He is unable to visit the area himself.
B. He is going to test the audience's abilities.
C. He does not know the answer to the question.
D. He is inviting the audience to look around.

Stop! This is the end of the Listening Comprehension Section of the exam. Turn to Part V.

You will have one hour and 15 minutes to complete Parts V, VI, and VII of the exam.

SECTION 2—READING COMPREHENSION

In the Reading Comprehension Section, you will read a variety of texts and answer different types of questions. The Reading Comprehension Section will last 75 minutes. There are three parts, and directions are given for each part. You are encouraged to answer as many questions as possible within the allotted time. Mark your answers on the separate answer sheet. Do no write them in the test book.

PART V: INCOMPLETE SENTENCES

Directions: There are 30 incomplete sentences below (questions 101–130). Four words or phrases are given below each one of them. You are to select the best answer (A), (B), (C), or (D) to complete the sentence. Then mark the letters on your answer sheet.

101. The marketing director's ________ on new media was better than expected.

- **A.** presentation
- **B.** presenting
- **C.** presently
- **D.** preventative

102. Because of the economic crisis in Europe, we have ________ off one-fifth of our staff.

- **A.** lays
- **B.** laid
- **C.** laying
- **D.** lay

103. The report from the sales manager ________ my supervisor's argument that the company needs restructuring.

- **A.** advancing
- **B.** advantage
- **C.** advanced
- **D.** advance

104. ________ our department had achieved the best results for the third quarter, we received a hefty bonus.

- **A.** As
- **B.** Even though
- **C.** Apart from
- **D.** Nevertheless

105. The CFO put his own financial interests ________ the well-being of his staff.

- **A.** above
- **B.** up
- **C.** away from
- **D.** along

106. Before he retired, Mr. Smith found a ________ professional to replace him as head of department.

- **A.** suit
- **B.** suitably
- **C.** suitability
- **D.** suitable

107. The construction workers stood together and ________ to renegotiate their contracts after being told there would be cuts in their sector.

A. reminded
B. rescinded
C. refused
D. restructured

108. Mrs. Malik was extremely worried ________ the lack of innovation in her design.

A. of
B. about
C. with
D. as

109. The Chinese market has been ________ all the commercial strategies of the firm.

A. influencing
B. influence
C. influenced
D. influences

110. The main aim was always to carry out the ________ with best professionals available in the pharmaceutical industry.

A. researching
B. researched
C. research
D. researches

111. The whole team was disappointed to hear that their proposal had been ________ by the CEO.

A. turned up
B. turned down
C. turned away
D. turned on

112. ________ Prof Park fired his old personal assistant, the environment has become less poisonous and more productive.

A. Since
B. While
C. For
D. Whenever

113. My boss sent the memo only ________ it had been approved and signed by the board.

A. so
B. but
C. after
D. until

114. The sales rep was kindly asked to ________ his presentation until next week.

A. put with
B. put off
C. put on
D. put in

115. Do ________ a client without checking the service order first.

A. never invoice
B. invoice never
C. not invoice ever
D. not ever invoice

116. Even though their service is usually poor, we were desperate and ________ them.

A. hire
B. weekly hire
C. had to hire
D. had better hire

GO ON TO THE NEXT PAGE.

117. Mrs. Jones has decided to _________ as governor.

A. step down
B. step out
C. step through
D. step in

118. The bank is expected to lower its _________ rates for new customers.

A. interesting
B. interested
C. interest
D. interests

119. When the managers _________ a profit, they will change their mind.

A. are seeing
B. see
C. might see
D. saw

120. Sales dropped sharply _________ the financial scandal was made public.

A. when
B. although
C. but
D. to

121. Due to the investors' budget _________, the factory will be able to hire new staff.

A. surplus
B. surprise
C. surrender
D. survive

122. Ms. Sorensen has opted not to _________ this meeting.

A. amend
B. ascend
C. attend
D. avenge

123. Our facilities look old and outdated. We should allocate funds to _________ the building.

A. modern
B. modernize
C. more modern
D. modernized

124. Offensive behavior against staff will not be tolerated and abusers will be _________.

A. implicated
B. accused
C. acquitted
D. prosecuted

125. Human Resources needs a new _________ to keep employees happy.

A. salary
B. secretaries
C. strategy
D. extraction

126. Mr. Souza made one bad investment after the other and ended up _________.

A. penniless
B. pointless
C. pitiless
D. careless

127. Factory ________ require all staff to wear gloves and helmets when operating machinery.

A. headlines

B. lines

C. guidelines

D. sidelines

128. The screen in our ________ is cracked, so we will have to postpone the presentation until it gets replaced.

A. smartest speaker

B. smart board

C. smart tablet

D. smart desk

129. The company has turned a ________ for the first time since the market crashed in 2001.

A. profit

B. profited

C. profiting

D. profitable

130. The new business strategy demonstrates a ________ shift in this company's mentality.

A. margin

B. maniac

C. mankind

D. monumental

PART VI: TEXT COMPLETION

Directions: Read the texts below. A word is missing in some of the sentences. You are to choose the best answer (A), (B), (C), or (D) to complete the text. Then mark the letters on your answer sheet.

Questions 131–134 refer to the letter that follows.

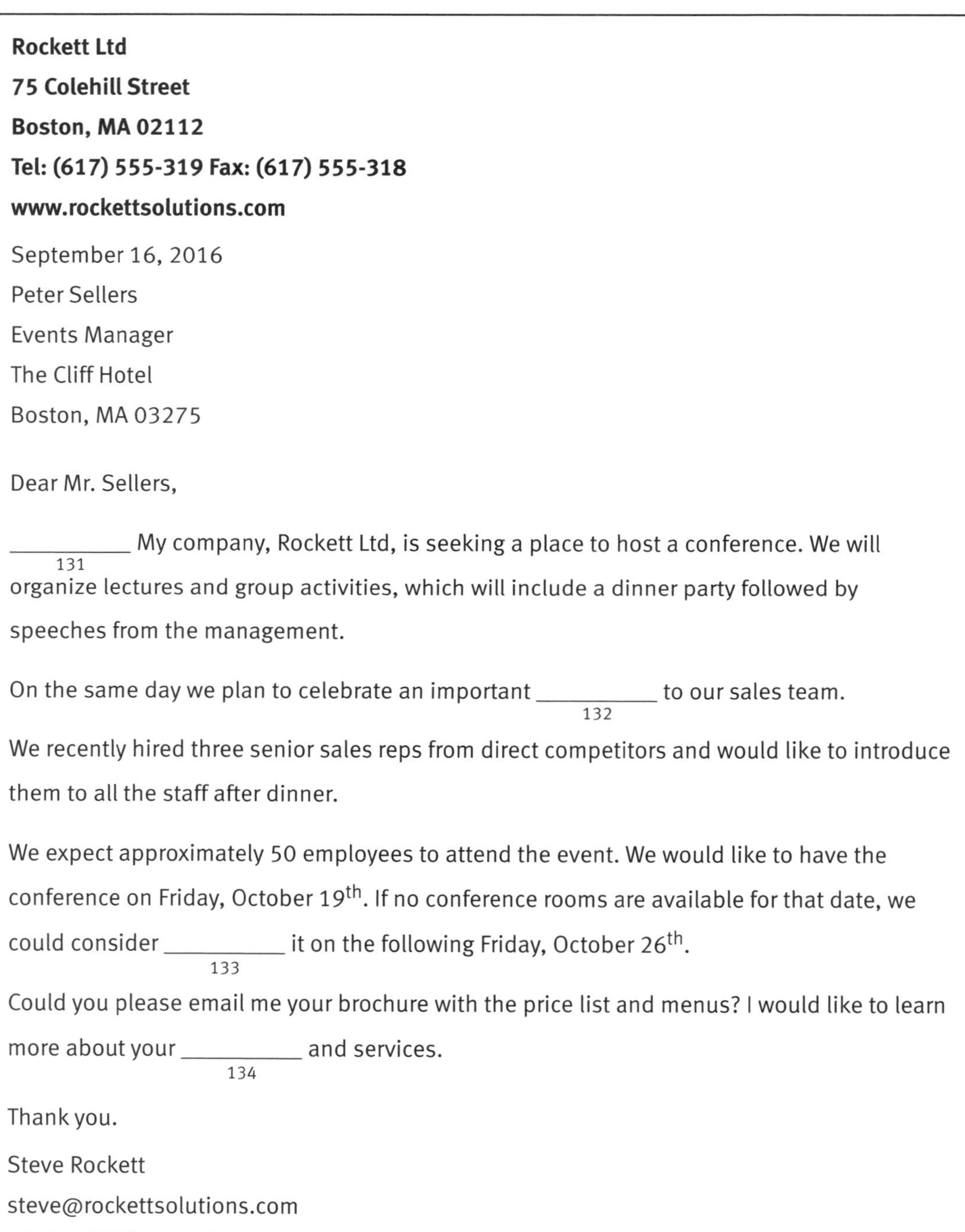

Rockett Ltd

75 Colehill Street

Boston, MA 02112

Tel: (617) 555-319 Fax: (617) 555-318

www.rockettsolutions.com

September 16, 2016

Peter Sellers

Events Manager

The Cliff Hotel

Boston, MA 03275

Dear Mr. Sellers,

__________ (131) My company, Rockett Ltd, is seeking a place to host a conference. We will organize lectures and group activities, which will include a dinner party followed by speeches from the management.

On the same day we plan to celebrate an important __________ (132) to our sales team.

We recently hired three senior sales reps from direct competitors and would like to introduce them to all the staff after dinner.

We expect approximately 50 employees to attend the event. We would like to have the conference on Friday, October 19th. If no conference rooms are available for that date, we could consider __________ (133) it on the following Friday, October 26th.

Could you please email me your brochure with the price list and menus? I would like to learn more about your __________ (134) and services.

Thank you.

Steve Rockett

steve@rockettsolutions.com

131. **A.** I hope this letter finds you well.
B. Please let me know your thoughts at the earliest opportunity.
C. I am interested in learning more about your products.
D. Yours sincerely.

132. **A.** addiction
B. addition
C. addicted
D. additive

133. **A.** have
B. to have
C. having
D. to having

134. **A.** facility
B. facilitate
C. facilitates
D. facilities

Questions 135–138 refer to the article below.

LOCAL CHEF NAMED TO "CHEF'S CHOICE AWARD 2016"

Tommy Lafayette, of *Modern Bistro*, was recently nominated as one of the 10 chefs who can win the prestigious award. He and the other 9 chefs ___(135)___ from a list of 1,000 candidates.

The 1,000 candidates had been nominated by a specialist magazine for ___(136)___ abilities to innovate and balance traditional and modern cuisine.

Mr. Lafayette is the first chef from Hawaii to ___(137)___ this honor.

The author is an exciting young talent who is never afraid to take risks and challenge traditional Mediterranean cuisine. His book, *Deconstructing Pepe*, ___(138)___.

135. **A.** will select
B. are selecting
C. been selected
D. were selected

136. **A.** them
B. themselves
C. theirs
D. their

137. **A.** give
B. be given
C. gave
D. be giving

138. **A.** is a collection of autobiographical poems about his early life.
B. is available to purchase in 20 different languages.
C. let me know what you think once you've read it.
D. will speak at the writer's and poet's conference in Hawaii next week.

Questions 139–142 refer to the following letter.

CYEF Ltd
481 Ringwood Street
Oakland, CA 94623
www.cyef.com

Office Express
Mrs. Penelope Bravo
2912 Capitol Lane
Los Angeles, CA 90016

Dear Mrs. Bravo

__________ (139) I work for CYEF Ltd, and we have a large demand for supplies on national level. I hope that we can __________ (140) partners and do business together.

We need some supplies to be delivered __________ (141) since our former supplier failed to fulfill our latest order.

We need 600 boxes of A4 110 mm quality paper for our laser printers. We would like them delivered as soon as possible because this is an urgent matter. I hope this can be the beginning of a long-lasting business partnership __________ (142) both companies can greatly benefit in the future.

Warm Regards,

Scott Drinkwater
HR Manager

139. **A.** I am writing to apply for the position of Office Manager at your company.
B. I wanted to congratulate you for your work on the Petrowski case.
C. A colleague recommended your company as the most reliable provider of quality office supplies.
D. Thank you for expressing interest in our products.

140. **A.** believe
B. belong
C. betray
D. become

141. **A.** quickly
B. quick
C. quicker
D. quickest

142. **A.** from which
B. at which
C. on which
D. which

Questions 143–146 refer to the article that follows.

A bright future for chiropractors

In the past, chiropractors were seen as an alternative last resort for those who had tried and failed more traditional medicines. ________ (143), however, more and more people choose chiropractic as a first option.

According to a survey involving more than 1,200 chiropractors in the US, 65 percent of their patients with back problems seek their professional advice without consulting their doctors.

Dr. Tommasi, who has been a chiropractor for over 35 years, describes chiropractic as ________ (144) "what traditional medicine doesn't, a heart."

Jake Brown, an apprentice chiropractor, now in his third year ________ (145) the supervision of Dr. Tommasi, believes that chiropractic is capable of transforming people's lives ________ (146)

143. **A.** Occasionally
B. Historically
C. Recently
D. Basically

144. **A.** have
B. to have
C. having
D. had

145. **A.** with
B. along
C. by
D. under

146. **A.** and is planning to officially protest the move in the coming weeks.
B. and does not hold out hope for the future of the profession.
C. and is waiting to hear if his job application is successful.
D. and that a bright future lies ahead for American chiropractors.

PART VII: READING COMPREHENSION

Directions: Read the selection of texts below. Each text is followed by a group of questions. Select the correct option and mark the letter (A), (B), (C), or (D) on your answer sheet.

Questions 147–149 refer to the job ad below.

CUSTOMER SERVICE

Boston-based company is looking for customer service professionals to expand its successful team in various regions in the US and Canada. Successful candidates will have a minimum of three years' experience in customer service or telemarketing, preferably in the cosmetics industry, as well as excellent communicative skills, good computer skills, and a college degree. Experience in sales is desirable but not essential. We offer an excellent salary and benefits package including life and health insurance, cycling allowance, and professional development courses. Send résumé to: W.F. Wilson, 418 Linskey Way, Boston, MA 02114. Closing date: March 29.

147. Who would most likely apply for this position?

A. a doctor

B. a teacher

C. a bus driver

D. a clerk in a department store

148. Which of the benefits is NOT mentioned in the job announcement?

A. life insurance

B. health insurance

C. cycling scheme

D. relocation allowance

149. Which of the following is mentioned as a requirement?

A. college degree

B. experience in sales

C. driving license

D. good appearance

Questions 150–153 refer to the following advertisement.

Stubble No-trouble

Stubble is a handsome addition to any men's looks, but it can often be difficult to keep under control. When does stubble end and a beard start? *Lumberjacks Unite*, the same company that has been providing you with top quality hair gel and other luxury grooming products for years, has developed a solution to the problem of losing your stubble and gaining a beard. Thorough research and careful testing of trial products has resulted in *Stubble No-trouble*, the fantastic new two-step, two-minute product that will keep your stubble short and shiny. Our special cream not only shortens your stubble, it also protects it from grease and food contamination in order to preserve that perfect natural, shiny stubble look.

If you have stubble, or plan to grow some, this product is an absolute must. It solves the problem every modern man has of keeping stubble from growing wild. We do all this at a price you can afford.

Stubble No-trouble sells for just $13 a box and is available at most drugstores and department stores.

150. What is the advertisement promoting?

A. shampoo and conditioner
B. hair gel
C. a facial hair cream
D. company supplies

151. How long does it take to use the product?

A. two minutes
B. four minutes
C. two weeks
D. four weeks

152. What problem does the product solve?

A. greasy beards
B. hair loss
C. gray beard
D. hairy ears

153. Where can you buy this product?

A. supermarkets
B. pharmacies
C. online
D. hair salons

Questions 154–156 refer to the form that follows.

Customer Satisfaction Research — [1] —

Are you pleased with the service offered by our staff? Did a member of our staff act in a manner which did not meet your expectations? We would love to know how you rate your experience with us. Please let us know by filling out this customer satisfaction form and dropping it in the green box by the store entrance. — [2] —

Name of staff member you would like to comment: ______________________

Service or Product Acquired: ______________________

Comments: ______________________

____

____

How could we improve the customer experience here at Tech Shop? ______________________

____

____

____

Name (optional): ______________ Email — [3] — (optional): ______________

Telephone number (optional): ______________________

— [4] — () Yes () No

154. Where would this form most likely be found?

A. a hotel

B. an airport

C. a computer store

D. a restaurant

155. In which of the positions marked [1], [2], [3], and [4] does the following sentence best belong?
"Would you like us to contact you about your experience?"

A. [1]

B. [2]

C. [3]

D. [4]

156. How should this form be submitted?

A. by leaving it in a special box

B. by sending it to the manager's office

C. by emailing the comments

D. by giving it to a member of staff.

Questions 157–159 refer to the following information.

Longleaf Home Offices
Office Solutions for Home-based businesses

Room Size	6 hours	A day (12 hours)	A week (5 days)
20 × 12m	$200	$360	$1,600
10 × 6m	$170	$310	$1,250
5 × 3m	$120	$200	$850
2 × 3m	$90	$140	$600

- Quoted prices are for January 2016.
- Coffee, tea, and water are included in the price of room.
- Bookings must be received 72 hours before the required date.
- Payment in full should be made with booking; payment by credit card or personal check is acceptable.

For longer-term bookings, please contact Theo Bessa at The Longleaf Home Offices, 88 Henry Street, San Diego.

157. When should bookings be made?

A. six hours in advance
B. a day in advance
C. three days in advance
D. a week in advance

158. Who is this information intended to help?

A. university students
B. multinationals
C. small businesses
D. motor companies

159. What policy is stated in the information?

A. Payment must be made at the time of booking.
B. Drinks are not included in room prices.
C. Credit cards are not accepted.
D. Longer-term bookings are not available.

Questions 160–163 refer to the following schedule.

OPERATION SCHEDULE FOR PLANT C

Saturday, August 12 — [1] —

	Sector A	Sector B	Sector C	Supervisor
09:00–15:00	Dr. Fisherman	Dr. Jones	Dr. Saunders	Prof. Smith
15:00–21:00	Dr. Wells	Dr. Saunders	Dr. Farrell	Dr. Campbell
21:00–03:00	Dr. Wells	Dr. Zaza	Dr. Beech	Prof. Challen
03:00–09:00	Dr. Zaza	Dr. Jones	Dr. Wastie	Prof. Challen

Engineering Team Members: Dr. Fisherman, Dr. Jones, Dr. Saunders, Dr. Wells, Dr. Williams, Dr. Farrell, Dr. Beech, Dr. Zaza, Dr. Wastie, Dr. Kcywoticz — [2] —

Team Leader: Dr. Campbell

Supervisors: Prof. Smith, Prof. Lilliput, Prof. Challen — [3] —

Each engineer is entitled to a 15-minute break with the authorization and operational cover of team leader or supervisor. — [4] —

160. What sector is Dr. Saunders responsible for in the morning shift?

A. sector A

B. sector B

C. sector C

D. sectors B and C

161. Who is NOT authorized to approve a break?

A. Dr. Wastie

B. Dr. Campbell

C. Prof. Challen

D. Prof. Lilliput

162. Who is allowed to cover engineers during their breaks?

A. Dr. Wastie

B. Dr. Campbell

C. Dr. Zaza

D. Dr. Beech

163. In which of the positions marked [1], [2], [3], and [4] does the following sentence best belong?
"Breaks must not be taken simultaneously."

A. [1]

B. [2]

C. [3]

D. [4]

Questions 164–166 refer to the memorandum that follows.

> **MEMO**
>
> To: All Staff
>
> Human Resources is organizing a *Green Day Out* at Central Park on Friday, September 22. There are no fees to be paid and each employee may bring two guests, family or friends. A picnic will be offered and we need to make sure everyone is catered for, so please call or email Lakesha in Human Resources by the end of the day on September 8 to confirm your presence and let her know if you have any guests. This should be a really fun event for everyone in the company!

164. When does an employee need to RSVP for this event?

A. before the end of the week
B. by September 22
C. by September 8
D. by the end of the day

165. Where is the event?

A. Human Resources
B. Central Park
C. Green Day Park
D. at the company

166. Who can employees invite?

A. no guests allowed
B. only friends
C. only family
D. family and friends

Questions 167–170 refer to the following email.

From: satoru@wfp.com
To: lindajp@ycfrecruitment.com
Subject: Recruitment–Lucas Johnson

Dear Ms. Peterson,

I am writing to you at the request of Mr. Johnson, who is applying for a position as a personal assistant through your agency.

Mr. Johnson worked for me as an administrative assistant from August 2004 to July 2012. My colleagues and I found him to be an extremely competent and reliable professional. His duties consisted of maintaining files, organizing meetings, appointments, and schedules, buying office supplies, and assisting visitors to the office. He always excelled at handling multiple tasks and working independently. He always assisted our customers in a friendly, patient, and professional manner. Moreover, he developed a high level of computer skills during his time at this company. We had hoped to keep him at our company, but he has decided to go through with his original plan of returning to Canada. We will miss Mr. Johnson here at WFP, but I am more than happy to recommend him as a valuable addition to any company he might be interested in joining as a PA. Please do not hesitate to contact me should you have any questions or require further information.

Sincerely,
Satoru Kagawa
WFP Studios

167. Why does the author of the email write "Please do not hesitate"?

- **A.** to explain that Mr Johnson will need to be hired quickly
- **B.** to encourage the reader to reach out to him
- **C.** to emphasize that Mr Johnson is a speedy worker
- **D.** to advise the reader to hire Mr Johnson

168. How long did Mr. Johnson work at WFP?

- **A.** 7 years
- **B.** 8 years
- **C.** 9 years
- **D.** 10 years

169. The word *reliable* in paragraph 2, line 2, is closest in meaning to

- **A.** independent.
- **B.** friendly.
- **C.** consistently good.
- **D.** skilled.

170. What kind of email is this?

- **A.** an email of complaint
- **B.** an email of recommendation
- **C.** a job inquiry
- **D.** an invitation

Questions 171–173 refer to the chart below.

DEFORESTATION

This chart shows the estimated deforestation by type of forest and time period, as well as experts' predictions for the next 20 years.

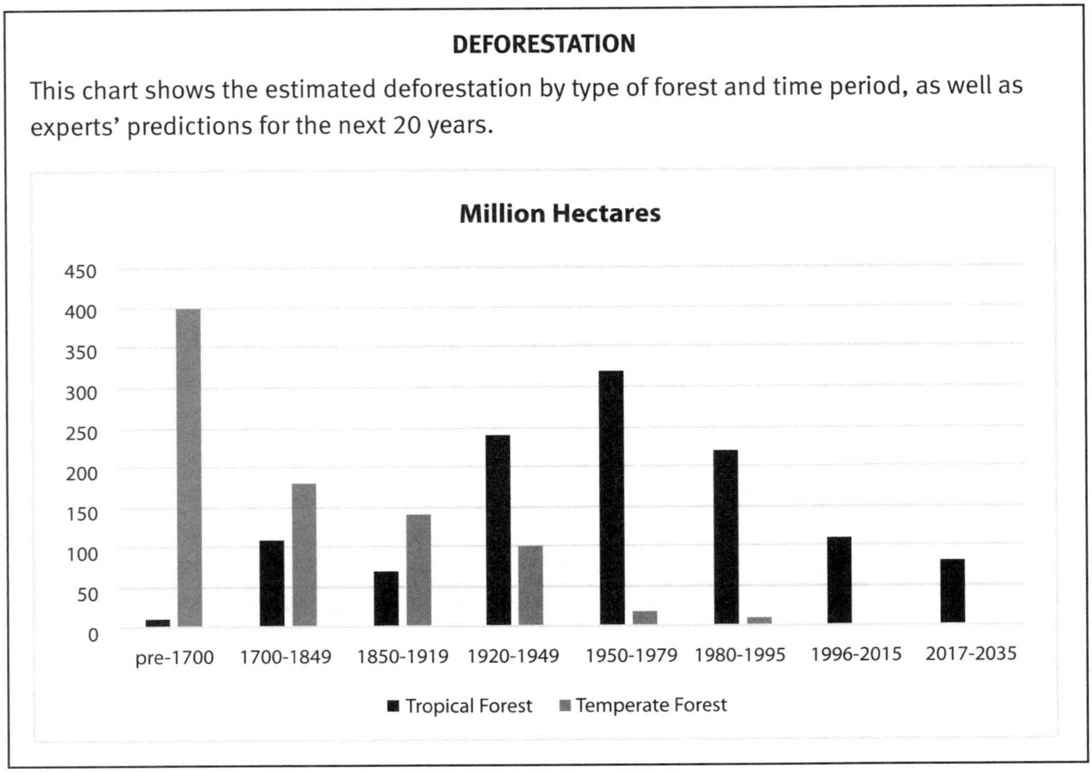

171. How many million hectares of temperate forest were cleared before the 18th century?

   A. between 150 and 200
   B. approximately 400
   C. between 400 and 500
   D. more than 400

172. In what period did tropical deforestation reach its peak?

   A. 1950–1979
   B. 1980–1995
   C. 1996–2015
   D. 1700–1849

173. When did tropical deforestation become greater than temperate deforestation?

   A. 1920–1949
   B. 1950–1979
   C. 1980–1995
   D. 1996–2015

Questions 174–175 refer to the bill that follows.

07/29/2016

3:28 P.M.

Your clerk is Patricia.

1	A4 110mm 500 sheets	$2.50	$2.50
3	Highlighter assorted	$4.00	$12.00
1	Ballpoint pen black	$0.40	$0.40
1	FX88GT Scientific Calculator	$13.50	$13.50
2	High Yield Ink Cartridge Black XL	$11.00	$22.00
2	High Yield Ink Cartridge Tri-color XL	$12.50	$25.00
	TOTAL		$75.40
	Tax @ 5%		$3.77
	Grand Total		**$79.17**

Thank you for your business.

174. How many items did the customer buy?

A. 8

B. 10

C. 12

D. 14

175. What kind of store is this bill from?

A. a restaurant

B. a computer store

C. a stationery store

D. a bar

Questions 176–180 refer to the following email and directory.

From: Gisele Fernandes
To: Samuel Barney
Subject: Things to do tomorrow

Hi Samuel,

I am really sick today and there are many things to be done in the store before the grand opening on Saturday. I really need your help as there are only 3 days left to do everything. I have outlined all the errands below. Please call me on my cell phone if you have any questions.

There are a lot of things to deliver to other floors of the store. All these items are in the staff room and it must be done today. You will find the screens and monitors in the blue containers, the perfumes in the yellow ones, and I am not sure what you will find in the red ones. However, just take them to the 2nd floor, as I am pretty sure I saw some red containers there yesterday.

The engineers from the software company had scheduled two training sessions for today. The first one is for the clerks and will take place in Screen B. Please put a sign by the store entrance so that everyone can find the room easily. The second one is for the management software and I need you to cancel it. There's a diary on my desk; you can find their number there.

Because everything is brand new and all the posters and signs won't be delivered until Friday, I have attached a copy of the store directory to help you find your way around. Thank you so much for your help with all of this. I hope to get better quickly and see you at the store tomorrow.

Gisele

Store Manager-ABC Megastores

STORE DIRECTORY

1st Floor
Perfume and Cosmetics
Purses and Bags
Beauty Experts

2nd Floor
Stationery
News
Books and Magazines
Toilets

3rd Floor
Children's Megastore
Tiny Theater
Screen A

4th Floor
Technology
Customers Service
Management
Screens B–F

5th Floor
Restaurant
Toilets

176. Where does Gisele work?

A. 1st floor
B. 2nd floor
C. 3rd floor
D. 4th floor

177. Which items will NOT be found in the red containers?

A. pens
B. dictionaries
C. hand soap
D. plastic spoons

178. To which floor should Samuel take the blue containers?

A. 1st floor
B. 2nd floor
C. 3rd floor
D. 4th floor

179. What would NOT be on the 4th floor that day?

A. yellow containers
B. Gisele's diary
C. clerk's training session
D. screen projectors

180. Why does Samuel need a store directory?

A. He hasn't been working at the store for long.
B. He has never been in the store before.
C. The store is being refurbished.
D. It's a new store.

Questions 181–185 refer to the email and invoice that follow.

From: lillyj@targetit.com
To: lochan@hdrwarehouse.com
Subject: Shipment and Invoice

Hi Lochan,

I'm glad I managed to reach you on the phone this morning before you shipped my order. As I told you earlier, I'd like to add a few things and change the delivery date to next Monday, February 18. In addition, instead of shipping the goods as they become available, please send the entire order to our warehouse at once. It makes things easier for us.

Can we have 20 of the small brown desks instead of 15? Also, I'd like to add 5 white chairs to go with the desks. As for the smart boards, I will also need an extra one, so it will be 5 of them after all.

By the way, I want to thank you again for recommending us to Havoc Investment as their potential IT suppliers. It's still early but I believe that it might be the beginning of a fruitful partnership. I'll let you know how it goes. Could you please send me a revised shipping order so I can forward it to finances?

Best,

Lilly Jameson

SHIPPING ORDER
BILL DATE: February 12
SHIPPING DATE: February 18

TO
Lilly Jameson
Target IT Ltd
1764 Commercial Road
San Diego, California

FROM
Lochan Verma
HDR Warehouse (Los Angeles)
81006 Ringwood Lane
Los Angeles, California

INVOICE TO
Margareth Wilshere
Target IT Ltd–Finances
1764 Commercial Road
San Diego, California

SHIPPER'S INSTRUCTIONS
DO NOT SPLIT ORDER. Send entire order when available.

	Articles	Unit Price	Total Charge
20	Boslik Desk Brown	$84.00	$1,680.00
20	Boslik Chairs White	$35.00	$700.00
100	DVD-RW Budget	$0.15	$15.00
5	UHD 4K Int Board 50'	$5,320.00	$26,600.00
			$28,995.00

Hi Lilly,
This is the revised order. Please let me know if there's anything else you need.
Lochan

181. Why did Lilly contact Lochan?

A. to cancel an order
B. to change a shipment date
C. to change an order
D. to change an order and shipment date

182. On which day will the order be delivered?

A. as soon as possible
B. the following Monday
C. the following day
D. as soon as all articles are ready for shipment

183. Which items were NOT amended in the new order?

A. the desks
B. the chairs
C. the DVDs
D. the boards

184. What is Havoc Investment?

A. a potential client
B. the shipment carrier
C. the supplier
D. a potential supplier

185. How much is the total cost of the merchandise?

A. $700.00
B. $1,680.00
C. $26,600.00
D. $28,995.00

GO ON TO THE NEXT PAGE.

Questions 186–190 refer to the following notice, email, and advertisement.

NOTICE

Both cafeterias for the main building will be closed at various times between December 23 and January 6 for renovations. The facilities are to be upgraded so that all the staff can have access to the facilities. Please use the cafeteria next to the parking garage or the main restaurant on the 2nd floor during this time. Make sure to book your lunch hour if going to the restaurant as it might be extremely busy during this period. We apologize for the inconvenience, but we have chosen to do the renovations for the benefit of everyone in the long-term future.

Note: Extra tables and chairs will be allocated to the cafeteria next to the parking garage. However, we kindly ask all our employees not to spend longer than 30 minutes so that everyone gets a chance to use the premises.

From: juliehr@morganbank.com

To: Undisclosed-Recipient:;

Subject: Cafeterias in the main building

Dear all,

I understand most of you are concerned about the renovations to take place in both cafeterias in the main building. Although I understand it is not ideal to have both cafeterias closed in the same period, we had no choice since the renovation plans involve merging them into one bigger and more modern restaurant.

Also, we understand that the Christmas period is usually quiet at the company since many of you will be taking your vacancies to enjoy the festivities. For those of you who are working in this period, we can assure you that both the restaurant and the old cafeteria will be able to accommodate everyone.

The improved facilities in the new restaurant will be able to offer better quality food at better prices to all our employees and this is the main reason why Human Resources has authorized the renovations. We want to offer the best to our employees.

Once again, we are truly sorry for the inconvenience but we believe that everyone will be happier than ever once the works have been completed.

Warm Regards,
Julie Walcott
Human Resources Director

Finance Department Restaurant Bookings	
Please make a note of your booking below. Note that no more than 5 members of the finance department are permitted to take their lunch break at the same time.	
Susanna	12:30
Priya	13:00
Derek	12:30
Ramona	12:00
Rashid	13:30
Branford	12:00
Vikesh	12:30

186. How long will the cafeterias be closed?

A. one week
B. two weeks
C. three weeks
D. four weeks

187. Why are the renovations taking place in that period?

A. because the company is not too busy
B. because it's cheaper
C. because people will have only 30 minutes
D. because employees chose this period

188. Which of the following is NOT a reason for the renovations?

A. better food
B. cheaper food
C. improved facilities
D. relaxing atmosphere

189. How many more members of the finance team can book their lunch for 12:30?

A. 5
B. 4
C. 3
D. 2

190. Which is NOT a recommendation for the renovations period?

A. skip lunch and finish work early
B. book a table at main restaurant
C. use the cafeteria next to the parking garage
D. spend 30 minutes or less at the cafeteria

Questions 191–195 refer to the following email, attachment, and advertisement.

The brand new **Fairies' Winter Garden** is one of the greatest attractions for both tourists and residents of New York this winter. Before this impressive theme park was open to the public last week, it had already generated enough public interest due to its innovative, and expensive, advertising campaigns. While new facilities like this are usually endorsed by celebrities on prime time TV commercials, the owners of the theme park decided to take an alternative route to promoting the park. Residents of Manhattan had known about the park since it started its construction 3 months ago. Fairies of all colors and sizes could be seen throughout the city inside cafes, shopping malls, book stores, and even cinemas.

But for all the park's success, its owners were worried about the extreme weather conditions that had afflicted New York during the past three winters. However, even though the weather is as cold as the previous winters, the park has been a success. Entire families have been waiting in two-hour lines for a chance to take their little ones to this magic land. This is understandable given the variety and quality of the facilities, including ice rinks, 5D cinemas, roller coasters and much more. Ticket prices range from $15 to $50 depending on add-ons such as express or VIP access.

Fairies' Winter Garden

Tinkerland	Rosalina's Resort	Ollie's Paradise	Fawn's Park
Three roller-coasters for all ages: *Peter Pirate (5+) *Tick Tock Time (5+) *The Lost Ones (8+)	Two indoor pools with various waterslides and an astonishingly realistic-looking artificial beach with palm trees and food kiosks.	High tech zone for Ollie and his friends: *Videogames mega screen *5D cinema *Build-a-tablet *Robot Ice Rink	Sports for all the family: *Ice Hockey with Fawn and his friends *Ice soccer *Snowball Fairy War

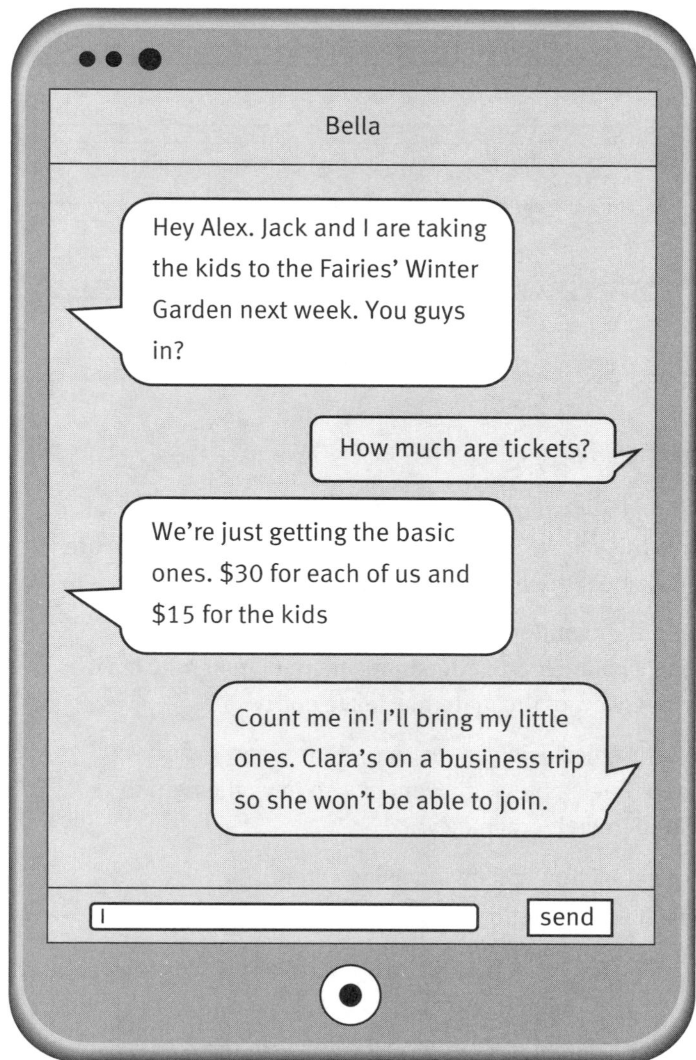

191. What does the article say about the opening of the park?

A. People weren't interested.
B. It was not advertised on TV.
C. It had to be delayed.
D. The weather didn't help.

192. What were people concerned about regarding the park?

A. its location
B. its cost of construction
C. ticket prices
D. weather conditions

193. In the text chain, why does Alex write "Count me in!"?

A. He wants to know how much money he needs to give Bella.
B. He can afford the tickets.
C. He will go to the Fairies' Winter Garden.
D. His wife won't be able to come.

194. Which of the facilities or activities are NOT mentioned in the texts above?

A. a swimming pool
B. a cinema room
C. a restaurant
D. a sport

195. How much does a basic adult ticket cost?

A. $5
B. $15
C. $30
D. $50

Questions 196–200 refer to the following email, attachment, and advertisement.

To:	eva.solaro@howson.com
From:	s.fitzpatrick@howson.com
Date:	August 25th
Subject:	Maternity Leave Information

Hi Eva

Congratulations on your pregnancy! We're all really excited for you.

I wanted to give you a bit more information about claiming maternity leave before you make your official request, so I've attached some further information to this email. The laws in the UK for maternity leave are quite different from those in the US, so feel free to ask me if there's anything you're uncertain about.

The attached document sets out Howson employee's staff entitlements and company procedures surrounding maternity leave. You should consult this document to understand length of maternity leave offered and payment for maternity leave. Here's an overview of the maternity leave policy:

1. Qualifying employees are entitled to up to 52 weeks of leave in connection with their pregnancy and/or the birth of their child. In addition to the 52 weeks, pregnant women also have the right to time off work for any doctors' appointments related to their pregnancy.
2. To qualify for maternity leave, employees must meet all three of the following criteria:
   a. be a Howson employee (freelancers and consultants do not qualify)
   b. be pregnant 15 weeks prior to your expected week of childbirth
   c. comply with the notification requirements and policies detailed in this document
3. Your right to take maternity leave is not dependent on your length of employment with Howson. However, employees must have completed 26 weeks of service to be entitled to Statutory Maternity Pay.

Let me know if you have any questions or wish to discuss further before you submit your formal leave request to HR.

Best,

Scarlet

Howson Maternity Leave Policy

Leave

1. The 4 weeks of maternity leave following the birth of your child for employees working in one of our factories is mandatory. For all other employees, 2 weeks of maternity leave must be taken immediately following the birth of your child.
2. All other maternity leave is optional and can be taken in full or in part.
3. The first 26 weeks of maternity is termed ‘Ordinary Maternity Leave’ and the final 26 weeks of maternity leave is termed ‘Additional Maternity Leave’.
4. Ordinary Maternity Leave can begin 11 weeks before your expected week of childbirth and no earlier.
5. You should notify your line manager of your pregnancy at the earliest opportunity and work with them to decide your maternity leave dates. If you wish to change your return to work date after deciding your dates, you must give your employer at least 8 weeks’ notice of this.

Payment

6. Statutory Maternity Pay is paid for a maximum of 39 weeks. Statutory Maternity Pay entitles employees to
   a. 90% of their weekly earnings for the first 6 weeks of maternity leave .
   b. £140.98 per week or 90% of their average weekly earnings (whichever is lower) for the remaining 33 weeks.
7. If you choose to take leave beyond the 39 weeks covered by Statutory Maternity Pay, this leave will be unpaid.

OPERATIONAL ADMINISTRATOR: 12 MONTH CONTRACT

Howson's is looking for a temporary employee to cover one of our existing staff's maternity leave.

Essential Skills:
* at least 1 year experience in a similar role
* familiarity with office computing software
* educated to college degree level

Desirable Skills:
* experience using RezCLNT booking software.

Please note that although this is not a role in one of our factories, you will be required to undergo basic factory emergency training. If you excel at this role, you may be asked to stay with the company after the maternity leave has finished.

To apply, email the Operations Director at s.fitzpartick@howsons.com with your C.V. and a cover letter.

196. What is the purpose of the letter?

- **A.** to inform a manager of a pregnancy
- **B.** to apply for a vacant role
- **C.** to provide staff with updates to a policy
- **D.** to inform a colleague about requesting specific leave

197. How long must an employee have worked at Howson's for to receive pay while on maternity leave?

- **A.** 11 weeks
- **B.** 26 weeks
- **C.** 39 weeks
- **D.** 52 weeks

198. What is the minimum amount of maternity leave that can be requested by an employee?

- **A.** 2 weeks
- **B.** 4 weeks
- **C.** 6 weeks
- **D.** 8 weeks

199. What is the earliest date that maternity leave can begin?

- **A.** 2 weeks before the due date of the child
- **B.** 4 weeks before the due date of the child
- **C.** 6 weeks before the due date of the child
- **D.** 11 weeks before the due date of the child

200. What is Scarlet's role in the company?

- **A.** HR manager
- **B.** Operational Administrator
- **C.** Operational Director
- **D.** Customer Service Advisor

Stop! If you finish before time is called, you may check your work on this section only. Do not turn to any other section in the test.

PRACTICE TEST 3 ANSWER KEY

Part I	Part II	Part III	Part IV	Part V	Part VI	Part VII
1. A	7. A	32. B	71. A	101. A	131. A	147. D
2. D	8. C	33. B	72. D	102. B	132. B	148. D
3. C	9. B	34. A	73. B	103. C	133. C	149. A
4. C	10. A	35. D	74. A	104. A	134. D	150. C
5. B	11. B	36. C	75. C	105. A	135. D	151. A
6. B	12. B	37. A	76. A	106. D	136. D	152. A
	13. A	38. B	77. B	107. C	137. B	153. B
	14. C	39. C	78. C	108. B	138. B	154. C
	15. A	40. B	79. D	109. A	139. C	155. D
	16. C	41. D	80. C	110. C	140. D	156. A
	17. B	42. B	81. D	111. B	141. A	157. C
	18. C	43. C	82. D	112. A	142. A	158. C
	19. C	44. A	83. B	113. C	143. C	159. A
	20. A	45. A	84. C	114. B	144. C	160. C
	21. A	46. D	85. D	115. D	145. D	161. A
	22. B	47. C	86. A	116. C	146. D	162. B
	23. C	48. B	87. A	117. A		163. D
	24. B	49. A	88. B	118. C		164. C
	25. A	50. D	89. D	119. B		165. B
	26. B	51. B	90. A	120. A		166. D
	27. B	52. C	91. C	121. A		167. B
	28. A	53. B	92. A	122. C		168. B
	29. C	54. B	93. C	123. B		169. C
	30. C	55. C	94. D	124. D		170. B
	31. A	56. B	95. C	125. C		171. B
		57. B	96. B	126. A		172. A
		58. A	97. C	127. C		173. A
		59. C	98. B	128. B		174. B
		60. B	99. B	129. A		175. C
		61. B	100. D	130. D		176. C
		62. D				177. D
		63. C				178. D
		64. C				179. A
		65. A				180. D
		66. A				181. D
		67. B				182. B
		68. C				183. C
		69. D				184. D
		70. C				185. D
						186. B
						187. A
						188. D
						189. D
						190. A
						191. B
						192. D
						193. C
						194. C
						195. C
						196. D
						197. B
						198. A
						199. D
						200. C

PRACTICE TEST 3 ANSWERS AND EXPLANATIONS

Section 1—Listening Comprehension

Part I: Photographs

1. (A)

The photograph shows paper documents piled up on a desk. **(A)** correctly describes the image. The files are on the *table* not in the *cupboard* **(B)**. There are not pens **(C)** visible in the image. The *documents* are on the *table*, not the *chair* **(D)**.

2. (D)

The photograph shows people standing in a line. **(D)** correctly describes the scenario. **(A)** confuses *line* with *decline*. The people are not walking **(B)**, they are standing. Some of the people are *carrying* bags, but none of them are *unloading* their bags **(C)**.

3. (C)

The photograph shows a doctor or nurse going through a booklet with a mother and daughter. The nurse is explaining the procedure **(C)**. There are no shoes in the picture **(A)**. There are only three people sitting, there is no *crowd gathering*. They are in a medical setting; the woman is not a *nail technician* **(D)**.

4. (C)

The photograph shows a man sanding the edges of a wooden chair. **(C)** correctly describes this. The man is *sanding* a chair, not *standing on* **(A)** a chair. The man is making a *chair*, not a *table* **(B)**. The man is holding a *chair*, not a *box* **(D)**.

5. (B)

The photograph shows a botanist pouring liquid from a test tube onto a plant. **(B)** correctly describes the image. The botanist is pouring liquid onto a *plant*, not a *tree* **(A)**. The botanist is *pouring* liquid from the test tube, not *measuring* the test tube **(C)**. The botanist is using the liquid to water the plant, she is not making herself a drink **(D)**.

6. (B)

The photograph shows a building with many broken glass windows. **(B)** correctly describes the photograph. The *building* is probably empty, but there are no *packets* in the photograph **(A)**. **(C)** confuses *broken* with *heartbroken*. **(D)** is a trap, in the photograph, the *windows* are *broken*, but the statement says the *widow* has *spoken*.

Part II: Question-Response

7. (A)

The questions asks *how soon can you solve the computer problem?* **(A)** correctly provides a time in the future (*after lunch*). **(B)** is incorrect as it gives a time in the past. **(C)** is incorrect as it discusses checking emails, which does not relate to the question.

8. (C)

The question asks *is your computer password locked?* this requires a yes/no answer. **(C)** is the only yes/no answer, and the answer also discusses the password. In **(A)**, the answer is not in the form of yes or no and discusses calling someone back, while the question asks about a *computer password.* **(B)** is not in the form of a yes or no answer and talks about a *desk* being *broken*, where the questions asks if a *computer password* is *locked.*

9. (B)

The question asks *why did you drive to work today?* This requires a reason in the form of an open answer. **(B)** correctly provides a reason (*subway workers and bus drivers are on strike*). **(A)** and **(C)** are yes/no answers and cannot be used to answer a More Information question.

10. (A)

The question asks *how long will the meeting last?* **(A)** is the only answer to provide a time frame (*2 hours*). **(B)** talks about a *report* which is not mentioned in the questions and **(C)** offers a solution to a possible problem which is not presented in the question.

11. (B)

The question asks *when do you have to send the report?* This requires an answer in the future tense. **(B)** correctly offers a future time expression (*before lunchtime*). **(A)** does not mention any times and addresses a specific problem (*the paper is not very good quality*) not mentioned in the question. **(C)** talks about a person preparing *dinner* which does not relate to the question.

12. (B)

The question asks *where's the nearest subway station?* This requires directions. **(B)** is correct. **(A)** and **(C)** do not mention directions.

13. (A)

The question asks *who is leading the development project?* The correct answer will name a person in charge. **(A)** correctly provides a name (*Mr. Patel*) and uses an expression for responsibility (*in charge*). **(B)** talks about a *woman* but also mentions a *baby* and does not discuss a *development project.* **(C)** talks about *preferences* but does not give a person.

14. (C)

The question asks *when did Mrs. Wilkins move back to England?* which requires an answer in the past tense. **(C)** correctly provides a past time expression (*six months ago*). **(A)** talks about a place and not time (*London*). **(B)** does not mention a time.

15. (A)

The question asks *do I need permission to park here?* This requires a yes/no response either allowing or denying permission to park. Although all the options say *yes*, **(A)** is the only option that correctly addresses the topic of *permission* (*a special permit from reception*). **(B)** does not relate to the topic of the question. **(C)** talks about a special day (*pancake day*) instead of *permission* and *parking*.

16. (C)

The question asks *whose desk is this?* This requires an answer addressing possessions. **(C)** is correct. **(A)** gives a suggestion which is not related to the question. **(B)** repeats *desk* but does not address who possesses the desk.

17. (B)

The question asks *when will the show begin?* This requires an answer containing a time expression. **(B)** is correct. **(A)** offers a future time expression (*next week*) but talks about a *secretary*, not a *show*. **(C)** mentions a *show* but fails to provide a time expression.

18. (C)

The question asks *who sent the package to the main office?* The answer will give a person responsible for the action. **(C)** is correct. **(A)** gives a person, but does not mention the package. **(B)** mentions the *package* but does not give a person.

19. (C)

The question asks *how many chairs are there on the* 5th *floor?* This requires an answer which gives a quantity. **(C)** is the only option to provide a number (*three of them*). **(A)** talks about *engineers*, not *chairs*. **(B)** repeats *desks* but does not provide the quantity.

20. (A)

The statement says *I don't have enough time to stay until the end of the meeting*. This requires a response addressing a predicament. **(A)** gives an appropriate response. **(B)** talks about *money* instead of a *meeting*. **(C)** repeats *meeting*, but discusses it in the past tense and does not address the statement.

21. (A)

The question asks *can you believe this building is 101 stories tall?* **(A)** correctly responds the question, by continuing to talk about *heights*. **(B)** talks about a *building* but does not mention the *height*. **(C)** talks about an *elevator*, which is related to the stories of a building, but does not respond to the question.

22. (B)

The questions asks *how often do we need to update the system*? This requires an answer about frequency. **(B)** is correct. **(A)** discusses a *cell phone*, not a *system*. **(C)** repeats *update* but does not answer the question of *how often*.

23. (C)

The question asks *can your assistant cancel my afternoon meeting, please?* **(C)** correctly responds to it by providing an reason why not (*he's not here today*). **(A)** is not relevant to the question. **(B)** repeats *secretary*, but does not answer the question.

24. (B)

The statement says *it's really hot today*. **(B)** is the only alternative to correctly respond to it by making a suggestion about cooling down (*take off your jacket*). **(A)** talks about a man's appearance and **(C)** fails to address the original statement and makes a comment about a *sweater*.

25. (A)

The question asks *where is your team presentation?* This requires an open answer about a place. **(A)** correctly provides a place (*in the conference room*). **(B)** and **(C)** give a yes/no response to a Where question.

26. (B)

The question asks *why are both the computer and the TV on?* **(B)** correctly answers the question by providing a reason (*I was writing my report*—that's why the computer is on—*when the match started*—that's why the TV is on). **(A)** fails to provide a reason and offers a place instead (*on the desk*). **(C)** repeats *computer* but does not answer the question.

27. (B)

The question asks *what is the best service offered by the consultants?* **(B)** is the only answer to mention a possible service offered by a company. **(A)** addresses the high number of people in a specific place. **(C)** repeats *consult* uses the word as a verb instead of a noun.

28. (A)

The question asks *what is the difference between a lift and an elevator?* The answer will compare the two words. **(A)** is correct. **(B)** repeats *lift* but uses the word as a verb instead of a noun. **(C)** expresses an opinion and not a comparison.

29. (C)

The question asks *what does this expression mean?* **(C)** addresses the topic of finding the meaning of an expression by suggesting the use of a *dictionary*. **(A)** does not relate to the question. **(B)** repeats *meaning* but discusses *life*, not *words*.

30. (C)

The question asks *why will Ms. Jenkinson be transferred to our New Jersey branch?* The answer requires a reason. **(C)** is correct. **(A)** talks about buying a *calculator* which is an inappropriate reason for moving to a different branch. **(B)** repeats *New Jersey* but does not offer a reason for the transfer.

31. (A)

The question asks *may I take the day off next Thursday?* **(A)** correctly replies to the request by granting permission (*I can't see why not...).* **(B)** repeats *Thursday*, but does not reply to a request. **(C)** talks about likes and dislikes, not permission or requests.

Part III: Short Conversations

32. (B)

The man asks the woman to *talk* him *through* her *role* in a *business training company* and asks her *how long* she *stayed in that role—both* of which are typical *job interview* questions, so **(B)** is correct. This means that **(A)**, **(B)** and **(C)** are incorrect.

33. (B)

The man says his previous *company* were *impressed with how well I did my job*, i.e. his *performance*, so **(A)** is incorrect. He also says *there are elements of project management in reception posts*, so he could use the *transferable skills* he *acquired*, so **(C)** is incorrect. Finally, he mentions his *Bachelor's degree in business administration*, i.e. his *education*, so **(D)** is wrong. **(B)** is correct because the man says he had *no experience*, so this is not a *reason for his career progression*.

34. (A)

The woman says about the *senior project manager* that she *passed away*, which means she *died*, so **(A)** is correct. She never says anything about the *senior project manager making her redundant* or *closing her business*, so **(B)** and **(C)** are wrong. **(D)** is incorrect because the woman says she was *assisting one of the senior project managers in her projects in North and Central America*, not that the woman *moved* there.

35. (D)

The woman says *Same table, please. Is chef here today?*, so **(D)** is the correct alternative. You wouldn't ask about a chef in a supermarket or office, so options **(B)** and **(C)** are wrong. The woman says *don't you think it's about time we told them we're selling the hotel and buying this place?*, so **(C)** is not possible either.

36. (C)

The woman says *We've just got back from the Andes and I'd like to talk to him about some of the small vineyards we visited there*, so **(C)** is the correct alternative. **(A)** is wrong because there's no mention of a resort. The woman talks about small vineyards but doesn't say they visited many places, so **(B)** is not possible either. They don't talk about a pool, so **(D)** is also incorrect.

37. (A)

The woman says *don't you think it's about time we told them we're selling the hotel and buying this place*, so **(A)** is the right answer. They went to the Andes on vacation, so **(B)** is incorrect. **(C)** is also wrong because they don't say anything about going to the same place. When the woman says *There's no point in buying this place if he won't work for us*, she's talking about the chef, not Arnold. This means **(D)** is not possible either.

38. (B)

(B) is the right answer because the man says *Have you seen a brown briefcase?* They don't talk about a cell phone, so **(A)** is wrong. **(C)** is also incorrect because even though the man asks *See you at the theater tonight?*, that doesn't mean he's looking for his theater tickets. The man says *brown briefcase*, so **(D)** is not possible either.

39. (C)

The man says *congratulations on your new position*, so **(C)** is the correct alternative. **(A)** is wrong because the woman says she might not go to the theater, but that doesn't mean she doesn't like it. **(B)** is also incorrect because the man says *You'll make a great Director of Operations*. The woman says Andy has the man's briefcase, but doesn't say she doesn't want to see him. Therefore, **(D)** is not possible.

40. (B)

To hit the sack means to go to bed, so **(B)** is the right answer. When asked about the theater, she replies *Not sure*. This means **(A)** is not possible. **(C)** is wrong because she doesn't say she might go to the theater after having a bath. There's no mention of a movie, so **(D)** is also incorrect.

41. (D)

(D) is the answer because the woman says *they usually have a street market in the square on Saturdays and Sundays, so the bus takes a different route*. **(A)** is not mentioned in the conversation. There's no reference to what time of the day it is, so **(B)** cannot be correct. The woman says *the bus takes a different route* when talking about weekends, but she doesn't mention a *new route* so **(C)** must be wrong.

42. (B)

The woman says *you can get the subway*. **(B)** is the correct answer. The only bus mentioned in the conversation is the *number 52*, so **(A)** is incorrect. The woman tells the man to take a *train* from Mulholland Avenue, not a *bus*, so **(C)** is not possible. **(D)** is not mentioned in the conversation.

43. (C)

(C) is the correct answer because the woman says *it's a five-minute walk from there. You'll see a lot of signs, so no need to worry*. The woman mentions the *market* when she explains why the bus won't stop at the square, so **(A)** is incorrect. **(B)** does not address the question and gives a *west bound* train, when the woman tells the man to take an *east bound train*. **(D)** is not possible because the woman tells the man it's *five minutes*, not *five miles* away.

44. (A)

The woman says *again? What does he want this time?* Clearly Mr Garcia calls regularly. **(A)** is the answer. **(B)**, **(C)**, and **(D)** are not mentioned in the conversation.

45. (A)

The man says *he says he's been taking the antibiotics for 10 days but still doesn't feel any better*. **(A)** is the answer. **(B)** repeats *10* but refers to days of sickness, not days of taking antibiotics. The woman says *I'll ask her to prescribe something stronger*, not that Mr. Garcia is feeling stronger, so **(C)** is incorrect. **(D)** is not mentioned in the conversation.

46. (D)

The woman says *I'll ask her to prescribe something stronger*. **(D)** is correct. The woman does not specify a time when she will ask *Dr Walker*, so **(A)** and **(B)** are incorrect. **(C)** is also incorrect because the woman says *I'll ask her to prescribe something stronger*, which indicates a new prescription and not a *copy* of the existing prescription.

47. (C)

The woman says *we've been expanding and moving some of our staff to our new office in Kyoto, so that's been causing some disruptions in customer's service lines*. **(C)** is correct. The woman answers *just fine* when asked about Tokyo, so **(A)** is incorrect. The woman says there is *nothing too serious* about customer service problems in Kyoto. **(D)** is not mentioned in the conversation.

48. (B)

The woman says *everything should get back to normal before the end of the week*. **(B)** is correct. The woman doesn't mention *the weekend*. The man tells the woman that they are *proud* of her, but this does not relate to the situation in Kyoto. The woman doesn't talk about going to Kyoto.

49. (A)

(A) is correct because the man says *you've been doing a great job, Sally*. **(B)** is not mentioned in the text. **(C)** repeats *Michigan* but does not provide an answer. The woman is the one who says *thanks Mr. Lee. I'm just doing my job*, so **(D)** is also incorrect.

50. (D)

The man says *they're downstairs in those two brown boxes by the front door*. **(D)** is the answer. **(A)** repeats *Chicago*, but does not answer where the store signs are. **(B)** repeats *furniture*, but there is not enough information in the text to know whether the *store signs* are next to the *furniture*. **(C)** is not mentioned in the conversation.

51. (B)

The woman says *we have to call the architect and let her know that both the signs and furniture are here*. **(B)** is the correct answer. The woman mentions that the *opening* is on *Monday*, but doesn't say that this is why she wants to call the architect. **(C)** and **(D)** are mentioned by the man, not the woman.

52. (C)

The woman says *I'm glad they got here in time for the opening on Monday*. **(C)** is correct. *Friday* **(A)** is the day the works need to be finished, not the day of the store opening. The man says *you can make any changes over the weekend*; **(B)** is incorrect. **(D)** is not mentioned in the conversation.

53. (B)

The man says *if you could go a bit slower and try to move to the right lane* and *please signal and try to turn right*. **(B)** is correct. **(A)**, **(C)**, and **(D)** are not mentioned in the text.

54. (B)

The man says *it's already 4:45*. **(B)** is correct. The only other time to be mentioned in the conversation is *5:00*. **(A)**, **(C)**, and **(D)** are not mentioned in the text.

55. (C)

The man says *the meeting starts at 5*. **(C)** is the correct answer. **(A)** and **(B)** are not mentioned in the conversation. The man says *our new office* **(D)** is incorrect because it says the office is *old*.

56. (B)

(B) is the right answer because the man says *I didn't fall asleep until after 4:30*. **(A)**, **(C)**, and **(D)** are not mentioned in the text.

57. (B)

The woman says *I usually need to sleep for at least 7 hours*. **(B)** is correct. The woman says *at least 7 hours*; **(A)** is incorrect. The woman doesn't say anything about *10 hours*, so **(C)** is not possible. The man is the one who says *I had to wake up at 8*, so **(D)** is wrong.

58. (A)

The man says *I have to finish this presentation by Monday and I can never get any work done from home*. **(A)** is correct. The man says *I can never get any work done from home*, so **(B)** is wrong. **(C)** is mentioned by the woman, not the man. **(D)** is not mentioned in the text.

59. (C)

The woman says *we live in that new building next to the old bagel store*. **(C)** is correct. The woman *used to* live near the supermarket, but doesn't anymore. The woman lives *in* Manhattan, not *outside*. The woman lives *10 minutes away* from the school, not *opposite* it.

60. (B)

The man says *I drive past it every day*. **(B)** must be correct; the man must drive by car to work. It's the woman who talks about *walking*, not the man. **(C)** and **(D)** are not mentioned in the conversation.

61. (B)

(B) is the correct option because the woman says *7:45 is just fine*. The only time mentioned in the conversation is 7:45, so all the other options, **(A)**, **(C)**, and **(D)**, are not possible.

62. (D)

The woman says *Are you meeting an artist? That building is mostly used as a workspace for creative people*, so **(D)** must be correct. **(A)** is incorrect as the man specifies that he is meeting a fashion designer, but the woman does not say that only fashion designers work there. **(B)** is incorrect as the man is meeting a client there, not the woman. **(C)** is incorrect as the man is a lawyer, but the building is not there for legal advice.

63. (C)

The man says *I'm his lawyer*, so **(C)** must be the answer. His client is the *fashion designer*, and the woman mentions that *artists* work at the same building, but neither of these are the man's profession.

64. (C)

The woman says *if you look on the map, you're here, on Rosencrantz street. You want to take the second left, and walk up that road... the building is on the corner of that block, on the right side of the road*. The building must be in the space indicated by the number 4. **(D)** is correct.

65. (A)

The man says *perhaps the first thing you'll notice is that our budget for this quarter is quite a bit higher than it was last year... that's because we've got some feedback from our digital trial, and our customers really loved the online options*. The budget has increased because they need to put more of their products online, so **(A)** is correct. The text doesn't mention that they need to *improve* their products, they just need to have more products online. It is also not stated that they are creating more products this year than last year, and their feedback was positive, not negative.

66. (A)

The woman says, *I can't believe we've waited so long to break into the online space* and the man replies *Right?* so he's agreeing with the woman; he's surprised that this didn't happen sooner. **(A)** is correct.

67. (B)

The woman says *I think we need to be spending more on actually creating our books, though... this figure doesn't seem to be high enough...* Production means the creation of new products, so this must be the budget that the woman doesn't think is correct. The correct answer is **(B)**.

68. (C)

The man calls the woman *honey* and refers to their children. They are most likely husband and wife. **(C)** is correct.

69. (D)

The man says *when we're visiting with your mum*, so **(D)** must be the answer. They are taking their children with them, not going to visit their children, and they are visiting an amusement park and looking at a house, not visiting a realtor and an owner of an amusement park.

70. (C)

The man says he *can't do any mornings next week* which means they must meet in the afternoon, so they can only meet on Monday or Thursday. The woman says *let's take the later day* so they must decide to schedule the meeting on Thursday.

Part IV: Short Talks

71. (A)

The question asks where the announcement would be most likely to be heard. **(A)** is correct; the words *captain*, *cabin*, *flight attendants* and *flight* are all related to flying on a plane. In **(B)**, the speaker mentions *seat belts* which would not be likely to be present at an airport. In **(C)**, *seat belts*, *hot snacks* and *drinks* are not likely to be present at a bus stop. In **(D)**, the speaker mentions *flight*, which does not relate to trains or train stations.

72. (D)

(A) and **(B)** would not be found working on a plane. **(C)** must also be incorrect, as the speaker refers to *the pilot* in third person. **(D)** must be correct.

73. (B)

The woman says *in a few moments, the flight attendants will be passing around the cabin to offer you hot or cold drinks, as well as a light meal or snack.* Food and drinks are usually served after take-off, so **(B)** is the best possible answer. Food is not commonly served on board before take-off **(A)**, before landing **(C)**, or after landing **(D)**.

74. (A)

The man says *this year we'll be holding it at the Hilton Hotel in San Diego on November 14*, so **(A)** is the answer. The man says *C&C will be holding a dinner party on Saturday November 16 as a closing ceremony for the conference*, so **(B)** gives the date, and **(D)** gives the day the conference ends. The man also says *our annual conference next month*, so **(C)** is incorrect.

75. (C)

The man says *please let Ms. Brown know if you are going to attend the conference and party by the end of next week*, so **(C)** is the correct answer. The man says *This year we'll be holding it at the Hilton Hotel in San Diego on November 14*, so **(A)** is the date the conference starts. **(B)** gives the date, and **(D)** gives the day the conference ends.

76. (A)

The speaker says *Everyone is invited to bring a spouse or date, but no children this time. Maybe next year.* The answer must be **(A)**, as the speaker will consider allowing children to attend next year.

77. (B)

The woman says *now we're about to enter the new section of the factory* and *we've developed a new line of frozen foods*, so **(B)** is the answer. **(A)** is incorrect because the woman doesn't say anything about computers. The woman talks about food, but says *we're about to enter the new section of the factory*, so they can't be in a restaurant and **(C)** is wrong. **(D)** is not possible because the woman doesn't say anything about a *laboratory*.

78. (C)

The woman says *a new line of frozen foods*, which makes **(C)** the correct answer. There's no mention of *research*, so **(A)** is incorrect. Although they're in a factory, the woman doesn't say anything about *machines*, so **(B)** is not possible. They are talking about frozen foods in a factory, but the woman doesn't say anything about *recipes*, so **(D)** is also incorrect.

79. (D)

The woman *says the same mouth-watering flavor Richmond Foods has been traditionally known for*, so **(D)** is the answer. The woman says *This new method allows us to use only the finest ingredients in offering high nutritional values* when talking about a *method* of production, not as the name of the company. This makes **(A)** and **(B)** not possible. **(C)** is also wrong because the woman uses the adjective *mouth-watering* to describe the products, not the name of the company.

80. (C)

The woman says *unfortunately, our offices are closed at the moment and we cannot take your call. Please call us back Monday to Friday between 8:00 A.M. and 7:00 P.M., or Saturdays from 9:00 A.M. to 3:00 P.M.* Most of the information given is about time (*opening hours*) so **(C)** is correct. **(A)** and **(D)** are not mentioned in the text. **(B)** repeats *emergency* but does not describe what the recording is mainly about.

81. (D)

(D) is the correct answer because the woman says *In case of an emergency call us at 518-485-1889 or visit our website*. The woman doesn't give an address so **(A)** is not possible. The woman mentions both **(B)** and **(C)** as a means to contact the company, not only one of them.

82. (D)

The woman says *Saturdays from 9:00 A.M. to 3:00 P.M.* **(D)** is the correct answer. **(A)** refers to the opening hours from Monday to Friday, so it is incorrect. **(B)** and **(C)** are wrong because the offices are never open during these hours.

83. (B)

The man says *lost or damaged items must be reported immediately to Health and Safety,* so **(B)** is the answer. *Supervisors* aren't mentioned, so **(A)** is wrong. The man says that *visitors are also required to wear the equipment*, not that workers can borrow their equipment. This makes **(C)** incorrect. **(D)** is also wrong because the man says *visitors without escorts or wearing the appropriate gear will be asked by security personnel to leave the building*, not that workers will be asked to leave the building.

84. (C)

The man says *please remember that visitors are also required to wear the equipment and must be accompanied at all times*, so **(C)** is the correct alternative. **(A)** and **(B)** are mentioned as requirements, but both of them, not one or the other. This makes them incomplete and incorrect. The man says *visitors are also required to wear the equipment'* but doesn't say *temporary equipment*, which makes **(D)** wrong.

85. (D)

The man says *visitors without escorts or wearing the appropriate gear will be asked by security personnel to leave the building*, so **(D)** is the answer. The man says *all workers are required to wear goggles* but doesn't say they might ask visitors to leave the building, which makes **(A)** incorrect. **(B)** is wrong because there isn't a *Mr. Lyndon* mentioned in the talk. *Lyndon Bros.* is the name of the company. **(C)** is not mentioned in the talk.

86. (A)

(A) is the correct option because the woman says *Sundown Hotels proudly announces the opening of its newest family resort in Acapulco*. The woman says *this modern resort designed by renowned leisure and hospitality architects* to describe the resort. She doesn't say anything about a leisure center, so **(B)** is wrong. The woman mentions *spa facilities* as part of the resort, which makes **(C)** incomplete and incorrect. The same applies to restaurants when she says *a choice of 5 restaurants* to describe the facilities, so **(D)** is also wrong.

87. (A)

(A) is the correct alternative because the woman mentions *two water parks* **(B)** and *24 hours room service* **(C)**. She also says *Call us now at 744-414-0171*, which is **(D)**. There's no mention of laundry services **(A)**.

88. (B)

The speaker says *Sundown Hotels proudly announces the opening of its newest family resort in Acapulco*. This means the hotel must come from the Sundown chain and be family friendly; the answer is **(B)**, June 16.

89. (D)

The man says *where your conference will be held*, so the only group that might be attending a conference is **(D)**. It's a guided bus tour so one might think that tourists **(A)** are on the bus, but it's not possible because the speaker mentions a conference and tourists don't usually attend conferences. **(B)** repeats *football*, but does not give the correct answer. **(C)** is wrong because the man says *it is extremely important to return on time as we will not be able to wait for latecomers*, which doesn't mean that everyone on the bus arrived or will arrive late.

90. (A)

(A) is the correct option because the man says *please be back on the bus before 4 o'clock*. The other means of transportation are not mentioned, so options **(B)**, **(C)**, and **(D)** are not possible.

91. (C)

The speaker says *So, it's noon now, and as I mentioned, we're going to start by taking a tour of the stadium. After that, we'll have a quick lunch, then we'll hear from some of our very own players, I know you're all excited about that! Then, we'll have a bit of a game in the stadium. Don't worry, it's going to be very casual, and then we'll all get our stuff together, visit the restroom, etc., and be back on the bus in time to go*. The speakers will be traveling on the bus at 16:00, so we can eliminate **(D)**, and they're playing after lunch, so we can eliminate **(A)**. After lunch and before they play football, the speaker says they will hear from some players, so that means they can't start playing immediately after lunch, so they must start at 14:30. **(C)** is the correct answer.

92. (A)

The man says *employee parking will not be permitted on the third level of the parking garage from tomorrow. This level will be allocated for visitors*. That's one level only, so **(A)** is the answer. The man says *please take note of the following: the yellow spaces on the second and fourth levels are no longer reserved for visitors*, but he doesn't say that there will be two **(B)** or four **(D)** levels reserved for visitors. This makes these two options wrong. **(C)** is also incorrect because the man says *employee parking will not be permitted on the third level*, but he doesn't say anything about three levels being allocated for visitors' parking.

93. (C)

The man says *red spaces are still reserved for management*, so **(C)** is the correct answer. The man *says employees are free to carry on parking on the second and fourth levels of the parking garage*, so **(A)** is incorrect. **(B)** is also wrong because the man says *this level will be allocated for visitors and should not be used by employees* when talking about level three. *Trucks* aren't mentioned, which makes **(D)** incorrect.

94. (D)

The man says *employees or visitors who fail to park in their designated areas will have their cars ticketed and towed*. **(D)** is correct. The man doesn't say anything about people losing their spaces **(A)** or jobs **(B)**, so these options are wrong. He doesn't say anything about cars being clamped either, so **(C)** is also incorrect.

95. (C)

The woman says *software developers can pick their schedules*, so **(C)** is the best possible answer. The woman doesn't mention or imply that she's addressing a group of *secretaries*, so **(A)** is incorrect. The woman says *as your managers will explain*, which means the listeners can't be managers and **(B)** is wrong. There's no mention of *lawyers* or anything related to *law*, so **(D)** is not possible.

96. (B)

The woman says *as long as they put in 35 hours of work per week*. **(B)** is correct. The numbers in options **(A)**, **(C)** and **(D)** are not mentioned by the speakers, so these options are incorrect.

97. (C)

(C) is the correct alternative because the woman says *the office is open 7 days a week from 07:00 A.M. to 09:00 P.M.* The woman says *the office is open 7 days a week*, which makes **(A)** and **(B)** incorrect. **(D)** is also wrong because she says *schedules are to be selected and handed in to HR four weeks in advance*, not that the office closes for four weeks.

98. (B)

The man says *welcome to New York Zoo*. **(B)** is the answer. **(A)**, **(C)**, and **(D)** are not mentioned in the talk.

99. (B)

The man says *get to know some of the amazing animals that lived before and after each one of them* so **(B)** is the correct answer. **(A)**, **(C)**, and **(D)** are not mentioned in the talk.

100. (D)

The speaker says *Can you tell me which animal survived the five major ice ages and still inhabit our planet as if nothing had happened? Visit our Ice Age exhibit and find out for yourself.* The man is asking the audience to look around and explore the exhibition. The answer is **(D)**.

Section 2—Reading Comprehension

Part V: Incomplete Sentences

101. (A)

Possessives (*director's*) are usually followed by a noun. **(A)** is the only answer choice which is a noun, and the word *presentation* fits with the sentence, so **(A)** must be correct. **(B)**, *presenting* is a verb and the sentence needs a noun. **(C)**, *presently* is an adverb and the sentence needs a noun. In **(D)**, the sentence needs a noun and *preventative* is an adjective.

102. (B)

The missing word is part of a verb phrase. *Have* is the auxiliary verb in the sentence and it needs a past participle to form the present perfect tense. *Laid* is the only past participle in the answers, so **(B)** must be the answer. **(A)** gives a verb in the present tense. **(C)**, *laying* is in the present continuous tense. **(D)**, *lay* is the root word, and is not conjugated.

103. (C)

Sales manager is a *singular subject* and **(C)** is the correct answer because it is the only verb form which can be used with a singular subject in a simple tense. **(D)** is conjugated in the plural form. We need a verb after the subject and **(B)** is a noun. **(A)** is a gerund and should be used in a continuous tense.

104. (A)

We need a *linking word* to connect both sentences. Both sentences are in agreement and **(A)** is the only conjunction not to express contrast (it expresses reason), so it is the correct answer. **(B)**, **(C)**, and **(D)** express contrast and are not possible here.

105. (A)

The gap word is a preposition part of a *verb expression*. *Put one's interests above something* or *someone* is a fixed expression so **(A)** is the only possible answer. **(B)** can have a similar meaning to **(A)** in some situations, but not here because *verb expressions* are usually fixed. **(C)** gives a preposition which would be used for a physical object. **(D)** is a preposition of movement commonly used for directions.

106. (D)

The word before the blank is an article, and the word after is a noun. We usually need an adjective between an article and a noun. **(D)** is the only adjective, so it is the correct alternative. **(A)** is a verb, **(B)** is an adverb, and **(C)** is a noun.

107. (C)

The answers for this question are all verbs and have different meanings. We need a verb that represents a *decision* and **(C)** is the only option that does that (it means *opposed*). **(A)** means *caused someone to remember*. **(B)** means *cancelled*. **(D)** means *rebuilt*.

108. (B)

The adjective *worried* needs the dependent preposition *about*, so **(B)** is the only possible answer. **(A)**, **(C)**, and **(D)** can be used with other adjectives but not with *worried*.

109. (A)

Has been indicates the present perfect continuous or present perfect passive. Since the object does not follow the preposition *by*, it can't be passive. This means that the sentence is in the present perfect continuous and that the gap should be verb in the gerund. **(A)** is the correct answer because it's the only gerund in the alternatives. **(B)** is infinitive, **(C)** is past, and **(D)** is conjugated in the third person singular.

110. (C)

The phrasal verb *carry out* should be followed by a noun. **(C)** is the correct option because it's the only noun. **(A)** is gerund, **(B)** is a verb in the past, and **(D)** is a verb in the third person singular.

111. (B)

We need a phrasal verb that means *reject*, so **(B)** is the correct answer. **(A)** means *arrive*, **(C)** usually means *look the other way*, and **(D)** often means *start*.

112. (A)

The present perfect use of *has become* indicates something that started in the past and is still true. **(B)** and **(D)** are incorrect as they would need the past simple. **(C)** is also incorrect as it would need to be followed by a period of time. Therefore, **(A)** is the only possible answer.

113. (C)

(C) is the correct alternative because the gap needs a conjunction showing a logical time relationship. **(A)** indicates purpose and **(B)** indicates contrast. **(D)** would mean the boss sent the memo *only before* it had been approved, but that does not make sense; he must have sent it *after*.

114. (B)

A phrasal verb which means *postpone* is required, so **(B)** is the correct answer. **(A)** means *to put near something else*. **(C)** is usually used with reference to clothes. **(D)** would not be used with a delay of time.

115. (D)

Do would not be followed by *never*, so **(A)** and **(B)** are incorrect. *Ever* should go before the main verb, which makes **(C)** also incorrect. Therefore, **(D)** is the correct answer.

116. (C)

The gap needs something that expresses the past tense, so **(C)** is the correct option. **(A)**, **(B)**, and **(D)** are not possible because they are in the present.

117. (A)

A phrasal verb which means *retire* is required, so **(A)** is the correct option. **(B)** means to *exit a space*. **(C)** means to *walk through*. **(D)** means to *become involved in a difficult situation*.

118. (C)

The possessive *its* should be followed by a noun. **(C)** is the correct answer because *interest* is the only noun. **(A)** and **(B)** are adjectives and **(D)** is a verb in the third person singular.

119. (B)

The gap is placed in a future-time clause. It requires a verb in the present tense, so **(B)** is the correct answer. **(C)** is future and **(D)** is past. *See* is a state verb in this sentence and should not be used in the continuous form, so **(A)** is not possible.

120. (A)

The gap requires a conjunction which means *at the same time*, so **(A)** is the correct answer. **(B)**, **(C)**, and **(D)** are not conjunctions of time and cannot be used here.

121. (A)

The gap needs a word which means *excess*, so **(A)** is the correct option. **(B)** means *an unexpected event*. **(C)** means *stop resisting*, and **(D)** means *continue to exist*.

122. (C)

The gap needs a verb that means *be present at*, so **(C)** is the correct answer. **(A)** means *make minor changes*, **(B)** means *go up*, and **(D)** means *inflict harm in return for*.

123. (B)

The gap follows the preposition *to*, which means an infinitive is required. **(B)** is the only verb among the options, which makes it the only possible answer. **(A)** is an adjective, **(C)** is also an adjective but in the comparative, and **(D)** is another adjective but this time in the form of a participle.

124. (D)

The gap requires an adjective with the meaning of *imposing legal proceedings against*. **(D)** is the correct answer. **(A)** means *have some of the responsibility*, **(B)** means to *be charged with a crime*, and **(C)** means *not guilty*.

125. (C)

The gap needs a word that means a *plan of action*, so **(C)** is correct. **(A)** means *a fixed regular payment*. **(B)** gives a plural and the sentence needs a singular. **(D)** means *the action of removing*.

126. (A)

The sentence could be completed with the adjective *bankrupt*. *Penniless* has a similar meaning, so **(A)** is the correct answer. **(B)** means *having little sense*, **(C)** means *showing no pity*, and **(D)** means *inattentive*.

127. (C)

The sentence requires a plural noun that means *general rules*, so **(C)** is the correct answer. **(A)** means the title of a news article. **(B)** does not make sense in the sentence. **(D)** would usually refer to a task of lesser importance.

128. (B)

Board is the only noun that collocates with the adjective *smart*, so **(B)** is the correct answer. **(A)** discusses a person, not an object with a screen. **(C)** and **(D)** cannot be correct as the presentation would not need to be postponed by a cracked screen; and desks don't contain screens.

129. (A)

The sentence should be completed with a noun, so **(A)** is the correct answer. **(B)** is a past verb, **(C)** is a gerund, and **(D)** is an adjective.

130. (D)

The gap needs a word could describe a difference in the *company's mentality*. **(A)**, **(B)**, and **(C)** do not express quantities, so these options are all incorrect. Therefore, **(D)** is the only possible answer, as it means *extremely large*.

Part VI: Text Completion

131. (A)

The gap comes at the beginning of the letter, so the sentence must be an introduction; eliminate **(B)** and **(D)**. **(C)** cannot be correct, as the writer of the letter wants to hire a room, not learn more about products. **(A)** must be the answer.

132. (B)

In this sentence, *important* is an adjective and should be followed by a noun. Only **(A)** and **(B)** are nouns. *Addiction* **(A)** is the condition of being addicted to a substance and is a trap answer because it sounds similar to *addition*, but does not make sense in the sentence **(A)** is incorrect. **(B)** gives the correct answer, *addition*, as the word is a noun, and describes that there is a new member of the sales team. **(C)** uses the incorrect word *addicted*. **(D)**, *additive* is either an adjective (and we need a noun) or it is a noun which does not fit within the context of the sentence (an additive is a substance which is added in small quantities to food, in order to preserve or enhance it.)

133. (C)

The word *consider* must be followed by a gerund—so *having* **(C)** is correct. **(B)** is the infinitive, which is not the right form. **(A)** and **(D)** give other incorrect forms of *have*.

134. (D)

The possessive adjective *your* needs to be followed by a noun. **(A)** and **(D)** are the only nouns, but **(A)** means a natural ability, which is inappropriate in the sentence. Facilities mean a place, amenity, or piece of equipment provided for a particular purpose, which makes **(D)** the correct answer. **(B)** and **(C)** are both wrong because they are verbs.

135. (D)

The article is about Tommy Lafayette, so the verb in the gap should be in the passive form. This is why **(D)** is the correct answer. **(C)** is also a passive form but the verb *been* usually follows the auxiliary *have*, which is not in the sentence. **(A)** and **(B)** are active, so these are options are not possible.

136. (D)

The only option that can be followed by a noun is the possessive adjective **(D)**. **(A)**, **(B)**, and **(C)** are pronouns and can't be followed by a noun.

137. (B)

Mr. Lafayette didn't give an award, he received one, which means the sentence should be in the passive. **(B)** is the correct answer because it's the only option in the passive form. **(A)** is infinitive and would make the sentence active, **(C)** is not possible because past verbs can't follow the preposition *to*, and **(D)** is wrong because it would also make the sentence active when it should be in the passive.

138. (B)

The beginning of the sentence discusses the book, so the gap must also talk about an aspect of the book; eliminate **(D)** as this is about the writer. **(C)** is also incorrect as it belongs in a letter, not an article. **(A)** cannot be correct, as the text mentions earlier that the author has written a book of recipes, not poetry. **(B)** must be the answer.

139. (C)

Scanning the email, the writer is looking to purchase supplies from the recipient. Therefore, only **(C)** can be the correct answer.

140. (D)

The gap requires a verb that means *begin to be*, so **(D)** is the correct answer. **(A)** means to have *faith* in something, **(B)** refers to something owned, and **(C)** means to *expose disloyally*.

141. (A)

The gap follows a verb and requires an adverb of manner, so **(A)** is the only possible answer. **(B)** is an adjective, **(C)** is also an adjective but in the comparative form, and **(D)** is the same adjective in the superlative form.

142. (A)

The gap requires a preposition which collocates with the main verb. The main verb is *benefit* and it collocates with the preposition *from.* **(A)** is the correct answer. **(B)** and **(C)** are incorrect because these preposition don't pair with the verb *benefit.* **(D)** is incorrect because it doesn't contain a preposition.

143. (C)

The sentence requires an adverb with the meaning of *not long ago*, so **(C)** is the correct option. **(A)** means *at irregular intervals*, **(B)** means *with reference to past events*, and **(D)** means *fundamentally.*

144. (C)

The word *as* is used in the form of a preposition in the sentence. Prepositions are usually followed by verbs in the gerund, so **(C)** is the correct answer. **(A)** is infinitive. **(B)** is also infinitive but should be paired with *to.* **(D)** gives the past tense of the verb.

145. (D)

The noun *supervision* collocates with the preposition *under* to form the noun phrase *under the supervision of.* **(D)** is the correct answer. The prepositions in **(A)**, **(B)**, and **(C)** do not pair with *supervision*.

146. (D)

The sentence discusses Dr. Tommasi's apprentice, who is positive about the field of chiropractic. **(A)** and **(B)** suggest the Jake Brown does not have a positive view of the subject, but he does. **(C)** cannot be correct as Jake already works in chiropractic. **(D)** must be the correct answer.

Part VII: Reading Comprehension

147. (D)

This questions asks you to choose which of the answer choices would be most likely to apply for the role. **(D)**, a clerk in a department store, would be most likely to apply for this job because he or she would have experience in customer service and possibly also cosmetics. **(A)**, a doctor, would only be likely to apply for a career in medicine, and the job is a role in customer service. The role is in *sales* and *cosmetics*; a teacher **(B)** would not be likely to apply for such a role. **(C)**, a bus driver, would not have *computer* or *telemarketing* skills.

148. (D)

This question asks you for a benefit which is not mentioned in the job announcement. **(A)** and **(B)** are mentioned in the text, so these answers are both incorrect. **(C)** means the same thing as the *cycling allowance* mentioned in the text, so **(C)** must also be incorrect. **(D)** is the correct answer, as *relocation allowance* is not mentioned in the text (the word allowance is used in the text, but only in relation to cycling).

149. (A)

The ad says *successful candidates will have a minimum of three years experience in customer service or telemarketing, preferably in the cosmetics industry, as well as excellent communicative skills, good computer skills, and a college degree.* **(A)** is the only option mentioned so it's the correct answer. **(B)** repeats *experience*, but the ad says that this is *required but not essential.* **(C)** and **(D)** are not mentioned in the ad.

150. (C)

Stubble means *short facial hair*. The word *beard* is also used in the text, so **(C)** is the correct answer. The text says *our special cream* which is different from *shampoo and conditioner* and *gel*. This makes **(A)** and **(B)** wrong. **(D)** is also wrong because the text doesn't say anything about *company supplies*.

151. (A)

The text describes the cream as a *two-minute product*. **(A)** is the correct answer. Options **(B)**, **(C)**, and **(D)** are wrong because they are not mentioned in the text. The only time reference is **(A)**.

152. (A)

The text says *it also protects it from grease*, so **(A)** is the correct answer. The text uses the words *stubble* and *beard*, which are related to facial hair rather the *hair loss* or *hairy ears*. **(C)** discusses *gray* hair, which is not specifically mentioned in the text.

153. (B)

The text says that the product *is available at most drugstores*. A *drugstore* is a synonym for a *pharmacy*. **(B)** is the correct answer. The text also says the product is available in *department stores*, but does not mention *supermarkets* **(A)**, *online stores* **(C)**, or *hair salons* **(D)**.

154. (C)

The text mentions the name of the company: *Tech Shop*, so **(C)** is the best possible answer. *Tech Shop* would be inappropriate as the name for a hotel **(A)**, airport **(B)**, or restaurant **(D)**.

155. (D)

The sentence is a Yes/No question, so the most appropriate place for it to appear is before the Yes/No boxes at the bottom of the form. **(D)** is correct.

156. (A)

The text says *dropping it in the green box*, so **(A)** is the correct option. The text asks the question *would you like a member of our management team to contact you about your experience?* but doesn't say that customers should submit the form to the manager's office. This makes **(B)** wrong. **(C)** is also incorrect because the text doesn't say anything about *emails*. The text mentions *staff*, but doesn't say that *forms* should be given to the staff.

157. (C)

The text says *bookings must be received 72 hours before the required date*, so **(C)** is the correct option. You can book a room for a period of 6 hours **(A)**, for a whole day **(B)**, or a whole week **(D)**. This doesn't mean that the booking have to be made that long in advance, which makes these options not possible.

158. (C)

The text says *office Solutions for Home-based businesses*. Options **(A)**, **(B)**, and **(D)** cannot be included in this category. This makes **(C)** the only possible answer.

159. (A)

The text says *payment in full should be made with booking*. **(A)** is the correct answer. **(B)** is wrong because the text says *coffee, tea, and water are included in the price of room*. It also says *payment by credit card or personal check is acceptable*, which makes **(C)** incorrect. **(D)** is also wrong because the text says *for longer-term bookings, please contact Theo Bessa*, which means that longer-term bookings are available.

160. (C)

Dr. Saunders is working in Sector C between 09:00 and 15:00. He is also working in Sector B, but not in the morning. This makes **(C)** the correct answer. Dr. Saunders doesn't work in *Sector A*, so option **(A)** is not possible. **(B)** and **(D)** are also wrong because Dr. Saunders works in *Sector B* in the afternoon shift, not in the morning.

161. (A)

The text says *with the authorization and operational cover of team leader or supervisor*. Dr. Wastie is neither a leader nor a supervisor. **(A)** is correct. Dr. Campbell **(B)**, Prof. Challen **(C)**, and Prof. Lilliput **(D)** are all supervisors, so these options are incorrect.

162. (B)

(B) is the only possible alternative since Dr. Wastie **(A)**, Dr. Zaza **(C)**, and Dr. Beech **(D)** are neither team leaders nor supervisors. The text says *operational cover of team leader or supervisor*.

163. (D)

The sentence could discuss breaks, but is not relevant to any of the other information in the text. The answer must be **(D)**.

164. (C)

The text says *by the end of the day on September 8*. **(C)** is correct. **(A)** is wrong because *the end of the week* is not mentioned in the memo. **(B)** gives the date that the event is taking place, not the date RSVPs are needed by. **(D)** is incorrect because the text says *by the end of the day on September 8*, not the end of the day *today*.

165. (B)

The memo says *Human Resources is organizing a Green Day Out at Central Park*. **(B)** is correct. **(A)** gives the department responsible for organizing the event, not the location of the event. **(C)** is also incorrect because it's the title of the event, not the location. The memo doesn't say anything about activities happening *at the company*.

166. (D)

The text says *each employee may bring two guests, family or friends*, so **(D)** is the correct option. Since guests can be invited, **(A)** is not possible. The text says *family or friends*, not only one or the other.

167. (B)

The phrase appears in the sentence *Please do not hesitate to contact me should you have any questions or require further information*; the author of the email is encouraging the reader to reach out to him and ask for clarification or additional information; **(B)** is the correct answer.

168. (B)

The email says *Mr. Johnson worked for me as an administrative assistant from August 2004 to July 2012*, which is 8 years. **(B)** is correct. No other periods of time are mentioned in the email, so options **(A)**, **(C)** and **(D)** not possible.

169. (C)

The word reliable means *consistently good in quality or performance*, so **(C)** is the correct alternative. *Reliable* people might be *independent* but the words do not have similar *meanings*, so **(A)** is wrong. You can *reliable* without being *friendly*, so **(B)** is also incorrect. The same applies to **(D)**. A person can be *reliable* but this doesn't mean that the person is *skilled*.

170. (B)

Paragraph 4, line 1 says *I am more than happy to recommend him*, so **(B)** is the correct answer. There are no *complaints* in the email, so **(A)** is not possible. Even though the email talks about *jobs*, **(C)** is incorrect because Mr. Kagawa writes *I am writing to you at the request of Mr. Johnson, who is applying for a position as a personal assistant through your agency*. This means he's writing on behalf of another person and it can't be a job inquiry. **(D)** is also incorrect because no *invitations* are mentioned in the email.

171. (B)

The only data that addresses a period before 18th century is *pre-1700*. The bar is close to the 400 million mark. **(B)** is correct. **(C)** and **(D)** are not possible because none of the bars go above the 400 million mark. **(A)** is wrong because it refers to the period of 1700–1849, which is not before the 18th century (1701–1800).

172. (A)

The meaning of *peak* in the question is *the highest number.* The darker bar represents tropical deforestation and its highest number is between 300 and 350 million in the period from 1950 to 1979. This makes **(A)** the correct answer. The other options are all wrong because the figures represented in the darker bars are much lower in periods **(B)**, **(C)**, and **(D)**.

173. (A)

The first period in which the darker bars (tropical deforestation) were higher than the lighter bars (temperate deforestation) was from 1920 to 1949, so **(A)** is the correct option. Even though tropical deforestation is much higher than temperate deforestation in alternatives **(B)**, **(C)**, and **(D)**, they do not represent the first time it happened. This makes these options not possible.

174. (B)

The customer buys five different types of items but *10 items in total* (3 highlighters, 1 pen, 1 calculator, 2 black cartridges and 2 tri-color cartridges). **(B)** is the correct answer. The numbers 8 **(A)**, 12 **(C)**, and 14 **(D)** are not mentioned in the receipt.

175. (C)

(C) is the only possible answer because **(A)** and **(D)** are places that sell food and drinks, and the items described in the bill don't fall into this category. You wouldn't buy pens or paper in a computer store, so **(B)** is also wrong.

176. (C)

Gisele signs the email as *store manager*. The directory says that management is situated on the 4th floor, so **(C)** is the correct answer. The directory doesn't mention any *offices* on any other floor, so options **(A)**, **(B)**, and **(D)** are not possible.

177. (D)

Gisele says that there were some red containers on the *2nd floor*. Plastic spoons should be delivered to the restaurant, which is on the 5th floor. This makes **(D)** the only possible answer. **(A)** is incorrect because *pens* can be found in *stationery*, which is on the 2nd floor. The same applies to **(B)** because dictionaries can be found in *books and magazines* on the 2nd floor. *Hand soap* would be needed for the toilets which are situated on the 2nd floor, so **(C)** is also incorrect.

178. (D)

Screens and monitors can be found in the blue containers. The best department for these items would be Technology on the 4th floor, so **(D)** is the correct answer. None of the other floors hold departments that may sell computer *screens and monitors*, so options **(A)**, **(B)**, and **(C)** are incorrect.

179. (A)

Perfumes are stored in the *yellow containers* and they belong on the *1st floor*, not on the *4th*. This makes **(A)** the correct option. **(B)** is wrong because Gisele's office in on the 4th floor (the directory says that *management* is on the *4th floor*). **(C)** is also incorrect because the email says *the first one is for the clerks and will take place in Screen B* and the directory tells us that *screen B* is on the *4th floor*. There are *screen projectors* on the *4th floor*, so **(D)** is also wrong.

180. (D)

Gisele mentions the *grand opening* in her email. She also says that *posters and signs won't be delivered until Friday*. This indicates that the store is new, so **(D)** is the correct answer. **(A)**, **(B)**, and **(C)** are not mentioned in the text.

181. (D)

Lilly says *I'd like to add a few things and change the delivery date.* **(D)** is the correct answer. Lilly says she wants to *change an order*, not cancel her order. **(B)** and **(C)** only give half of the reason for Lilly contacting Lochan.

182. (B)

Lilly asks Lochan to change the *delivery date to next Monday, February 18.* **(B)** is the correct answer. **(A)**, **(C)**, and **(D)** are not mentioned in the text.

183. (C)

The question asks for the items NOT amended in the new order. Lilly says *can we have 20 of the small brown desks instead of* 15 **(A)**; *I'd like to add 5 white chairs* **(B)**; and *as for the smart boards, I will also need an extra one, so it will be 5 of them after all* **(D)**. There's no mention of *DVDs*, so **(C)** is the only possible answer.

184. (D)

Lilly says *I want to thank you again for recommending us to Havoc Investment as their potential IT suppliers.* **(D)** is the correct answer. A *supplier* is not a *client*, so **(A)** is incorrect. **(B)** is not mentioned in the text. **(C)** is incorrect because *Havoc Investment* might become a supplier in the future, but isn't one yet.

185. (D)

(A), *Boslik Desk White*; **(B)**, *Boslik Chairs Brown*; and **(C)**, *UHD 4K Int Board 50* are the total charges for each of the articles in the order. The total cost of the *merchandise* is **(D)**.

186. (B)

The notice says *both cafeterias for the main building will be closed at various times between December 23 and January 6.* This is a period of *two weeks.* **(B)** is the correct answer. No other period of time is mentioned in the notice or email, so options **(A)**, **(C)**, and **(D)** are not possible.

187. (A)

The email says *the Christmas period is usually quiet at the company. Quiet* and *not too busy* are synonyms. **(A)** is correct. **(B)** and **(C)** are mentioned in the text but are not given as reasons for the renovations taking place. **(D)** is not mentioned in the text.

188. (D)

The question asks for the answer choice not given in the text as a reason for the renovations. The email says *the improved facilities* **(C)** *in the new restaurant will be able to offer better quality food* **(A)** at *better prices* **(B)**. There's no mention of a *relaxing atmosphere*, so **(D)** is the only possible answer.

189. (D)

The table shows that 3 people have booked their lunch for 12:30, and the information explains that a maximum of 5 people can book their lunch at the same time. Therefore, 2 more people can book their lunch at 12:30. **(D)** is correct.

190. (A)

The notice says *please use the cafeteria next to the parking garage* **(C)** or *the main restaurant on the 2nd floor during this time* **(B)**. The notice also says *we kindly ask all our employees not to spend longer than 30 minutes* **(D)**. Neither the notice nor the email mention the possibility of *finishing work early*, so **(A)** is the correct answer.

191. (B)

The article says *while new facilities like this are usually endorsed by celebrities on prime time TV commercials, the owners of the theme park decided to take an alternative route.* **(B)** is the correct answer. The article says *it had already generated enough public interest.* **(C)** is not mentioned in the text. The article says *even though the weather is as cold as the previous winters, the park has been a success,* so **(D)** is also incorrect.

192. (D)

The article says *its owners were worried about the extreme weather conditions that had inflicted New York in the past three winters*. **(D)** is correct. The article talks about the park's location (*Residents of Manhattan*) but doesn't mention any *worries* about this. The only costs mentioned in the article are *ticket prices*. **(C)** is not mentioned in the text.

193. (C)

The phrase *count me in* means *I will come with you,* so **(C)** must be the correct answer.

194. (C)

The question asks for the facility or activity not mentioned. There are *two indoor* swimming *pools* in Rosalina's Resort **(A)**. **(B)** is also wrong because there's a *cinema room* in Ollie's Paradise. You can play *sports* in Fawn's Park, so **(D)** is incorrect. Although there is a mention of *food kiosks* in Rosalina's Inn, nothing is said about *restaurants*. This makes **(C)** the only possible answer.

195. (C)

Bella writes *We're just getting the basic ones. $30 for us and $15 for the kids*, the adults basic tickets must cost $30 each. **(C)** is correct.

196. (D)

Scarlet writes *I wanted to give you a bit more information about requesting maternity leave before you make your official request, so I've attached some further information.* The answer is **(D)**.

197. (B)

The email states *employees must have completed 26 weeks of service to be entitled to Statutory Maternity Pay.* The answer is **(B)**.

198. (A)

The document states *For all other employees, two weeks of maternity leave must be taken immediately following the birth of your child.***(A)** is correct.

199. (D)

The document states *Ordinary Maternity Leave can begin 11 weeks before your expected week of childbirth and no earlier.* The answer is **(D)**.

200. (C)

The advertisement gives the Scarlet's email address, and says that this is the Operational Director's email, so Scarlet must be the Operational Director. **(C)** is correct.

PRACTICE TEST 4

 **Track 18**

Play Track 18 to hear the audio for Part I.

SECTION 1—LISTENING COMPREHENSION

In the Listening Comprehension Section, you will have the chance to demonstrate how well you understand spoken English. The Listening Comprehension Section will take approximately 45 minutes. There are four parts, and directions are given for each part. You must mark your answers on the answer sheet. Do not write them in the test book.

PART I: PHOTOGRAPHS

Directions: For each question, you will hear four statements about the photograph in your test book. When you hear the statements, choose the one statement that best describes what you see in the photograph. Then, find the number of the question on your answer sheet and mark your answer. The statements will not be written in your test book and will be spoken just once

Now listen to the four statements. 

Choice (D), "They're having a meeting," best describes what you see in the picture. Therefore, you should fill in choice (D) in your answer sheet.

1.

2.

3.

4.

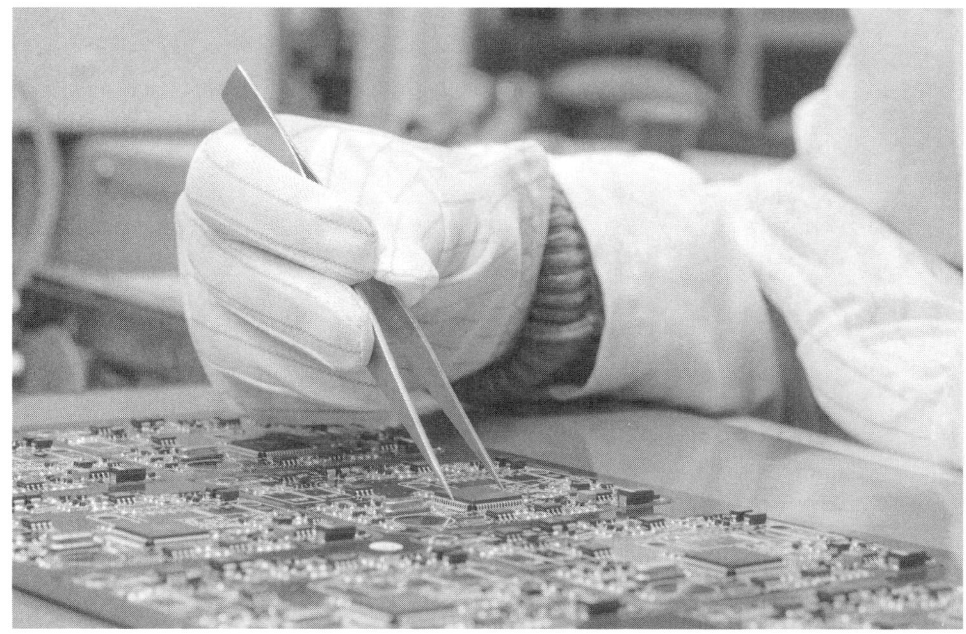

5.

6.

 **Track 19**

Play Track 19 to hear the audio for Part II.

PART II: QUESTION-RESPONSE

Directions: You will hear a question or statement and three responses spoken in English. They will be spoken only once and will not be printed in your test book. Choose the best response to the question or statement and mark the letter on your answer sheet.

Listen to a sample question:

Sample Answer

Choice (C), "They go in the paper recycling box," best answers the question. Therefore, you should fill in choice (C) in your answer sheet.

7. Mark your answer on your answer sheet.

8. Mark your answer on your answer sheet.

9. Mark your answer on your answer sheet.

10. Mark your answer on your answer sheet.

11. Mark your answer on your answer sheet.

12. Mark your answer on your answer sheet.

13. Mark your answer on your answer sheet.

14. Mark your answer on your answer sheet.

15. Mark your answer on your answer sheet.

16. Mark your answer on your answer sheet.

17. Mark your answer on your answer sheet.

18. Mark your answer on your answer sheet.

19. Mark your answer on your answer sheet.

20. Mark your answer on your answer sheet.

21. Mark your answer on your answer sheet.

22. Mark your answer on your answer sheet.

23. Mark your answer on your answer sheet.

24. Mark your answer on your answer sheet.

25. Mark your answer on your answer sheet.

26. Mark your answer on your answer sheet.

27. Mark your answer on your answer sheet.

28. Mark your answer on your answer sheet.

29. Mark your answer on your answer sheet.

30. Mark your answer on your answer sheet.

31. Mark your answer on your answer sheet.

GO ON TO THE NEXT PAGE.

 **Track 20**

Play Track 20 to hear the audio for Part III.

PART III: SHORT CONVERSATIONS

Directions: You will hear a number of conversations between two people. You will be asked to answer three questions about what the speakers say in each conversation. Select the best response to each question and mark the letter on your answer sheet. The conversations will be spoken only once and will not be printed in your test book.

32. What are the speakers mainly discussing?

- **A.** where to find fresh lobster
- **B.** what to eat for dinner
- **C.** why the steaks are from Montana
- **D.** which type of wine to drink

33. What does the woman suggest for the man?

- **A.** Maine lobster
- **B.** clam chowder
- **C.** Brooklyn cheesecake
- **D.** Caesar salad

34. Who will pay for the meal?

- **A.** the man
- **B.** the man's company
- **C.** the woman's firm
- **D.** the man and the woman

---

35. What is the woman doing?

- **A.** researching new server system
- **B.** replacing the existing server system
- **C.** selling used IT servers
- **D.** maintaining the new server system

36. What does the woman need?

- **A.** advice on purchasing IT server systems
- **B.** feedback on the old computers
- **C.** computer software sales
- **D.** information on available computers

37. What does the man suggest the woman do?

- **A.** consult with a computer specialist
- **B.** ask Caitlin for some suggestions
- **C.** locate a different vendor than Ingram Computers
- **D.** find a company that offers good service support

---

38. What is the relationship between the speakers?

- **A.** manager-investor
- **B.** waiter-customer
- **C.** employer-candidate
- **D.** professor-student

39. What does the woman ask the man?

- **A.** to give her a higher salary
- **B.** to explain about benefits
- **C.** to disclose trade secrets
- **D.** to clarify a contract section

40. What will the woman probably do next?

- **A.** ask a question
- **B.** decline an offer
- **C.** sign the contract
- **D.** phone her attorney

---

41. How is the woman traveling?

- **A.** by car
- **B.** by subway
- **C.** on foot
- **D.** by bus

42. What problem does the woman have?

A. She cannot find her map.
B. She does not know where she is.
C. She is walking the wrong direction.
D. She is at the wrong station.

43. What does the man suggest?

A. calling Jim's office for assistance
B. walking to Central Street Station
C. getting in a taxi
D. heading east on Broadway

---

44. Why won't Marie eat the pasta?

A. She doesn't like pasta.
B. She doesn't eat meat.
C. She doesn't like tomatoes.
D. She doesn't eat ham.

45. What can be inferred from the conversation?

A. Marie is coming to the dinner alone.
B. Marie is the wife of the woman's boss.
C. Umit is teasing the woman.
D. The woman is not good at cooking.

46. How does the woman feel?

A. anxious
B. amused
C. disturbed
D. befuddled

---

47. What are the speakers mainly discussing?

A. a weekend
B. a concert
C. a musician
D. an award

48. When does the conversation take place?

A. on Saturday
B. on Sunday
C. on Monday
D. on Tuesday

49. What does the woman say about the Screaming Lizards?

A. They were average.
B. They were awesome.
C. They were too loud.
D. They were exciting.

---

50. Why was the woman unavailable?

A. She was away from the country.
B. She was on holiday.
C. She was ill.
D. A family member was in the hospital.

51. Why did the man go ahead with the presentation?

A. He thought the woman wouldn't be able to do it.
B. The client insisted on it.
C. He wanted to have an informal chat with the client.
D. He was threatened by his boss to do it.

52. Why does the woman say "Oh, brilliant"?

A. She's happy with something she's been told.
B. She's describing how something went.
C. She's calling Mark smart.
D. She's complaining about something.

---

53. What's the problem the woman is facing?

A. Her laptop is offline.
B. Her laptop doesn't recognize her credentials.
C. She can't get into the system.
D. Her password has expired.

54. What can be inferred from the conversation?

A. Ian works in IT.
B. The IT meeting will be over soon.
C. The woman plans to call IT again.
D. None of the IT people are in the office.

55. Why does the woman say "yes, of course" at the end?

A. She confirmed something.
B. She remembered something.
C. She agreed with something.
D. She agreed to do something.

---

56. Who most likely are the speakers?

A. employer and employee
B. banker and client
C. salesman and customer
D. husband and wife

57. What does the man suggest?

A. reducing the house payment
B. increasing expenses
C. listening to the radio
D. borrowing some money

58. What does the woman ask the man to do next?

A. drive to the bank
B. schedule a meeting
C. spend $100
D. save 5 percent

---

59. Where is Thomas now?

A. in a meeting
B. at her desk
C. at a branch office
D. out to lunch

60. What problem is he dealing with?

A. an angry client
B. a paperwork mix-up
C. a stocking mistake
D. a cancelled flight

61. How does the woman suggest contacting Thomas?

A. by visiting his office
B. by leaving a message with a secretary
C. by sending him an email
D. by calling his phone

---

62. What does the woman ask the man to do?

A. Manage the new advertising project
B. Recommend an option
C. Check with the head of marketing
D. Show her the different marketing options

63. Why does the man say "You should probably check with Maria"?

A. He doesn't think she is authorized to share the information.
B. He doesn't have time to look into it.
C. He thinks Maria can give her a better answer.
D. He thinks Maria will know where to find it.

64. Look at the graphic below. How much does the man think they should spend?

A. $6,000
B. $15,000
C. $45,000
D. $60,000

Type	Budget
Radio	$45,000
Billboard	$6,000
Internet	$60,000
Magazine	$15,000

---

65. What is happening next week?

A. They are inviting clients to share a meal with them.

B. They are having an office party.

C. They are going for dinner with their employees.

D. They are inviting their families to work.

66. Look at the graphic below. Which seating area does the woman choose?

A. 1

B. 2

C. 3

D. 4

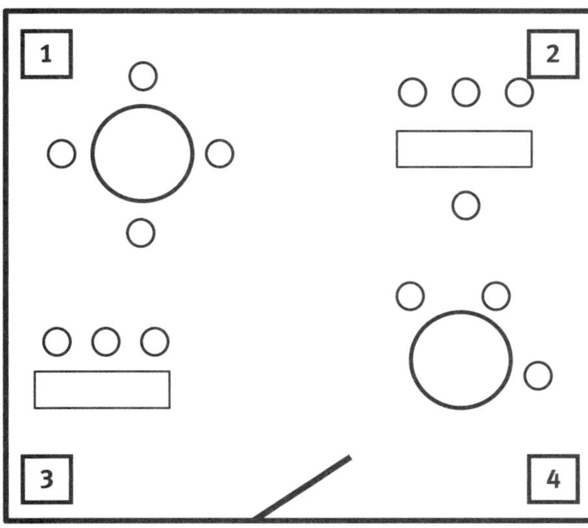

67. What changed about the clients the man was inviting?

A. One of them can't make it.

B. He had to ask an additional client to attend.

C. None of them are available now.

D. He wasn't planning on inviting any of them.

68. Where does the man most likely work?

A. a restaurant

B. an office

C. a diet center

D. a supply center

69. Why is the woman calling?

A. to cancel a reservation

B. to order some food for delivery

C. to check details about a booking

D. to check how many people will attend

70. Look at the graphic below. Which booking did the woman make?

A. Booking 1

B. Booking 2

C. Booking 3

D. Booking 4

	Time	Description
Booking 1	18:30	2 people, 1 x vegetarian, quiet corner
Booking 2	19:00	7 people, 1 x lactose intolerance, pre ordered deserts
Booking 3	19:30	6 people, 1 x nut allergy, round table
Booking 4	20:00	4 people, wheelchair access. no dietary requirements

Track 21

Play Track 21 to hear the audio for Part IV.

PART IV: SHORT TALKS

Directions: You will hear some talks given by a single speaker. You will be asked to answer three questions about what the speaker says in each talk. Select the best response to each question and mark the letter (A), (B), (C), or (D) on your answer sheet. The talks will be spoken only once and will not be printed in your test book.

71. Where is this talk most likely being broadcast?

A. on the radio
B. at a technology fair
C. in a train station
D. on an airplane

72. What is being offered?

A. low credit
B. free delivery
C. used mattresses
D. a special sale

73. Look at the table. What is the item number for the dining table discussed?

A. 3052
B. 3456
C. 3678
D. 3890

On Sale Items

Item number	Original Price	New Price	Origin	Material
3052	$199	$179	USA	hardwood
3456	$389	$220	Europe	oak
3678	$179	$150	USA	hardwood
3890	$220	$179	Europe	oak

74. Where would this announcement most likely be heard?

A. at a stadium
B. in a cinema
C. in a restaurant
D. at a concert

75. What is the speaker offering?

A. an autographed ball
B. free gifts
C. ticket stubs
D. a free car wash

76. Look at the list of tickets. Who won the prize draw?

A. Sajeda
B. Frank
C. Amna
D. Charlie

Ticket Holders

Name	Seat	Section	Row
Sajeda	186	23	F
Frank	200	34	F
Amna	186	34	E
Charlie	200	23	E

77. What is the main purpose of the radio announcement?

A. to warn about a big snowstorm
B. to remind drivers of icy roadways
C. to inform people of schedule changes
D. to publicize the city's web site

78. What should students who take the bus do?

A. get a ride with their parents
B. wait at special bus stops
C. get to their bus stop early
D. take the bus as usual

79. When will community colleges begin?

A. at the normal time
B. three hours later
C. they have been cancelled
D. two hours later

80. Who is probably making this speech?

A. a college professor
B. a business recruiter
C. a company executive
D. an external specialist

81. Which of the following is a possible date for the employees to be paid on?

A. at the middle and end of each month
B. by 5 P.M. each Friday
C. after they work overtime
D. Mondays and Wednesdays every week

82. What is the main purpose of the speech?

A. to discuss customers
B. to persuade a patron
C. to debate policy
D. to explain a problem

83. Where is this report most likely being broadcast?

A. television
B. the internet
C. radio
D. an MP3 player

84. What does the speaker say about traffic?

A. It is flowing smoothly everywhere.
B. It is very congested.
C. It is lighter than usual.
D. It is a commute.

85. Who is sponsoring this report?

A. Pat Sullivan
B. WKRP Radio
C. the Westside shopping center
D. Kangaroo Cola

86. Who is the speaker most likely speaking to?

A. new employees
B. potential investors
C. unhappy customers
D. department managers

87. What excuse do staff members have for not taking computer classes?

A. They cannot afford them.
B. They see no advantages to them.
C. They have not heard about them.
D. They lack time and energy.

88. What is the plan to improve attendance?

A. hire a consultant
B. provide a motivational speaker
C. add more classes
D. change to another technology school

89. What is suggested about Wild Waters Adventures Theme Fun Park?

A. It is relatively small.
B. It is open throughout the year.
C. It is not very well known.
D. It has area competitors.

90. What discount is being offered?

A. a family ticket package
B. a boogie board
C. a children's ticket
D. a bathing suit

GO ON TO THE NEXT PAGE.

91. Why does the speaker say "Don't wait!"?

A. He does not think that anything is coming.
B. He is advising the listeners to book now.
C. He thinks that they should visit the park immediately.
D. He wants the listeners to continue without him.

---

92. Why does the speaker say "Sometimes I wonder myself"?

A. She sometimes questions her motivations for running a business.
B. She doesn't know why there aren't more people like her.
C. She wants to understand what makes some companies successful.
D. She doesn't know what she would have done differently.

93. How many start-up companies has the speaker formed?

A. six
B. twelve
C. thirteen
D. fifty-five

94. What does the speaker say about his future?

A. He is ready to retire.
B. He is going to sell his assets.
C. He will work for five more years.
D. He will remain in the same field.

---

95. What is the main purpose of the advertisement?

A. to sell a product
B. to announce a public service
C. to promote alcohol
D. to warn criminals

96. Who is the intended audience?

A. adults
B. children
C. women
D. friends

97. What is being offered?

A. a little bit of good cheer
B. designated drivers
C. tough winter driving
D. free cab rides for drunk drivers

---

98. Who is probably speaking?

A. a new employee
B. a movie star
C. a flight attendant
D. a football coach

99. What does the speaker say about the coaching staff?

A. They have too many choices.
B. They are talented enough to win.
C. They will treat the team fairly.
D. They are disappointed in the team's failures.

100. What is the main purpose of the speech?

A. to motivate
B. to inform
C. to entertain
D. to educate

Stop! This is the end of the Listening Comprehension Section of the exam. Turn to Part V.

You will have one hour and 15 minutes to complete Parts V, VI, and VII of the exam.

SECTION 2—READING COMPREHENSION

In the Reading Comprehension Section, you will read a variety of texts and answer different types of questions. The Reading Comprehension Section will last 75 minutes. There are three parts, and directions are given for each part. You are encouraged to answer as many questions as possible within the allotted time. Mark your answers on the separate answer sheet. Do no write them in the test book.

PART V: INCOMPLETE SENTENCES

Directions: In this TOEIC practice section there are 30 questions. For each question you will see an incomplete sentence. Four words or phrases, marked A–D, are given beneath each sentence. You are to choose the one word or phrase that best completes the sentence. The correct answer for each sentence has been highlighted below.

101. The IT engineers ________ investigated the latest server malfunction.

A. are just
B. still
C. have already
D. have yet

102. Financial ________ are predicting that a reduction in consumer activity will adversely impact corporate profits.

A. analysis
B. analytical
C. analyze
D. analysts

103. Hardly ________ of the components that we ordered are in stock.

A. none
B. few
C. any
D. all

104. The logistics manager is currently unable to account ________ the missing inventory.

A. by
B. for
C. to
D. with

105. Sales executives ________ performance is considered exceptional will be awarded an annual incentive bonus.

A. whose
B. who
C. which
D. whom

106. Transferring our ________ facilities to areas with lower labor costs will lead to greater long term profitability.

A. manufactured
B. manufacture
C. manufacturing
D. manufacturer

107. Many analysts feel that the latest economic data indicates that the threat of inflation has ________ slightly over the past six months.

A. rising
B. risen
C. rose
D. raised

108. All staff are required to report for work, ________ of existing weather conditions.

A. although
B. despite
C. even
D. regardless

109. The increase in overall sales in the fourth quarter was ________ due to a national online marketing campaign.

A. almost
B. most
C. mostly
D. much

110. ________ a flex-time work schedule was introduced in 2015, overall productivity has risen by a remarkable 25% in the last fiscal year.

A. As
B. Before
C. Since
D. While

111. The security guards ________ on duty for the late night shift at midnight every evening.

A. coming
B. to come
C. comes
D. come

112. Ms. Nolan wants to ________ the marketing campaign costs estimate by this evening.

A. final
B. finally
C. finalize
D. finality

113. Ms. Wainwright has recommended that we________ more hotel reception staff.

A. hire
B. hired
C. hiring
D. to hire

114. A call center representative ________ at our customer support number.

A. always shall available
B. is always available
C. was available always
D. is being always available

115. Could you briefly meet with us ________ 10:30?

A. on
B. for
C. at
D. in

116. The general manager advocated ________ a project analysis team.

A. organized
B. organizing
C. organizes
D. to organize

117. The personal assistant ________ a message if you are unable to answer your office telephone.

A. will take
B. took
C. take
D. taken

118. A list of compatible software programs and applications ________ with your new PC tablet.

A. includes
B. is including
C. is included
D. included

119. The total cost of all tour ________ includes airfare and other transportation.

A. travels
B. packages
C. boxes
D. parcels

120. ________ we didn't arrive on time; we could not enter the concert venue.

A. Although
B. Therefore
C. Because
D. However

121. When you require office supplies or equipment, ________ an official invoice with the person in charge.

A. filling
B. fell
C. fallen
D. file

122. The hotel bell captain suggested that more guest porters ________ recruited.

A. were
B. have
C. be
D. do

123. The last passenger express train to Naples ________ at 15:45.

A. depart
B. departs
C. to depart
D. departing

124. The vice president will be seated ________ the CEO at the awards dinner.

A. as
B. on
C. beside
D. in

125. The restaurant manager required his employees ________ last Sunday.

A. to work
B. was working
C. workable
D. worked

126. The online journal expects overall circulation ________ next year.

A. to ascend
B. to hike
C. to escalate
D. to rise

127. The chief of IT system administration ________ to the annual conference.

A. going

B. are going

C. go

D. is going

128. Cuts in the travel budget ________ us to reduce our costs for international travel.

A. admire

B. require

C. hire

D. transpire

129. The ticketholders for the concert could be ________ about the change of date.

A. reused

B. refused

C. confused

D. unused

130. Mr. Moss is the most ________ member of our marketing team.

A. instep

B. innersole

C. innumerable

D. innovative

PART VI: TEXT COMPLETION

Directions: Read the texts that follow. A word or phrase is missing in some of the sentences. Four answer choices are given below each of the sentences. Select the best answer to complete the text. Then mark the letter (A), (B), (C), or (D) on your answer sheet.

Questions 131–134 refer to the following notice.

BEWARE OF PICKPOCKETS AND THEFT OF PERSONAL ITEMS

The management of FANTASIA'S would like to __________ (131) all patrons to beware of pickpockets.

A spate of thefts have taken place in the __________ (132) weeks, and in order to avoid a ruined evening, we urge you to be extra vigilant with your personal property.

We have our suspicions as to who is guilty of these thefts, and would like to make this fact known. FANTASIA'S has a city-wide __________ (133) as a nightclub of the highest quality, and we do not appreciate the efforts of those working to damage this reputation. We have notified the police of the current situation and will not hesitate to encourage anyone who falls victim to theft while on our __________ (134) to press full charges, should the thief be identified.

131. **A.** attention
B. apprehend
C. alert
D. announce

132. **A.** previous
B. next
C. coming
D. following

133. **A.** certification
B. reputation
C. notoriety
D. representation

134. **A.** promises
B. preamble
C. premises
D. practices

Questions 135–138 refer to the following announcement.

Dear MTT Customer:

MTT and the state of Virginia are pleased to bring you Enhanced 911, a new emergency __________ (135) system which will soon be in your area. This new system, provided by MTT, will help the Virginia Emergency Response Units to serve you more efficiently. When you call 911 in an emergency, this system automatically displays and relays your __________ (136) number, address and any other special conditions or instructions you need to provide to police, fire, or ambulance services __________ (137) to your location.

To help state officials serve you better, if someone in your family has a special medical condition, or if your home or business has __________ (138) materials, please complete the closed form and mail the information as soon as possible. All information provided will be held in the strictest confidence.

If you have questions about the new Enhanced 911 system, please call Jonathan Appleton, Emergency 911 Director at (804) 555-5771.

PLEASE NOTE: If you or family members have no special conditions, it is not necessary to return this information card.

135. **A.** response
B. engagement
C. reaction
D. communicate

136. **A.** transfer
B. total
C. house
D. telephone

137. **A.** transmuted
B. dispatched
C. deported
D. ejected

138. **A.** hostile
B. beneficial
C. nondescript
D. hazardous

Questions 139–142 refer to the following memorandum.

To: Helen Browning, Sandra Daly & Hank Sahota
From: Roxanne Benning
Re: Tardiness at Work
Date: September 3, 2016

Everyone,

It has been __________ (139) to my attention that in the last month or so, a significant proportion of the staff have been getting slack about arriving on time. Please remind everyone in your division that all bank employees are expected to be at their desk and ready to start work at least 10 minutes before the bank opens. We cannot __________ (140) staff members running in the back door at the same time as we are opening the front doors to customers. Tardiness inevitably causes errors, which in turn means that we are all held up going home at the end of the day. __________ (141) the problem continues, we will consider introducing penalties to deal with offenders. Please make sure all staff are __________ (142) of this.

Roxanne Benning
Senior Manager

139. **A.** bring
B. caught
C. brought
D. alerted

140. **A.** appreciate
B. tolerate
C. communicate
D. obligate

141. **A.** Because
B. Since
C. When
D. If

142. **A.** aware
B. alert
C. concern
D. awareness

Questions 143–146 refer to the following email.

TO: robbierat@mailpal.com

FROM: romley.rebecca@sercoin.com

SUBJECT: Job Offer

Dear Robert Ratner,

Further to our recent discussions, I am writing to ___(143)___ our offer of employment regarding the post of Senior Analyst with Sercoin TFD.

Your salary will be $74,000 per annum. Please note that this offer is subject to our receiving at least one satisfactory reference. These will be ___(144)___ using the details provided prior to your commencing employment.

Earlier today, we discussed a start date of 09/15/18 at 9:00 A.M. ___(145)___, please state your name at reception, and ask for Karen Bukowski. If the given start date should be inconvenient please let us know.

Please find attached your contract of employment which sets out the terms and conditions of your employment. Please review the document and return one signed copy to me prior to your start date. Should you have any questions about your role or the terms in this contract prior to your start date, please do not hesitate to contact me. ___(146)___

Yours sincerely,

Rebecca Romley

143. **A.** remark
B. query
C. confirm
D. reteam

144. **A.** found
B. divulged
C. delivered
D. sought

145. **A.** At the same time
B. Upon arrival
C. In addition
D. Under duress

146. **A.** We look forward to welcoming you to the team.
B. I am honored to accept the position.
C. You should expect to receive your contract in two working days.
D. Thank you for your support.

PART VII: READING COMPREHENSION

Directions: In this part you will read a selection of texts, such as magazine and newspaper articles, letters, and advertisements. Each text is followed by several questions. Select the best answer for each question and mark the letter (A), (B), (C), or (D) on your answer sheet.

Questions 147–150 refer to the following article.

Klankstown Train Station Renovations

Train commuters should seek alternative routes, as Klankstown Station is set to close for two weeks starting next Monday. The closures are a result of ongoing renovations to the stations, which were begun at the close of last year and are expected to continue until next February.

Klankstown Station operates as a hub for many major stations and cities in the state, so most routes will be affected as a result. — [1] — Some routes will still be running with diversions via Wakon Station, but passengers should expect a delay of at least 30 minutes to their usual journey.

So far, the train station has remained open, with various platform closures but no significant impact on services. However, as changes to the layout of the station progress, the two week closure will allow the station to complete various installations and renovations to the site as a whole. — [2] —

— [3] — Changes to the services were officially announced last month, and will include high-speed trains running every 15 minutes to both Croonsden Station and Marina Stretch Station. The changes will also include the construction of a luxury shopping mall, with a capacity for 50 new store openings and 25 restaurants. — [4] —

For more information on the Klankstown Station renovations, visit www.klankstownstation.com.

147. What is being announced in the article?

A. a two-week closure of a station
B. the opening of a high-speed train
C. future renovations to a shopping mall
D. the construction of a new train

148. Which of the following will still be open during Klankstown Station's closure?

A. the luxury shopping mall
B. Wakon Station
C. Croonsden Station
D. Marina Stretch Station

149. Who should expect to experience a 30-minute delay?

A. passengers using Klankstown Station during the period of closure
B. passengers using the high speed trains
C. passengers visiting the luxury mall
D. passengers traveling through Wakon

150. In which of the positions marked [1], [2], [3], and [4] does the following sentence best belong?
"Klankstown station's renovations will create a more streamlined service for passengers."

- **A.** [1]
- **B.** [2]
- **C.** [3]
- **D.** [4]

Questions 151–153 refer to the following notice.

WATER SHORTAGE WARNING AND WATER USAGE ANNOUNCEMENT:

Princeton municipal government officials have announced that restrictions on water usage will be introduced starting next Wednesday. Due to an unusually low amount of rainfall, water reserves are now at their lowest levels in the last fifty years. The water management authorities have issued the following water conservation measures: All water users are required to restrict their water use! Public and privately owned water utilities shall limit the monthly usage of water by their customers. They may do this by interrupting supply or by advising their clients on guidelines to encourage reductions in their use of water. The usage of water for residential gardens and yards is permitted on Wednesdays and on Saturdays for residents with even-numbered house addresses, and on Mondays and on Thursdays for residents with odd-numbered house addresses. For agricultural businesses, irrigation is now restricted between the hours of 7 P.M. and midnight.

151. What is the purpose of this notice?

- **A.** to inform residents of water conservation measures
- **B.** to warn residents of weather conditions
- **C.** to announce water pollution levels
- **D.** to promote mineral water sales

152. What actions are water utility companies authorized to take?

- **A.** increase their fees
- **B.** cut water supply
- **C.** supply more water
- **D.** develop new water reserves

153. When can farmers water their crops?

- **A.** anytime
- **B.** Monday and Thursdays
- **C.** weekends
- **D.** evenings

Questions 154–157 refer to the following announcement.

> **ATTENTION!**
>
> **EMERGENCY PROCEDURES FOR MINOR CHEMICAL SPILLS**
>
> Certain experiments require the handling of dangerous and toxic chemicals and materials. Please be familiar with the following emergency procedures.
>
> **GET AWAY.** Extinguish any ignition source (burners, appliances, and other equipment) and move to a safe distance.
>
> **DETERMINE** the nature of the substance spilled, the extent of the spill, and the degree of danger. Block off the area.
>
> **GET HELP.** If the spill cannot be handled safely using the equipment and personnel present, activate the fire alarm and call 911 for emergency assistance.
>
> **ASSESS INJURIES.** If anyone is injured, call 911.
>
> **CLEAN UP THE SPILL WITH PROPER EQUIPMENT AND MATERIALS.** Select the appropriate protective equipment and clean-up materials for the chemical spill. Place contaminated materials in the container designated for hazardous waste.
>
> **DISPOSAL.** Contact Environmental Health and Safety personnel. Absorbed materials remain hazardous. Treat them with care.

154. Where would this notice be posted?

- **A.** a laboratory
- **B.** a health food store
- **C.** a restaurant kitchen
- **D.** a garage

155. In case of a chemical spill, what should be done first?

- **A.** put on protective gear
- **B.** contact the janitor
- **C.** turn off open flames and sources of electricity
- **D.** call the health authorities

156. How should contaminated materials be disposed of?

- **A.** They should be burned.
- **B.** They should be rinsed thoroughly with water.
- **C.** They should be placed outside.
- **D.** They should be placed in special containers.

157. Which personnel should be contacted prior to disposal?

- **A.** the police department
- **B.** the fire department
- **C.** medical emergency personnel
- **D.** environmental health authorities

Questions 158–160 refer to the following letter.

Dear Wildlife Conservation Society Member,

Following the Annual General Meeting, we agreed to proceed with the election of two new members of the board of directors. Society board members are elected for a three-year term and may not serve more than two consecutive terms. As an active and registered member of the society, you are entitled to vote for the candidate of your choice by secret ballot.

The profiles of the four candidates standing for election are enclosed in a separate document. You will also find a postal ballot form and a stamped addressed envelope. Photocopies of the ballot forms will not be accepted.

Please return your enclosed vote to us by midnight on November 16th. The results of the secret ballot will be published on our website and in the December newsletter.

If you have any questions on the above, please feel free to contact us at the earliest convenience.

Sincere Regards,

Nathaniel Bronstein

Chairman

158. What is the maximum number of years that an elected member can serve on the board?

A. two years
B. four years
C. six years
D. ten years

159. How can society members vote in this election?

A. by attending the annual meeting
B. by submitting a postal vote
C. by connecting to the society's website
D. by calling Norris Williams

160. What is NOT included with this letter?

A. a newsletter
B. a postal ballot form
C. a profile of the candidates
D. a stamped addressed return envelope

Questions 161–163 refer to the following survey.

Executives Most Productive in the Mornings According to Survey

The majority of top management work most effectively outside typical office hours. This survey by the Vermillion Consulting Group involved the participation of 100 chief executives from the top 300 corporations all across the country. The hours before other employees usually arrive at work were most favored by 47 executives, while 24 preferred to work when the other staff had left the office. The remaining 39 executives considered normal business hours to be their most productive time during the business day.

Moreover, 75% of the executives polled favored working during mornings over afternoons. Close to 85% of those surveyed said that they worked at home in the evenings, and 65% worked over the weekends. In addition, 55% mentioned that weekends were also a very effective time to complete their tasks in the office. The overall survey results revealed that top managers were very adept at using time effectively to complete their job tasks.

161. Who participated in the survey?

- **A.** Vermillion's top one hundred managers
- **B.** presidents from each of five hundred companies
- **C.** one hundred executives of the top firms in the nation
- **D.** forty-seven executives of the watch industry

162. What did the survey reveal?

- **A.** when executives do their best work
- **B.** how many hours most businesses are open
- **C.** what brands of watches top managers wear
- **D.** how close workers lived to their jobs

163. What percentage of those surveyed work on Saturdays or Sundays?

- **A.** 47
- **B.** 65
- **C.** 75
- **D.** 85

Questions 164–166 refer to the following memorandum.

MEMORANDUM

To: All Office Employees

From: Eloise Rogers

Subject: New Phone Communications System

Date: March 12

As you know, we badly need to modernize our office communications system. I have enclosed with this memo some descriptions of some phone systems sent by sales representatives. Please read the materials carefully and send your recommendations to me.

The system should be able to handle at least one hold line and eight extension lines. My opinion is that a built-in answering machine system is necessary. Conference calls and speed-dialing features are now standard in many systems and could prove useful for our business going forward.

At the present time our office uses twelve phones, and although we do not have a fixed limit for the unit price, it should be in mid-price range. Recommendations should be in my office by the end of the week so an order can be placed through the Supplies and Equipment Department by the first of the month.

Eloise Rogers

President and Founder

Enclosures

164. What does the memorandum discuss?

- **A.** holding a conference on telecommunications
- **B.** repairing old telephone units
- **C.** communicating by telephone less frequently
- **D.** choosing a new telephone system

165. What should people do after reading the memorandum?

- **A.** organize a conference to discuss the matter
- **B.** order new phones right away
- **C.** share suggestions with Eloise Rogers
- **D.** contact Supplies and Equipment as soon as possible

166. What is a criterion for selecting equipment?

- **A.** use of standard colors
- **B.** one hold line and at least eight extension lines
- **C.** twenty phones
- **D.** low price per unit

Questions 167–170 refer to the following invitation.

We would like to welcome you to the TRT Cloud Technology International Symposium. TRT employees from over thirty countries will be in attendance at this year's event, so if you would like to meet your colleagues from overseas on a more personal level be sure to sign up at the registration desk for insightful seminars, special dinners, lunches, or breakfast meetings that are described below. Whether you are in Personnel, Sales, Management, or Research, you'll be able to discuss topics of common interest with counterparts of diverse backgrounds. Find out what your Indian, Japanese, or Moroccan colleagues can suggest for your department's current challenges. Help your French, Colombian, or Russian colleagues on an issue that you've dealt with before. Take advantage of this rare opportunity to collaborate with your international partners. All meetings will be held in the Main Lounge.

SCHEDULE & SYMPOSIUM TOPICS:

Monday Breakfast – 7:00–9:00	Legal Implications of Establishing Branch Offices in Asia
Tuesday Lunch – 12:00–14:00	Emerging Technologies and Emerging Challenges
Wednesday Dinner – 19:00–21:00	International Personnel and HR Management Issues
Thursday Breakfast – 7:00–9:00	New Markets and Opportunities in Eastern Europe

167. Who is the conference aimed at?

- **A.** international politicians
- **B.** people learning foreign languages
- **C.** international chefs
- **D.** employees of a technology company

168. What is the purpose of the invitation?

- **A.** to give a list of participants
- **B.** to indicate room changes
- **C.** to announce special events
- **D.** to cancel several sessions

169. Which session would most likely deal with human resources?

- **A.** Wednesday dinner
- **B.** Tuesday lunch
- **C.** Monday breakfast
- **D.** Thursday breakfast

170. How many nationalities are expected to attend the symposium?

- **A.** 10
- **B.** 15
- **C.** 30
- **D.** 35

Questions 171–172 refer to the following announcement.

AURORA IT SOLUTIONS NEW SECURITY PROTOCOLS ON DATA STORAGE DEVICES

All USB flash drive data storage devices must be scanned immediately upon entry to this building. Aurora IT Solutions Corporation updated security policy prohibits the possession of any USB flash drives on site. USB Flash devices authorized for business use must be declared, accompanied by a security pass, and scanned for viruses. When entering the facility, failure to declare USB flash drives will result in immediate confiscation. The term USB "flash drive" refers to any portable data storage flash memory device.

171. Where would this notice most likely be seen?

- **A.** a health clinic
- **B.** a computer terminal
- **C.** the entrance of Aurora IT solutions
- **D.** the company cafeteria

172. What will happen if the flash drive is not declared?

- **A.** It will be erased.
- **B.** It will be scratched.
- **C.** It will be duplicated.
- **D.** It will be taken away.

Questions 173–175 refer to the following invitation.

TELECOMMUNICATIONS EQUIPMENT & INFRASTRUCTURE EXHIBITION
HO CHI MINH CITY, VIETNAM
SEPTEMBER 2~27, 2021

Rapid economic development, strong GDP performance, an attractive environment for FDI, and geographic proximity to China and ASEAN make VIETNAM an extremely attractive market for US and EU manufacturers of telecommunications equipment and infrastructure. Sales of these products are projected to climb from USD $261 million this year and peak at nearly $800 million by FY 2026, reflecting not only large increases in the amount and variety of telecom equipment purchased, but also significant upgrading of current and existing infrastructure and installations.

Call 450-555-3981 for more information.

173. Who is this notice intended for?

A. United States and European manufacturers

B. Vietnamese distributors and exporters

C. manufacturers from all Southeast Asian countries

D. United States and European importers

174. Which of the following mentioned as a key factor in making Vietnam an attractive market?

A. a lack of trade restrictions

B. a nationwide communications system

C. accelerated economic growth

D. significant revenues from oil

175. When are sales expected to level off?

A. this year

B. next year

C. in two years

D. in five years

Questions 176–180 refer to the following registration, notice, and email.

To: Registrants
From: Program Director
Subject: Course Deposits and Withdrawal Policy
Date: March 12

Dear Registrants;

A $100 deposit per person is required for the 5-day course on Website Design and $50 per person for the 2-day Social Media Marketing course. Deposits are refundable if notice of cancellation is received at least 14 days prior to the reservation period, less a $10 handling charge. Deposit will not be refunded if cancellation is received less than 14 days prior to the reservation period. Deposit may be transferred to another session if notice of change is received at least 7 days prior to original date of enrollment. Transfer of deposit to another session is contingent upon availability of space in that session.

Please contact the Program Director at pd@seminars.com

To: Program Director
From: Grant Hayhurst
Subject: Course Refund
Date: March 12

Dear Sir or Madam;

I originally intended to participate in the 2-day Social Media and Marketing course and send my $100 deposit as required. However, I had to cancel my attendance and notified your organization more than 3 weeks prior to the course and am waiting to receive a full refund (less the handling fee of $10).

However, I have not received my refund as of now and would like to inquire about the current status of my refund and when I am going to receive notice from your organization about my deposit.

Looking forward to receiving your reply on the above issue.

Kind regards,

Grant Hayhurst

176. Which of the following would be the best heading for this notice?

A. Procedures for Depositing Checks
B. Availability of Registration Forms
C. Spring Course Offerings
D. Policy on Withdrawals

177. How much must you pay if you cancel three weeks before a session begins?

A. nothing
B. $5
C. $10
D. $50

178. What determines if your deposit can be transferred to a different course?

A. if you paid the handling charge
B. if there is any space left in the second course
C. if the first course is cancelled because of low enrollment
D. if your original suit can be fitted

179. What is the time limit for transferring the deposit for another training course?

A. 5 days
B. 7 days
C. 10 days
D. 14 days

180. What is the customer requesting in the email?

A. a reply about his refund request
B. an update on his training course
C. a request on the training fee
D. a complaint about the instructor

GO ON TO THE NEXT PAGE.

Questions 181–185 refer to the following announcement and email.

ESTATE AUCTION

An auction for the estate of Martin McDonald has been set for Sunday, June 29, at 12:00 noon. A preview of the estate starts at 10:00 A.M. at the McDonald residence at 825 Somerset Boulevard. Some of the Items to be auctioned include:

- 1963 Convertible Sports Car
- Billiards Table
- Oriental Carpets and Area Rugs
- Stamp and Coin Collection
- Hand-Carved Ceremonial Totem Pole
- Antique China and Silverware from Scotland
- Aviator Goggles Collection

Inquiries? Please call Estate Planners Partners & Associates at 384-986-8000 or info@eppassociates.com. The McDonald Family requests that you do not contact their home or solicit their residence prior to the auction.

To: Estate Planners Partners & Associates

From: Paul Landau

Subject: Pre-Auction Bid Inquiry

Date: June 22

Dear Estate Planners Partners & Associates;

I am contacting you with regards to the upcoming estate auction that was recently announced by your firm for the estate of Martin McDonald on the 29th of June.

I am representing a client who is an avid collector who wishes to keep his identity secret at this time and who has expressed some keen interest in one of the items listed. Specifically, my client would be prepared to purchase the Aviator Goggles Collection at a premium by bank certified check before the auction takes place.

Could you please find out if the McDonald Family would be interested selling the above item beforehand? We would be prepared to make an immediate offer once we have received your reply.

Sincerely,

Paul Landau

Attorney at Law

181. What event is being advertised?

- **A.** a party for the McDonald family
- **B.** a fund raising event at the Municipal Building
- **C.** a sale of the possessions of Martin McDonald
- **D.** a private viewing of museum pieces

182. Where will the event be held?

- **A.** the Municipal Building
- **B.** 825 Somerset Boulevard
- **C.** the Estate Planners Associates office
- **D.** the city parking lot

183. Which is NOT available at the auction?

- **A.** Aviator Goggles Collection
- **B.** Oriental Rugs
- **C.** 1963 Hatchback Car
- **D.** Stamp and Coin Collection

184. Which item is the man inquiring about in his email?

- **A.** Billiards Table
- **B.** Aviator Goggles Collection
- **C.** Antique China and Silverware
- **D.** Hand-Carved Ceremonial Totem Pole

185. How is the man trying to pay for this auction item?

- **A.** cash
- **B.** credit card
- **C.** money order
- **D.** certified check

Questions 186–190 refer to the following two letters and voucher.

DELIVERED 20th AUGUST 2019

Mr. Fred Browning

Excel Freight Forwarding

5454 Western Avenue

Detroit, MI 48210

Dear Mr. Browning:

We have just received a complaint about a mishandled shipment from one of our trusted customers, Mr. C. Benson of Magnolia Beauty Care in Dublin, Oregon.

Apparently, a member of your staff delivered two boxes of goods to the Magnolia Beauty Care facility that had been damaged in transit. You will find an enclosed copy of the transmittal form signed by Mr. Benson, on which he clearly indicated that he noticed the damaged packages while your driver was still on the premises.

We can only conclude that they were damaged during shipment. We expect you to pick up the boxes immediately at absolutely no cost to Mr. Benson or Satin Smooth Skin Care. We are far from satisfied with the quality of your service. Considering that this is the third complaint we have received in the last six months, any further incidents of this will force us to reconsider the renewal of our contract with your firm.

Sincerely

Susannah Anderson

Deputy Shipping Manager

DELIVERED 25th AUGUST 2019
Susannah Anderson

Satin Smooth Skincare

2822 Richter Street

Orillia, CA 90271

Dear Ms. Anderson:

On behalf of IFS Freight Forwarding, I would like to sincerely apologize for the poorly handled shipment by one of our employees to Magnolia Beauty Care in Dublin, Oregon. This situation should have never occurred as we always attempt to provide the very highest quality of delivery and customer service to each and every one of our customers.

Please accept the enclosed voucher as compensation. I have not dated the voucher, so please write in the date that you receive this letter. Furthermore, a notice has been sent to all employees about this incident and our shipping department will be inspected regularly in order to ensure the highest quality of handling of all items. We will make the utmost effort to make certain that this never occurs again.

Your business is very important to us and we hope to continue our long standing relationship with you going forward. Once again, please accept my sincere apologies for this mishap and I hope to hear from you soon on the above matter.

Sincerely

Fred Browning

President

Excel Freight Forwarding

ENTERPRISE VOUCHER

This voucher entitles the bearer to one free shipment of an order, up to a shipping value of $100.00.

If using this voucher when booking online, use the code FREE100SHIP. You can also quote this code over the phone, or via email.

We hope you accept this voucher, and hope to do business with you again soon.

Issued and authorized by

Fred Brown

Valid for 1 year from date of issue. Date issued:

____

186. What was sent to Mr. Browning with this letter?

A. a voucher

B. two boxes

C. a new contract

D. a shipping document

187. According to the letter, what actually happened?

A. Smooth Skin was responsible for the damage.

B. Butterfly Beauty should file a complaint.

C. The shipment was damaged in transit.

D. IFS should refund the customer's money.

188. How does Ms. Anderson want the firm to respond to her letter?

A. contact her directly

B. renew the contract

C. retrieve the goods

D. pay for the damage

189. How does Mr. Browning attempt to apologize to Ms. Anderson?

A. offering her a free shipment next time

B. replacing the damaged goods

C. punishing his employee

D. offering Ms. Anderson free beauty supplies

190. When will the voucher expire?

A. 20th August 2019

B. 25th August 2019

C. 20th August 2020

D. 25th August 2020

Questions 191–195 refer to the following advertisement, instructions, and email.

To: Ursula Pennington

From: Richard Seymour

Subject: Arrival in Santiago and Accommodations

Date: January 10

Dear Ms. Pennington,

We will be pleased to welcome you to our headquarters for the end of year auditing procedures.

Paula Jenkins tells us that you will arrive in Santiago on Flight TA 209 on Monday, January 31, at 11:20 A.M. I have instructed my assistant, Carmen Sierra, to drive you directly to our office and make sure that all the arrangements for your stay are satisfactory. We will set up a PC workstation with LAN access at your disposal in a private office. If you have any special requirements or requests, I would appreciate it if you would contact us by phone or email us to let us know before your arrival.

We have booked a room at the Los Cristinos Hotel in the center of downtown Santiago, which serves complimentary breakfast and dinner. Alternatively, we can recommend many fine restaurants in the center of town. We have arranged for you to have prepaid lunches at our staff cafeteria. Ms. Sierra will take care of the transport arrangement for your return to the airport on Saturday the fifth.

I look forward to meeting you next month.

Sincerely,

Richard Seymour

Financial Director

To: Richard Seymour, Carmen Sierra

From: Ursula Pennington

Subject: Arrival in Santiago and Special Requirements

Date: January 20

Dear Mr. Seymour and Ms. Sierra,

Thank you for your message and your thoughtful arrangements for my stay in Santiago during the audit. Unfortunately, due to an urgent personal matter, my schedule has suddenly changed to a different flight on a different day. I've attached my updated flight itinerary. Would it be possible to have someone from your firm meet me at the airport?

In addition, I need to inform you that I am a vegetarian (including no dairy or eggs) and would like to request that my food requirements are taken care of while working at your office during the audit.

Thank you again for your cooperation in advance.

Sincere regards,

Ursula

FLIGHT ITINEARY

Airline:	United Airways
Flight number:	72
Departure Date:	Feb 1st (Tues)
Depart From:	Chile
Destination:	Santiago
Departure:	19:30
Arrival:	21:30 (same day)

191. Why is Ms. Pennington going to Santiago?

A. to visit a drilling site
B. to upgrade a computer system
C. to conduct an audit
D. to review various restaurants

192. Why does Ms. Pennington contact Mr. Seymour prior to her arrival?

A. to arrange to use a computer
B. to confirm her travel schedule
C. to reserve hotel accommodations
D. to find out if she will have access to a copy machine

193. Where will Ms. Pennington probably have her midday meals?

A. the company's cafeteria
B. the Los Cristinos hotel
C. one of the town's restaurants
D. a local coffee shop

194. When will Ms. Pennington actually arrive in Santiago?

A. Tuesday
B. Thursday
C. Friday
D. Monday

195. What special requests did Ms. Pennington make?

A. special sleeping arrangements
B. special travel arrangements
C. special dietary arrangements
D. special work arrangements

Questions 196–200 refer to the following advertisement, instructions, and email.

BANKING WITH ROOIBOS

Here at Rooibos Bank we take pride in putting our customers first. With your needs in mind, we have created a range of different current accounts to suit the needs of all our clients.

Rooibos Basic Account:	A current account to fulfill your everyday needs without costing you a penny, our Basic Account comes with free internet banking, mobile alerts, and a daily limit of £300 in cash withdrawals.
Rooibos Simple Account:	Our most popular account. Affordable at just £3 a month (which can be waived if you deposit over £1,000), the Simple Account comes with everything the Basic Account offers, plus a planned overdraft of up to £500. It also includes a free anti-virus program for your computer and access to our mobile banking app.
Rooibos Special Account:	For those who enjoy that little something extra, our Special Account is the perfect choice. For only £6 per month (or a minimum monthly deposit of £1,500), Rooibos Special gives you a daily limit of £700 in cash withdrawals and a planned overdraft of up to £1,000. In addition to all the benefits included in a Rooibos Simple Account, Special Account members will also receive a membership gift of their choice in addition to free mobile phone or laptop insurance. Please specify your choice of membership gift when you apply.
Student Account:	Available to all students in full-time education for more than 1 year and aged 17 or over, our Student account comes with all the features of Rooibos Simple, and also includes a fee-free student overdraft of up to £2,000.

HOW TO OPEN AN ACCOUNT WITH US

You can now open a Rooibus Basic or Simple Account online, just click on **this link** and fill in your personal details. You will receive an answer within 90 seconds. If your application is successful, you'll need to visit one of our branches with a form of ID* and a proof of address**. You do not need to book an appointment for this.

Please remember to bring the following documents with you to your appointment:

1. A form of ID. This can include:
   - a valid passport
   - a valid UK/EEA driving license
   - a birth certificate
   - a registration or naturalisation certificate
2. A proof of address. This can include:
   - a valid UK driving license
   - a bank statement from another bank, dated within the last three months
   - a utility bill dated within the last six months
   - a council tax statement dated within the last year
3. If you are opening a Student Account, you will also need to bring a stamped and dated letter from your education provider offering you a place to study with them or confirming that you are currently studying with them.

To:	rudy.horowitz@email.com
From:	agnes.drew@rooibusbanks.com
Date:	August 25th
Subject:	RE: Banking with Rooibus

Dear Rudy

Thanks for getting in touch with your questions about one of our accounts.

Our current membership gift options include:

- Subscription to a magazine of your choice
- 6 pairs of cinema tickets
- 3 £20 vouchers redeemable at over 250 restaurants across the UK
- A year's subscription to an online movie streaming provider

Please note that only one choice is permitted per customer. For more information on our range of membership gift options, visit www.rooibosmembership.co.uk.

If you'd like to make an appointment, bear in mind that following our commitment at the start of 2018 to provide our staff with better working hours and conditions, only ten, centrally-located branches nationwide remain open on Saturdays. We do, however, continue to offer late appointments on weekdays for those who are unable to visit any of our weekend branches. To check if there is a weekend branch near you, please check our online branch locator by visiting our website.

Let me know if I can be of further assistance.

Agnes

Customer Service Advisor

196. Which account offers the largest planned overdraft?

A. Rooibos Basic Account
B. Rooibos Simple Account
C. Rooibos Special Account
D. Rooibos Student Account

197. What is the maximum amount that can be withdrawn in one day when using the Basic Account?

A. £300
B. £500
C. £1,000
D. £2,000

198. Why does the author of the email write "bear in mind"?

- **A.** to explain the banking laws in the UK
- **B.** to remind the reader of the items he needs to bring to his appointment
- **C.** to highlight the fact that not all bank branches are open on Saturday anymore
- **D.** to explain that many bank branches have been closed

199. What is the purpose of the email?

- **A.** to request information about the different accounts
- **B.** to arrange an appointment with a new customer
- **C.** to advertise a new banking account to an existing customer
- **D.** to provide additional information to a potential customer

200. Which account is Rudy most likely to have requested further information about?

- **A.** Rooibos Basic Account
- **B.** Rooibos Simple Account
- **C.** Rooibos Special Account
- **D.** Rooibos Student Account

Stop! If you finish before time is called, you may check your work on this section only. Do not turn to any other section in the test.

PRACTICE TEST 4 ANSWER KEY

Part I	Part II	Part III	Part IV	Part V	Part VI	Part VII
1. B	7. B	32. B	71. A	101. C	131. C	147. A
2. D	8. C	33. A	72. D	102. D	132. A	148. B
3. C	9. A	34. C	73. D	103. C	133. B	149. D
4. A	10. A	35. B	74. A	104. B	134. C	150. C
5. A	11. C	36. A	75. B	105. A	135. A	151. A
6. B	12. B	37. D	76. C	106. C	136. D	152. B
	13. B	38. C	77. C	107. B	137. B	153. D
	14. C	39. D	78. B	108. D	138. D	154. A
	15. B	40. C	79. D	109. C	139. C	155. C
	16. C	41. C	80. C	110. C	140. B	156. D
	17. B	42. B	81. B	111. D	141. D	157. D
	18. B	43. D	82. A	112. C	142. A	158. C
	19. C	44. B	83. C	113. A	143. C	159. B
	20. A	45. C	84. B	114. B	144. D	160. A
	21. A	46. A	85. D	115. C	145. B	161. C
	22. B	47. B	86. D	116. B	146. A	162. A
	23. C	48. D	87. D	117. A		163. B
	24. A	49. A	88. B	118. C		164. D
	25. A	50. C	89. D	119. B		165. C
	26. C	51. B	90. A	120. C		166. B
	27. B	52. B	91. B	121. D		167. D
	28. C	53. C	92. A	122. C		168. C
	29. B	54. A	93. B	123. B		169. A
	30. A	55. B	94. D	124. C		170. C
	31. B	56. D	95. B	125. A		171. C
		57. A	96. A	126. D		172. D
		58. B	97. D	127. D		173. A
		59. A	98. D	128. B		174. C
		60. B	99. C	129. C		175. D
		61. D	100. A	130. D		176. D
		62. B				177. C
		63. C				178. B
		64. D				179. B
		65. A				180. A
		66. D				181. C
		67. B				182. B
		68. A				183. C
		69. C				184. B
		70. B				185. D
						186. D
						187. C
						188. C
						189. A
						190. D
						191. C
						192. B
						193. A
						194. A
						195. C
						196. D
						197. A
						198. C
						199. D
						200. C

PRACTICE TEST 4 ANSWERS AND EXPLANATIONS

Section 1—Listening Comprehension

Part I: Photographs

1. (B)

The photograph shows carrots covered in dirt being pulled out of the earth. **(B)** correctly describes the photograph. There are no *flowers* in the photograph **(A)**. There is no *forest* in the photograph **(C)**. There plants are *vegetables* (carrots), not *trees* **(D)**.

2. (D)

The photograph shows builders putting up scaffolding for building construction. **(D)** describes the photograph; they are building a frame. **(B)** confuses *frame* with *game*. They are building a frame, not *making some dinner* **(C)**.

3. (C)

The photograph shows a man helping a toddler to take her first steps. **(C)** describes the photograph correctly. They are *walking* not *hiking* **(A)**. He is holding the toddler, not *picking a flower* **(B)**. **(D)** confuses *walk* with *talk*.

4. (A)

The photograph shows a technician using tweezers to remove a piece of machinery. **(A)** correctly describes the photograph; the use of tweezers suggests the work is intricate (precise). **(B)** is incorrect, as there is no *document* in the photograph. The technician is using tweezers on computer *hardware*, not *software* **(C)**, and it is being *fixed*, not *downloaded*. There is not sculpture in the photograph and the work is not complete **(D)**.

5. (A)

The photograph shows two people standing with a box in between them. **(A)** correctly describes the image. There is no cabin **(B)** in the photograph. **(C)** confuses *case* with *casing*. The box is sealed, and is not being *unpacked* **(D)**.

6. (B)

The photograph shows a group of people barbecuing food. **(B)** correctly describes the photograph; the group of six is split into two conversations between three people. There is food in the photograph on people's plates and on the barbeque, so **(A)** cannot be correct. The guests are standing and talking, not *leaving* **(C)**. There are no crossed wires in the photograph **(D)**.

Part II: Question-Response

7. (B)

The statement says *I suggest consulting a lawyer before signing a contract.* **(B)** gives a logical response in agreement. **(A)** repeats *consult.* **(C)** repeats *law.*

8. (C)

The question asks *have you ever used this type of device?* **(C)** gives an appropriate Yes/No response. **(A)** discusses *computers* when a single *device* is asked about. **(B)** discusses *trousers*, not a *device*.

9. (A)

The question asks *when can you deliver the shipment to our logistics center?* **(A)** gives a logical time (*next week*). **(B)** gives a mode of transport (*courier*) but does not answer When. **(C)** gives a location (*Main Street*), not a time.

10. (A)

The question asks *where do we keep the expense vouchers?* **(A)** gives an appropriate location as a response. **(B)** answers a Yes/No question. **(C)** discusses *pouches*, which sounds like *vouchers* but is not mentioned in the question.

11. (C)

The statement says *this CD-ROM isn't working right.* **(C)** gives an appropriate response by asking a follow up question (*what's wrong with it?*). **(A)** discusses *DVDs*. **(B)** confuses the meaning of *working* in the sentence.

12. (B)

The question asks *when will you go on vacation?* **(B)** gives an appropriate time in the future. **(A)** gives a destination, not a time. **(C)** gives a time in the past, but the question asks about the future.

13. (B)

The question asks *have you read any good books lately?* **(B)** gives a logical positive response (*I just purchased one online*). **(A)** discusses books (*novels*) but doesn't answer the question. **(C)** discusses the amount of books generally read per month, but doesn't answer the question.

14. (C)

The question asks *can I borrow that pair of scissors on your desk?* **(C)** gives a positive yes/no answer. **(A)** replies to a request to borrow a *desk*, not a *pair of scissors*. **(B)** discusses *scissors* but doesn't answer the question.

15. (B)

The question asks *when are you meeting Mr. Xang next week?* **(B)** gives a logical date. **(A)** repeats *Mr. Xang*, but doesn't answer a When question. **(C)** gives a time *today*, but the question asks about *next week*.

16. (C)

The question asks *how long have you wanted to work for yourself?* **(C)** gives a logical time in the past. **(A)** does not make grammatical sense, and *until* suggests the future, while the question asks about the past. **(B)** answers a Yes/No question.

17. (B)

The question asks *where should we put these boxes?* **(B)** gives a logical location as a response. **(A)** discusses *carrying*, which could relate to moving *boxes*, but does not answer the question.

18. (B)

The question asks *why don't you take a short break?* **(B)** gives an appropriate positive response. **(A)** confuses the meaning of the word *break* in the sentence. **(C)** discusses *work*, but does not answer the question.

19. (C)

The question asks *excuse me, where can I catch the subway going uptown?* **(C)** gives an appropriate location. **(A)** tells them where they are *now*, but the question asks where to go. **(B)** answers a When question, but the question asked is a Where question.

20. (A)

The question asks *you haven't seen the Jenkins report, have you?* Only answer **(A)** makes logical sense. **(B)** and **(C)** are incorrect as they do not make sense.

21. (A)

The question asks *haven't you heard about our merger?* **(A)** gives an appropriate Yes/No response. **(B)** and **(C)** repeat *hear*, but do not answer a Yes/No question.

22. (B)

The question asks *would you please tell him that I called?* Only **(B)** gives a Yes/No answer. **(A)** repeats *tell/told* and **(C)** repeats *call.*

23. (C)

The question asks *do you want juice or milk?* **(C)** responds with an appropriate choice. **(A)** gives an answer in the past tense, but the question is about the future. **(B)** repeats *juice* but does not answer a Choice question.

24. (A)

The question asks *whose car are you driving?* **(A)** gives an appropriate person (*my friend*) in response. **(B)** answers a Where question. **(C)** is irrelevant to the question.

25. (A)

The question asks *which dates will you be overseas next quarter?* **(A)** gives appropriate dates in response. **(B)** gives days of the week, but the question asks about *next quarter*, so dates are required. **(C)** specifies a time frame, but does not give dates.

26. (C)

The question asks *whose jacket is that navy one?* **(C)** gives an appropriate person and response. **(A)** names a person, but does not answer the *jacket* question. **(B)** answers a Where question.

27. (B)

The question asks *who's Mr. Duvall speaking with?* **(B)** gives an appropriate person. **(A)** answers a Where question. **(C)** says Mr. Duvall is not available, but does not answer Who he is speaking with.

28. (C)

The question asks *how many copies of the report do you need?* **(C)** gives an appropriate amount. **(A)** confuses *copies* with the similar sounding *coffee*. **(B)** answers a Yes/No question.

29. (B)

The question asks 'When will we leave for Toronto?' **(B)** gives an appropriate date. **(A)** answers a where question. **(C)** answers in the past, but the question asks about the future.

30. (A)

The question asks *who's in charge of marketing?* **(A)** gives an appropriate person in response. **(B)** answers a Yes/No question. **(C)** answers a Where question.

31. (B)

The question asks *where are you going this evening?* **(B)** gives an appropriate response. **(A)** answers a When question, but does not say Where the speaker is going. **(C)** answers a Why question.

Part III: Short Conversations

32. (B)

This is a Gist question, asking what the speakers were mainly discussing. The man says 'everything on this menu looks amazing. I'm not sure what to order.' **(B)** is correct. *Lobsters*, *steaks*, and *wine* are mentioned in the conversation, but they are not the main topic of conversation.

33. (A)

The woman says *Personally, I recommend the lobster. It's fresh from Maine and it is simply fantastic!* **(A)** is correct. *New York cheesecake* is mentioned, but not *Brooklyn cheesecake* **(C)**. **(B)** and **(D)** are not mentioned in the conversation.

34. (C)

The woman says *have anything you like. It's on the company*. **(C)** is correct. **(A)**, **(B)**, and **(D)** are incorrect as the woman says her company will pay.

35. (B)

This is a Gist question, asking what the woman is doing. The man says *Rebecca, I heard from the head office that you're now in charge of replacing our IT system servers*. **(B)** is correct. **(A)** and **(C)** are not mentioned in the text. **(D)** repeats *server system*, but the old severs are being *replaced*, rather than the *new* severs being *maintained*.

36. (A)

The woman says *I still have some research to do because I want to change vendors as well.* **(A)** is correct. **(B)**, **(C)**, and **(D)** are not mentioned in the conversation.

37. (D)

The man says *I know that Sympatico Solutions have an excellent reputation for 24-hour customer service and support*. **(D)** is correct. **(A)**, **(B)**, and **(C)** are not mentioned in the conversation.

38. (C)

This Gist question asks for the relationship between the two speakers. The man says *once you start working for us*, so the woman is a *candidate* and the man is an *employer*. **(C)** is correct. There is no evidence in the conversation to suggest **(A)**, **(B)**, or **(D)** are correct.

39. (D)

The woman says *I didn't completely understand the non-disclosure agreement clause*. **(D)** is correct. **(A)**, **(B)**, and **(C)** are not mentioned in the conversation.

40. (C)

The woman says *everything looks like it's in order and I am ready to put my signature on the dotted line*. **(C)** is correct. The woman asked a question earlier, but as she says *everything looks like it's in order*, she is unlikely to ask another question. The woman says she's ready to sign a contract, so she is likely to *accept*, not *decline*, the offer. **(D)** is not mentioned in the conversation.

41. (C)

The man says *walk down Trafalgar Street*, so the woman must be traveling on foot; **(C)** is correct. **(A)**, **(B)**, and **(D)** are not mentioned in the conversation.

42. (B)

The woman says *I'm a bit confused right now and I may be lost*. **(B)** is correct. The woman needs directions, but a *map* is not mentioned in the conversation. **(C)** and **(D)** are incorrect as the woman needs to know where to *go*, but she is not in the *wrong place*.

43. (D)

The man says *the best thing to do would be to go east on Broadway*. **(D)** is correct. The woman is going to *Jim's office*, but the man does not suggest that she call Jim. The woman is currently at *Central Street Station*; the man does not suggest that she walk there. **(C)** is not mentioned in the conversation.

44. (B)

The woman says *Marie is vegetarian* and that *she's not going to touch the pasta if there's minced meat on it*. A *vegetarian* is a person who *doesn't eat meat*, so **(B)** is correct. **(A)** is wrong because the woman never says that *Marie doesn't like pasta*. **(C)** is wrong because the man says he will make *pasta* with *tomatoes* for *Marie*, which he wouldn't if she didn't *like* them, and **(D)** is wrong because there's no *ham* on the *pasta—ham* is only mentioned as part of a *joke* about the *starters*.

45. (C)

The man mentions *Marie and her husband*, so **(A)** is incorrect. Since the woman is obsessing over *Marie*, it's likely she is the *boss*, not the *wife* of the *boss*. Finally, while it's true that the man is *cooking*, neither the man nor the woman says this is because *the woman is not good* at it. **(C)** is the correct answer because the man *promises* to make *no tacky jokes*, which must mean he's a *jokester*.

46. (A)

The woman asks about the food the man is preparing and then about the *clothes* he's going to wear. She also says *this is my boss we're talking about* and suggests it will be bad if things don't go well. The man tells her to *relax* because she is stressing herself out. All of this suggests the woman is *anxious*, so **(A)** is correct. It's unlikely the woman is *amused*, as she doesn't seem to find the man's *jokes* funny, and there's no reason to be *disturbed* or *befuddled*, i.e. confused.

47. (B)

The woman says *yesterday we saw a concert by the Screaming Lizards*. **(B)** is correct. The speakers are discussing a *weekend*, not a *weekday*. The speakers discuss a *music concert*, not a *musical*. A *Lemmy* could be a type of award, but this is not their main topic of conversation.

48. (D)

This is an inference question, asking when their conversation takes place. The man asks the woman if she enjoyed her *three-day weekend*, and the woman responds by saying *on Saturday and Sunday we went hiking and camping up on Grouse Mountain and had a picnic while enjoying the splendid scenery, and yesterday we saw a concert*. The conversation must take place on a Tuesday. **(D)** is correct.

49. (A)

The woman says *the band wasn't as exciting as I thought it would be*. **(A)** is correct. **(B)** repeats *awesome*, but the man says this. **(D)** repeats *exciting*, but the woman says *the band wasn't as exciting* as she expected. **(C)** is not mentioned in the conversation.

50. (C)

The woman says *I was in the hospital* and *I wasn't away on holiday or anything*, meaning that **(A)** and **(B)** are wrong. The man then says *I didn't mention you were sick*, which means it was her, not a *family member* who was *ill*, so **(C)** is correct.

51. (B)

The man says *they threatened to go to a competitor if we didn't present something to them*. This means *the client insisted*, so **(B)** is correct. The man never says *he thought the woman wouldn't be able to do it*. While the meeting is described as an *informal chat* by the other woman, the man never says he was the one who *wanted* it—and it was the *client* who *threatened* the man, not *his boss*.

52. (B)

The woman asks: *how was the presentation?* And the other woman replies, *oh, brilliant. They loved it.* This means she's *describing how* it *went*, so **(B)** is correct. **(A)** is wrong because the woman has not been *told* anything—she is the one *telling* something. While the woman says *Mark smashed it*, she never *calls* him *smart*, and there is nothing to *complain about*, as the meeting went well.

53. (C)

The woman asks: *is something wrong with the system? I've been trying to get in for the past ten minutes but it's been kicking me out*. If the *system* has been *kicking* her *out*, it means *she can't get onto* it, so **(C)** is correct. **(A)** and **(B)** are wrong because the woman is experiencing issues with the *system*, not her *laptop*, and **(D)** is wrong because the woman says the *system* doesn't *recognize* her *credentials*, not that *her password has expired*.

54. (A)

The man mentions *IT* are in a *meeting*, and then he says *from what Ian told me, their meeting's going to last three hours*. If Ian is in the *meeting*, he must *work in IT*, so **(A)** is correct. **(B)** is wrong because, according to the woman, *they're going to be in there all day*. **(C)** is wrong because the woman says she will *make phone calls* to others while she *waits* for the *meeting* to finish, and **(D)** is wrong because, while the *IT people* are not *at their desks*, they must be *in the office* if they are having a *meeting*.

55. (B)

One woman asks *what sort of meeting is this* and the other woman says, *oh, yes, of course! It's that planning meeting they mentioned, isn't it?* The question tag (*isn't it*) at the end suggests she is seeking *confirmation*, not offering it, so **(A)** is wrong. It also means she has just *remembered* someone *mentioned* the *meeting* to her, so **(B)** is correct. While *of course* can be used to *agree with something* or *agree to do something*, there is nothing to suggest this is the case here.

56. (D)

This Gist question asks who the speakers are. The man says *we need to drastically reduce our home expenses*. As they live together, the most likely option is that they are *husband and wife*. **(D)** is correct. **(A)**, **(B)**, and **(C)** are not mentioned in the text.

57. (A)

The man says *we could reduce our monthly mortgage payment*. **(A)** is correct. **(B)**, **(C)**, and **(D)** are not mentioned in the conversation.

58. (B)

The woman says *send them an email and make an appointment with them*. **(B)** is correct. **(A)**, **(C)**, and **(D)** are not mentioned in the conversation.

59. (A)

The woman says *he had to go to a branch meeting to clear up a problem*. **(A)** is correct. **(B)** and **(D)** are not mentioned in the conversation. **(C)** repeats *branch*, but it is not specified whether or not Thomas is in a *branch office*.

60. (B)

The woman says *they sent us the wrong emails in the post*. **(B)** is correct. **(A)**, **(C)**, and **(D)** are not mentioned in the conversation.

61. (D)

The woman says *you should call him on his cell.* **(D)** is correct. **(A)** and **(B)** are not mentioned in the text. The woman says Thomas would *rather* be called than emailed.

62. (B)

The woman says *can you look at this list and tell me which type of advertising you think would be the best one for us to spend money on this month?* so the answer must be **(B)**.

63. (C)

The man says *Oh! Sorry, but, are you sure this is a question for me? I'm the project manager, I don't really have any experience with advertising. You should probably check with Maria, in marketing.* He thinks Maria can answer the question better than he can; **(C)** is correct.

64. (D)

The man says *I know it's expensive, but I think we've got to go online*. Looking at the graphic, *internet* is the best match for *go online*, so the man is recommending they spend $60,000. **(D)** is correct.

65. (A)

The man says *I'm just putting together the seating plan for our client dinner next week*. The answer must be **(A)**.

66. (D)

The man says *Bianca and Ewa have already reserved the two rectangular tables for themselves and their clients*, so eliminate **(B)** and **(C)**. The woman says *Let's see, hmm... okay, so I invited 3 clients but one of them can't make it, so this table should be fine for me*. She only has two clients coming, so she only needs three seats, so **(D)** must be correct.

67. (B)

The man says *Well that was the plan, but one of them let me know that they told another of my clients, so I had to quickly invite them too, otherwise it would have been a bit awkward*, so the answer is **(B)**.

68. (A)

The woman says *Sure, so it was for... 6 to 8 people, not sure what I said specifically, and I remember I mentioned a dietary requirement... one of the party can't have lactose, milk, cheese, that sort of thing... I also put in an order for chocolate soufflés for everyone*, so the man most likely works at a restaurant. **(A)** is correct.

69. (C)

The woman says *Hello, I just wanted to call, because I made a reservation for tonight last week, but I didn't make a note of it, and now I've forgotten the time!* The answer is **(C)**.

70. (B)

The woman says *Sure, so it was for... 6 to 8 people, not sure what I said specifically, and I remember I mentioned a dietary requirement... one of the party can't have lactose, milk, cheese, that sort of thing... I also put in an order for chocolate soufflés for everyone*, so the answer is Booking 2; **(B)** is correct.

Part IV: Short Talks

71. (A)

This Gist question asks where the advertisement is most likely being broadcast. The speaker says *from now through this Saturday you can get amazing deals*. The talk is an advertisement offering *discount furniture*. A radio station is the only appropriate location for this to be broadcast. The talk is advertising *furniture*, not *technology*, *train* tickets, or *airline* merchandise. **(B)**, **(C)**, and **(D)** are incorrect.

72. (D)

The Detail question asks what is being offered. The speaker says f*rom now through this Saturday, you can get tremendous deals*. **(D)** is correct; the speaker is offering a special sale. **(A)** repeats *low credit*, but *furniture* is being offered, not *credit*. **(B)** and **(C)** are not mentioned in the talk.

73. (D)

The speaker says *Or this European designed dining table and chairs for only $179*. The region of origin must be Europe, and the new, or sale, price must be $179, so the answer must be **(D)**, item number 3890.

74. (A)

The speaker says *official team jersey, before the end of the game*, and *section 34, row E, seat 186*. **(A)** is correct, the announcement would be most likely to be heard in a stadium. **(B)**, **(C)**, and **(D)** are incorrect as they do not host *games*.

75. (B)

The speaker says *you'll receive a wonderful prize package*. **(B)** is the correct answer. **(A)** is related to sporting games, but is not mentioned in the text. **(C)** repeats *ticket stubs*, but these must be used to receive gifts; they are not being offered. The speaker offers *$10 off a regular car wash*, not a completely free car wash.

76. (C)

The speaker says *Tonight's winner is in section 34, row E, seat 186*, so the winner must be Amna. **(C)** is the correct answer.

77. (C)

The speaker says *the Seabrook City School board has just announced delays and closures*. **(C)** is correct. the *snowstorm* is mentioned, but this is not the purpose of the talk. **(B)** repeats *ice on roads*, but this is not the purpose of the talk. **(D)** is incorrect, as the talk mentions a *website* only to raise awareness of the schedule changes.

78. (B)

The speaker says *buses will pick children up at specially designated bus stop locations*. **(B)** is correct. *Parents are requested to avoid driving and parking*, not to pick their children up. **(C)** and **(D)** are not given as options in the talk.

79. (D)

The speaker says *community colleges, as well as City University, will begin two hours later this morning*. **(D)** is correct. **(A)** is not mentioned in the talk. **(C)** repeats *cancelled*, but it is *after-school activities*, not *community colleges*, that are cancelled. **(B)** repeats *three*, but *schools*, not *community colleges* will open *two to three hours later*.

80. (C)

The speaker says *for a company such as ours*. **(C)** must be correct. **(A)** is incorrect as the speaker discusses a *company*, not a *school*. **(B)** and **(D)** are incorrect, as the speaker is part of the company (*a company such as ours*), not an outside recruiter or specialist

81. (B)

The speaker says *we distribute staff salaries on a weekly basis*. **(B)** is the only possible option. **(A)** is less than weekly. **(C)** is not mentioned in the talk. **(D)** is more than weekly.

82. (A)

The speaker says *the most important question that we need to ask ourselves is how do we attract and retain customers?* **(A)** is correct. **(B)** discusses a single *patron*, but the speaker discusses many customers. **(C)** and **(D)** are not mentioned in the text.

83. (C)

The speaker says *This is Pat Sullivan with the evening traffic report for WKRP traffic radio*. **(C)** is correct. The speaker specifies that it is being broadcast on *radio*, so **(A)**, **(B)**, and **(D)** cannot be correct.

84. (B)

The speaker says *the commute tonight is extremely slow*. **(B)** is correct. **(A)** and **(C)** are incorrect as the best route is *moving slowly*, so the traffic is not *flowing smoothly* anywhere, and is not *lighter than usual*. **(D)** mistakes the meaning of *commute* and *traffic*.

85. (D)

The speaker says *this report is brought to you by Kangaroo Cola*. **(D)** is correct. **(A)**; Pat Sullivan is the radio host, not the sponsor. **(B)** gives the radio station, not the sponsor. **(C)** repeats an area which is experiencing delays, but is not the sponsor.

86. (D)

The speaker says *workers in your department* and *as managers, it's your duty*. **(D)** must be correct. **(A)** repeats *employees* but there is no suggestion that the speaker is addressing *new* employees. **(B)** and **(C)** are incorrect, the speaker is addressing *managers* at the company, not *customers or investors.*

87. (D)

The speaker says *staff have complained that they are too tired and too busy*. **(D)** is correct. **(A)** and **(C)** are not mentioned in the talk. **(B)** repeats *advantage*, but confuses the meaning of the word in the text.

88. (B)

The speaker says *I propose that we hire a presenter, Tom Thompson, to give our employees a motivational lecture*. **(B)** is correct. **(A)** repeats *hire*, but a *motivational speaker* will be hired, not a *consultant*. **(C)** repeats *classes*, but the speaker is highlighting lack of attendance at classes, not suggesting they add more. **(D)** repeats *technology*, but the speaker does not suggest switching to a different *technology school.*

89. (D)

The speaker says *bigger and more exciting than any other water parks in the state*. **(D)** is correct. **(A)** and **(C)** are not mentioned in the talk. The speaker says *we are open for the summer*, suggesting the park is not open throughout the year.

90. (A)

The speaker says *we are now offering special discount family packages*. **(A)** is correct. *boogie boards* are part of the water park, and are not being offered as a discount. **(C)** and **(D)** are not mentioned in the talk.

91. (B)

The speaker says *This offer is only until June 30th so to order please call 333–5464 or access our website at www.wildwatersadventures.com and receive an additional 5% off the package price! We're the best value Water Park in the area. Don't wait!* The speaker is not advising listeners to visit the water park immediately, but he is advising them to book the offer now. **(B)** is the correct answer.

92. (A)

The speaker says *The question I'm probably asked the most by people I meet is: Why do you do it? Sometimes I wonder myself. It's hard work to start any business from nothing but an idea or a dream*. The woman is saying that she's not always sure why she runs her own business. The answer is **(A)**.

93. (B)

The speaker says *this current venture is my 12th start-up company*. **(B)** is correct. **(D)** is the speaker's age. **(A)** and **(C)** are not mentioned in the talk.

94. (D)

The speaker says *honestly, I can't imagine doing anything else for the rest of my life*. **(D)** is correct. **(A)**, **(B)**, and **(C)** are not mentioned in the talk.

95. (B)

The speaker says *I have a special public service message*. **(B)** is correct. The service offered is *free*, the speaker is not selling anything. The speaker warns against *drinking alcohol* while driving. **(D)** is not mentioned in the talk.

96. (A)

The speaker talks about *drinking alcohol* and *driving*. The intended audience must be adults. Children would not be old enough to drink alcohol or drive. Woman are not specifically mentioned. **(D)** repeats *friends*, but the service is for anyone.

97. (D)

The speaker says *if you do happen to find yourself too drunk to drive, please call 555-TAXI for a special, free holiday taxi ride anywhere with the city limits*. **(D)** is correct. **(A)** repeats *a little bit of good cheer*, but this is not being offered. **(B)** repeats *designated drivers*, but arranging this is being recommended, not offered. **(C)** is not mentioned in the talk.

98. (D)

The speaker says *me and the other members of this coaching staff*, and also says *you can win the games this season* and *win the championship*. The speaker is likely to be the coach of a sports team. **(D)** is correct. **(A)**, **(B)**, and **(C)** are not mentioned in the talk.

99. (C)

The speaker says *whatever happened under the previous regime will not affect how you're treated by me and the other members of the coaching staff.* **(C)** is correct. **(A)** and **(B)** are addressed to the team, not the coaching staff. **(D)** repeats *failures*, but the speaker says these can be moved on from.

100. (A)

The speaker says *the most important thing is for you to believe that you can win games this season.* **(A)** is correct. The speaker is attempting to motivate the team, not inform, educate or entertain. **(B)**, **(C)**, and **(D)** are incorrect.

Section 2—Reading Comprehension

Part V: Incomplete Sentences

101. (C)

This is a grammar question. *Investigated* requires a phrase in the past tense. **(C)** must be correct. **(A)** and **(B)** give the present tense. **(D)** gives the future tense.

102. (D)

This is a grammar question. The sentence needs a noun which could *predict*, most likely an employee. **(D)** must be correct. **(A)** gives a noun, but means detailed examination, not a type of employee. **(B)** gives an adjective. **(C)** gives a verb.

103. (C)

This is a vocabulary question. The missing word must pair with the negative word *hardly*. *Any* is used in negative sentences, so must be correct. *None* and *all* would not make sense paired with *hardly*, which means very little. *Few* would be used with countable nouns and would not pair with *hardly*.

104. (B)

This is a vocabulary question. The missing word must pair with *account*. *For* must be correct. *By* does not pair with account and does not describe the *missing inventory*. *To* would be used if the manager was accounting information to someone else, but the manager is accounting for *missing inventory*. The manager could not account *with* missing inventory.

105. (A)

This is a grammar question. The missing word must pair with a group of people (*sales executives*). **(A)** must be correct. **(C)** does not pair with people, but objects. **(B)** and **(D)** would be used for one person, not many.

106. (C)

This is a grammar question. The missing word must describe *facilities*. The gerund *manufacturing* pairs with *facilities* correctly. *Manufacturer* is a noun. *Manufactured* and *manufacture* are verbs.

107. (B)

This is a grammar question. The correct answer must give the past tense of *rise* which pairs with *has*. **(B)** is correct. **(C)** gives the past tense, but *rose* would not be paired with *has*. **(A)** gives the present tense. **(D)** gives the past tense, but it does not pair with *has* and would typically be used with a physical object, not the *threat of inflation*.

108. (D)

This is a vocabulary question. *Regardless* is the only word which would pair with *of*. **(A)**, **(B)**, and **(D)** would never be followed by *of*.

109. (C)

This is a grammar question. The missing word must modify *due* in the sentence. **(B)** and **(D)** would not be used to modify *due*. **(A)** could be used, but would mean that the increase in sales had been avoided being caused by the *marketing campaign*. This does not make sense in the sentence, so **(C)**—which also pairs with *due*—is correct.

110. (C)

This is a vocabulary question. The missing word is a connective. As the first clause of the sentence causes the second clause of the sentence, the missing word must signify this. **(C)** is correct. **(A)**, **(B)**, and **(D)** would not make sense in the sentence.

111. (D)

The missing word is a verb in the present continuous tense which must pair with the plural noun *security guards*. **(D)** is correct. **(C)** would be used for one *security guard*. **(A)** and **(B)** would be used for a future event.

112. (C)

This is a grammar question. The missing word must be a verb which means *complete*. **(C)** is correct. **(A)** and **(D)** are nouns. **(B)** is an adverb.

113. (A)

This is a grammar question. The missing word is a verb in the present tense. **(A)** is correct. **(B)** could not be used in the sentence without a modifier. **(C)** gives the past tense. **(D)** gives the root verb.

114. (B)

This is a grammar question. **(B)** is the only phrase to make sense in the sentence. **(A)** and **(D)** are not correct English. **(C)** gives the past tense.

115. (C)

This is a vocabulary question. The missing word is the preposition which is used to with a specific time in the day (*10:30*). **(C)** is correct. **(A)** would be used for a date (let's meet *on* the 4th of December). **(D)** would be used for a month (I can see you *in* August). **(B)** would not be used for time.

116. (B)

This is a grammar question. The missing word is a verb in the future tense which pairs with *advocated*. **(B)** is correct. **(A)** gives the past tense. **(C)** gives the present tense. **(D)** gives the root verb.

117. (A)

This is a grammar question. The missing phrase or word will be in the future conditional. **(A)** is correct. **(B)** and **(D)** are in the past tense. **(C)** is in the present tense.

118. (C)

This is a grammar question. The sentence explains that additional items come with *your new PC tablet*. **(C)** gives the correct answer. **(A)** would be used if the included items followed the missing word, but they come before it. **(B)** gives the present tense, but the past is needed. **(D)** gives the past tense, but does not include the preposition *is*.

119. (B)

This is a vocabulary question. The missing word must describe a travel deal which includes *airfare and other transportation*. **(B)** is correct. **(A)** gives a similar meaning to *tour*. **(C)** and **(D)** have a similar meaning to *packages*, but while *packages* can be used for physical items as well as pricing plans, *boxes* and *parcels* are used for physical items only and could not contain *transportation* or *airfare*.

120. (C)

This is a vocabulary question. The missing word is a connective which should show that the first clause of the sentence causes the second. **(C)** is correct. **(A)** and **(D)** would be used if the clauses were negative. **(B)** would be used in the middle of the sentence, not the beginning.

121. (D)

This is a vocabulary question. The missing word must be a verb in the future tense. **(D)** is correct. **(B)** and **(C)** sound similar to *file* but mean to trip over. **(A)** gives the present tense.

122. (C)

This is a vocabulary question. The missing word must give the future tense, as the *guest porters* will be *recruited* in the future. **(C)** is correct. **(A)** and **(B)** give the past tense. **(D)** does not make sense in the sentence.

123. (B)

This is a grammar question. The verb must pair with a singular *train* in the future tense. **(B)** is correct. **(A)** would be used for more than one train departing at 15:45. **(C)** gives the root verb. **(D)** gives the present tense.

124. (C)

This is a vocabulary question. It only makes sense for the *vice president* to sit next to (*beside*) the *CEO at the awards dinner*. **(C)** is correct. **(A)** would mean that the vice president took on the role of CEO for the dinner. **(B)** and **(D)** do not make sense in the sentence, as the vice president could not sit inside or on top of the CEO.

125. (A)

This is a grammar question. The sentence requires the root verb *to work* as the past tense has been given. **(B)** and **(D)** give the past tense, but this is already given in the sentence, so the root verb is required. **(C)** is a noun, and the sentence needs a verb.

126. (D)

This is a vocabulary question. All of the answer choices mean to go up in a physical sense (for example, when climbing a mountain), but the sentence talks about the increase of *overall circulation*, which is not a physical increase. Only **(D)** can be correct.

127. (D)

This is a grammar question. The correct answer will give the future tense for one person (*the chief of IT system administration*). *Is going* is the correct answer. **(A)** needs a preposition, but does not give one. **(B)** would be used if more than one person *was going*. **(C)** gives the present tense.

128. (B)

This is a vocabulary question. The missing word will mean 'to make necessary'. *Require* gives this meaning, and is therefore the correct answer. **(A)** means 'to regard with approval'. **(C)** means 'to procure more staff'. **(D)** means 'to become known'.

129. (C)

This is a vocabulary question. The correct answer will give an appropriate emotion for the *ticketholders*, as a result of the *change of date*. Only **(C)**, *confused*, is appropriate. None of the other answers give emotions.

130. (D)

This is a vocabulary question. The correct answer will describe one of *Mr. Moss*'s personal qualities. Only **(D)** could be used to describe a person. **(A)** and **(B)** relate to footwear. **(C)** means many.

Part VI: Text Completion

131. (C)

This is a vocabulary question. The missing word is a verb which should relate to *patrons* being aware of *thieves*. **(C)** is correct. **(A)** is a noun. **(B)** means to arrest, which would relate to the *thieves*, but not the patrons. **(D)** could be used if followed the preposition *to*.

132. (A)

This is a vocabulary question. The missing word must mean in the past, as the thefts have already occurred. Only **(A)** means in the past. **(B)**, **(C)** and **(D)** would all be used to refer to weeks in the future.

133. (B)

This is a vocabulary question. The missing word will be a noun which relates to the *nightclub* being of the *highest quality*. **(B)** is correct. **(A)** would be used if a certificate had been issued, but this is not mentioned in the text. **(C)** would be used if the nightclub was low-quality, rather than high quality. **(D)** sounds like *reputation* but means to act or speak on behalf of someone else.

134. (C)

This is a vocabulary question. The answer will give a location. **(C)** must be correct. **(A)** means to give word to do something. **(B)** means to introduce. **(D)** means to make attempts.

135. (A)

This is a vocabulary question. The correct answer will give a noun which will pair with emergency. **(A)** is correct. **(B)** is incorrect, as it means an arrangement to do something at a specific time. **(C)** means to react to. **(D)** means to talk with.

136. (D)

This is a vocabulary question. The correct answer must pair with *number* and relate to the rest of the text. **(D)** is correct.

137. (B)

This is a vocabulary question. The missing word must be a noun which means *sent*. **(B)** must be correct. **(A)** is incorrect as it means changed. **(C)** is incorrect as it means removed. **(D)** is incorrect as it means expelled.

138. (D)

This is a vocabulary question. The correct answer must be a word which could describe *materials*. **(D)** is correct. **(A)**, **(C)**, and **(D)** could not be used to describe materials.

139. (C)

This is a vocabulary question. The correct answer will pair with *to my attention*. **(C)** is correct. **(A)** gives the correct meaning but is in the present tense, and the information has been discovered in the past. **(B)** rhymes with *brought*, but does not give the correct meaning. **(D)** has a similar meaning, but would not pair with *to my attention*.

140. (B)

This is a vocabulary question. The correct answer will give a synonym for *allow*. **(B)** is correct. **(A)** means to be thankful for. **(C)** means to talk with. **(D)** means to be forced to do something.

141. (D)

This is a vocabulary question. The correct answer will connect the two clauses of the sentence. As the second clause will be the result of the first clause, **(D)** is correct. The other answers are all unsuitable connectives.

142. (A)

This is a vocabulary question. The correct answer will give a synonym for *know* which will make sense in the sentence. **(A)** is correct. **(B)** means to warn. **(C)** means to be worried about something or someone. **(D)** gives the correct meaning, but uses a noun when the sentence needs a verb.

143. (C)

The sentence needs a word that means 'make sure of' or 'give officially'. Only *confirm* offers an appropriate word to complete the sentence. **(A)** means *say*, which is inappropriate in the sentence. **(B)** means *ask*, but the email is giving information, not asking for information. **(D)** means to form a team again, so is inappropriate in the sentence.

144. (D)

The paragraph with the missing word discusses that the company will need to receive at least one reference in order for Robert to accept the job. As such, these references will be *looked for or requested* before Robert's employment. Only **(D)** offers an appropriate word to complete the sentence. **(A)** is inappropriate, as the details need to be asked for, not simply *found*. **(B)** and **(C)** are words that mean *told* and *given*, but the references need to be *asked for* or *taken*.

145. (B)

The paragraph discusses what will happen on Robert's first day at work. The sentence tells Robert what he should do when he first gets to work, therefore the idiom *upon arrival* is most appropriate. **(A)** and **(C)** describe doing something at the same time as another, but Robert is not being asked to do anything else. **(D)** means *when pressured*, which has a negative connotation, and is unlikely to happen on Robert's first day.

146. (A)

The text needs a sentence to complete the last paragraph, so a concluding sentence about Robert starting work would be most appropriate. **(A)** gives the only appropriate response. **(B)** would be a response given by Robert, not a concluding sentence given by Rebecca. **(C)** cannot be correct, as the email says that the contract is attached to the email, so Robert will not receive the contract in the future. **(D)** is a concluding sentence, but it thanks someone for their support, and as Robert has not yet started to work with Rebecca, it is unlikely that he has offered her support yet.

Part VII: Reading Comprehension

147. (A)

This question asks for the gist of the article. The first sentence of the article says 'Klankstown Station is set to close for two weeks;' **(A)** is correct. **(B)** are **(C)** are incorrect; although high-speed trains and a shopping mall are mentioned, this information has already been 'officially announced last month', so the purpose of the article is not to announce this. **(D)** is incorrect as a train station is being renovated, a new train is not being constructed.

148. (B)

This question asks which station will be open when Klankstown Station is closed. The text says 'some routes will still be running with diversions via Wakon Station,' so Wakon Station must be open while Klankstown is closed. **(B)** is correct. **(A)** mentions a shopping mall, which has not yet been built. **(C)** and **(D)** mention stations which will be connected to Klankstown by high-speed trains *after* construction is finished, but it is not said that they will be open during renovations.

149. (D)

This question asks who will experience a 30-minute delay. Scanning the text, 30-minute delays are mentioned in the second paragraph. The text says 'routes will still be running with diversions via Wakon Station, but passengers should expect a delay of at least 30 minutes;' passengers traveling through Wakon will experience a 30-minute delay, **(D)** is correct. **(A)** cannot be true, as passengers cannot use Klankstown Station while it is closed. **(B)** and **(C)** are mentioned in the article, but not in relation to a 30-minute delay.

150. (C)

This question asks you to choose the best position in the text for the sentence. Scanning the sentence, the keywords are *Klankstown Station's renovations and streamlined service. Service* is mentioned in the fourth paragraph, which also mentions *high-speed*, which has a similar meaning to *streamlined*. As the beginning of this paragraph discusses the high-speed service, whereas the end of the paragraph discusses a new mall, this sentence should appear at the beginning of the paragraph. The sentence should occupy position [3]; **(C)** is correct.

151. (A)

This is a Gist question, asking for the purpose of the notice. The text says *WATER SHORTAGE WARNING AND WATER USAGE ANNOUNCEMENT.* The correct answer is **(A)**. **(B)**, **(C)**, and **(D)** are not mentioned in the text.

152. (B)

This is a Detail question, asking about the actions the water utility companies are authorized to take. The text says *public and privately owned water utilities shall limit the monthly usage of water by their customers. They may do this by interrupting supply*. The answer is **(B)**. **(A)**, **(C)**, and **(D)** are not mentioned in the text.

153. (D)

This is an Inference question, asking when farmers can water their crops. The text says *for agricultural businesses, irrigation is now restricted between the hours of 7 P.M. and midnight.* The correct answer is **(D)**. **(A)** and **(C)** are not mentioned in the text. **(B)** gives the times when *residents with odd-numbered houses* can use the water supply.

154. (A)

This is a Gist question, asking where the notice would be posted. The text says *certain experiments require the handling of dangerous and toxic chemicals and materials*. The correct answer is **(A)**, as experiments would only be carried out in a lab. **(B)**, **(C)**, and **(D)** are all inappropriate places for experiments to be carried out.

155. (C)

This is a Detail question, asking for the first thing to be done after a chemical is spilled. The text says *extinguish any ignition source (burners, appliances, and other equipment) and move to a safe distance.* **(C)** is correct. **(A)** and **(D)** are actions to be taken **after** the first step. **(B)** is not mentioned in the text.

156. (D)

This is a Detail question, asking how contaminated materials should be disposed of. The text says *place contaminated materials in the container designated for hazardous waste*. The answer is **(D)**. **(A)**, **(B)**, and **(C)** are not mentioned in the text.

157. (D)

This is a Detail question, asking who should be contacted for disposal. The text says *Contact Environmental Health and Safety personnel.* **(D)** is correct. **(A)**, **(B)**, and **(C)** are mentioned elsewhere in the text, but are not related to disposal.

158. (C)

This is an Inference question, asking for the maximum number of years an elected member can serve on the board. The text says *society board members are elected for a three-year term and may not serve more than two consecutive terms*. **(C)** is correct. **(A)**, **(B)**, and **(D)** are not mentioned in the text.

159. (B)

This is a Detail question, asking how society members can vote in the election. The text says *please return your enclosed vote to us by midnight on November 16th* and mentions a *stamped addressed envelope* to be used. **(B)** is correct. **(A)** is mentioned, but has already occurred, and the voting has not yet occurred. **(C)** and **(D)** are not mentioned in the text.

160. (A)

This is a Detail question, asking what is not included with the letter. The text says *the profiles of the four candidates standing for election are enclosed in a separate document. You will also find a postal ballot form and a stamped addressed envelope*. The only answer not mentioned is **(A)**, which must be correct.

161. (C)

This is a Detail question, asking who participated in the survey. The text says *this survey by the Vermillion Consulting Group involved the participation of 100 chief executives from the top 300 corporations all across the country*. **(C)** is correct. **(A)** and **(B)** are not mentioned in the text. **(D)** repeats *47 executives* from the text but does not answer the question.

162. (A)

This is a Gist question, asking what the survey revealed. The text says *the majority of top management work most effectively outside typical office hours*. **(A)** is correct. **(B)**, **(C)**, and **(D)** are not mentioned in the text.

163. (B)

This is a Detail question, asking for the percentage of people who worked on Saturday and Sunday. The text says *65% worked over the weekends*. **(B)** is correct. **(A)** gives the number of executives who work before office hours. **(C)** gives the percentage of executives who preferred working in the mornings to afternoons. **(D)** gives the percentage of executives who work at home in the evenings.

164. (D)

This is a Gist question, asking what the memorandum discusses. The email says *Subject: New Phone Communications Systems*. **(D)** is correct. **(A)**, **(B)**, and **(C)** all discuss *telephones* and *telecommunications*, but do not talk about buying new phones, which is the purpose of the email.

165. (C)

This is a Detail question, asking what people should do after reading the email. The text says *please read the materials carefully and send your recommendations to me*. **(C)** is correct, as the sender's name (*Eloise Rogers*) is given at the bottom of the email. **(A)**, **(B)**, and **(D)** are not mentioned in the text.

166. (B)

This is a Detail question, asking for a criterion for selecting the equipment. The text says *the system should be able to handle at least one hold line and eight extension lines*. **(B)** is correct. **(A)**, **(C)**, and **(D)** are not mentioned in the text.

167. (D)

This is a Gist question, asking who the conference is most likely to be aimed at. The text says *we would like to welcome you to the TRT Cloud Technology International Symposium. TRT employees from over thirty countries will be in attendance at this year's event*. **(D)** is correct. **(A)**, **(B)**, and **(C)** are not mentioned in the text.

168. (C)

This is a Detail question, asking for the purpose of the invitation. The text says *sign up at the registration desk for insightful seminars, special dinners, lunches, or breakfast meetings that are described below*. **(C)** is correct. **(A)**, **(B)**, and **(D)** are not mentioned in the text.

169. (A)

This is an Inference question, asking which session would be most likely to deal with human resources. The Wednesday Dinner will discuss *International Personnel and HR Management Issues*. **(A)** is correct. **(B)**, **(C)**, and **(D)** do not discuss human resources.

170. (C)

This Detail question asks how many nationalities are expected to attend the symposium. The text says *TRT employees from over thirty countries will be in attendance*. **(C)** is correct. **(A)**, **(B)**, and **(D)** are not mentioned in the text.

171. (C)

This Gist question asks you where the notice would most likely be seen. The text says *Aurora IT Solutions New Security Protocols* and later says that *devices must be scanned upon entry to this building*. **(C)** is correct. **(A)**, **(B)**, and **(D)** are not mentioned in the text.

172. (D)

This is a Detail question, which asks what will happen if a flash drive is not declared. The text says *failure to declare USB flash drives will result in immediate confiscation*. **(D)** is correct. **(A)**, **(B)**, and **(C)** are not mentioned in the text.

173. (A)

This Gist question asks who the notice is intended for. The text says *rapid economic development, strong GDP performance, an attractive environment for FDI, and geographic proximity to China and ASEAN make VIETNAM an extremely attractive market for US and EU manufacturers*. **(A)** is correct. **(B)** is discussed in the text, but the notice is intended for EU and US manufacturers. **(C)** and **(D)** are not mentioned in the text.

174. (C)

This is a Detail question, which asks what makes Vietnam an attractive market. The text says *rapid economic development, strong GDP performance, an attractive environment for FDI, and geographic proximity to China and ASEAN make VIETNAM an extremely attractive market for US and EU manufacturers*. **(C)** is correct. **(A)**, **(B)**, and **(D)** are not mentioned in the text.

175. (D)

This Inference question asks when sales are expected to level off. The text says *sales of these products are projected to climb from USD $261 million this year and peak at nearly $800 million by FY 2021*. The current date is given at the top of the notice as *2016*, so the answer is **(D)**, five years. **(A)**, **(B)**, and **(C)** are not mentioned in the text.

176. (D)

This Gist question asks for the best heading for the notice. The text says *Course Deposits and Withdrawal Policy*, **(D)** is correct. **(A)**, **(B)**, and **(C)** are not mentioned in the text.

177. (C)

This is a Detail question. The text says *deposits are refundable if notice of cancellation is received at least 14 days prior to the reservation period*, *less a $10 handling charge*. **(C)** is correct. **(A)** and **(B)** are not mentioned in the text. **(D)** is the total deposit.

178. (B)

This is a Detail question. The text says *transfer of deposit to another session is contingent upon availability of space in that session.* **(B)** is correct. **(A)** repeats *handling charge* but does not relate to *transferring courses*. **(C)** and **(D)** are not mentioned in the text.

179. (B)

This is a Detail question. The text says *deposit may be transferred to another session if notice of change is received at least 7 days prior to original date of enrollment.* **(B)** is correct. **(A)**, **(C)**, and **(D)** are not mentioned in the text.

180. (A)

This Gist question asks you what the customer's email requests. The email says *I have not received my refund as of now and would like to inquire about the current status of my refund and when I am going to receive notice from your organization about my deposit.* **(A)** is correct. **(B)**, **(C)**, and **(D)** relate to *training* and *courses*, but do not answer the question.

181. (C)

This Gist question asks you what event is being advertised. The text says *an auction for the estate of Martin McDonald has been set for Sunday, June 29, at 12:00 noon.* **(C)** is correct. **(A)**, **(B)**, and **(D)** are not mentioned in the text.

182. (B)

This Detail question asks where the event will be held. The text says *a preview of the estate starts at 10:00 A.M. at the McDonald residence at 825 Somerset Boulevard.* **(B)** is correct. **(A)**, **(C)**, and **(D)** are not mentioned in the text.

183. (C)

This Detail question asks for the answer which is not available at the auction. The text says the auction will include a *1963 Convertible Sports Car*. **(C)**, a *1963 Hatchback Car*, is not included in the items mentioned for sale, so must be incorrect. **(A)**, **(B)**, and **(D)** are all mentioned in the listing.

184. (B)

This Detail question asks you what the man is enquiring about in his email. The text says *my client would be prepared to purchase at a premium by bank certified check the Aviator Goggles Collection before the auction takes place.* **(B)** is correct. **(A)**, **(C)**, and **(D)** are mentioned in the listing, but not in the email.

185. (D)

This Detail question asks how the man would like to pay for the auction item. The email says *my client would be prepared to purchase at a premium by bank certified check.* **(D)** is correct. **(A)**, **(B)**, and **(C)** are not mentioned in the text.

186. (D)

This Detail question asks what was sent to Mr Browning with the letter. The text says *you will find an enclosed copy of the transmittal form signed by Mr. Benson. Transmittal* is a synonym for *shipping*, so **(D)** is correct. **(A)**, **(B)**, and **(C)** are not mentioned in the text.

187. (C)

This Gist question asks for the event which occurred. The text says *a member of your staff delivered two boxes of goods to the Magnolia Beauty Cure facility that had been damaged in transit.* **(C)** is correct. **(A)** and **(B)** places blame and give directions, but do not explain what happened. **(D)** suggests an action, but does not explain what happened.

188. (C)

This Detail question asks what Ms. Anderson wants Mr. Browning to do. The email says *we expect you to pick up the boxes immediately at absolutely no cost to Mr. Benson or Satin Smooth Skin Care.* **(C)** is correct. **(A)**, **(B)**, and **(D)** are not mentioned in the text.

189. (A)

This Detail question asks how Mr. Browning attempts to apologize to Ms. Anderson. The email says *you will receive a full refund and the next shipment that you will make with our company will be free of charge.* **(A)** is correct. **(B)** mistakes the apologies in the *email* for apologies in *person*, which is not mentioned. **(C)** and **(D)** are not mentioned in the text.

190. (D)

Fred writes *I have not dated the voucher, so please write in the date that you receive this letter*. The letter is received on August 25th, 2019. The voucher states that it will expire in one year, so it will expire on August 25th, 2020. **(D)** is correct.

191. (C)

This Gist question asks why Ms. Pennington is going to Santiago. The text says *we will be pleased to welcome you to our headquarters for the end of year auditing procedures*. **(C)** is correct. **(A)**, **(B)**, and **(D)** are not mentioned in the text.

192. (B)

This Detail question asks why Ms. Pennington might need to contact Mr. Seymour prior to her arrival. Ms. Pennington's email says *unfortunately, my schedule has suddenly changed due to an urgent personal matter so I will be arriving in Chile on a different flight and on a different day*. **(B)** is correct. **(A)**, **(C)**, and **(D)** are not mentioned in the email.

193. (A)

This Inference question asks where Ms. Pennington is likely to have her midday meals. The text says *we have arranged for you to have prepaid lunches at our staff cafeteria*. **(A)** is correct. **(B)** and **(C)** are mentioned in the email, but as Ms. Pennington also offers the company dietary information, and requests that her *food requirements* are taken care of while working at the office, it is most likely that Ms. Pennington will eat at the staff cafeteria. **(D)** is not mentioned in the text.

194. (A)

This Detail question asks when Ms. Pennington will arrive in Santiago. The text says *I intend to arrive in Santiago on United Airways Flight 72 on Tuesday, February 1st at 9:30 P.M.* **(A)** is correct. **(B)** and **(C)** are not mentioned in the text. **(D)** is the date Ms. Pennington was originally scheduled to arrive, but her email mentions that she will travel on Tuesday instead

195. (C)

This Detail question asks for Ms. Pennington's special requests. The email says *I need to inform you that I am a vegetarian (including no dairy or eggs) and would like to request that my food requirements are taken care of.* **(C)** is correct. **(A)**, **(B)**, and **(D)** are not mentioned in the text.

196. (D)

The student account offers up to £2,000 for an overdraft, which is the greatest amount. **(D)** is correct.

197. (A)

The information in the Basic Account states *a daily limit of £300 in cash withdrawals*. **(A)** is correct.

198. (C)

The text says *If you'd like to make an appointment, bear in mind that following our commitment at the start of 2018 to provide our staff with better working hours and conditions, only ten, centrally located branches nationwide remain open on Saturdays*, so the author is reminding the reader that some branches will not be open on Saturday. **(C)** is correct.

199. (D)

The email states *Thanks for getting in touch with your questions about one of our accounts* and provides further information. The answer is **(D)**.

200. (C)

The email gives further details about the membership gift choices, which are only available for those opening a special account, so the answer is **(C)**.

PART SIX

Listening Scripts

CHAPTER 3 LISTENING SCRIPTS

Track 1

(Narrator)	Let us begin with sample directions for the Listening Comprehension Section of the TOEIC exam.
(Narrator)	For each question, you will hear four statements about the picture in your test book. When you hear the statements, choose the one statement that best describes what you see in the picture. Then, find the number of the question on your answer sheet and mark your answer. The statements will not be written in your test book and will be spoken just once.
(Narrator)	Now listen to the four statements.
(Narrator)	*A.*
(Woman A)	*They're leaving the office.*
(Narrator)	*B.*
(Woman A)	*They're turning off the machine.*
(Narrator)	*C.*
(Woman A)	*They're gathered around the table.*
(Narrator)	*D.*
(Woman A)	*They're eating at a restaurant.*
(Narrator)	Choice (C), "They're gathered around the table," best describes what you see in the picture.
(Narrator)	Let us begin with number one. Go on to the next page.

(Narrator)	Number 1
(Narrator)	Look at the picture marked number 1 in your book.
(Man A)	**A** He is sorting envelopes into the boxes.
	B All of the boxes are filled to capacity.
	C He is writing letters to his colleagues.
	D The squares are stacked on top of each other.

(Narrator)	Number 2
(Narrator)	Look at the picture marked number 2 in your book.
(Woman A)	**A** The cable is old and rusty.
	B The wire is in front of the school.
	C The cable is coiled on spools.
	D The spools are being delivered by truck.

(Narrator)	Number 3
(Narrator)	Look at the picture marked number 3 in your book.
(Man B)	**A.** Several parking spots are available.
	B. A parking attendant is counting the cars.
	C. The people are getting into their cars.
	D. The parking lot is completely filled.

(Narrator)	Number 4
(Narrator)	Look at the picture marked number 4 in your book.
(Woman B)	**A.** The woman is watching television.
	B. The woman is sending a business contract from her cell phone.
	C. The phone is being used.
	D. The woman is walking down the staircase.
(Narrator)	Number 5
(Narrator)	Look at the picture marked number 5 in your book.
(Man A)	**A.** He is taking inventory at the store.
	B. He is putting pants on the hanger.
	C. He is hanging the pictures on the wall.
	D. He is hemming the pants at the shop.
(Narrator)	Number 6
(Narrator)	Look at the picture marked number 6 in your book.
(Woman A)	**A.** They are checking all the boxes.
	B. They are looking at the departure board.
	C. They have just departed from the plane.
	D. They are all looking bored.
(Narrator)	Number 7
(Narrator)	Look at the picture marked number 7 in your book.
(Man B)	**A.** The housekeeper is making the bed.
	B. The woman is going to bed.
	C. The sheets need changing.
	D. The maid is folding towels.
(Narrator)	Number 8
(Narrator)	Look at the picture marked number 8 in your book.
(Woman B)	**A.** The equipment is full of dirt.
	B. The vehicle is being driven on the highway.
	C. He's working under the trees.
	D. The man is operating construction equipment.
(Narrator)	Number 9
(Narrator)	Look at the picture marked number 9 in your book.
(Man A)	**A.** The man is leaving the store with the boards.
	B. The boards are being sawed in the back room.
	C. The store sells lumber.
	D. The store is filled with many customers.

(Narrator)	Number 10
(Narrator)	Look at the picture marked number 10 in your book.
(Woman A)	**A.** The women are being shown to their table.
	B. The waitress has spilled soup on her sleeve.
	C. The women are getting ready to leave.
	D. The waitress is serving dessert to her customers.
(Narrator)	Number 11
(Narrator)	Look at the picture marked number 11 in your book.
(Man B)	**A.** He is looking at his watch.
	B. He watches his step while he walks.
	C. He is watching something below.
	D. He is washing the glass under the railing.
(Narrator)	Number 12
(Narrator)	Look at the picture marked number 12 in your book.
(Woman B)	**A.** The nurse is entering patient information into the computer.
	B. She attends to the sick patient all by herself.
	C. She is standing patiently while she waits for the doctor.
	D. The nurse is writing notes on the paper.
(Narrator)	Number 13
(Narrator)	Look at the picture marked number 13 in your book.
(Man A)	**A.** He is cooking meat at the restaurant.
	B. The butcher packs meat on small trays.
	C. He meets his deadline for unpacking the trays.
	D. The chef is chopping the meat into small pieces.
(Narrator)	Number 14
(Narrator)	Look at the picture marked number 14 in your book.
(Woman A)	**A.** She is stacking boxes on top of each other.
	B. She is putting groceries on the shelf.
	C. She is getting a refund at the store.
	D. She is purchasing office supplies.
(Narrator)	Number 15
(Narrator)	Look at the picture marked number 15 in your book.
(Man B)	**A.** The man is buying a new tennis racquet.
	B. The woman is writing a check for the merchandise.
	C. The woman is helping a couple move furniture.
	D. The woman is assisting the customers with a purchase.

(Narrator) Number 16

(Narrator) Look at the picture marked number 16 in your book.

(Woman B)
A. He is driving his car to the construction site.
B. The truck is leaving the construction area.
C. He is burning garbage at the construction site.
D. The construction debris is being loaded into the trash container.

(Narrator) Number 17

(Narrator) Look at the picture marked number 17 in your book.

(Man A)
A. The shoes are stacked on the floor.
B. She is trying the shoes on for size.
C. The shoes are all on sale.
D. She is walking into the shoe store.

(Narrator) Number 18

(Narrator) Look at the picture marked number 18 in your book.

(Woman A)
A. The material is displayed on racks.
B. The material is stacked on pallets.
C. The stack of materials is wet.
D. The man is stacking the material.

(Narrator) Number 19

(Narrator) Look at the picture marked number 19 in your book.

(Man B)
A. The package fell out of the truck.
B. There is no room in the truck for the package.
C. The package has already been opened.
D. He's loading the package into the truck.

(Narrator) Number 20

(Narrator) Look at the picture marked number 20 in your book.

(Woman B)
A. He wears headphones while he is on the air.
B. The air inside the studio is chilly.
C. He is using a remote to change the channel.
D. He is speaking into a telephone.

(Narrator) Number 21

(Narrator) Look at the picture marked number 21 in your book.

(Man A)
A. The pharmacist is taking an order for a prescription.
B. The farmer is buying fertilizer for her crops.
C. The woman is reaching for a bottle from the shelf.
D. The pharmacist is filling a customer's prescription.

(Narrator) Number 22

(Narrator) Look at the picture marked number 22 in your book.

(Woman A)
A. The camera crew is carrying the equipment.
B. The camera man is talking on the phone.
C. The camera crew is taking a break.
D. The camera man is loading film into the camera.

(Narrator) Number 23

(Narrator) Look at the picture marked number 23 in your book.

(Man B)
A. They are balancing the company's books.
B. The woman waits while the man looks.
C. The man and woman are reviewing a document.
D. The woman watches the man prepare the invoice.

(Narrator) Number 24

(Narrator) Look at the picture marked number 24 in your book.

(Woman B)
A. The boys are ignoring the speaker.
B. The boys listen and watch while the man speaks.
C. He's teaching the boys how to paint the fence.
D. The man is coaching a football team.

CHAPTER 4 LISTENING SCRIPTS

Track 2

(Narrator) **Part II**

(Narrator) You will hear a question or statement and three responses spoken in English. They will be spoken only once and will not be printed in your test book. Choose the best response to the question or statement and mark the letter on your answer sheet.

(Narrator) Listen to a sample question:

(Man A) *Where are we meeting?*

(Narrator) *A.*

(Woman B) *To meet the new supervisor.*

(Narrator) *B.*

(Woman B) *It's the second room on the left.*

(Narrator) *C.*

(Woman B) *No, at three o'clock.*

(Narrator) Choice (B), "*It's the second room on the left*," best answers the question.

(Narrator) Number 1

(Woman A) Is there anything good on TV tonight?

(Man B)
A. The news comes on in about an hour.
B. Yes, the plant is on top of the television.
C. Please find a different station.

(Narrator) Number 2

(Man A) Why did they cancel the reception for Mr. Chang?

(Woman B)
A. Her secretary did.
B. He received the invitation.
C. He got sick.

(Narrator) Number 3

(Woman A) Where can I buy a magazine?

(Man A)
A. A cab just went by.
B. The store takes credit cards, I think.
C. The newsstand on the corner.

(Narrator) Number 4

(Man B) What type of business are you in?

(Woman A)
A. Because I sold the house.
B. I'm a banker.
C. I'll type it tomorrow.

(Narrator) Number 5
(Woman B) Would you like to work overtime tonight?
(Man A)
A. No thanks, I have one.
B. I'd rather begin at 8.
C. Sure, I need the hours.

(Narrator) Number 6
(Woman A) Where is your final destination today?
(Man B)
A. I'll be flying there.
B. I'm leaving this afternoon.
C. I'm going to Rome.

(Narrator) Number 7
(Woman B) It'll be a long trip, won't it?
(Man B)
A. She tripped on the stairs, yes.
B. No, I leave next week.
C. Yes, about four weeks.

(Narrator) Number 8
(Woman A) Why don't we take a short break?
(Man B)
A. My car got new brakes last summer.
B. Yes, Lisa broke the plate by accident.
C. Good idea, I'm getting tired.

(Narrator) Number 9
(Man B) When will the earnings report be issued?
(Woman B)
A. It will be published in the newspaper.
B. At the end of the first quarter.
C. Because the stock went up last week.

(Narrator) Number 10
(Man B) You subscribe to *Business Monthly Magazine*, don't you?
(Man A)
A. No, but my office does.
B. Yes, I heard the news on the radio.
C. The mail is late today.

(Narrator) Number 11
(Woman B) How are the contract negotiations coming along?
(Woman A)
A. Our attorneys are reviewing the proposed changes.
B. We're almost finished with the progress report.
C. They returned the rental car last night.

(Narrator)	Number 12
(Man B)	Who should we send to Buenos Aires?
(Woman A)	**A.** I'd recommend next week.
	B. Let's send out for lunch.
	C. Jaime should go.
(Narrator)	Number 13
(Man A)	Does Ali rent that house, or does he own it?
(Woman B)	**A.** He used to rent a house in Alexandria.
	B. His cousin just bought a home downtown.
	C. He has a one-year lease.
(Narrator)	Number 14
(Woman B)	Has Ms. Matala finished with the samples?
(Man A)	**A.** Yes, she was right on schedule.
	B. No, she was born in Finland.
	C. She felt his action was justified.
(Narrator)	Number 15
(Man A)	What's the training workshop about?
(Woman A)	**A.** Sometime tomorrow afternoon.
	B. Somewhere in the new building.
	C. Something to do with team building.
(Narrator)	Number 16
(Man B)	Why don't you apply for that new job posting?
(Woman B)	**A.** I worked on the second shift.
	B. I don't think I'm qualified.
	C. I'm walking to the post office.
(Narrator)	Number 17
(Man A)	Is that pollution or just morning haze?
(Woman B)	**A.** The latter; it should be gone by noon.
	B. The industrial zone is located in the valley.
	C. The afternoon rain keeps the air clean.
(Narrator)	Number 18
(Woman A)	Why don't we take a cruise for vacation?
(Man B)	**A.** Because the food is so good.
	B. So that we can get a free ticket.
	C. That might be a nice change.

(Narrator)	Number 19	
(Man A)	Will Mr. Yoon write the report, or does he want me to do it?	
(Woman A)	**A.**	He was right last time.
	B.	I think he reports directly to Mr. Yoon.
	C.	He'll do it himself.
(Narrator)	Number 20	
(Woman B)	How many workers will we need for the Johnston building?	
(Man A)	**A.**	Construction has been ongoing for two years.
	B.	I estimate around a hundred.
	C.	We'll need to work overtime to finish.
(Narrator)	Number 21	
(Woman A)	Why don't you think about taking early retirement?	
(Man B)	**A.**	I thought you retired.
	B.	Actually, I've been considering it.
	C.	I've worked for over thirty years.
(Narrator)	Number 22	
(Woman B)	Who's your favorite author?	
(Man A)	**A.**	I prefer short stories over novels.
	B.	Her favorite books are usually fiction.
	C.	It's hard for me to pick just one.
(Narrator)	Number 23	
(Man B)	Don't you think interest rates will continue to go up?	
(Woman B)	**A.**	In the short term, I suppose so.
	B.	No, I am very interested.
	C.	I had to drive up the hill.
(Narrator)	Number 24	
(Woman A)	What should we do with these files for the Wallrock lease?	
(Man A)	**A.**	Leave them until Tuesday.
	B.	Your secretary has them.
	C.	No, I sent them to Mr. Wallrock.

CHAPTER 5 LISTENING SCRIPTS

Track 3

(Narrator) **Part III**

(Narrator) You will now hear a number of conversations between two people. You will be asked to answer three questions about what the speakers say. Select the best response to each question and mark the letter on your answer sheet. The conversations will be spoken only once and will not be printed in your test book.

(Narrator) Practice 1

(Narrator) Questions 1 through 3 refer to the following conversation.

(Man A) You're not working on Monday? You didn't work on Thursday, either! How many vacation days do you get? You certainly seem to get more than I do!

(Woman A) Well, actually I get twenty-five days of vacation, just like you, but my company allows us to work weekends and trade that for weekdays off. I worked two Saturdays in February and three Sundays in March, so now I have five extra days to take.

(Man A) I wish my company was flexible like that, but our office is totally closed on weekends.

(Woman A) Oh yeah? My company just keeps on going, twenty-four hours a day, seven days a week.

(Narrator) Number 1. What are the speakers mainly discussing?

(Narrator) Number 2. What about the woman surprised the man?

(Narrator) Number 3. Look at the graphic. Which company does the woman work at?

(Narrator) Practice 2

(Narrator) Questions 4 through 6 refer to the following conversation.

(Woman B) Well, Mr. Donahue, I think that's all we have to ask you. Now it's your turn to do the speaking! Do you have any questions you'd like to ask us about the job?

(Man B) Well, yes, there are few things. For example, you asked me earlier if I had any project management experience. Does that mean that you're looking for people with this kind of experience?

(Woman B) Oh, not necessarily, although clearly it would be an advantage. But no, what we're looking for is the potential for leadership. Obviously the most important skills for the current job are the necessary computer programming expertise, but if we think someone has the necessary skills set for a leadership role in the future—things like organizational and communication skills, then we're interested.

(Man B) I see. Because, you see, although I haven't actually done any project management, I did learn the principles when I was in university.

(Narrator) Number 4. Who is the man?

(Narrator) Number 5. What kind of experience are the speakers talking about?

(Narrator) Number 6. What kind of job is being offered?

(Narrator) Practice 3

(Narrator) Questions 7 through 9 refer to the following conversation.

(Man A) I can't believe it! Someone's moved the file for that new German contract, the JDK job. I put it in the contract files cabinet only last week. Why don't people put things back where they belong? I can't understand it.

(Woman B) Oh, sorry Mike. I forgot to tell you. I've changed the filing system slightly. There wasn't room anymore for all the contract files in one cabinet. You couldn't find anything, so I've split them up.

(Man A) Oh, what do you mean?

(Woman B) Well, I've put all the foreign contracts in a separate cabinet—that one over there by the window. You'll find the JDK file there, because it's a German contract. It's in the second drawer from the top. All the U.S. contracts are in the cabinet by your desk. And by the way, I think we need to reorganize the finance files, too!

(Narrator) Number 7. Why does the man say "I can't believe it!"?

(Narrator) Number 8. What has the woman changed?

(Narrator) Number 9. Look at the graphic. Where is the JDK contract file?

(Narrator) Practice 4

(Narrator) Questions 10 through 12 refer to the following conversation.

(Man B) Now we've got your camera connected directly to the projector, so we actually don't need to copy the photos onto the computer at all. You can project directly from your camera!

(Woman A) Oh, that's great. It's just that I have no idea at all how to use the projector.

(Man B) Don't worry. It's really very easy. First of all, use the red button here to switch it on and off. The green button puts the projector on standby, which is very convenient for presentations and that kind of thing. These blue arrows here control the color and the brightness of the image and then there's this little wheel here. If you turn the wheel towards you, the image gets bigger, and if you turn it away from you, the image gets smaller.

(Woman A)	Okay, that looks easy!
(Narrator)	Number 10. What is the woman learning about?
(Narrator)	Number 11. Why does the man say, "Don't worry"?
(Narrator)	Number 12. How can users change the size of the image?
(Narrator)	Practice 5
(Narrator)	Questions 13 through 15 refer to the following conversation.
(Woman B)	Oh, good evening. We're the party from Limo Car Rentals. We've reserved tables for this evening.
(Man B)	Oh dear, I'm sorry, but we were expecting you tomorrow. Let me just check... yes, Limo Cars, party of five for seven-thirty on Tuesday. The reservation was made by a Mr. Robert Jones on Friday.
(Woman B)	Oh yes, originally we reserved for Tuesday, but we changed the reservation for Monday instead. Didn't you get a call to change it to this evening?
(Man B)	No, I'm sorry, we weren't informed. At least, there's no record of that change here in the list. Perhaps Mr. Jones forgot to call us. However, don't worry too much. It's seven-thirty now and we may have a table free at eight o'clock, if you'd like to wait until then.
(Narrator)	Number 13. What do the speakers want to reserve?
(Narrator)	Number 14. When was the reservation made?
(Narrator)	Number 15. How long do the speakers need to wait?
(Narrator)	Practice 6
(Narrator)	Questions 16 through 18 refer to the following conversation.
(Woman A)	Excuse me officer, I've just come from the airport and I need to get to the train station. I have absolutely no idea how to get there. Is it walking distance from here?
(Man A)	Well, it's not too far on foot, no, but I see you have quite a bit of luggage there. It could take ten minutes to walk from here, so I think you'd be best using public transportation to be honest. There isn't a subway station near here, but there's the number fifteen bus that stops across the street and the train station is just two or three stops down.
(Woman A)	Oh really? Well how frequent are the buses. I mean, will I have to wait long?
(Man A)	Let's see. Well, the last number fifteen came by about five minutes ago, and they're quite frequent. I mean, they come by every eight minutes or so. Yeah, there should be one coming in about three minutes.

(Narrator) Number 16. Who is the woman speaking to?

(Narrator) Number 17. Where does the woman want to go?

(Narrator) Number 18. How many minutes will the woman need to wait for the next bus?

(Narrator) Practice 7

(Narrator) Questions 19 through 21 refer to the following conversation.

(Woman B) Rory, I've just spoken to Ann Hanson, the external consultant, and it seems that she can't make it to Thursday's planning meeting. I can't do Friday because we've got a safety inspection at the new manufacturing facility, and that can't be changed. So we'll have to postpone until next week.

(Man B) Oh dear. Well, I'd better contact the people from Elgar Plastics then, and find out their availability for next week. I'll email them explaining the problem.

(Woman B) No, I'd prefer you to call them. They're not going to be very happy about this, and on the phone you'll be able to explain the situation better than in an email message. Sometimes it's better to contact clients by phone.

(Man B) Okay, but I'll also email our team to announce the postponement.

(Narrator) Number 19. What are the speakers mainly discussing?

(Narrator) Number 20. Who will Rory call?

(Narrator) Number 21. How will Rory contact their team?

(Narrator) Practice 8

(Narrator) Questions 22 through 24 refer to the following conversation.

(Man A) Hi Kelly. It's Tony Buckby from service supplies here. Listen, I've got a bit of a problem here and I'm not sure what to do. You see, the maintenance department is here now making some repairs, and they need a spare part for one of the lacquering machines down on the shop floor. Well, anyway we don't have that particular part in stock, and we have to order a new one.

(Woman A) Oh? Well just go ahead and order one. What's the problem exactly? Don't you have the catalogue?

(Man A) No, that's not the problem. It's just that last week Mr. Logan, my supervisor, told me not to order anything without asking him first... and he's not here today.

(Woman A) Oh yes, you're right. He's away at a product training in Baltimore.

(Narrator) Number 22. Where does Tony work?

(Narrator) Number 23. What is Tony's problem?

(Narrator) Number 24. Why are Mr. Logan and Tony not together?

(Narrator) Questions 25 through 27 refer to the following conversation with three speakers.

(Woman B) Hey guys, Aidan wants to talk to both of you.

(Man B) Oh! Has he sorted out the contract with the new clients?

(Woman B) Actually, that's what he wants to talk to you about... he's still trying to find common ground with their lawyers. Apparently they're being quite difficult.

(Woman A) Well, those clients aren't exactly easy, are they? Matteo, did you tell Giulia what they wanted us to do, initially?

(Man B) No, get this, they wanted us to drive to their headquarters, so that we could do every talk, *every talk*, in person. Not just, like, formal meetings, but any little talk about anything. They wanted it in person, at their office... I think they're worried about confidentiality.

(Woman A) Yeah, so Aidan told them that we could possibly make it work, but that, obviously, we'd have to expense them for the travel, you know, the mileage and also the time it would take, because they're way out in the middle of nowhere... they decided after that that they could do without it.

(Narrator) Number 25. Why haven't the contracts been signed?

(Narrator) Number 26. Why does the man think the clients liked meeting in person?

(Narrator) Number 27. What does the woman imply about the clients changing their mind?

(Narrator) Questions 28 through 30 refer to the following conversation with three speakers.

(Man A) Hello you two! I had no idea you were coming tonight.

(Man B) Hlynur! Bego, weren't we just talking about Hlynur the other day? We were saying it's been too long. Honestly, I know it's our fault... we almost never get out of the house in the evening, now that we've got our two little barnacles.

(Woman B) Oh, please don't call them that, Pedro! He's pretending to be glad to be free, but he was so worried about leaving them on the way here that he had to call his mother in the cab, to make sure they were both okay. We hadn't even been gone for an hour. How are you, Hlynur?

(Man A) I'm good. I've missed you guys. But what do you think of the show? I think the lead woman is fantastic.

(Woman B) Isn't she? She's so passionate, so convincing. It's hard to believed that it was written over two hundred years ago, isn't it? She just gives the words relevance.

(Man B) I'm not sure she did that for me, to be honest, I had no idea what was happening in that last scene.

(Narrator) Number 28. Where are the speakers?

(Narrator) Number 29. What does the woman say about Pedro?

(Narrator) Number 30. What do two of the speakers agree about?

CHAPTER 6 LISTENING SCRIPTS

Track 4

(Narrator)	**Part IV**
(Narrator)	You will now hear short talks given by a single speaker. You will be asked to answer three questions about what the speaker says. Select the best response to each question and mark the letter on your answer sheet. The talks will be spoken only once and will not be printed in your test book.
(Narrator)	Practice 1
(Narrator)	Questions 1 through 3 refer to the following talk.
(Man A)	Welcome to the twelfth annual trade conference. One of the key themes of this year's conference is Ireland's position in the world marketplace. I was recently asked why I feel so strongly about Irish businesses exporting their products. My answer was straightforward and simple: If you don't sell abroad, you are selling your company short. There are lots of reasons why Irish firms should look to overseas markets to sell their goods, and it has never made more sense to be exporting than it does right now. For example, exchange rates over the last eighteen months have made our prices highly attractive to overseas buyers. Also, recent government innovations are making it easier than ever to reach foreign markets.
(Narrator)	Number 1. What is the speaker promoting?
(Narrator)	Number 2. Where does this talk take place?
(Narrator)	Number 3. According to the speaker, why are foreign buyers interested in Irish products?
(Narrator)	Practice 2
(Narrator)	Questions 4 through 6 refer to the following news report.
(Woman A)	Good evening and welcome to Business News Nightly. Coming up in a few minutes, the latest developments in the SmartShares fraud scandal. A judge orders the company to close, but we find out how SmartShare's creditors are reacting to the news. And later on, our East Asia correspondent has been to Thailand to learn more about the novel ways companies there are increasing the productivity of their workforces. Plus, in 20 minutes, Jane Withers reports from Berlin's twenty-first technology fair where the very latest must-have business gadgets are on display, including the world's lightest laptop computer. But first, here's Mark Francis with the latest on the stock markets.
(Narrator)	Number 4. Why is the SmartShares company in the news?
(Narrator)	Number 5. According to the report, what is improving in Thailand?
(Narrator)	Number 6. Look at the graphic. What time will the East Asia report begin?

(Narrator) Practice 3

(Narrator) Questions 7 through 9 refer to the following advertisement

(Man B) Dunthrops' big summer sale is now going on. Yes, our annual July sale bonanza starts July first, and there are literally hundreds of bargains to be had. Reductions of up to fifty percent on menswear. Men's suits have been slashed from $400 down to $300. Men's coats regularly selling for $200 are now just $150. It's crazy! But it's not just men who have reasons to be pleased. There are bargains galore for the ladies, too, with up to thirty percent off on top brand names. And this year we've extended our sale to other departments too. There are huge savings available in kitchenware and home furnishings. But don't delay! Dunthrops' big summer sale starts July 1st and ends July 31st!

(Narrator) Number 7. What kind of store is Dunthorps?

(Narrator) Number 8. Why does the speaker say, "it's crazy!"?

(Narrator) Number 9. When does the sale end?

(Narrator) Practice 4

(Narrator) Questions 10 through 12 refer to the following talk.

(Woman B) In our next gallery you will see *Island Life*, one of the artist's most famous works. The artist conceived of the idea while vacationing in the Caribbean, where he stayed for two months. He didn't actually begin work on the piece, however, until he had returned home to Paris. It's oil on canvas, and because of its intricate design and detail, it took the artist six years to complete. You're actually very lucky to be able to see this masterwork, in fact, because the museum currently has it on loan from the Austrian National Gallery in Vienna. It will be on display here for only another two weeks and then it goes back home.

(Narrator) Number 10. Where did the artist get the idea for his piece?

(Narrator) Number 11. What kind of artwork is being discussed?

(Narrator) Number 12. Who is the speaker addressing?

(Narrator) Practice 5

(Narrator) Questions 13 through 15 refer to the following talk.

(Man A) Good afternoon. I'm pleased that so many of you could attend our ceremony despite the threat of rain, and I thank you all for coming. Ira Levinson would have been proud to see our new building complete and ready for occupancy. Who could have thought that the family business he started back in 1952 would grow into the thriving company it is today, with nearly a thousand employees, or that our products would rank among the very best in the industry worldwide. This beautiful new office building will house the company headquarters, and provide workspace for a very lucky staff of 250 people, including all of you who have come this morning. And so, it's my great pleasure to name this building the Levinson Building in honor of Ira Levinson, whose innovation and hard work built the company that we know today.

(Narrator) Number 13. Who is Ira Levinson?

(Narrator) Number 14. How many people will work in the building?

(Narrator) Number 15. What is the purpose of the talk?

(Narrator) Practice 6

(Narrator) Questions 16 through 18 refer to the following news report.

(Woman A) The number of recorded traffic violations decreased in the metropolitan area last year in keeping with a five year decline nationally. But does this mean that drivers are becoming more law-abiding? Not according to some. The transportation department suspects that the lower number is due to fewer police officers rather than fewer traffic offenders. During the last three years, traffic citations have dropped 27% in the city. The Transportation Department says budget cuts and an increasing population have led to fewer patrol hours for police throughout the metropolitan area. A police department spokesperson agreed that the figures do not necessarily indicate that drivers' behavior is changing.

(Narrator) Number 16. For how many years have traffic violations been decreasing nationally?

(Narrator) Number 17. Why does the speaker say, "Not according to some?"

(Narrator) Number 18. What did the police spokesperson say about the figures?

(Narrator) Practice 7

(Narrator) Questions 19 through 21 refer to the following recorded announcement.

(Woman B) Thank you for calling MoneyWise Savings Bank's automated teller service. If you have a MoneyWise account, you can also access your account via our online e-banking services. For e-banking, go to www.moneywise.com. To access your savings account through our automated teller service, please press one now. To access your checking account, please press two now. To access your credit card account, please press three now. To access your retirement funds, money market accounts, or other investment accounts, please press four now. To transfer funds between accounts, please press five now. To speak with a customer service representative, please press zero now. To repeat this menu option, please press nine now.

(Narrator) Number 19. Which number should a customer press for checking account access?

(Narrator) Number 20. What does pressing 5 allow customers to do?

(Narrator) Number 21. What do customers find out?

(Narrator) Practice 8

(Narrator) Questions 22 through 24 refer to the following advertisement.

(Man B) Jet Lines makes the difference. That's why more business people choose to fly to South East Asia destinations from New York with Jet Lines than any other airline. Perhaps it's the peace and quiet of our executive lounges, with free internet access and complementary drinks and snacks. Perhaps it's the comfort of Jet Lines business class seating, with more leg room than any of our competitors. Perhaps it's the fact that all Jet Lines business class passengers enjoy a good night's sleep on seats that recline 180 degrees to form flat beds. Perhaps it's our award-winning in-flight menus or maybe just that little extra courtesy that makes Jet Lines crews stand out from the rest. Whatever it is, Jet Lines makes a difference. Isn't it time you found out why for yourself?

(Narrator) Number 22. Who is the intended audience for the advertisement?

(Narrator) Number 23. What do Jet Lines executive lounges have?

(Narrator) Number 24. Look at the graphic. Which flight is most likely operated by Jet Lines?

(Narrator) Practice 9

(Narrator) Questions 25 through 27 refer to the following voicemail message.

(Woman A) Hello Mr. Rushman. It's Amy Richardson here calling from Seiler Logistics. I'm sorry I wasn't able to speak to you earlier when you called. I'm afraid I was in a meeting all afternoon. I thought I might just catch you before you went home for the evening, but it seems I've just missed you. Anyway, I just wanted to let you know that we have located the missing package. I spoke to the driver who was supposed to deliver it to you today, and it seems he left the package with the security guard in the building lobby. That was at seven thirty this morning, so perhaps the guard forgot to contact you about the delivery? I'll be at my desk first thing tomorrow, so do please contact me if the item still hasn't turned up. Thank you.

(Narrator) Number 25. What relationship does Mr. Rushman have with Seiler Logistics?

(Narrator) Number 26. Why has Amy Richardson called?

(Narrator) Number 27. When has Amy Richardson probably called Mr. Rushman?

(Narrator) Practice 10

(Narrator) Questions 28 through 30 refer to the following announcement.

(Man A) Welcome aboard the Metropolitan Airport Express. This is a non-stop service for Metropolitan Airport North Terminal. We will be departing in a few moments. Our travel time will be thirty-five minutes. Those of you without tickets can purchase a single fare ticket from a conductor who will be passing through the train. We accept both cash and most major credit cards. Frequent flyers may be interested to know that advance purchase discount tickets are available for the Metropolitan Airport Express, offering a ten percent discount on fares. Ask the conductor for more details. Thank you for choosing the Metropolitan Airport Express.

(Narrator) Number 28. How long does it take to get to the airport?

(Narrator) Number 29. What is true about the single fare tickets?

(Narrator) Number 30. What is learned about the advance purchase discount tickets?

PRACTICE TEST 1 LISTENING SCRIPTS

(Narrator) In the Listening Comprehension Section, you will have the chance to demonstrate how well you understand spoken English. The Listening Comprehension Section will take approximately 45 minutes. There are four parts, and directions are given for each part. You must mark your answers on the answer sheet. Do not write them in the test book.

Part I: Photographs

Track 6

(Narrator) Directions: For each question, you will hear four statements about the photograph in your test book. When you hear the statements, choose the one statement that best describes what you see in the photograph. Then, find the number of the question on your answer sheet and mark your answer. The statements will not be written in your test book and will be spoken just once. Look at the example item below.

(Narrator)	Now listen to the four statements.
(Narrator)	A.
(Woman A)	They're scraping the walls.
(Narrator)	B.
(Woman A)	The woman is watching the football.
(Narrator)	C.
(Woman A)	The girl is painting a picture.
(Narrator)	D.
(Woman A)	They're making some food.
(Narrator)	Choice (C), "She's painting a picture," best describes what you see in the picture. Therefore, you should fill in choice (C) in your answer sheet.
(Narrator)	Now let us begin Part 1 with question number 1. Go on to the next page.

(Narrator) Number 1.

(Narrator) Look at the picture marked number 1 in your test book.

(Man A)

A. A technician is using some equipment.

B. The equipment has all been unwired.

C. A technician is writing over some equipment.

D. The equipment is being unloaded from a car.

(Narrator) Number 2.

(Narrator) Look at the picture marked number 2 in your test book.

(Woman B)

A. The patio doors are open to the garden.

B. The flower pot is in the middle of the table.

C. The plant is on top of the stool.

D. The chair is in the corner of the room.

(Narrator)	Number 3.
(Narrator)	Look at the picture marked number 3 in your test book.
(Man B)	**A.** He's getting up from his chair.
	B. He's bent over his work table.
	C. He's cleaning up his office.
	D. He's turning on the desk light.
(Narrator)	Number 4.
(Narrator)	Look at the picture marked number 4 in your test book.
(Woman B)	**A.** The truck is parked alongside the building.
	B. The truck is being loaded in the rain.
	C. The man is getting out of the truck.
	D. They are moving into a new house.
(Narrator)	Go on to the next page.
(Narrator)	Number 5.
(Narrator)	Look at the picture marked number 5 in your test book.
(Man A)	**A.** The photographer is putting film into the camera.
	B. The scientist is watching birds through binoculars.
	C. The journalist is interviewing the woman for a story.
	D. The man is taking a picture.
(Narrator)	Number 6.
(Narrator)	Look at the picture marked number 6 in your test book.
(Woman A)	**A.** The dishes are below the cutlery in the drawers.
	B. The plates are in the top drawer.
	C. There are five place settings on the table.
	D. The dishwasher is full of clean dishes.

Part II: Question-Response

Track 7

(Narrator) Directions: You will hear a question or statement and three responses spoken in English. They will be spoken only once and will not be printed in your test book. Choose the best response to the question or statement and mark the letter on your answer sheet.

(Narrator)	Listen to a sample question:
(Man B)	Where are we meeting?
(Narrator)	A.
(Woman A)	To meet the new supervisor.
(Narrator)	B.
(Woman A)	It's the second room on the left.
(Narrator)	C.

(Woman A) No, at three o'clock.

(Narrator) Choice (B), "It's the second room on the left," best answers the question. Therefore, you should fill in choice (B) on your answer sheet.

(Narrator) Now let us begin Part II with question number 7.

(Narrator) Number 7.

(Man A) Do you have an additional pair of bookends?

(Woman B)
A. Yes, this pear is delicious.
B. Yes, I have some spare time.
C. Yes, I have an extra pair.

(Narrator) Number 8.

(Woman B) Are gratuities already added in, or are they separate?

(Man A)
A. They're included in the price.
B. You can pack whatever you like.
C. Yes, the price includes all meals.

(Narrator) Number 9.

(Woman A) Why do you want to advertise in the trade publications?

(Man B)
A. No, let's skip the trade show this year.
B. A lot of our trade is done overseas.
C. It's a good way to attract customers.

(Narrator) Number 10.

(Man B) What are the arrangements for publicising the general's visit?

(Woman A)
A. We've arranged a hotel room.
B. The television station is sending a reporter.
C. All public buildings are open to visitors.

(Narrator) Number 11.

(Man A) You've had experience with this particular software, haven't you?

(Woman B)
A. No, I'm not familiar with it all.
B. Menswear is located on the second floor.
C. Yes, I think it's very expensive.

(Narrator) Number 12.

(Man B) Why didn't she attend the medical conference yesterday?

(Woman B)
A. There was a conflict in her schedule.
B. She will attend to it immediately.
C. There wasn't any medicine in here.

(Narrator)	Number 13.
(Woman A)	When will payroll be finished?
(Man B)	**A.** We get paid every two weeks.
	B. I had the last roll with my coffee.
	C. I hope to have everything done by Wednesday.
(Narrator)	Number 14.
(Woman B)	Did you send an invitation to Mr. Maxwell?
(Man A)	**A.** No, I registered late.
	B. Yes, he was on my list.
	C. No, it's on back order.
(Narrator)	Number 15.
(Man B)	Who will be taking notes at the meeting?
(Woman A)	**A.** The receptionist sent a note about the meeting.
	B. I'll be taking the day off.
	C. Mr. Lorenzo's secretary will do it.
(Narrator)	Number 16.
(Man A)	What would you like to drink with your meal?
(Woman A)	**A.** I'll have some iced tea.
	B. Could I have a piece of chocolate cake, please?
	C. I'd prefer a table next to the window, if possible.
(Narrator)	Number 17.
(Woman B)	How is your new assistant working out?
(Man B)	**A.** That was a tough work out.
	B. I need a lot of assistance.
	C. He's learning fast and doing well.
(Narrator)	Number 18.
(Woman A)	The uniforms have been ordered already, haven't they?
(Woman B)	**A.** Yes, the waitress took our order.
	B. Yes, the soup is ready.
	C. Yes, they're arriving on Thursday.
(Narrator)	Number 19.
(Woman B)	Who should I contact to get the sink repaired?
(Man A)	**A.** Call the building superintendent.
	B. There's a good car mechanic across town.
	C. I like my apartment.

(Narrator)	Number 20.
(Man B)	Where is your office in New York?
(Woman A)	**A.** We moved about two months ago.
	B. Downtown, in the financial district.
	C. We do a lot of business there.
(Narrator)	Number 21.
(Man A)	When's a good time to telephone Mr. Boros?
(Woman B)	**A.** It's not what you thought.
	B. It's best to call early.
	C. It was yesterday morning.
(Narrator)	Number 22.
(Woman A)	Are you going to print new business cards, or keep your old ones?
(Man A)	**A.** The old ones are fine for now.
	B. I have the printer's card in my file.
	C. No, you can't use the printer, because it's broken.
(Narrator)	Number 23.
(Woman B)	Where did you leave the Zurich invoices?
(Man B)	**A.** I hear voices in the conference room.
	B. I am going to leave with you.
	C. I put them in the gray cabinet.
(Narrator)	Number 24.
(Man B)	How did you get here so quickly?
(Woman A)	**A.** The elevator took forever.
	B. I took a taxi directly from work.
	C. I heard about it on the radio.
(Narrator)	Number 25.
(Man A)	You have a computer at home, don't you?
(Man B)	**A.** Yes, it's a laptop.
	B. Yes, but I left it in my wallet.
	C. No, I don't have my phone with me.
(Narrator)	Number 26.
(Woman A)	Would you like the lunch special, or will you stick with your regular order today?
(Man A)	**A.** It's especially delicious.
	B. I'll have my usual meal.
	C. I'll have lunch early today.

(Narrator) Number 27.
(Woman B) How much do we have left in our mailing budget?
(Man A)
A. We still have about 2,000 dollars.
B. Because I left a copy of the budget for Mr. Wilson.
C. No, because the mailing costs didn't go over budget.

(Narrator) Number 28.
(Man B) How much vacation do you get this year?
(Woman B)
A. In September.
B. At the shore.
C. Two weeks.

(Narrator) Number 29.
(Man A) I think they're going to finish before the deadline, don't you?
(Woman A)
A. Yes, the checkout line is pretty short.
B. Yes, the work seems to be going pretty fast.
C. No, this street turns into a dead end.

(Narrator) Number 31.
(Woman B) When is the tour group from Brazil due to arrive?
(Man B)
A. They should be here at noon.
B. My plane lands in Brazil at 1:30.
C. I get back form my tour on the 22nd.

(Narrator) Number 31.
(Woman A) What's at the top of our agenda this morning?
(Man B)
A. That's on the top shelf.
B. First we need to discuss pay raises.
C. The agent needs the invoices by noon.

Part III: Short Conversations

Track 8

(Narrator) Directions: You will now hear a number of conversations between two people. You will be asked to answer three questions about what the speakers say. Select the best response to each question and mark the letter on your answer sheet. The conversations will be spoken only once and will not be printed in your test book.

(Narrator) Now let us begin Part III with question number 32.

(Narrator) Questions 32 through 34 refer to the following conversation.
(Man A) We need to know the final count before we can call the caterer. Originally, we were supposed to have fifty, but I know the number has

	gone up since last week. Do you have any idea how many people we're going to have?
(Woman A)	It's sixty-five. Ms. Colby also invited the instructors to lunch, so that's another eight people. Plus we've decided to invite people from the administration team, so that's another seven.
(Man A)	Thanks. And are we staying with the same time?
(Woman A)	Yes, that hasn't changed; we're still scheduled to start serving at one-thirty.
(Narrator)	Number 32. What are the speakers planning?
(Narrator)	Number 33. How many people are expected to attend?
(Narrator)	Number 34. What has changed?
(Narrator)	Questions 35 through 37 refer to the following conversation with three speakers.
(Man A)	I'm so sorry I'm late. Traffic is pretty bad with all the snow and the subway is a nightmare too.
(Man B)	I know. It took me nearly three hours to get to work this morning. This is ridiculous. I know they're doing the best they can, but...
(Woman A)	I get that Mr. Wells, but this has gone too far. This is not the first time you're late, and you only joined us three weeks ago. I don't know what things were like with Royal Investments but we run things on schedule here.
(Man A)	I know and I'm terribly sorry. It won't happen again, I promise.
(Woman B)	I appreciate you apology, Mr. Wells. Okay, shall we get started? Who has the agenda?
(Man B)	I've got it here, Susan. So, let's review our notes from last week...
(Narrator)	Number 35. What is described as a nightmare?
(Narrator)	Number 36. Why is the woman angry?
(Narrator)	Number 37. Where are the speakers?
(Narrator)	Questions 38 through 40 refer to the following conversation.
(Man A)	Hello. My name's Eric Jansen from API insurance. I'd like to speak to Kate Brody, please.
(Woman A)	I'm sorry, but Ms. Brody's in a meeting right now. Would you like to leave a message?
(Man A)	Yes, could you please tell her that she's covered for her trip to China next week, but that she needs to send me a message with the details of her trip—I mean the cities that she'll be visiting. It's urgent, so she needs to get those details to me before the end of today. If she wants to call me, I'll be in the office all day. She has my number.
(Woman A)	Okay, Mr. Jansen. I'll let her know. Thanks for calling.

(Narrator) Number 38. What has Mr. Jansen called about?

(Narrator) Number 39. Where is Ms. Brody?

(Narrator) Number 40. What does Mr. Jansen need to know regarding Ms. Brody's trip?

(Narrator) Questions 41 through 43 refer to the following conversation with three speakers.

(Man A) I can't find my memory stick. Do you mind if I borrow yours?

(Woman B) Sorry, Ahmed. I lent mine to Serena last week and she hasn't returned it. Oh! There you are Serena. You okay? I heard you'd been doing some late nights.

(Woman A) Yeah, I'm not too bad. I mean, we're slammed in accounting at the moment, making sure everything's okay for our audit, but I'm good.

(Man A) Oh of course! I'd forgotten about that. Do you think you'll manage to get everything ready in time?

(Woman A) Yeah, I mean everything's kind of ready at the moment, we just really need to check through to make sure it's all up to standard.

(Woman B) Of course I'm sure you'll get there... Oh! I almost forgot—can you give my memory stick to Ahmed? He needs it to back up some files from the old system.

(Man A) Actually, I need it to move some files from the cloud... I've run out of space on my computer for storage.

(Woman A) Of course! Sorry, we'd been using it for showing people our video testimonials... it's in our filing cabinet, you know, the one by Greta's office?

(Woman B) Oh yeah, you know, I thought it was on your desk all this time. I'll go grab it now, thanks!

(Narrator) Number 41. Why has Serena been working late?

(Narrator) Number 42. What does Ahmed want the memory stick for?

(Narrator) Number 43. Where is the memory stick?

(Narrator) Questions 44 through 46 refer to the following conversation.

(Man A) I hear that her work is exhibited all over the world. She must be very well known.

(Woman B) Oh yes, she's quite a celebrity in the art world. Her works are in most of the big galleries in New York, London, and Paris. Although, I have to admit that until a week ago I'd never heard of her.

(Man A) Me neither, but then I don't know much about sculpture. I prefer paintings. Anyway, it's quite an honor to have someone so famous come and speak here in Glasgow.

(Woman B) Yes, she's supposed to be a very entertaining speaker. I think it will really make a big difference to the dinner.

(Narrator) Number 44. Who are the speakers talking about?

(Narrator) Number 45. Where are the speakers?

(Narrator) Number 46. What event do the speakers refer to?

(Narrator)	Questions 47 through 49 refer to the following conversation.
(Man A)	I'm going to need ten more feet of wire to install these overhead lights. This piece doesn't reach the ceiling. We've got some more in a blue box in the truck. Could you go and bring it, Greg?
(Man B)	Yeah, sure. Do you want me to bring the whole box or just cut ten feet?
(Man A)	Well, bring the whole box. We'll need some more wire for the switches in the bedrooms and the kitchen.
(Man B)	Okay. I'll be right back.
(Narrator)	Number 47. Who are the men?
(Narrator)	Number 48. Where is the blue box?
(Narrator)	Number 49. Where are the men working?
(Narrator)	Questions 50 through 52 refer to the following conversation with three speakers
(Woman A)	Excuse me, can you tell me when the elevator will be working again? It's got an 'out of order' sign on it.
(Man B)	Er... sorry, I have no idea, actually. I always take the stairs. Rosa, do you know?
(Woman B)	Well, I've just been talking to Frank in maintenance, and he says that they were planning to do a routine check-up and then replace the button panel which would have taken just a couple of weeks. Then they found that some of the machinery is a bit worn, so they need to replace those parts now, which could take a month.
(Woman A)	Oh! That's not good! I have all this paper for our printer, and we're on the 11th floor. I don't think I can get it up the stairs.
(Man B)	Yeah... 11 floors with two crates of paper might be a bit of a stretch! You know you can use the service elevator though, right?
(Woman B)	Service elevator?
(Man B)	Yeah, it's round the back, by the cafeteria. Here, it'll be easier if I just show you, come with me.
(Narrator)	Number 50. What are the speakers discussing?
(Narrator)	Number 51. Why is the lift out of order?
(Narrator)	Number 52. What will the man do?
(Narrator)	Go on to the next page.
(Narrator)	Questions 53 through 55 refer to the following conversation.
(Man A)	I just received an email from Colleen Rankin. She said she'd love to see you when you're in Australia next week. Do you think you'll have time?
(Woman B)	I'm not sure, to be honest. I'd love to see her, but it's going to be a very busy three days. I've got meetings with five different clients, plus I'll be at the Trade and Commerce Center. Still, it would be a shame to go all the way there and not see Colleen. I'll email her and tell her my

program. Maybe we can meet up on Friday evening before my flight back on Saturday.

(Man A) Yes, I think you should... Listen, why don't you stay an extra night and fly back on Sunday? As your boss, I can approve the cost of another night's accommodation this afternoon. After all those years working out there, I'm sure that Colleen has some useful contacts and it would be good for us if you could meet with her.

(Woman B) Really? That's a great idea. Thanks, Jim.

(Narrator) Number 53. Why is Colleen Rankin in Australia?

(Narrator) Number 54. When will the woman return from Australia?

(Narrator) Number 55. Who is the man in relation to the woman?

(Narrator) Questions 56 through 58 refer to the following conversation.

(Woman A) Have you heard any news on that shipment of sportswear from Shanghai? I'm getting a bit worried. The ad campaign is due to start in two weeks and we need to deliver to stores well before then.

(Man B) Don't worry, Jane. The ship hasn't sunk in Hong Kong harbor or anything like that. The container's actually here in Dublin, but there's been a problem in customs—they needed extra time to review the paperwork, or something. I didn't understand the issue, exactly.

(Woman A) So when can we expect delivery to the stores?

(Man B) The official I spoke to said we should get customs clearance by Wednesday, and then all the stores will receive delivery by Friday at the latest.

(Narrator) Number 56. What goods are the speakers talking about?

(Narrator) Number 57. Where has the shipment come from?

(Narrator) Number 58. What has caused the delay?

(Narrator) Questions 59 through 61 refer to the following conversation.

(Man A) I've heard you have a special deal on the Verity 540. Can you tell me more about it?

(Woman B) Yes, that's right, sir. If you buy the 540 we'll throw in a free carrying case and a choice between a memory upgrade or a graphics software package.

(Man A) Oh, I see. And how much is the software or the memory upgrade worth in dollars? I mean, can't I just get a reduction in the price instead of the software or the memory upgrade? To be honest I don't really need either of those.

(Woman B) Well, the offer is worth about 120 dollars, but I'm afraid a straight discount isn't available with this particular model. And to be honest, this is already a great price on a quality laptop. You won't find one with the same features for much cheaper.

(Narrator)	Number 59. What are the speakers talking about?
(Narrator)	Number 60. What does the special offer include?
(Narrator)	Number 61. What does the man ask for?
(Narrator)	Questions 62 to 64 refer to the following conversation and graphic.
(Woman B)	So, what did you think of the plan for the break room?
(Man B)	I like it—it's about time we got some new chairs and tables!
(Woman B)	I know, the old ones are so worn! But do you think the layout's right?
(Man B)	Hmm... let me have a look at the plan... well, I'm not sure about this, see, the kitchen's right next to the door. I think that will be too busy, because everyone always ends up standing around there. I think we should move it so that it's on the opposite side of the room from the door, next to the sofas.
(Woman B)	That's actually a really good idea. You should suggest that to Ricardo. He's in charge of the redesign and was asking for feedback this morning.
(Narrator)	Number 62. What do the speakers imply about the current furniture?
(Narrator)	Number 63. Look at the graphic. Which area does the man think the kitchen should be in?
(Narrator)	Number 64. What does the woman suggest?
(Narrator)	Questions 65 through 67 refer to the following conversation and graphic.
(Woman B)	Larry, we need to choose which evening to have the staff party on in the last week of the month. When's best for your team?
(Man B)	Probably Saturday, but have you checked the venue's fees for each night? I think the cost varies depending on the day.
(Woman B)	Are you sure?
(Man B)	Yeah, Sofia was looking at their website yesterday. Apparently some nights are more popular, so they charge more.
(Woman B)	That's annoying. Well, Damien said we couldn't spend more than $800 on the venue, and if possible, it would be better to have the party after we submit the new client's contract on Friday morning.
(Man B)	OK... I'll take a look at the prices over lunch and let you know which night to book the venue for.
(Narrator)	Number 65. What does the woman ask the man?
(Narrator)	Number 66. Why does the woman say, "That's annoying"?
(Narrator)	Number 67. Look at the graphic. Which night will they book the venue for?
(Narrator)	Questions 68 through 70 refer to the following conversation and graphic.
(Man B)	Okay, so we've got our pitch sorted, so now we just need to schedule a time with the investors to present it. I have a really good feeling about this, Trupti; I think they're gonna go for it.

(Woman A)	I know, Vikesh, it's really good... so let's take a look at their calendars, Rhonda and Leroy shared them with me earlier today.
(Man B)	Great, okay, so we've got a couple of options here.
(Woman A)	Well, yeah but we can't schedule it for the weekend, not everyone's as fond of work as you!
(Man B)	Of course, okay so that narrows it down... I can't do the first couple of days next week, either.
(Woman A)	Well, there's only one day left, then. I'll shoot them an email.
(Man B)	Brilliant, will you copy me in?
(Narrator)	Number 68. What are the speakers most likely to be doing?
(Narrator)	Number 69. Why does the man say "Of course"?
(Narrator)	Number 70. Look at the graphic. On which day will they schedule the meeting?

Part IV: Short Talks

Track 9

(Narrator) Directions: You will hear some talks given by a single speaker. You will be asked to answer three questions about what the speaker says in each talk. Select the best response to each question and mark the letter A, B, C or D on your answer sheet. The talks will be spoken only once and will not be printed in your test book. Now let us begin Part IV with question number 71.

(Narrator)	Questions 71 through 73 refer to the following talk.
(Woman B)	We hope you will come and help us welcome the Colombian National Symphony for the first time to Seattle on Saturday May 28th at 7 o'clock in the Municipal Concert Hall. Tickets are 18, 24, and 30 dollars. A ten percent discount is available to holders of student union membership cards and to school or university staff. Tickets are available at the Municipal Concert Hall. You can also buy seats for all our events online, at www.seattlearts.com where you can search for details of upcoming concerts and reserve seats.
(Narrator)	Number 71. What event will occur on May 28th?
(Narrator)	Number 72. How much is the cheapest ticket without the discount?
(Narrator)	Number 73. Where can people buy tickets?
(Narrator)	Questions 74 through 76 refer to the following talk.
(Man A)	Tomorrow, John Park, the vice president, will be coming to make an inspection that he would like to include as a part of his annual report. As some of you may remember from last year, his reports are very thorough. Last year he focused on our menu items, and this year he will be concentrating on customer service. This means he will be carefully observing the host, waiters, bus boys, and anyone else who has direct contact with the customers. He will also be looking at how we present the food. I hope you will work hard, smile, and demonstrate how well we treat our customers.

(Narrator) Number 74. What is Mr. Park's title?

(Narrator) Number 75. What will Mr. Park mainly focus on this year?

(Narrator) Number 76. What does the speaker want the employees to do?

(Narrator) Questions 77 through 79 refer to the following talk.

(Woman A) I'd like to introduce you to our new vice president of operations, Mr. Frank Nazar. Mr. Nazar has been with the company for 15 years. He started as an account representative and then quickly moved up to sales executive. For the last five years he has been Regional Manager and under his direction, domestic sales have increased by 30 percent. As vice president of operations, Mr. Nazar will be looking at ways to lower expenses and increase production. I'm sure all of the store managers will join me in welcoming Mr. Nazar.

(Narrator) Number 77. Where is this introduction taking place?

(Narrator) Number 78. What is one of Mr. Nazar's accomplishments?

(Narrator) Number 79. What is one of Mr. Nazar's goals in his new role?

(Narrator) Go on to the next page.

(Narrator) Questions 80 through 82 refer to the following talk and graphic.

(Man B) The weather in Zurich today: rain at times, highs in the lower teens. In the Central Valley, a mostly cloudy day with some areas of mixed rain and snow over the mountains, highs around nine degrees. In the southern mountains, lots of snow, possibly 30 centimeters today with the snow level around elevations of 1,000 meters. And in southeastern Switzerland, snow there too, about 15 to 25 centimeters are possible today. Seven to 13 centimeters of snow are already reported along the Italian-Austrian border.

(Narrator) Number 80. Where is it expected to rain?

(Narrator) Number 81. Look at the graphic. Which area shows the weather forecast for the Central Valley?

(Narrator) Number 82. Where has snow already been reported?

(Narrator) Questions 83 through 85 refer to the following talk.

(Woman A) Thank you for that introduction, Mr. Hausman. Today I would like to speak about financial services and how they affect the planning process for business and industry. As we are aware, tremendous changes have been made in the financial services sector over the past decade, and they are set to continue. These changes, especially those in the areas of regulation and industry management, have created new challenges for business planning.

(Narrator) Number 83. What did Mr. Hausman do?

(Narrator) Number 84. What does the woman mean when she says, "As we are aware"?

(Narrator) Number 85. What is this talk mainly about?

(Narrator) Questions 86 through 88 refer to the following talk.

(Man A) As you know I just returned from Europe where I spent two months visiting our hotel units. I spent approximately three days at each unit, evaluating the services, staff, and accommodations. My goal was to evaluate the architectural structure of both the interiors and exteriors. Very briefly, we surpass the competition in customer service, but many of our units need structural updating. I feel we should have a team of interior designers redecorate the lobbies and rooms. I'd like to suggest to the board that they make these improvements a priority and that sufficient sums be allocated for each unit.

(Narrator) Number 86. What kind of company does the speaker work for?

(Narrator) Number 87. Why does the speaker say, "Very briefly"?

(Narrator) Number 88. What does the speaker ask the board of directors to make available?

(Narrator) Questions 89 through 91 refer to the following talk.

(Woman B) Well folks, that concludes our show for this evening. You have been listening to "Contemporary Management," broadcast every Monday night on these affiliated radio stations. We have been talking with Dr. Julia McDermott, the renowned management consultant and expert in the field of employee motivation. Dr. McDermott's new book is *Motivating Your Staff*. Please listen again next week when we will visit with Mr. Peter Thompson, the noted author of the best-selling book, *Managing Change*. Until next week, thank you for listening.

(Narrator) Number 89. What is the purpose of this announcement?

(Narrator) Number 90. Who will be the guest next week?

(Narrator) Number 91. What topic was probably discussed on the program?

(Narrator) Questions 92 through 94 refer to the following talk and graphic.

(Woman B) Thanks for coming, everyone. As usual, I'm going to begin by briefly summarizing what we'll try and cover over the next hour. You can see that there are five agenda items on the meeting invitation I sent out, but there's also another important item to add to the list, which Katherine wants to talk to you about towards the end of today's meeting. She'd like to talk about project budgets for the next financial year. After this summary, we'll do a quick update of what everyone's been working on, then I've reserved 20 minutes for us to talk about changes to our policy. Once we've covered that, we'll discuss project planning, and then look at our job advertisements for the new hire. Any questions before we move forward?

(Narrator) Number 92. What is the speaker doing?

(Narrator) Number 93. How many agenda items are there?

(Narrator) Number 94. Look at the graphic. When will they discuss policy changes?

(Narrator) Questions 95 through 97 refer to the following talk.

(Man A) Good morning ladies and gentlemen. On behalf of Captain Smith and the rest of the crew, I'd like to welcome you aboard LinkLines flight L-K nine seventy from London Gatwick to Edinburgh. My name is James Watts and I'm your lead flight attendant on today's flight. We'd like to apologize for the slight delay this morning, which has been due to fog grounding flights most of the morning up in Edinburgh. We thank you for your patience and understanding. I'm pleased to be able to report that the fog has lifted now and we'll be pushing away from the gate in the next few minutes.

(Narrator) Number 95. Who is speaking?

(Narrator) Number 96. Where is the flight going?

(Narrator) Number 97. What delayed the flight?

(Narrator) Questions 98 through 100 refer to the following talk.

(Woman A) This next slide shows how the different elements of our research fit together. First of all, we have the stakeholder interviews. The principle stakeholders were the tour operators, the hotel managers, and their clients—that is, the tourists themselves. However, we also interviewed local residents because the industry has a huge impact on their lives, too. And this actually leads into the second of our research elements, which involved empirical measurement of the impact visitors have on the local environment. We did this in a number of ways. One was to gather data on changes in demand for local resources such as water and electricity. Other quantifiable data came from measurements of erosion on pathways and increases in pollution of various kinds. Next slide, please.

(Narrator) Number 98. What is the talk mainly about?

(Narrator) Number 99. What is the speaker's main interest?

(Narrator) Number 100. What was measured?

Stop! (Narrator) This is the end of the Listening Comprehension Section of the exam. Turn to Part V. (Narrator) End of recording..

PRACTICE TEST 2 LISTENING SCRIPTS

(Narrator) In the Listening Comprehension Section, you will have the chance to demonstrate how well you understand spoken English. The Listening Comprehension Section will take approximately 45 minutes. There are four parts, and directions are given for each part. You must mark your answers on the answer sheet. Do not write them in the test book.

Part I: Photographs

Track 10

(Narrator) Directions: For each question, you will hear four statements about the photograph in your test book. When you hear the statements, choose the one statement that best describes what you see in the photograph. Then, find the number of the question on your answer sheet and mark your answer. The statements will not be written in your test book and will be spoken just once. Look at the example item below.

(Narrator) Now listen to the four statements.

(Narrator) A.

(Woman A) He's driving the car.

(Narrator) B.

(Woman A) The car is traveling under the bridge.

(Narrator) C.

(Woman A) He's turning the wheel.

(Narrator) D.

(Woman A) The mechanic is under the car.

(Narrator) Choice (C), "The mechanic is under the car," best describes what you see in the picture. Therefore, you should fill in choice (C) in your answer sheet. Now let us begin Part I with question number 1.

(Narrator) Go on to the next page.

(Narrator) Number 1.

(Narrator) Look at the picture marked number 1 in your test book.

(Man A)
A. He's looking for apples.
B. He's counting the items.
C. He's eating an orange.
D. He's checking the fruit.

(Narrator) Number 2.

(Narrator) Look at the picture marked number 2 in your test book.

(Woman A)
A. The screw needs three turns.
B. The nails have all been hammered.
C. The middle screw is being turned.
D. The wood is not secure.

(Narrator) Number 3.

(Narrator) Look at the picture marked number 3 in your test book.

(Man B)
A. The books are stacked on shelves.
B. The wooden crates are full.
C. The customer is making a purchase.
D. The library is open all day.

(Narrator) Number 4.

(Narrator) Look at the picture marked number 4 in your test book.

(Woman B)
A. The man is counting vegetables.
B. The chefs are preparing vegetables.
C. The teacher is listening to his students.
A. The food has been overcooked.

(Narrator) Go on to the next page.

(Narrator) Number 5.

(Narrator) Look at the picture marked number 5 in your test book.

(Man A)
A. They are home from work.
B. The man is staying at the hotel.
C. The realtor is showing them around.
D. The couple are visiting an acquaintance.

(Narrator) Number 6.

(Narrator) Look at the picture marked number 6 in your test book.

(Woman A)
A. They are giving a speech.
B. They are having lunch together.
C. He is writing a proposal.
D. They are discussing a project.

Part II: Question-Response

Track 11

(Narrator) Directions: You will hear a question or statement and three responses spoken in English. They will be spoken only once and will not be printed in your test book. Choose the best response to the question or statement and mark the letter on your answer sheet.

(Narrator) Listen to a sample question:

(Man B) Are you free to talk?

(Narrator) A.

(Woman A) No, it has a $5.00 fee.

(Narrator) B.

(Woman A) Yes, what can I help you with?

(Narrator) C.

(Woman A) I think he's spending the day in the office.

(Narrator) Choice (B), "Yes, what can I help you with?" best answers the question. Therefore, you should fill in choice (B) in your answer sheet.

(Narrator) Now let us begin Part II with question number 7.

(Narrator) Number 7.

(Man A) This is a great hotel, isn't it?

(Woman B)
A. It's not time yet.
B. I'm hungry too.
C. It is. We always come here in the summer.

(Narrator) Number 8.

(Woman A) Who sent the email?

(Man B)
A. I'll call you later.
B. I looked for the files.
C. My secretary did.

(Narrator) Number 9.

(Woman B) Have the contracts arrived yet?

A. Yes, we came by train.
B. He didn't get the contract.
C. Yes, they came yesterday.

(Narrator) Number 10.

(Man B) Who did you think would come?

(Woman A)
A. I'll have to come back some other time.
B. I expected my partner to come.
C. I thought it was my turn.

(Narrator) Number 11.

(Man A) How many candidates are there in the group dynamics?

(Woman B)
A. The dynamics starts at 5.
B. There are about 20.
C. The candidates arrived really early.

(Narrator) Number 12.

(Man B) Where shall we go?

(Woman B)
A. They go there every Friday.
B. Before dinner would be better.
C. How about that small Indian restaurant in the square?

(Narrator) Number 13.
(Woman A) How much does this TV cost?
(Man B)
A. It's 500 dollars.
B. This is a smart TV.
C. I have 3 TVs at home.

(Narrator) Number 14.
(Woman B) What time are you leaving today?
(Man A)
A. I'll leave at about 4:30 if that's OK with you.
B. I left early yesterday.
C. The leaves are falling because it's fall.

(Narrator) Number 15.
(Man B) How busy is the lecture theater today?
(Woman A)
A. It's very crowded in there.
B. Yes, she was busy in the morning.
C. She'll lecture you when you get home.

(Narrator) Number 16.
(Man A) Where's the supervisor's office?
(Woman A)
A. There's one supervisor for the morning and another one for the afternoon.
B. It's on the 5th floor.
C. She was placed under the supervision of a probation officer.

(Narrator) Number 17.
(Woman B) What color shirt would you like to buy?
(Man B)
A. I'd like the one with the black and white pattern.
B. I bought a really nice shirt yesterday.
C. The parks are really green this time of year.

(Narrator) Number 18.
(Woman A) Did the new assistant order more black toners?
(Woman B)
A. Black is my favorite color.
B. I don't like your tone. I's rude.
C. Yes, they'll be delivered tomorrow.

(Narrator) Number 19.
(Woman B) Would you like to play basketball after work?
(Man A)
A. I'm sorry but I'm not very good at sports.
B. He used to be a famous basketball player.
C. Can you please grab a shopping basket?

(Narrator)	Number 20.
(Man B)	Where should I file this report?
(Woman A)	**A.** If I were you, I'd report him straightaway.
	B. You should eat more healthily.
	C. In the filing cabinet next to my desk.
(Narrator)	Number 21.
(Man A)	Where did you buy those shoes?
(Woman B)	**A.** At the new shopping mall.
	B. Yes, they're very comfortable.
	C. I don't know where my shoes are.
(Narrator)	Number 22.
(Woman A)	What did Mrs. Nomoto email you about?
(Man A)	**A.** I will check the mail later.
	B. Mrs. Nomoto's email is nomotop@youroffice.com
	C. I was asked not to tell anyone until our meeting on Friday.
(Narrator)	Number 23.
(Woman B)	Why isn't Mr. Amorim here yet?
(Man B)	**A.** He might be stuck in the traffic.
	B. He's the new financial manager.
	C. She's not here today. Sorry.
(Narrator)	Number 24.
(Man B)	Who won the tender?
(Woman A)	**A.** The turkey was really tender.
	B. We did. Let's celebrate!
	C. Not really. They won it last year, though.
(Narrator)	Number 25.
(Man A)	Where do you keep the spare keys?
(Man B)	**A.** I am worried that we might not be able to keep him.
	B. Under the purple vase by the back door.
	C. No, we don't have to do that.
(Narrator)	Number 26.
(Woman A)	What did you think of the play?
(Man A)	**A.** I don't play any sports, sorry.
	B. I thought it was excellent.
	C. I think I'm tired of playing games.

(Narrator) Number 27.
(Woman B) I can help you do the typing if you need help with the invitation letters.
(Man A)
A. Thank you, but Larry's assistant is doing it for me.
B. Yes, I can type really fast.
C. No, I wasn't invited to his party.

(Narrator) Number 28.
(Man B) What kind of workshops are they planning for the conference?
(Woman B)
A. She doesn't work in that shop anymore.
B. Team development, presentation skills and personal marketing, I've been told.
C. That was very kind of her.

(Narrator) Number 29.
(Man A) How many candidates responded to our newspaper ad?
(Woman A)
A. More than a hundred.
B. I don't read newspapers.
C. She's an exceptional candidate.

(Narrator) Number 30.
(Woman B) Can you show me how to use the new system?
(Man B)
A. Yes, she called you earlier today.
B. No, I've seen that show already but thanks for asking.
C. Of course. Can we do it tomorrow morning? I'm really busy today.

(Narrator) Number 31.
(Woman A) Will you be in Florida this time next year?
(Man B)
A. Next year is the year of the dragon.
B. I will! We're moving there after I retire.
C. I'm going on vacation next week.

(Narrator) Go on to the next page.

Part III: Short Conversations

Track 12

(Narrator) Directions: You will now hear a number of conversations between two people. You will be asked to answer three questions about what the speakers say in each conversation. Select the best response to each question and mark the letter (A), (B), (C), or (D) on your answer sheet. The conversations will not be printed in your test book and will be spoken only one time. Now let us begin Part III with question number 32.

(Narrator) Questions 32 through 34 refer to the following conversation with three speakers.
(Man A) Thandie, I heard you're moving back to LA. What's going on?

(Woman B) Hi, Mustafa. The rumors are true. I applied for the VP of Marketing position and they offered me the job. Thing is, I have to start next week, so I only have this weekend to pack and sort everything.

(Man A) And where are you staying? My cousin lives in Los Angeles. I can ask her if you could stay there for a couple of nights until you find a place of your own.

(Woman B) Thanks. I really appreciate your offer, but the company has booked a hotel room for the first month so I can find an apartment or something.

(Man A) That's amazing.

(Man B) Isn't it? And you know what's even more amazing?... I'm going to LA with her. Thandie's asked me to come along and keep working as her assistant.

(Man A) What?

(Woman B) That's right. There's no way I'd go back to Los Angeles without this guy, I've spent too long showing him the ropes to let him go. So I told Mr. Albright that I would only take the job if I they could find a place for Stuart.

(Man A) Wow! Congratulations both of you! I'll have to come visit.

(Narrator) Number 32. What does Thandie say about Los Angeles?

(Narrator) Number 33. Who is Stuart?

(Narrator) Number 34. What do we know Mr. Albright?

(Narrator) Questions 35 through 37 refer to the following conversation.

(Man B) Could you tell me where you keep the staples? I've looked everywhere but I can't seem to find them.

(Woman B) There must be one in your desk. Did you check the top drawer?

(Man B) We must have run out of them then. What I'll do is ask Mrs. Silva to order some more with the rest of the office supplies. How many should we order? Three boxes, maybe four?

(Woman B) Oh, you wanted staples, not a stapler. I'm sure there are at least 2 boxes in the supply closet. Let me get them for you.

(Man B) OK, great. Thank you.

(Narrator) Number 35. What is the man looking for?

(Narrator) Number 36. Where is what he is looking for?

(Narrator) Number 37. What does the woman offer to do?

(Narrator) Questions 38 through 40 refer to the following conversation.

(Woman A) If the snow doesn't stop in the next few hours we should consider canceling the lecture.

(Man B) I think it's too late to cancel it. There might be people in the building already so we'd better come up with an alternative if Professor Turan can't make it here.

(Woman A) Why don't we show them that video about some of his latest projects? We could do that and then invite them to his other lecture next week. I'm sure they'd understand.

(Man B) OK. I'll go to my office and try to contact the professor. If I can reach him, I'm sure he'll be able to tell us where to find the video.

(Narrator) Number 38. What is the problem with the lecture?

(Narrator) Number 39. What suggestion does the woman make?

(Narrator) Number 40. Why does the man disagree with the woman?

(Narrator) Questions 41 through 43 refer to the following conversation with three speakers.

(Man B) Have you heard about the new project? The one in Auckland?

(Woman B) No, I haven't. What's he talking about, Cindy?

(Woman A) Are you talking about the new office in New Zealand, Michel?

(Man B) Of course I am. Isn't that exciting? They'll let us apply for the positions as soon as they become available. They'll only advertise jobs externally two weeks after they become available. Wouldn't it be amazing to live in New Zealand?

(Woman B) Wow! That's very good news indeed. My sister lives there with her husband and kids and they love it!

(Woman A) Is Auckland on the South Island?

(Woman B) No. It's on the North Island. Actually, it's the biggest city on the North Island. My sister's just outside Auckland and she says it's one of the best places to live in the world. And trust me, she's been everywhere.

(Man B) So are you going to apply for a position there, Louise?

(Woman B) Why not? I have no family here in Denver. My sister's there, the weather's amazing. So if I see something that suits me, I'll definitely apply. And you're coming too, right Cindy?

(Woman A) I'm not so sure yet. We'll see, we'll see.

(Narrator) Number 41. What do the man and woman tell the other woman about?

(Narrator) Number 42. What does Michel say about New Zealand?

(Narrator) Number 43. What does Louise NOT say about New Zealand?

(Narrator) Questions 44 through 46 refer to the following conversation with three speakers.

(Woman A) Do you think Malik made the right decision?

(Man A) He didn't have a choice. It was pretty much a done deal the moment Oliver's son applied for the position.

(Man B) It's just so frustrating. Monika's been doing such a great job and she would've been perfect in the role.

(Man A) Oh, I know. Between us, I think Peter's going to fail. He doesn't treat his current job with respect—what do you think he's going to do with the new role?

(Woman A) Well, his previous role was an entry-level position, so he might've thought it was beneath him. Not that this justifies his behavior.

(Man B) It's hard for any role to be beneath you when you've got zero experience and no qualifications whatsoever—just your dad pulling the strings.

(Woman A) I'm going to speak to Monika. I hope she's taken it well.

(Man A) I spoke to her already. She's not stupid—she anticipated it, like the rest of us. Doesn't make it sting any less, of course, but...

(Narrator) Number 44. Whose job application was unsuccessful?

(Narrator) Number 45. What does the woman say about Peter?

(Narrator) Number 46. What does the man say about the recruitment decision at the end?

(Narrator) Questions 47 through 49 refer to the following conversation.

(Man B) This is the worst film I've ever seen. Who recommended it to you? Probably Abdullah, am I right?

(Woman B) I really don't remember but it was definitely someone from work. We don't have to see it until the end if you don't want. We can watch something else.

(Man B) All right. Let's find something else then. We should get one of those streaming services. Then we wouldn't have to rent DVDs we don't like and end up with nothing to watch.

(Woman B) All right, all right, calm down. I'll ask my sister which one they use and we can sign up tomorrow.

(Narrator) Number 47. Who recommended the film to the woman?

(Narrator) Number 48. What does the man say about DVDs?

(Narrator) Number 49. What does the man want to do?

(Narrator) Questions 50 through 52 refer to the following conversation.

(Woman A) What a beautiful jacket. I've never seen you wear it before. When did you get it?

(Man B) I've had it for years. You probably haven't seen me wearing it because it was too tight but now that I've lost weight...

(Woman A) You look so handsome in it. And the color goes really well with your eyes. You should wear it more often. Anyway, we should get going now or we'll miss the play.

(Man B) Absolutely. Are we driving or shall we call a taxi? We might struggle to find a space downtown.

(Woman A) A taxi it is then. Can you call one? I'll go get my scarf.

(Man B) Will do.

(Narrator) Number 50. What does the man say about his jacket?

(Narrator) Number 51. Where are they going?

(Narrator) Number 52. What is the woman's opinion of the jacket?

(Narrator) Go on to the next page.

(Narrator) Questions 53 through 55 refer to the following conversation.

(Man A) It sure is cold today. Does the building not have any central heating? I can't remember the last time it was this cold in November.

(Woman B) You really think so? It is winter, you know. I'm toasty. Are you wearing enough layers?

(Man A) Well, I wanted to put a jumper on, but I wasn't sure it was smart enough. I'm still getting to know the dress code.

(Woman B) A lot of people are pretty relaxed about the dress code here! You're still new; you'll get used to it. I'm sure our bosses would rather you were warm enough, even if it meant you looked a little less formal. Bring a jumper with you tomorrow.

(Man A) Well, I suppose that makes sense. I mean, I'll be more productive if I feel more comfortable. My fingers are so cold they feel stiff today! I'm typing much slower than usual.

(Woman B) Poor you! Why don't you check the lost and found? There might be a spare jumper you can wear for today.

(Narrator) Number 53. What do the man and woman disagree about?

(Narrator) Number 54. What does the woman think their bosses would prefer?

(Narrator) Number 55. What does the woman suggest?

(Narrator) Questions 56 through 58 refer to the following conversation.

(Man A) How was your weekend, Carla?

(Woman A) Not very good, Luke. We were going on a hiking trip in the Rockies but my husband had a stomach bug and couldn't leave the bathroom for the whole weekend so you can get a pretty good idea of how great my weekend was. What about you? Did you go to that party in the end?

(Man A) I did. I must say the party wasn't that good but I'm not going to complain after what you've just told me. Anyway, is he better now?

(Woman A) Who?

(Man A) Your husband, Carla. What planet are you on?

(Woman A) Oh, Pedro? Yes, he's much better now. Thanks for asking. Anyway, what time's the meeting?

(Narrator) Number 56. Why didn't the woman have a good weekend?

(Narrator) Number 57. Where did the man go at the weekend?

(Narrator) Number 58. Who's Pedro?

(Narrator) Questions 59 through 61 refer to the following conversation.

(Woman B) What do you want for lunch, boss? I was thinking about Japanese. Any thoughts?

(Man B) I had Japanese yesterday, Susan. How about Chinese? It's been years since I last had some good fried rice.

(Woman B)	I love Chinese, but I'm really trying to cut down on cholesterol. Let's just order a salad or a sandwich from Phillipo's, shall we?
(Man B)	Okay. So can you please get one of those tuna melt sandwiches for me? But no mayo, please.
(Woman B)	Of course. I'll call them straightaway. I'll have the avocado salad.
(Man B)	I didn't know they made an avocado salad. It sounds nice, can you order one for me too, instead of the sandwich?
(Narrator)	Number 59. What does the man suggest they order for lunch?
(Narrator)	Number 60. Why doesn't the woman accept the man's suggestion?
(Narrator)	Number 61. What does the man decide to have for lunch?
(Narrator)	Questions 62 through 64 refer to the following conversation and graphic.
(Woman A)	Hi Igwe, thanks for taking my call.
(Man B)	No worries Niko, what's happening? You've got your meeting in 15 minutes, right?
(Woman A)	Absolutely, that's why I'm calling. So, I'm on the corner of Gerard Street and Bleacher, but I can't see the Madison Building. Am I in the wrong place?
(Man B)	Hang on, I'll check online. Ah, okay... so, I'm really sorry about this, Niko, but we gave you the wrong address... the good news is you're not far away from where you need to be...
(Woman A)	Uh-oh! Okay, good thing I got here early. So where do I need to go?
(Man B)	I'll talk you through it... okay, so you want to go down Bleacher street, and when you get to the Post Office... don't cross the road to it, turn right and walk down the road, then keep straight and cross the road once, and that should get you to the Madison Building, it will be on your right, on the corner once you've crossed the road.
(Woman A)	Got it, thanks Igwe!
(Narrator)	Number 62. What is the woman doing?
(Narrator)	Number 63. Why does the man say "the good news is"?
(Narrator)	Number 64. Look at the graphic below. Which number shows the location of the Madison Building?
(Narrator)	Questions 65 through 67 refer to the following conversation and graphic.
(Man A)	Have you checked your emails yet? Head Office has just sent out our profits for the last quarter.
(Woman A)	Oh! I'm just logging in, let me check now... Well, it looks like our overall profits are up from the last quarterly report.

(Man A) True, but look at the individual products. We're doing really well with laptop sales, but it looks like profits have dropped in other areas.

(Woman A) Yes, you're right... Tripti said that if anything's making less than $5,000 in profits per quarter we'll have to discuss rebranding options.

(Man A) Honestly, looking at the figures, I think if anything's making less than $3,000 at this point they should just scrap it entirely.

(Woman A) Maybe they will. In the meantime, we should call a departmental meeting to discuss the figures with the rest of the team.

(Narrator) Number 65. What is the conversation mainly about?

(Narrator) Number 66. What does the man say is doing well?

(Narrator) Number 67. Look at the graphic below. Which product does the man think should be discontinued?

(Narrator) Questions 68 through 70 refer to the following conversation and graphic.

(Man A) We need to schedule a time to meet with Ramona, the CEO of WhisperTech, for sometime next week.

(Woman B) WhisperTech?! They're our biggest competitors! Why do we need to meet them?

(Man A) Well, Ramona called me last night, apparently, she's stepping down from her position, because she wants to spend more time with her family... she didn't want to call it retirement, but I guess that's what it is... Anyway, the owner doesn't think he can do it without her, so he's going to try and sell.

(Woman B) And you think we can buy? Wow! That would be a real game changer... can we afford it?

(Man A) I guess we'll find out next week. So, here, is your online calendar up to date?

(Woman B) Er, yes, yes that's right.

(Man A) Okay, so I can't do any mornings next week, because I'm overseeing the user trial sessions then... so I guess that just leaves us two days. Any preference?

(Woman B) I'd like to have as much time to prepare as possible, so let's take the later day.

(Man A) Good idea, we want to come in from a position of strength.

(Narrator) Number 68. What does the woman imply about WhisperTech?

(Narrator) Number 69. Why are the speakers meeting Ramona?

(Narrator) Number 70. Look at the graphic below. When will they schedule the meeting?

Part IV: Short Talks

Track 13

(Narrator) Directions: In this part of the test you will hear some talks given by a single speaker. You will have to answer 3 questions about each talk. Choose the correct option and mark the answer (A), (B), (C), or (D) on your answer sheet.

(Narrator) Questions 71 through 73 refer to the following talk.

(Man B) Hello, Mr. Bashar. This is Youssef Ginola from FDP. I'm calling about the video conference that is scheduled for Thursday morning. My assistant is going to email you the agenda so we can get everything done quickly. We've got a lot to cover, so if you would like to add anything to the agenda, please email her before the end of the day. It is a very important meeting and I just want to make sure that all those involved in the acquisition have a say before the business is concluded. If there is anything you would like to discuss with me before the video conference, you can reach me in my Boston office at 617-555-6106. Thank you and see you on Thursday.

(Narrator) Number 71. Why did Mr. Ginola call?

(Narrator) Number 72. What is the video conference about?

(Narrator) Number 73. Why does Mr. Ginola give his office number?

(Narrator) Questions 74 through 76 refer to the following talk and table.

(Woman B) Attention, passengers waiting to board flight AA178 to Seattle. Your plane has been delayed due to heavy rain and we expect it to arrive here in New York within the next two hours. We deeply apologize for the inconvenience and we'll keep you updated should anything change. Again, passengers waiting to board American Airways flight 178 to Seattle. Because of bad weather conditions, the aircraft left Seattle two hours late, and boarding will not take place before 3:45 P.M.

(Narrator) Number 74. Where are you most likely to hear this announcement?

(Narrator) Number 75. Why is there a delay?

(Narrator) Number 76. Look at the table. Which flight is the speaker discussing?

(Narrator) Questions 77 through 79 refer to the following talk.

(Woman A) First of all, I would like to thank Mrs. Takeda for her contribution to our conference tonight. It is always good to hear such innovative insight on the current market situation; I'm sure you must have hundreds of questions which you would like to ask her. However, we must stick to our schedule. I believe Mrs. Takeda won't mind answering some of your questions during lunchtime. However, when I say lunchtime, please show her some Brazilian courtesy and let our guest finish her lunch before you approach her. Anyway, now it's time to move on to our next presentation, which is due to start in 10 minutes in the main auditory hall. There are refreshments outside, but please don't be late.

(Narrator) Number 77. What was Mrs. Takeda's speech about?

(Narrator) Number 78. What does the speaker mean when she says, "please show her some Brazilian courtesy"?

(Narrator) Number 79. When's the next presentation?

(Narrator) Go on to the next page.

(Narrator) Questions 80 through 82 refer to the following talk.

(Woman B) Thank you for calling Las Vegas Tourist Information. We are sorry to inform you that our office is closed until 27 November due to very unlikely circumstances. We're doing the best we can to get our lines open again, and provide out-of-town visitors with local hotel information, theater reservations, and guided tours. We deeply regret the inconvenience. If you would like to make a theater reservation you can contact our partner agency Vegas Shows on 702-555-0410. For hotel information you can still access our website: www.lasvegasinfo.com. The guided tours will resume on 27 November. Once again we'd like to apologize for the inconvenience and hope you enjoy your stay in Las Vegas.

(Narrator) Number 80. What is the recording mainly about?

(Narrator) Number 81. How can callers make a theater reservation?

(Narrator) Number 82. What service do they NOT offer?

(Narrator) Questions 83 through 85 refer to the following talk.

(Man B) Good evening. I would like to welcome you all to our professionals of Human Resources dinner party. We have a wonderful night to look forward to. Firstly, another amazing dinner experience provided by Chef Lafayette and the catering staff here at the club. We also have a special guest with us tonight. Former president Harold Clipton is our guest of honor and has prepared a fantastic speech for the closing ceremony. In order to get the night going, I would like to invite our first speaker on stage. She has given seminars all over the world and worked in professional development for 30 years before she retired. I am more than pleased that she has agreed to join us on this special occasion. She will share some of her experience and even take us through some more practical activities to help us rethink our traditional HR practices. But that's enough from me. Ladies and gentlemen, I give you Michelle Lucas.

(Narrator) Number 83. What is the event?

(Narrator) Number 84. Who has worked in professional development for more than 30 years?

(Narrator) Number 85. What's the topic of Michelle Lucas's seminar?

(Narrator) Questions 86 through 88 refer to the following talk.

(Man A) Attention all university students. Attention all job seekers. Attention all pensioners. Are you struggling with your finances at the moment? Are you looking for some extra income or maybe a full-time job? Do you have basic computer skills? Your problems are history! If you know how to check and reply to emails, answer a telephone and build a good rapport with people, we have some more work for you. Actually, we have a lot of work for you. Pick up your phone right now and call us on 1 (800) 555-3667 to speak to one of our agents. Office Wizards has hundreds of available positions ranging from well-established Wall Street firms to local small businesses that need someone just like you. Do not be put off by a lack of skills or experience, these companies are constantly looking for people they can shape according to their own needs. The next person could be you. Call us on 1 (800) 555-3667 and say goodbye to your financial problems. Office Wizards. No magic, just work.

(Narrator) Number 86. Where would you be most likely to hear this talk?

(Narrator) Number 87. What requirement is NOT mentioned?

(Narrator) Number 88. What's the name of the company responsible for the recording?

(Narrator) Questions 89 through 91 refer to the following talk.

(Man B) Now that our bring-and-share breakfast is nearly finished, please go back to your seats for a final word from our master of ceremony, Noor Bilal. You will find the welcome packs in front of your seats. Please check if your name on the envelope is spelt correctly. If not, please contact a member of staff before going home this morning. Anyway, you will find the course schedule, notepad and training manual inside your welcome packs. Ms. Bilal's notes for the closing speech can be found on the first page of the manual. So, if you could go back to your seats, find your welcome packs and open the manuals on the first page I'll ask Ms. Bilal to join us for her final speech.

(Narrator) Number 89. Who is giving this announcement?

(Narrator) Number 90. What is the event?

(Narrator) Number 91. What can be found in the welcome pack?

(Narrator) Questions 92 through 94 refer to the following talk.

(Woman A) Dear colleagues. During the past 3 months we conducted a comprehensive survey to assess our products and look into how we could make these products more attractive to current and potential customers. Previous surveys told us that customers still preferred watching their favorite shows at fixed times and on specific days to making use of streaming services which instantly gave them access to what they call 'box sets'—essentially packages which contain all the episodes and seasons of a show. Well, this scenario has changed, and the results of our latest survey point out that people are getting more and more interested in using streaming services. The main reason given for this is convenience. Even if the content is not so up-to-date and the image quality not so clear, people are now getting used to fitting their favorite shows around their own schedules. This is why ETV is proud to announce its new product, ETV Go.

(Narrator) Number 92. Where is this speech taking place?

(Narrator) Number 93. What was the survey about?

(Narrator) Number 94. What were the survey's main findings?

(Narrator) Questions 95 through 97 refer to the following talk.

(Man A) This is your local weather report with Javier Poole. We can look forward to an incredible weekend, with warm temperatures and lovely sunshine. This means beach, beach, beach. We couldn't ask for a better day for the first day of summer. Right now it's twenty-eight degrees and clear, and we can expect temperatures to rise above thirty-five for tomorrow and Sunday, so the next two days will be boiling hot people! We're also expecting blue skies throughout the entire weekend. Though there is only a ten percent chance of showers, this good weather can't last forever. It's pouring up north, so we should see some rain by Tuesday morning. Now, stay tuned for the local news.

(Narrator) Number 95. What is the recording about?

(Narrator) Number 96. What does the speaker expect to happen throughout the weekend?

(Narrator) Number 97. When does the recording take place?

(Narrator) Questions 98 through 100 refer to the following talk.

(Woman B) *Dixon Records* is going out of business. This is our final week and everything must go. Come in today for the best bargains you have ever seen. You'll find our lowest price ever on CDs, LPs, MDs, and half off throughout our entire electronics department. This means MP3 players, DVD and Blu-Ray players, and much more for half the price. So stop what you're doing and go down to *Dixon Records* before we are gone forever. We're located at the corner of 52nd and Broadway. We're open every day, and that means from today until Saturday, from 9 A.M. to 10 P.M. Closed forever on Sunday.

(Narrator) Number 98. What kind of sale is the store having?

(Narrator) Number 99. Which products are discounted 50%?

(Narrator) Number 100. Look at the table. Which store is being discussed?

Stop! (Narrator) This is the end of the Listening Comprehension Section of the exam. Turn to Part V. (Narrator) End of recording.

PRACTICE TEST 3 LISTENING SCRIPTS

(Narrator) In the Listening Comprehension Section, you will have the chance to demonstrate how well you understand spoken English. The Listening Comprehension Section will take approximately 45 minutes. There are four parts, and directions are given for each part. You must mark your answers on the answer sheet. Do not write them in the test book.

Part I: Photographs

Track 14

(Narrator) Directions: For each question, you will hear four statements about the photograph in your test book. When you hear the statements, choose the one statement that best describes what you see in the photograph. Then, find the number of the question on your answer sheet and mark your answer. The statements will not be written in your test book and will be spoken just once.

(Narrator) Now listen to the four statements.

(Narrator) A.

(Woman A) They're leaving the office.

(Narrator) B.

(Woman A) They're turning off the machine.

(Narrator) C.

(Woman A) They're gathered around the table.

(Narrator) D.

(Woman A) They're eating at a restaurant.

(Narrator) Choice (B), "They're gathered around the table," best describes what you see in the picture. Therefore, you should fill in choice (B) in your answer sheet.

(Narrator) Now let us begin Part 1 with question number 1.

(Narrator) Go on to the next page.

(Narrator) Number 1.

(Narrator) Look at the picture marked number 1 in your test book.

(Man A)
A. The papers are stacked on the desk.
B. The files are stored in the cupboard.
C. The office is well stocked with pens.
D. The books are on the chair.

(Narrator) Number 2.

(Narrator) Look at the picture marked number 2 in your test book.

(Woman A)
A. They are on a decline.
B. They are walking next to each other.
C. They are unloading their bags.
D. They are waiting in line.

(Narrator) Number 3.

(Narrator) Look at the picture marked number 3 in your test book.

(Man B)
A. They are tying their shoes.
B. The crowd is gathering in the hall.
C. The nurse is explaining the procedure.
D. The nail technician is training the women.

(Narrator) Number 4.

(Narrator) Look at the picture marked number 4 in your test book.

(Woman B)
A. He's standing on the chair.
B. He's making the table.
C. He's sanding the chair.
D. He's handling the box.

(Narrator) Go on to the next page.

(Narrator) Number 5.

(Narrator) Look at the picture marked number 5 in your test book.

(Man A)
A. She's grown a tree.
B. She's pouring the liquid.
C. She's measuring the test tube.
D. She's making a drink.

(Narrator) Number 6.

(Narrator) Look at the picture marked number 6 in your test book.

(Woman A)
A. The packets are empty.
B. The glass is broken.
C. The people are heartbroken.
D. The widow has spoken.

Part II: Question-Response

Track 15

(Narrator) Directions: You will hear a question or statement and three responses spoken in English. They will be spoken only once and will not be printed in your test book. Choose the best response to the question or statement and mark the letter on your answer sheet.

(Narrator) Listen to a sample question:

(Man B) What time is the finance meeting?

(Narrator) A.

(Woman A) It's this afternoon, at two.

(Narrator) B.

(Woman A) No, I work in marketing.

(Narrator) C.

(Woman A) It's in the safe on the 5th floor.

(Narrator) Choice (A), "It's this afternoon, at two," best answers the question. Therefore, you should fill in choice (A) in your answer sheet.

(Narrator) Now let us begin Part II with question number 7.

(Narrator) Number 7.

(Man A) How soon can you solve the computer problem?

(Woman B)
A. It will be ready after lunch.
B. About ten minutes ago.
C. I will check my emails now.

(Narrator) Number 8.

(Woman A) Is your computer password locked?

(Man B)
A. I need to call her back later.
B. My desk is broken.
C. Yes, and the password is 456123.

(Narrator) Number 9.

(Woman B) Why did you drive to work today?

(Man A)
A. No, today is Saturday.
B. Both subway workers and bus drivers are on strike.
C. Not at the moment. Maybe on Friday.

(Narrator) Number 10.

(Man B) How long will the meeting last?

(Woman A)
A. Almost two hours.
B. I won't be able to write the report.
C. I can make you some if you're late.

(Narrator) Number 11.

(Man A) When do you have to send the report?

(Woman B)
A. The paper is not very good quality.
B. Before lunchtime.
C. Dinner's almost ready.

(Narrator) Number 12.

(Man B) Where's the nearest subway station?

(Woman B)
A. We need to replace the headlights.
B. Three blocks that way.
C. I have left my keys at home.

(Narrator)	Number 13.
(Woman A)	Who is leading the development project?
(Man B)	**A.** I heard Mr. Patel is in charge.
	B. She's had a baby boy.
	C. I prefer the laptop computer if you don't mind.
(Narrator)	Number 14.
(Woman B)	When did Mrs. Wilkins move back to England?
(Man A)	**A.** Her family lives in London.
	B. She wouldn't tell me what to do.
	C. Almost six months ago, I think.
(Narrator)	Number 15.
(Man B)	Do I need permission to park here?
(Woman A)	**A.** Yes, you need a special permit from reception.
	B. Yes, she keeps asking the same thing all the time.
	C. Yes, tomorrow is pancake day.
(Narrator)	Number 16.
(Man A)	Whose desk is this?
(Woman A)	**A.** You should answer the phone first.
	B. The desks are all second hand.
	C. It belongs to Mr. Akita.
(Narrator)	Number 17.
(Woman B)	When will the show begin?
(Man B)	**A.** The new secretary will begin working next week.
	B. It always begins 5 to 10 minutes later than advertised.
	C. This is a new show.
(Narrator)	Number 18.
(Woman A)	Who sent the package to the main office?
(Woman B)	**A.** She looks really worried.
	B. The package came from China.
	C. I believe the courier took it this morning.
(Narrator)	Number 19.
(Woman B)	How many chairs are there on the 5th floor?
(Man A)	**A.** Both engineers will be here later today.
	B. The new chairs look amazing.
	C. There are only three of them.

(Narrator) Number 20.
(Man B) I don't have enough time to stay until the end of the meeting.
(Woman A)
A. Don't worry. He'll understand.
B. I can lend you some money if you want.
C. The meeting was very productive.

(Narrator) Number 21.
(Man A) Can you believe this building is 101 stories tall?
(Woman B)
A. You're lucky you're not afraid of heights.
B. I am sure this is the wrong building.
C. This elevator is too old.

(Narrator) Number 22.
(Woman A) How often do we need to update the system?
(Man A)
A. I want to get a new cell phone.
B. Every three months I believe.
C. I updated mine last year.

(Narrator) Number 23.
(Woman B) Can your assistant cancel my afternoon meeting, please?
(Man B)
A. I prefer phone calls to emails.
B. My secretary invited me to be his best man.
C. He's not here today. Sorry.

(Narrator) Number 24.
(Man B) It's really hot today.
(Woman A)
A. He's not that handsome.
B. Take off your jacket, then.
C. I love her new sweater.

(Narrator) Number 25.
(Man A) Where is your team presentation?
(Man B)
A. It'll take place in the conference room.
B. No, I can't do that.
C. Yes, of course I will help with your presentation.

(Narrator) Number 26.
(Woman A) Why are both the computer and the TV on?
(Man A)
A. It's on my desk.
B. I was writing my report when the match started.
C. I need to buy a new computer.

(Narrator)	Number 27.
(Woman B)	What is the best service offered by the consultants?
(Man A)	**A.** There are too many people in here.
	B. Each company is assigned their very own consultant.
	C. You'll have to consult a specialist.
(Narrator)	Number 28.
(Man B)	What is the difference between a lift and an elevator?
(Woman B)	**A.** One is British English and the other is North American English.
	B. I'll lift you up if you need it.
	C. I think so.
(Narrator)	Number 29.
(Man A)	What does this expression mean?
(Woman A)	**A.** You shouldn't ask that.
	B. The meaning of life is a question asked by many.
	C. I'm not really sure. Let me get a dictionary.
(Narrator)	Number 30.
(Woman B)	Why will Ms. Jenkinson be transferred to our New Jersey branch?
(Man B)	**A.** She had to buy a new calculator.
	B. New Jersey is a wonderful city.
	C. She's the new regional manager now.
(Narrator)	Number 31.
(Woman A)	May I take the day off next Thursday?
(Man B)	**A.** I can't see why not, as long as the report is finished by then.
	B. Thursday is the first day of summer.
	C. No, he doesn't like them either.
(Narrator)	Go on to the next page.

Part III: Short Conversations

Track 16

(Narrator) Directions: You will hear a number of conversations between two people. You will be asked to answer three questions about what the speakers say in each conversation. Select the best response to each question and mark the letter (A), (B), (C), or (D) on your answer sheet. The conversations will not be printed in your test book and will be spoken only one time. Now let us begin Part III with question number 41.

(Narrator)	Questions 32 through 34 refer to the following conversation with three speakers.
(Woman A)	It says here that you worked for three years at a business training company. Can you talk me through your role there a bit?
(Man A)	Certainly. It was actually a variety of roles, as I started out as a receptionist and moved up the ranks within six months when there was an opening for a junior project manager.
(Man B)	That's quite a leap, isn't it?
(Man A)	They were impressed with how well I did my job—if you think about it, there are elements of project management in reception posts—and I did have the qualification, even though I had no experience. I had my Bachelor's degree in business administration.
(Woman A)	That's very good. And how long did you stay in that role?
(Man A)	I was in that role for the rest of my stay at the company, assisting one of the senior project managers in her projects in North and Central America and managing my own small projects locally, too.
(Woman A)	So, why did you decide to leave?
(Man A)	In all honesty, it was out of loyalty. The senior project manager I worked with, she opened her own business and asked me to come with her. Her plan was to take me under her tutelage and teach me the skills required to become a senior project manager.
(Woman A)	And you stayed with her for two years, right?
(Man A)	Yeah. Sadly, she passed away recently so I had to look for a new position.
(Narrator)	Number 32. Where is this conversation likely to take place?
(Narrator)	Number 33. Which of the following reasons does the man NOT give for his career progression?
(Narrator)	Number 34. What happened to the senior project manager the man worked with?
(Narrator)	Questions 35 through 37 refer to the following conversation between three speakers.
(Man B)	Welcome back, Mr. Klinsmann. Same table?
(Man A)	Hi, Arnold. What do you think, dear? Or would you like to sit outside today?
(Woman A)	Hi, Arnold. Oh, same table, please. Don't you think dear? Is the chef here today, Arnold?
(Man B)	He certainly is. I'll let him know you're here.
(Woman A)	Thanks. We've just got back from the Andes and I'd like to talk to him about some of the small vineyards we visited there.
(Man B)	I think he'd love to hear all about that. Please, sir. If you could follow me.
(Man A)	After you, dear.
(Woman A)	Thanks, darling.
(Man B)	Here you are, sir. I'll be back in a minute with the wine list.

(Man A) Thanks, Arnold. Honey, don't you think it's about time we told them we're selling the hotel and buying this place?

(Woman A) I do. That's why I wanted to talk to Chef Lavoisier. There's no point in buying this place if he won't stick around. We need to make sure he stays. No matter what.

(Man A) I agree.

(Man B) Here's the wine list, sir.

(Narrator) Number 35. Where's the conversation taking place?

(Narrator) Number 36. What do we learn about the couple's vacations?

(Narrator) Number 37. What do we learn about the couple?

(Narrator) Questions 38 through 40 refer to the following conversation.

(Man A) Have you seen a brown briefcase? I had it with me when I came in this morning but I can't seem to find it anywhere.

(Woman B) I think Andy was asking around about a briefcase. Why don't you ask him?

(Man A) Thanks. By the way, congratulations on your new position.

(Woman A) Thank you.

(Man A) They couldn't have appointed anyone better. You'll make a great director of operations, Margaret.

(Woman B) That's very kind of you, Sean. Ah... and there's Andy.

(Man A) With my briefcase under his arm. What a relief! See you at the theater tonight?

(Woman B) Not sure. Had a really long week so I'll probably take a hot bath and hit the sack.

(Man A) Nothing like a good night's sleep.

(Woman B) Absolutely.

(Narrator) Number 38. What's the man looking for?

(Narrator) Number 39. What do we learn about the woman?

(Narrator) Number 40. What does the woman mean when she says "I'll probably take a hot bath and hit the sack"?

(Narrator) Questions 41 through 43 refer to the following conversation.

(Man B) Does the 52 bus stop at Central Square?

(Woman A) It normally does, but not at weekends. They usually have a street market in the square on Saturdays and Sundays, so the bus takes a different route.

(Man B) Is there any other way to get there?

(Woman A) Of course. You can get the subway. Take the west bound train until Mulholland Avenue. Then you'll have to change trains. Take the yellow line and get off Grand Street It's a five-minute walk from there. You'll see a lot of signs, so no need to worry.

(Man B) Ok. Thanks for your help. I really appreciate it.

(Narrator) Number 41. Why won't the 52 bus stop at Central Square?

(Narrator) Number 42. According to the woman, how can the man get to Central Square?

(Narrator) Number 43. Why shouldn't the man worry?

(Narrator) Questions 44 through 46 refer to the following conversation.

(Man B) Please tell Dr. Walker that Mr. Garcia is on the line.

(Woman B) Again? What does he want this time?

(Man B) He says he's been taking the antibiotics for 10 days but still doesn't feel any better.

(Woman B) That's too bad. Dr. Walker won't be back for the next 2 or 3 hours but tell Mr. Garcia that I'll ask her to prescribe something stronger, and then I'll send the prescription to his pharmacy so he doesn't have to come all the way here.

(Man B) Perfect! I'll tell him he can pick it up after 4 then.

(Narrator) Number 44. Who is Mr. Garcia?

(Narrator) Number 45. Why is Mr. Garcia calling?

(Narrator) Number 46. What does the woman offer to do?

(Narrator) Questions 47 through 49 refer to the following conversation.

(Man A) How are things going at the Tokyo office, Sally?

(Woman A) Just fine. We've been expanding and moving some of our staff to our new office in Kyoto, so that's been causing some disruptions in customer's service lines, but nothing too serious. Everything should get back to normal before the end of the week.

(Man A) That's good to hear. I was concerned business might not have been so good in Japan, but now you're telling me otherwise, so that's a big relief. You've been doing a great job Sally and we're all very proud of you here in Michigan.

(Woman A) Thanks Mr. Lee. I'm just doing my job.

(Narrator) Number 47. What is affecting customer's service lines?

(Narrator) Number 48. When does Sally expect things to get back to normal?

(Narrator) Number 49. What does the man say about Sally?

(Narrator) Go on to the next page.

(Narrator) Questions 50 through 52 refer to the following conversation.

(Woman B) We ordered the new store signs over a month ago, didn't we? Haven't they come back from Chicago yet?

(Man A) They got here yesterday. They're downstairs in those two brown boxes by the front door.

(Woman B)	Excellent! I'm glad they got here in time for the opening on Monday. We have to call the architect and let her know that both the signs and furniture are here.
(Man A)	I'll do that straightaway. I'll make sure everything gets done before Friday so you can make any changes over the weekend if necessary.
(Narrator)	Number 50. Where are the store signs?
(Narrator)	Number 51. Why does the woman want to call an architect?
(Narrator)	Number 52. When does the store open?
(Narrator)	Questions 53 through 55 refer to the following conversation.
(Man B)	Now, if you could go a bit slower and try to move to the right lane because you'll have to take the third exit at the roundabout. That's the street that goes past the cathedral and toward our new office.
(Woman A)	But how do I do that with all those cars waiting in line to go right? You should have told me earlier.
(Man B)	I'm sorry but that's the only way. We don't have time to miss the exit. We won't be able to turn around for the next 20 kilometers and it's already 4:45. The meeting starts at 5. Please, signal and try to turn right. I'm sure they'll understand.
(Woman A)	Well, I'll do as you say but next time you're driving!
(Narrator)	Number 53. In which direction does the man want to go?
(Narrator)	Number 54. What time is it now?
(Narrator)	Number 55. Where are the speakers going?
(Narrator)	Questions 56 through 58 refer to the following conversation.
(Man B)	I'm exhausted. I've been sitting in front of this computer for nearly 14 hours now and I didn't get much sleep last night.
(Woman B)	Really? That's not healthy, you know.
(Man B)	I did try to go to bed earlier but my neighbor was having a party last night. They're usually very quiet but last night the noise was just too loud. I didn't fall asleep until after 4:30 and I had to wake up at 8.
(Woman B)	That wouldn't be enough for me, either. I usually need to sleep for at least 7 hours. But anyway, why did you have to wake up so early? It's Saturday today. You could've stayed in bed longer.
(Man B)	Not really. I have to finish this presentation by Monday and I can never get any work done from home.
(Narrator)	Number 56. What time did the man go to bed?
(Narrator)	Number 57. How many hours of sleep does the woman need?
(Narrator)	Number 58. Why did the man get up early?
(Narrator)	Questions 59 through 61 refer to the following conversation.
(Man A)	Don't you live by the new supermarket?

(Woman B)	I used to, but I didn't really like the area, so last year we decided to move back to Manhattan. Now we can go anywhere on foot; even the kids' school is only a ten-minute walk. We live in that new building next to the old bagel store.
(Man A)	Oh, that's great. It's an amazing building. I drive past it every day to get here to the office.
(Woman B)	I have to say we're quite lucky. Actually, I know it's quite near but since you drive past my building every day, maybe you could give me a lift when the weather's bad.
(Man A)	Absolutely! And they're saying it's going to rain all day tomorrow. What time shall I pick you up? Is 7:45 too early for you?
(Woman B)	Not at all. 7:45 is just fine. See you tomorrow, then.
(Man A)	See you.
(Narrator)	Number 59. Where does the woman live?
(Narrator)	Number 60. How does the man get to work?
(Narrator)	Number 61. What time will the woman meet the man tomorrow?
(Narrator)	Questions 62 through 64 refer to the following conversation and graphic.
(Man A)	Excuse me, can you help me find the Bernard Building? I'm supposed to be meeting a client there
(Woman A)	Yes, I know where that is. Are you meeting an artist? That building is mostly used as a workspace for creative people.
(Man A)	I guess you could say that, yeah, he's a designer. Clothes, y'know? I'm his lawyer.
(Woman A)	Oh! That's pretty cool. Right, okay, so if you look on the map, you're *here*, on Rosencrantz street. You want to take the second left, and walk up that road... the building is on the corner of that block, on the right side of the road.
(Narrator)	Number 62. What does the woman say about the Bernard Building?
(Narrator)	Number 63. What is the man's profession?
(Narrator)	Number 64. Look at the graphic below. Which number shows the location of the Bernard Building?
(Narrator)	Questions 65 through 67 refer to the following conversation and graphic.
(Woman A)	Right, let's talk about this budget. Muhammed, thanks for putting it together.
(Man B)	Not at all... right, so perhaps the first thing you'll notice is that our budget for this quarter is quite a bit higher than it was last year ... that's because we've got some feedback from our digital trial, and our customers really loved the online options.

(Woman A) To be honest, I can't believe we've waited so long to break into the online space.

(Man B) Right? So that's going to be our main cost for this quarter, we're going to get some extra people on board, and pay some upfront costs, and also increase our server capacity so that we can get all of our content online, too.

(Woman A) Gotcha, so that makes sense, I think that should all be fine... I'm glad we're putting the research for new projects into the budget now, too, it's good to see what we're spending on that... I think we need to be spending more on actually creating our books, though... this figure doesn't seem to be high enough...

(Man B) Well, we typically allow $2,000 for each book, and we've got five projects, so that's where that figure came from.

(Woman A) Right, but remember that one of the projects is a kit, so there are actually three books in that project?

(Man B) Oh yeah, of course! I'm so sorry, we should definitely change that, then.

(Narrator) Number 65. Why has the budget increased?

(Narrator) Number 66. Why does the man say "Right?"?

(Narrator) Number 67. Look at the graphic. Which budget does the woman think should change?

(Narrator) Questions 68 through 70 refer to the following conversation and graphic.

(Man A) Hey honey, do you still want to take the kids to that amusement park next week when we're visiting with your mom?

(Woman A) Oh, definitely! Thanks for reminding me... let me check the forecast for next week, so we can decide on the day. Here, look... well, we can't go when it's raining, because everything's outside at this place, and I don't wanna get soaked.

(Man A) Right, and remember Thursday and Friday your mom wants us to look at those houses with her... Also, I think anything over 90 degrees is going to be way too hot for the kids.

(Woman A) Definitely! Holly is no good in the heat. Okay, so that just leaves one day. Sorted!

(Narrator) Number 68. What is most likely the relationship between the two speakers?

(Narrator) Number 69. Who are the speakers visiting next week?

(Narrator) Number 70. Look at the graphic below. When will they go to the amusement park?

Part IV: Short Talks

Track 17

(Narrator) Directions: In this part of the test you will hear some talks given by a single speaker. You will have to answer 3 questions about each talk. Choose the correct option and mark the answer (A), (B), (C), or (D) on your answer sheet.

(Narrator) Questions 71 through 73 refer to the following talk.

(Woman A) Ladies and gentlemen, the captain has turned off the Fasten Seat Belt sign, and you may now move around the cabin. However, we always recommend to keep your seat belt fastened while you're seated. In a few moments, the flight attendants will be passing around the cabin to offer you hot or cold drinks, as well as a light meal or snack. Alcoholic drinks are also available with our compliments. Now, sit back, relax, and enjoy the flight. Thank you.

(Narrator) Number 71. Where would this announcement most likely be heard?

(Narrator) Number 72. Who is speaking?

(Narrator) Number 73. When is the announcement being made?

(Narrator) Questions 74 through 76 refer to the following talk.

(Man B) Hello everyone. My name is Brad Sullivan and I am the new Sales Manager at C&C Ltd. I wanted to come down personally to introduce myself and invite you all to our annual conference next month. This year we'll be holding it at the Shilton Hotel in San Diego on November 14. Everyone from the department is invited and, although it is not compulsory, I would love to see you all there. Also, for the first time in its brief but successful history, C&C will be holding a dinner party on Saturday November 16 as a closing ceremony for the conference. Everyone is invited to bring a spouse or date, but no children this time. Maybe next year. Anyway, please let Ms. Brown know if you are going to attend the conference and party by the end of next week. I hope to see you all there.

(Narrator) Number 74. When is the annual conference?

(Narrator) Number 75. When should the employees confirm their presence?

(Narrator) Number 76. What is the speaker talking about when he says, "maybe next year"?

(Narrator) Questions 77 through 79 refer to the following talk.

(Woman A) Now we're about to enter the new section of the factory. Our company places a great deal of importance on health and quality and this is the main reason why we have chosen to upgrade our facilities. We've developed a new line of frozen foods that carry no preservatives or coloring so that you can offer it to your customers with the maximum guarantee. This new method allows us to only use the finest ingredients while also offering high nutritional values and maintaining the same mouth-watering flavor Richmond Foods has traditionally been known for.

(Narrator) Number 77. Where is the speaker?

(Narrator) Number 78. What is the speaker discussing?

(Narrator) Number 79. What is the name of the company?

(Narrator) Go on to the next page.

(Narrator) Questions 80 through 82 refer to the following talk.

(Woman B) You have reached Coastline Televron Customers' Helpline. Unfortunately, our offices are closed at the moment and we cannot take your call. Please call us back Monday to Friday between 8:00 A.M. and 7:00 P.M. or Saturdays from 9:00 A.M. to 3:00 P.M. Our offices are closed on Sundays. In case of an emergency call us at 518-485-1889 or visit our website on www.coastlinetelevron.com/help/emergency. Have a good day.

(Narrator) Number 80. What is the recording mainly about?

(Narrator) Number 81. How can the listener contact the company in case of an emergency?

(Narrator) Number 82. What time are the offices open on Saturday?

(Narrator) Questions 83 through 85 refer to the following talk.

(Man A) All workers are required to wear goggles and a helmet at all times. Lost or damaged items must be reported immediately to Health and Safety. Replacement items will be promptly requested for you, and a temporary pair of goggles and a helmet will be available. Items are property of Lyndon Brothers and a replacement fee may be charged in cases of repeated loss or damage. Please remember that visitors are also required to wear the equipment and must be accompanied at all times. Visitors who are without escorts or are not wearing the appropriate gear will be asked by security personnel to leave the building. Thank you for your cooperation.

(Narrator) Number 83. What should workers do if equipment is damaged or lost?

(Narrator) Number 84. What are the requirements for visitors entering the building?

(Narrator) Number 85. Who might ask visitors to leave the building?

(Narrator) Questions 86 through 88 refer to the following talk and table.

(Woman A) Sundown Hotels proudly announces the opening of its newest family resort in Acapulco. This modern resort, designed by renowned leisure and hospitality architects, has its own private beach and is only 5 minutes away from Acapulco's bustling city center. It offers a complete family resort experience with a children's club, two water parks, spa facilities, and a choice of 5 restaurants. Like other Sundown Hotels, our bedrooms offer maximum comfort with memory foam mattresses, air conditioning, cable TV, mini bar, and 24-hour room service. Call us now at 744-414-0171 and find out more about our special packages for summer 2017.

(Narrator) Number 86. What is opening?

(Narrator) Number 87. What is not mentioned by the speaker?

(Narrator) Number 88. Look at the table. What is the opening date for the hotel being discussed?

(Narrator) Questions 89 through 91 refer to the following talk.

(Man B) Coming up on your right is the Nigel's Stadium, home of the 49ers, the greatest football team in the world. On your left you will find the Santa Clara Convention Center where your conference will be held from tomorrow. We will now take a brief tour of the stadium. Please stay with your guide at all times, and please be back on the bus before 4 o'clock. It is extremely important to return on time as we will not be able to wait for latecomers. In case you fail to return to the bus by the stipulated time, you will be responsible for returning to the hotel on your own. So, it's noon now, and as I mentioned, we're going to start by taking a tour of the stadium. After that, we'll have a quick lunch, then we'll hear from some of our very own players, I know you're all excited about that! Then, we'll have a bit of a game in the stadium. Don't worry, it's going to be very casual, and then we'll all get our stuff together, visit the restroom, etc., and be back on the bus in time to go. Everyone ready?

(Narrator) Number 89. Who is listening to this announcement?

(Narrator) Number 90. How is the group traveling?

(Narrator) Number 91. Look at the itinerary. What time will they start playing football?

(Narrator) Questions 92 through 94 refer to the following talk.

(Man A) Attention all staff. Attention all staff. Employee parking will not be permitted on the third level of the parking garage from tomorrow. This level will be allocated for visitors and should not be used by employees. Visitors' parking permits must be requested at reception at least 24 hours prior to the visit. Failure to do so might not guarantee visitors an allocated space and cause embarrassment to the company. Employees are free to carry on parking on the second and fourth levels of the parking garage. Please take note of the following: the yellow spaces on the second and fourth levels are no longer reserved for visitors and can be used by all staff. Red spaces are still reserved for management and should not be used without written authorization.

Employees or visitors who fail to park in their designated areas will have their cars ticketed and towed.

(Narrator) Number 92. How many levels are reserved for visitor parking?

(Narrator) Number 93. Who may park in the red spaces?

(Narrator) Number 94. What will happen to employees who park in wrong spaces?

(Narrator) Questions 95 through 97 refer to the following talk.

(Woman A) Good morning everybody, and welcome to M&T Technologies. We've got a lot of information to cover today, so I'll be as brief as I can. My name is Julia Perez and I have been the HR Director at M&T for the past 20 years. Here at M&T we take great pride in our laidback approach to working hours but at the same time there is a great demand for productivity. As your managers will explain to you later today, working hours are flexible as long as both short and long-term goals are consistently met. The office is open 7 days a week from 7:00 A.M. to 9:00 P.M., and software developers can pick their schedules as long as they put in 35 hours of work per week. Schedules are to be selected and handed in to HR four weeks in advance.

(Narrator) Number 95. Who are most likely to be the listeners?

(Narrator) Number 96. How many hours do employees work a week?

(Narrator) Number 97. When is the office closed?

(Narrator) Questions 98 through 100 refer to the following talk.

(Man B) Welcome to New York Zoo. You are probably already familiar with the zoo's traditional exhibits. However, we are proud to announce the opening of our Ice Age exhibit displayed in sector C. The exhibit is made of 3 rooms that will take you through one of the most amazing, and coldest, periods in the history of our planet. You will get a chance to not only understand the causes of major ice ages, but also get to know some of the amazing animals that lived before and after each one of them. Can you tell me which animal survived the five major ice ages and still inhabit our planet as if nothing had happened? Visit our Ice Age exhibit and find out for yourself.

(Narrator) Number 98. Where is the talk probably being given?

(Narrator) Number 99. What will the listeners have the opportunity to do?

(Narrator) Number 100. Why does the speaker say "find out for yourself"?

Stop! (Narrator) This is the end of the Listening Comprehension Section of the exam. Turn to Part V. (Narrator) End of recording.

PRACTICE TEST 4 LISTENING SCRIPTS

(Narrator) In the Listening Comprehension Section, you will have the chance to demonstrate how well you understand spoken English. The Listening Comprehension Section will take approximately 45 minutes. There are four parts, and directions are given for each part. You must mark your answers on the answer sheet. Do not write them in the test book.

Part I: Photographs

Track 18

(Narrator) Directions: For each question, you will hear four statements about the photograph in your test book. When you hear the statements, choose the one statement that best describes what you see in the photograph. Then, find the number of the question on your answer sheet and mark your answer. The statements will not be written in your test book and will be spoken just once.

(Narrator) Now listen to the four statements.
(Narrator) A.
(Woman A) He's waving at them.
(Narrator) B.
(Woman A) They're learning to dance.
(Narrator) C.
(Woman A) They're singing in tune.
(Narrator) D.
(Woman A) They're having a meeting.
(Narrator) Choice (D), "They're having a meeting," best describes what you see in the picture. Therefore, you should fill in choice (D) in your answer sheet.
(Narrator) Now let us begin Part 1 with question number 1.

(Narrator) Go on to the next page.

(Narrator) Number 1.
(Narrator) Look at the picture marked number 1 in your test book.
(Man A)
A. The plants have flowered.
B. There is dirt on the carrots.
C. There are vegetables in the forest.
D. The trees are being uprooted.

(Narrator) Number 2.
(Narrator) Look at the picture marked number 2 in your test book.
(Woman A)
A. They are building furniture.
B. They are creating a game.
C. They are making some dinner.
D. They are constructing a building frame.

(Narrator) Number 3.
(Narrator) Look at the picture marked number 3 in your test book.
(Man B)
A. They are going hiking.
B. He is picking a flower.
C. She is learning to walk.
D. They are trying to talk.

(Narrator) Number 4.
(Narrator) Look at the picture marked number 4 in your test book.
(Woman B)
A. The technician's work is intricate.
B. The document is confusing.
C. The computer software has downloaded.
D. The sculpture is complete.

(Narrator) Go on to the next page.

(Narrator) Number 5.
(Narrator) Look at the picture marked number 5 in your test book.
(Man A)
A. The box is between the people.
B. The cabin is packed.
C. The casing is coming loose.
D. The box is being unpacked.

(Narrator) Number 6.
(Narrator) Look at the picture marked number 6 in your test book.
(Woman A)
A. The food is all finished.
B. There are two separate conversations.
C. The party guests are leaving.
D. The wires are crossed.

Part II: Question-Response

Track 19

(Narrator) Directions: You will hear a question or statement and three responses spoken in English. They will be spoken only once and will not be printed in your test book. Choose the best response to the question or statement and mark the letter on your answer sheet.

(Narrator) Listen to a sample question:
(Man A) Where should I put these empty coffee cups?
(Narrator) A.
(Woman B) There's a new coffee shop a couple of blocks away.
(Narrator) B.
(Woman B) No thanks, I've just had some tea.

(Narrator)	C.
(Woman B)	They go in the paper recycling box.
(Narrator)	Choice (C), "They go in the paper recycling box," best answers the question. Therefore, you should fill in choice (C) in your answer sheet.
(Narrator)	Now let us begin Part II with question number 7.
(Narrator)	Number 7.
(Man A)	I suggest consulting a lawyer before signing a contract.
(Woman B)	**A.** No, I don't want to work in consulting.
	B. Yes, that's what I'm planning to do.
	C. He studied international law.
(Narrator)	Number 8.
(Woman A)	Have you ever used this type of device?
(Man B)	**A.** The new computers are great.
	B. I've never seen a pair of trousers like this.
	C. Yes, a couple of weeks ago.
(Narrator)	Number 9.
(Woman B)	When can you deliver the shipment to our logistics center?
(Man A)	**A.** By the end of the week.
	B. By courier would be fastest.
	C. It's on Main Street by the university.
(Narrator)	Number 10.
(Man B)	Where do we keep the expense vouchers?
(Woman A)	**A.** They're in Mr. Doran's office.
	B. Yes, they're very expensive.
	C. I don't have any pouches.
(Narrator)	Number 11.
(Man A)	This CD-ROM isn't working right.
(Woman B)	**A.** I hate DVDs.
	B. Yes, I'm working tonight.
	C. What's wrong with it?
(Narrator)	Number 12.
(Man B)	When will you go on vacation?
(Woman B)	**A.** To Hong Kong.
	B. The week of the 12th.
	C. I was going on the 24th.

(Narrator) Number 13.
(Woman A) Have you read any good books lately?
(Man B)
A. I really enjoy reading detective novels.
B. Well, I just purchased one online.
C. I usually read six books every month.

(Narrator) Number 14.
(Woman B) Can I borrow that pair of scissors on your desk?
(Man A)
A. Sorry, but I'm using my desk.
B. I never use scissors anymore.
C. Of course you can!

(Narrator) Number 15.
(Man B) When is your meeting with Mr. Xang next week?
(Woman A)
A. Mr. Xang travels to work by foot every day.
B. Next Wednesday in the late afternoon.
C. At 2 P.M. today, I think.

(Narrator) Number 16.
(Man A) How long have you wanted to work for yourself?
(Woman A)
A. Until five years.
B. Yes, I am self-employed.
C. Ever since college.

(Narrator) Number 17.
(Woman B) Where should we put these boxes?
(Man B)
A. We shouldn't carry them in the rain.
B. How about in that room down the hall?
C. These boxes are quite heavy.

(Narrator) Number 18.
(Man A) Why don't you take a short break?
(Woman B)
A. I broke my coffee cup last week.
B. That's a good idea!
C. You've been working too hard.

(Narrator) Number 19.
(Woman B) Excuse me, where can I catch the subway going uptown?
(Man A)
A. You are in the middle of downtown.
B. It leaves at 6:23.
C. At the 23rd Street Station.

(Narrator)	Number 20.
(Man B)	You haven't seen the Jenkins report, have you?
(Woman A)	**A.** No, I haven't.
	B. No, I have.
	C. Yes, I haven't.
(Narrator)	Number 21.
(Man A)	Haven't you heard about our merger?
(Woman B)	**A.** No, nobody told me.
	B. I couldn't hear anything.
	C. I had heard it once.
(Narrator)	Number 22.
(Woman A)	Would you please tell him that I called?
(Man A)	**A.** I'm not sure if I told him.
	B. Yes, I'll let him know.
	C. I'll tell him you will call.
(Narrator)	Number 23.
(Woman B)	Do you want juice or milk?
(Man B)	**A.** I did want milk.
	B. Thanks, it's really juicy.
	C. I'd like juice.
(Narrator)	Number 24.
(Man B)	Whose car are you driving?
(Woman A)	**A.** It belongs to my friend.
	B. My car is getting fixed.
	C. Yes, I like it very much.
(Narrator)	Number 25.
(Man A)	Which dates will you be overseas next quarter?
(Man B)	**A.** May 23rd to June 5th.
	B. From Thursday to Wednesday.
	C. I'll be gone for two weeks.
(Narrator)	Number 26.
(Woman A)	Whose jacket is that navy one?
(Man A)	**A.** Jack Green is our new manager.
	B. It's hanging up near the window.
	C. I believe it belongs to William.

(Narrator) Number 27.
(Woman B) Who's Mr. Duvall speaking with?
(Man A)
A. He's in his office right now.
B. A potential new corporate client.
C. He's not available at this time.

(Narrator) Number 28.
(Man B) How many copies of the report do you need?
(Woman B)
A. I don't drink coffee.
B. No problem.
C. I'd like 50, please.

(Narrator) Number 29.
(Man A) When will we leave for Toronto?
(Woman A)
A. At the airport lounge now.
B. On Wednesday the 14th.
C. We left last Tuesday.

(Narrator) Number 30.
(Woman B) Who's in charge of marketing?
(Man B)
A. That would be Ms. Williams.
B. No thanks, I'll pay cash.
C. It's at First and Broad.

(Narrator) Number 31.
(Woman A) Where are you going this evening?
(Man B)
A. I'm leaving the office at eight sharp.
B. I have a dinner event with the managing director.
C. Because I have a doctor's appointment.

(Narrator) Go on to the next page.

Part III: Short Conversations

Track 20

(Narrator) Directions: You will hear a number of conversations between two people. You will be asked to answer three questions about what the speakers say in each conversation. Select the best response to each question and mark the letter (A), (B), (C), or (D) on your answer sheet. The conversations will not be printed in your test book and will be spoken only one time.

(Narrator) Questions 32 through 34 refer to the following conversation.
(Man B) Wow, everything on this menu looks amazing! I'm not sure what to order.

(Woman B)	Have anything you like. It's on the company. Personally, I recommend the lobster. It's fresh from Maine and it is simply fantastic! The steaks are also excellent, as this restaurant serves only grass-fed Angus beef from Montana. For dessert, you've got to order the New York Cheesecake!
(Man B)	That all sounds delicious. I think I'll have the lobster and a bowl of clam chowder. What about you?
(Woman B)	I'm going to order a medium rare steak and a Caesar salad. Now, would you like to take a look at the wine menu?
(Narrator)	Number 32. What are the speakers mainly discussing?
(Narrator)	Number 33. What does the woman suggest for the man?
(Narrator)	Number 34. Who will pay for the meal?
(Narrator)	Questions 35 through 37 refer to the following conversation.
(Man A)	Rebecca, I heard from the head office that you're now in charge of replacing our IT system servers.
(Woman A)	When the system crashed last Friday, Mr. Simpson gave me the green light to order and install the new system. I'm trying to get all of the servers operational by the end of this month, but I still have some research to do because I want to change vendors as well.
(Man A)	I know that Sympatico Solutions have an excellent reputation for 24-hour customer service and support along with a comprehensive warranty. During the warranty period, if something goes wrong they'll replace your servers immediately and you can maintain operations with their own servers.
(Woman A)	Really? I've heard really good things about that firm too. We should contact them and arrange a meeting to find out more.
(Narrator)	Number 35. What is the woman doing?
(Narrator)	Number 36. What does the woman need?
(Narrator)	Number 37. What does the man suggest the woman do?
(Narrator)	Questions 38 through 40 refer to the following conversation.
(Man B)	Did you have a chance to go through the contract yet?
(Woman A)	Yes I did, but I didn't completely understand the non-disclosure agreement clause.
(Man B)	Basically, once you starting working for us, you cannot disclose any confidential information about our products, even if you choose to leave the company for any reason in the future.
(Woman A)	Ah, yes, I understand now and that actually makes a lot of sense. You do need to protect your trade secrets and intellectual property. Well then, everything looks like it's in order and I am ready to put my signature on the dotted line.

(Narrator) Number 38. What is the relationship between the speakers?

(Narrator) Number 39. What does the woman ask the man?

(Narrator) Number 40. What will the woman probably do next?

(Narrator) Questions 41 through 43 refer to the following conversation.

(Woman B) Hello, Bill? This is Akiko. I'm on my way to Jim's office, but I'm a bit confused right now and may be lost!

(Man A) Where are you right now?

(Woman B) I'm at the main entrance of Central Street Station. Should I go east or west on Broadway?

(Man A) Actually, the best thing to do would be to go east on Broadway another two more blocks to the corner of Broadway and Trafalgar Street and turn left. Walk down Trafalgar Street about two more blocks and turn right when you see the bookstore in front of you. Jim's office will be a half-block down on the right-hand side.

(Narrator) Number 41. How is the woman traveling?

(Narrator) Number 42. What problem does the woman have?

(Narrator) Number 43. What does the man suggest?

(Narrator) Questions 44 through 46 refer to the following conversation with three speakers.

(Man B) Are you going to the supermarket? Don't forget to get some minced meat!

(Woman B) What do you need the minced meat for?

(Man B) For the pasta for tomorrow.

(Woman B) Umit, I told you. Marie is vegetarian. She's not going to touch the pasta if there's minced meat on it.

(Man B) I know, I remember. I was going to do two versions: one with minced meat and one with cherry tomatoes and asparagus for her.

(Woman B) What about the starters?

(Man B) A ham platter... I'm joking! A selection of stuff: cheese, olives, some salad, bread and dips... Don't worry, I've got it all under control. It's all going to go well.

(Woman B) I hope so. This is really important. This is my boss we're talking about. If she doesn't like the food, or if she...

(Man B) Relax. You're stressing yourself out. It's all going to be fine. We've got the whole evening planned out and the food's going to be great. I'm going to be on my best behavior and Marie and her husband are going to love me.

(Woman B) No tacky jokes.

(Man B) No tacky jokes, I promise.

(Woman B) What about your clothes? Have you picked them up yet from the dry-cleaner?

(Man B) Oh, no... Yes! Yes! I'm joking. Stop panicking.

(Woman B) One of these days, Umit, one of these days.

(Narrator) Number 44. Why won't Marie eat the pasta?

(Narrator) Number 45. What can be inferred from the conversation?

(Narrator) Number 46. How does the woman feel?

(Narrator) Questions 47 through 49 refer to the following conversation.

(Man A) Good morning, Helena. Did you have a nice three-day weekend?

(Woman A) Yes, I most certainly did. On Saturday and Sunday we went hiking and camping up on Grouse Mountain and had a picnic while enjoying the splendid scenery, and yesterday we saw a concert by the Screaming Lizards.

(Man A) Oh, I've seen them live before. Aren't they amazing? When I went, their instrumentals were awesome! And I think Richard Evans should win the Lemmy for best live performance!

(Woman A) Yeah, He. was pretty good on stage. But I thought their newest music was so-so. The songs were too long, and the band wasn't as exciting as I thought it would be.

(Narrator) Number 47. What are the speakers mainly discussing?

(Narrator) Number 48. When does the conversation take place?

(Narrator) Number 49. What does the woman say about the Screaming Lizards?

(Narrator) Questions 50 through 52 refer to the following conversation with three speakers.

(Man B) Look, I know you're upset, but...

(Woman B) You're absolutely right, I'm upset. We were supposed to pitch this client together and you went and pitched behind my back.

(Man B) I didn't do it behind your back. You were away and...

(Woman B) I was in the hospital. I wasn't away on holiday or anything.

(Man B) But I told them that you were unavailable for personal reasons—I didn't mention you were sick—and I was clear that this is as much your pitch as it is mine.

(Woman A) It's true, Florence. Your name was prominent everywhere and Mark pointed out all your contributions and your ideas and made it clear that there can't be another meeting until you're available, and our meeting was less of a pitch and more of an informal chat.

(Man B) We were pressured, that's all. They threatened to go to a competitor if we didn't present something to them before the deadline they gave us, and I panicked.

(Woman B) You should've called me. You should've run it by me first.

(Man B) I know. I didn't call you because I thought you had enough on your plate and I didn't want to stress you out, but I can understand why you're upset.

(Woman B) How was the presentation?

(Woman A) Oh, brilliant. They loved it. Mark smashed it.

(Man B) Well, I wouldn't say I smashed it, but... We've got another meeting in two weeks. Which you're coming to, obviously.

(Woman B) Obviously. All right, show me what you presented to them so we can prepare for the next meeting.

(Narrator) Number 50. Why was the woman unavailable?

(Narrator) Number 51. Why did the man go ahead with the presentation?

(Narrator) Number 52. Why does the woman say "Oh, brilliant"?

(Narrator) Questions 53 through 55 refer to the following conversation with three speakers.

(Woman B) Hey guys, can I ask you something?

(Man A) Sure, what's up?

(Woman B) Is something wrong with the system? I've been trying to get in for the past 10 minutes but it's been kicking me out.

(Woman A) It's all fine for me.

(Man A) What do you mean, 'kicking you out'?

(Woman B) I'm putting in my password and it tells me the system's offline or that it doesn't recognize my credentials. I've tried every single combination I can think of but nothing works.

(Man A) That's strange. My laptop's been fine.

(Woman A) Have you tried calling IT?

(Woman B) I did, but no one's at their desk.

(Woman A) Oh, right, they've got a meeting right now—but you can interrupt them if it's an emergency.

(Woman B) I know, I know, I just didn't want to be a nuisance if it's something simple. Besides,

I've got a couple of phone calls to make today so I can make them now while I wait.

(Man A) They'd better be long phone calls, then. From what Ian told me, their meeting's going to last three hours.

(Woman B) Three hours! What sort of meeting is this?

(Woman A) Oh, yes, of course! It's that planning meeting they mentioned, isn't it? Yeah, you'd better go and interrupt them, they're going to be in there all day.

(Narrator) Number 53. What's the problem the woman is facing?

(Narrator) Number 54. What can be inferred from the conversation?

(Narrator) Number 55. Why does the woman say "yes, of course" at the end?

(Narrator)	Questions 56 through 58 refer to the following conversation.
(Man B)	I've been thinking. We need to drastically reduce our home expenses. I think we should consider getting a second mortgage. I saw an online ad yesterday and they offered generous terms on house refinancing with a fixed interest rate of only 3 percent on the loan.
(Woman B)	Hmm... That might be an idea worth looking into. What's our current payment now, about $1,500 a month?
(Man B)	Yes. I sent the company an email this morning and they replied that we could reduce our monthly mortgage payments by about $400 if we refinance soon.
(Woman B)	Send them an email and make an appointment with them later this week. We certainly could use the additional money in case we have an emergency.
(Narrator)	Number 56. Who most likely are the speakers?
(Narrator)	Number 57. What does the man suggest?
(Narrator)	Number 58. What does the woman ask the man to do next?
(Narrator)	Questions 59 through 61 refer to the following conversation.
(Man A)	Do you know where Thomas is? I've been trying to phone him and have been sending emails all afternoon.
(Woman A)	He had to go to our branch office to clear up a problem. For some reason, they sent us the wrong invoices for September.
(Man A)	Right, okay. By the way, I have some excellent news. We have signed up a new customer, and I would like Thomas to be in charge of their account.
(Woman A)	That's great news! You should call him on his phone. I'm sure he'd rather hear the good news from you than read it in an email.
(Narrator)	Number 59. Where is Thomas now?
(Narrator)	Number 60. What problem is he dealing with?
(Narrator)	Number 61. How does the woman suggest contacting Thomas?
(Narrator)	Questions 62 through 64 refer to the following conversation and graphic.
(Woman B)	Hey Roman, can you look at this list and tell me which type of advertising you think would be the best one for us to spend money on this month?
(Man B)	Oh! Sorry, but, are you sure this is a question for me? I'm the project manager; I don't really have any experience with advertising. You should probably check with Maria, in marketing.
(Woman B)	Actually, Maria's the one who asked me to check with you. She said you might have some thoughts about the target market, as you've worked so closely with the project. It won't take a minute. Just tell me, what's your gut reaction?

(Man B) Hmm... well, I know it's expensive, but I think we've got to go online... we definitely shouldn't use radio, because the target market's young... they'd never hear it.

(Narrator) Number 62. What does the woman ask the man to do?

(Narrator) Number 63. Why does the man say "You should probably check with Maria"?

(Narrator) Number 64. Look at the graphic below. How much does the man think they should spend?

(Narrator) Questions 65 through 67 refer to the following conversation and graphic.

(Man A) Okay, so Corinne, I'm just putting together the seating plan for our client dinner next week. Bianca and Ewa have already reserved the two rectangular tables for themselves and their clients. That leaves you and me, and our clients. Any preference?

(Woman B) Let's see, hmm... okay, so I invited 3 clients but one of them can't make it, so this table should be fine for me.

(Man A) Awesome, that works out great because I've got three clients, so I'll need more seats. I'll go over on the remaining table.

(Woman B) I thought you just had the two clients coming?

(Man A) Well that was the plan, but one of them let me know that they told another of my clients, so I had to quickly invite them too, otherwise it would have been a bit awkward.

(Narrator) Number 65. What is happening next week?

(Narrator) Number 66. Look at the graphic below. Which seating area does the woman choose?

(Narrator) Number 67. What changed about the clients the man was inviting?

(Narrator) Questions 68 through 70 refer to the following conversation and graphic.

(Woman B) Hello, I just wanted to call, because I made a reservation for tonight last week, but I didn't make a note of it, and now I've forgotten the time!

(Man A) That's not a problem, Madame. We're a small place, so there aren't too many reservations in our book for this evening... can you give me some details about the party?

(Woman B) Sure, so it was for... 6 to 8 people, not sure what I said specifically, and I remember I mentioned a dietary requirement... one of the party can't have lactose, milk, cheese, that sort of thing... I also put in an order for chocolate soufflés for everyone ahead of time, because they're delicious but they take quite a while to make, so I thought that might speed things up a bit.

(Man A) Perfect. I've found your reservation, Madame. Now, do you have a pen handy this time? You made an order for... [fade]

(Narrator) Number 68. Where does the man most likely work?

(Narrator) Number 69. Why is the woman calling?

(Narrator) Number 70. Look at the graphic below. Which booking did the woman make?

Part IV: Short Talks

Track 21

(Narrator) Directions: You will hear some talks given by a single speaker. You will be asked to answer three questions about what the speaker says in each talk. Select the best response to each question and mark the letter (A), (B), (C), or (D) on your answer sheet. The talks will not be printed in your test book and will be spoken only one time. Now, let us begin Part IV with question number 71.

(Narrator) Questions 71 through 73 refer to the following talk and table.

(Man A) Bad credit, low credit or no credit? It simply doesn't matter during "Furniture Frenzy Week" on now at Divine Furnishings and Interiors. From now through this Saturday, you can get tremendous deals, like this luxurious hardwood bookshelf for just $199! Or this European designed dining table and chairs for only $179. Do you have children? How about this set of study desks and chairs imported from Denmark that has been dramatically reduced from $389 down to the amazing low price of just $220. Divine Furnishings and Interiors now has three locations to serve you better: Woodhaven Mall, North Fork South Mall, and Missoula Center. Visit "Furniture Frenzy Week" on now at Divine Furnishings and Interiors.

(Narrator) Number 71. Where is this talk most likely being broadcast?

(Narrator) Number 72. What is being offered?

(Narrator) Number 73. Look at the table. What is the item number for the dining table discussed?

(Narrator) Questions 74 through 76 refer to the following talk and itinerary.

(Woman B) Ladies and gentlemen, could I have your attention please? It's time for this evening's 'Lucky Fantasy Fan' draw. If your ticket is called, you'll receive a wonderful prize package consisting of an official team jersey, an autographed team poster, a $200 gift certificate to Big Ribs and Burgers Steakhouse, and two tickets to an upcoming game against Seattle. Tonight's winner is in section 34, row E, seat 186. Congratulations! To claim your prize, bring your ticket stub to the fan information booth adjacent to tunnel 23F before the game. To all of you who missed out on tonight's draw, remember to keep your ticket stubs from tonight's game as it entitles you to $10 off a regular car wash at any Green Hornet Auto Wash and Wax locations throughout the city. Our team appreciates your support!

(Narrator) Number 74. Where would this announcement most likely be heard?

(Narrator) Number 75. What is the speaker offering?

(Narrator) Number 76. Look at the itinerary. What time will they start playing football?

(Narrator) Questions 77 through 79 refer to the following talk.

(Woman A) The Seabrook City School board has just announced delays and closures for all of its schools due to the huge snowstorm and blizzard this morning. All private elementary, middle and high schools have cancelled school today. Community colleges, as well as City University, will begin two hours later this morning. All public elementary, junior and high schools will begin two to three hours later today. Due to ice on the roads, buses will pick children up at specially designated bus stop locations today and possibly tomorrow. If you do not know where your child's designated bus stop is, please call the district transportation office at 555-3343 or access the school board's website. Schools will end at the regular time, but all after-school activities today have been cancelled. Buses will deliver students to their designated bus stop locations and parents are requested to avoid driving and parking at the bus stop locations to avoid traffic congestion. For updated information on the snowstorm, visit the city website at www.seabrookcityschoolboard.com.

(Narrator) Number 77. What is the main purpose of the radio announcement?

(Narrator) Number 78. What should students who take the bus do?

(Narrator) Number 79. When will community colleges begin?

(Narrator) Go on to the next page.

(Narrator) Questions 80 through 82 refer to the following talk.

(Man B) For a company such as ours, the most important question that we need to ask ourselves is: how do we attract and retain customers? First of all, we focus our attention on details such as the overall appearance of our stores; the quality of lighting; and the cleanliness of our facilities both inside and outside. Second, we invest in our employees. We distribute staff salaries on a weekly basis; we provide merit-based pay increases; we pay annual performance bonuses; and we make contributions to their health insurance and retirement plans. We believe that satisfied employees equals satisfied clients. In addition, we have just introduced a new service we call supreme shopping. Customers who visit our stores will be able to access our staff instantly via a smartphone application for a personalized and fast service even during our busiest hours when store traffic is at its heaviest. We receive feedback from about 100,000 customers each week, and they rate us on a number of attributes. Their comments are an invaluable source of information and insight into doing things better.

(Narrator) Number 80. Who is probably making this speech?

(Narrator) Number 81. Which of the following is a possible date for the employees to be paid on?

(Narrator) Number 82. What is the main purpose of the speech?

(Narrator) Questions 83 through 85 refer to the following talk.

(Woman A) This is Pat Sullivan with the WKRP evening traffic report. The commute tonight is extremely slow on all major routes leaving the city. The Fairburn Highway is experiencing delays of up to 30 minutes from downtown to the Bay City Street exit. The interstate freeway is currently backed up all the way from the Westside Shopping Center to the end of the freeway as road crews are attempting to deal with signal light malfunctions. We're getting a report of a two-car collision on Highway 22 just south of the Kennedy Street exit that's blocking the left two lanes there. The only route that looks pretty good right now is Interstate 73 with both directions moving slowly but without delays at this time. This report is brought to you by Kangaroo Cola, the drink that gives you a hop in your step. This is Pat Sullivan with the evening traffic report for WKRP traffic radio and we will update you again at the top of the hour.

(Narrator) Number 83. Where is this report most likely being broadcast?

(Narrator) Number 84. What does the speaker say about traffic?

(Narrator) Number 85. Who is sponsoring this report?

(Narrator) Questions 86 through 88 refer to the following conversation.

(Woman B) As you know, we've been negotiating with the SCS Technology Institute to provide discount computer classes for our department staff. Even though these classes are free to all of our non-managerial employees, some of you have complained that workers in your department aren't taking advantage of them. Staff have complained that they are too tired and too busy to drive to the SCS campus after work. But I have a feeling that most of them don't recognize the benefits such expanded computer skills will have for their overall job performance. I can understand this, since most of them already have the ability they need to perform their current jobs at a very competent level. As managers, it's your duty to ensure your staff are motivated. So, I propose that we hire a presenter, Tom Thompson, to give our employees a motivational lecture about why continued learning is important in their career development.

(Narrator) Number 86. Who is the speaker most likely speaking to?

(Narrator) Number 87. What excuse do staff members have for not taking computer classes?

(Narrator) Number 88. What is the plan to improve attendance?

(Narrator) Questions 89 through 91 refer to the following talk.

(Man A) Are you ready to have some fantastic family fun in the sun? Then come and visit Wild Waters Adventure Theme Fun Park just off the I-99 highway exit in Brentwood. We have something fun for everyone in the family to enjoy. Toddlers will love our splash-and-tumble pool. Older kids can surf with their boogie boards in our giant wave pool. We have water slides for all ages, including our famous "Typhoon Tumble" and "Niagara Falls Extravaganza." Our newest slides are bigger and more exciting than those offered by any other water parks in the state. We are open for the summer from the 21st of June and we are now offering special discount family packages which are up to 35% off our regular prices. This offer is only until June 30th so to order please call 333–5464 or access our website at www.wildwatersadventures.com and receive an additional 5% off the package price! We're the best value water park in the area. Don't wait! Wild Waters Adventure Theme Fun Park: Fantastic Family fun in the sun for everyone!

(Narrator) Number 89. What is suggested about Wild Waters Adventures Theme Fun Park?

(Narrator) Number 90. What discount is being offered?

(Narrator) Number 91. Why does the speaker say "Don't wait!"?

(Narrator) Questions 92 through 94 refer to the following talk.

(Woman A) The question I'm probably asked the most by people I meet is: Why do you do it? Sometimes I wonder myself. It's hard work to start any business from nothing but an idea or a dream. So why do I work so hard to create a new start-up venture, make it profitable, and then walk away to start another one from scratch...? I really don't know why I do it and it's certainly not for the money! Some people say that this is my DNA, since I love the challenge of seeing my dreams become a reality! However, I do have a tendency to get bored quickly so I often lose interest. Once the venture is off the ground and begins growing then I am ready for a new challenge. I have had several successes and several failures and I truly believe that you learn more from your failures than from your successes. This current venture is my 12th start-up company and I am just as excited about this venture as I was about my first start-up. I am only 55 and am still in good health—and I still love what I do. Honestly, I can't imagine doing anything else for the rest of my life.

(Narrator) Number 92. Why does the speaker say "Sometimes I wonder myself"?

(Narrator) Number 93. How many start-up companies has the speaker formed?

(Narrator) Number 94. What does the speaker say about his future?

(Narrator) Questions 95 through 97 refer to the following talk.

(Man B) I'm Michael Jacobs and I have a special public service message from the Ontario provincial police. During this year's holiday season, it's okay to celebrate with family and friends with a little bit of good cheer. However, it's definitely not okay to get behind the wheel of a car after you've been drinking alcohol. If you plan to drink, please arrange a designated driver beforehand and leave your vehicle at home or at the office. If you see someone who shouldn't be driving, please talk them into giving you their keys and help them out by ordering a taxi or arranging for someone to give them a ride home. If they refuse, please call 911. Remember, friends don't let friends drive while intoxicated. Finally, there is a special holiday taxi service that offers people a free lift during the holiday season. If you do happen to find yourself too drunk to drive, please call 555-TAXI for a special, free holiday taxi ride anywhere with the city limits. That's 555-TAXI. for a free ride anywhere in the county. The Ontario provincial police wishes everyone a happy, and safe, holiday season.

(Narrator) Number 95. What is the main purpose of the advertisement?

(Narrator) Number 96. Who is the intended audience?

(Narrator) Number 97. What is being offered?

(Narrator) Questions 98 through 100 refer to the following talk.

(Man A) The first thing you need to know is that everybody here has a clean slate with me. Whatever happened under the previous regime will not affect how you're treated by me and the other members of this coaching staff. You are all in good standing with us until you give us reason not to be. The most important thing is for you to believe that you can win games this season. I know that you didn't win many games during the past four years and I don't really have the answer for this squad's past failures but I do believe that you have the talent to win. I repeat: you are talented enough to win the championship! I want you to think about something my high school coach said to me. He said, "Whether you think you can, or whether you think you can't, you're right." The choice is up to you!

(Narrator) Number 98. Who is probably speaking?

(Narrator) Number 99. What does the speaker say about the coaching staff?

(Narrator) Number 100. What is the main purpose of the speech?

Stop! (Narrator) This is the end of the Listening Comprehension Section of the exam. Turn to Part V. (Narrator) End of recording.